UPENDING THE IVORY TOWER

Upending the Ivory Tower

Civil Rights, Black Power, and the Ivy League

Stefan M. Bradley

NEW YORK UNIVERSITY PRESS

New York

NEW YORK UNIVERSITY PRESS

New York

www.nyupress.org

References to Internet websites (URLs) were accurate at the time of writing. Neither the author nor New York University Press is responsible for URLs that may have expired or changed since the manuscript was prepared.

An earlier and partial version of chapter 2 was previously published as "The Southern-Most Ivy: Princeton University from Jim Crow Admission to Anti-Apartheid Protests, 1764–1969," in *American Studies* 51, no. 3/4 (2010): 109–130; reprinted by permission.

An earlier and partial version of chapter 4 was published as "Black Power and the Big Green: Dartmouth College and the Black Freedom Movement in the Postwar Era," in *Journal of Civil and Human Rights* 1, no. 1 (2015): 25–55; reprinted by permission.

ISBN: 978-1-4798-7399-9 (hardback) | ISBN: 978-1-4798-0602-7 (paperback)

For Library of Congress Cataloging-in-Publication data, please contact the Library of Congress.

New York University Press books are printed on acid-free paper, and their binding materials are chosen for strength and durability. We strive to use environmentally responsible suppliers and materials to the greatest extent possible in publishing our books.

Manufactured in the United States of America

10 9 8 7 6 5 4 3 2 1

Also available as an ebook

CONTENTS

LIST OF ABBREVIATIONS

AAAAS: Association of African and Afro-American Students
AAS: Afro-American Society
ABC: Association of Black Collegians
Afro: Association of African and Afro-American Students
APBA: Association of Black Princeton Alumni
ASRC: Africana Studies and Research Center
AWC: Area-Wide Council
BGLO: Black Greek-Letter Organization
BOSS: Barnard Organization of Soul Sisters
BSAY: Black Student Alliance of Yale
CCC: Columbia Citizenship Council
CEO: Committee on Equal Opportunity
CIC: Community Involvement Council
CORE: Congress of Racial Equality
COSEP: Committee on Special Education Projects
FIGHT: Freedom Integration God Honor Today
HBCU(s): Historically Black Colleges and Universities
HRAAAAS: Harvard and Radcliffe Association of African and Afro-American
   Students
IDA: Institute for Defense Analyses
KKK: Ku Klux Klan
MCP: Mantua Community Planners
MHI: Morningside Heights, Inc.
NAACP: National Association for the Advancement of Colored People
NSSFNS: National Scholarship and Service Fund for Negro Students
OBU: Organization of Black Unity
OIC: Opportunities Industrialization Center
OPHR: Olympic Project for Human Rights
PIDC: Philadelphia Industrial Development Center
PSCP: Princeton Summer Cooperative Program

PWI: Predominantly White Institution
RAM: Revolutionary Action Movement
ROTC: Reserve Officers Training Corps
SAS: Students' Afro-American Society (Columbia University)
SAAS: Students' Afro-American Society (University of Pennsylvania)
SCLC: Southern Christian Leadership Conference
SDS: Students for a Democratic Society
SNCC: Student Nonviolent Coordinating Committee
SROs: Single Room Occupancy units
TSP: Transitional Summer Project
UNCF: United Negro College Fund
VFW: Veterans of Foreign Wars
WPC: West Philadelphia Corporation

GERALD HORNE

I was born in 1949 in a now defunct Jim Crow hospital in St. Louis, Missouri, the Homer G. Phillips Hospital. I did not find out until years later that the actual Homer G. Phillips was an activist black lawyer in St. Louis who was murdered in 1931 under circumstances that continue to remain murky.[1]

I grew up in the Mound City neighborhood known as Mill Creek Valley, the son of a teamster. Perhaps I should use the past tense since that neighborhood has long since been obliterated as a result of "urban renewal"—or "Negro removal"—a direct result not least of pressures exerted by Professor Stefan Bradley's former employer, Saint Louis University, in whose shadow I came to a kind of maturity.

Like many of that era, I was a sports fan. I rooted for the St. Louis Cardinals but my Mississippi-born parents, whose taste of the acidulous bitterness of apartheid was more direct than mine, refused to do so and instead cheered for the Brooklyn—then Los Angeles—Dodgers because of the presence of Jackie Robinson, the African-American athlete who spearheaded the desegregation of baseball in the twentieth century. I have toyed over the years with the notion of writing a play with this conflict over baseball between parent and child standing in for a larger dramatic tension.

Ironically, sports led me to Princeton in 1966. During my senior year at now defunct Beaumont High School in North St. Louis, Bill Bradley of neighboring Crystal City, Missouri, was much in the news because of his exploits on the basketball court for the Princeton Tigers.[2] It was not as if I intended to play ball at Princeton, but I was then—and still am—an avid consumer of the news and Bradley's heroics placed this Ivy League school in my field of vision. Thus, I decided to apply and then was accepted.

This was a propitious moment in that the U.S. elite was under pressure during the Cold War as Moscow pointed the finger of accusation at Washington because of Jim Crow and the U.S. attempt to win "hearts and minds" in a rapidly decolonizing world was compromised as a result.[3] These tailwinds propelled me to New Jersey by the fall of 1966.

Assuredly there were classmates of mine during my four-year stay there who felt a sense of isolation in being in central Jersey at an all-male school, disproportionately comprised of Euro-Americans of a certain affluence. However, I confess that I was not among them. After all, I was in the center of a megalopolis and recall early on visiting jazz clubs in Manhattan with my late black classmate and fellow Missourian (Kansas City in his case) Darryl Johnson, checking out Ornette Coleman, Archie Shepp, and Albert Ayler and developing a lifelong interest in their jazz music.[4] It was because of Darryl's influence that I studied the Romance languages—he was fluent, I only had reading ability—that subsequently enhanced my academic research.[5]

I do not recall how, but at some point during my early tenure at Princeton I met Larry Frazier, now a prominent attorney in Washington, D.C., but then a student at Columbia. In the argot of the day, he allowed me to "crash" at his dorm room in Morningside Heights.[6]

During the late summer of 1968, I was "quasi-homeless" after my summer gig in Washington, D.C., expired. I had worked as an intern on Capitol Hill for then Congressman Bill Clay of St. Louis (his son now holds the seat). That year, I recall hanging out at the Penn Relays in Philadelphia, which was a magnet for black students from the Ivy League and other students from the region and as well, and spending time at "Q by the Sea" in Atlantic City, a festive occasion headed by the African American fraternity Omega Psi Phi (I think I learned about this from Frazier, who had pledged at Columbia).

If one could reach a nearby city, one often could find a place to "crash" almost instantaneously. Thus, I recall an annual event, "Spook Weekend," hosted by black Yale students in New Haven where African American students flocked for a round-robin of parties. My contact there was Randy Hudson, my "homeboy" from St. Louis, whose father, George Hudson, was one of the leading Negro musicians of his—or any other—era.[7]

Lest one think that I was a mere social butterfly during that time, readers should know that during my time at Princeton I recall helping to raise funds for students then beleaguered at South Carolina State University in Orangeburg and, along with my classmate Rod Hamilton, dropping the money off in Philadelphia, then to be transported southward. I was at Columbia during the tumult of 1968 and was actually inside an occupied building for a while with black comrades. At the urging of my classmate Preston Holmes, now a Hollywood producer, I attended the massive rally in New Haven on behalf of Black Panthers then on trial, which then led me as a law student at Berkeley to do legal work for the BPP and teach classes at Vacaville State Prison.[8]

And, of course, I was part of the building takeover at Princeton in protest of the university's holdings in institutions invested in apartheid South Africa. I recall certain students opposed to our presence—there and in general—imploring us to "go home," though somehow I do not think they meant returning to our dorm rooms necessarily. That episode helped to solidify within me an abiding interest in global trends, particularly in Africa, which led me to eventually reside in Zimbabwe.[9]

Of course, hovering like a cloud above black Princeton was the memory and majesty of Paul Robeson, who grew up there. My classmate then known as Paul Williams was named after him. Williams, to no avail, implored the then retired actor and activist to come back home for a special occasion.[10] Robeson went to Rutgers because he could not go to Princeton, so he retained no enchantment with the Ivy League university.

After Princeton I attended another Ivy, Columbia, for graduate school in history. By then I was also an attorney and, thus, aided students there in the 1980s protesting the university's ties to apartheid, coming full circle in the process. I was then moonlighting as the leader of the National Conference of Black Lawyers, headquartered across Morningside Park in "Black Harlem." It was from there that I was able to raise funds from the Council on Namibia of the United Nations and arrange for the U.S. visit of the recently freed political prisoner Andimba Toivo ya Toivo, founder of the Southwest Africa Peoples Organization (SWAPO) of Namibia, then under illegal occupation by apartheid South Africa. Readers who detect a tie between my peripatetic perambulating at Princeton and my subsequent career are not far wrong.

Retrospectively, I think I was relatively immune to the imprecations tossed at students like myself suggesting that somehow we did not belong or were not qualified to enter the hallowed halls of Ol' Nassau. First of all, I was well aware that this concession, granting my admission to Princeton, was adopted under tremendous global pressure—the U.S. elite were trying to save themselves as much as they were trying to help those like myself; they also realized that giving the illusion that Negroes (as we were then called) had a "stake in the system" would be a stabilizing force for the system designed to profit them handsomely. Second, I was well aware of measures akin to alumni preference—that is, affirmative action for the sons and daughters of alumni and the affluent and generous donors and the like—and shared many a classroom with some of the dimmest bulbs among this variegated grouping.

Looking back, I think some of the most valuable lessons I learned at Princeton and Columbia were outside the classroom, such as how to navigate seemingly awkward situations (being quasi-homeless), how to raise funds for causes (Orangeburg, Namibia), how to use personal experience to enhance understanding of book topics (African liberation, Hong Kong, the South Seas, labor history, etc.), and most of all, how to survive in a society where white supremacy remains more than a cipher. Over the years I have conducted primary research on virtually every continent and I feel that paving the way for this wanderlust was my experience at Princeton particularly, being plopped in the middle of a megalopolis at the age of seventeen, having never traveled beyond Illinois and Kansas before then, and—as a result—being consumed by the new vistas opened to me. The papers and research notes I have accumulated over the years, with a particular emphasis on my Princeton and post-Princeton years, are now sited at the Schomburg Center for Research in Black Culture of the New York Public Library and, as a consequence, may help future generations to shed light on the experience of African Americans in the twentieth and twenty-first centuries. Further, they may illuminate a time when we upended the Ivory Tower.

Guest commentators on MSNBC's *All In with Chris Hayes* usually have the luxury of a calm, well-lit, studio, and scholars typically have the comfort of distance when covering significant moments. On the night of November 24, 2014, I did not. Minutes into my conversation with Hayes in Ferguson, Missouri, I abruptly concluded the interview. I had been responding to his questions about the nonindictment of Officer Darren Wilson for the shooting death of Ferguson teenager Michael Brown Jr. I explained that more than angry or shocked, I was saddened because the narrative of that night would be that the lawless, ungrateful, black youth delighted in destroying other people's property. I wanted to express that more than anything what I sensed was hopelessness, but the chaotic scene unfolding off camera behind me demanded that I shift my attention elsewhere. I hastily wrapped up the MSNBC interview, crawled under the fence of a locked-down compound to race to my car, which was parked twenty feet from the Public Storage building on West Florissant Avenue that was going up in flames. I pulled on the hot door handle and entered the smoke-filled vehicle, driving through red lights and weaving to the wrong side of the road to avoid the burning garbage cans in the street. I looked warily at the seemingly endless number of police officers and national guardsmen. As I drove, I remembered hearing the moans of mothers (including Brown's) and the defiant shouts of young angry people earlier in the night after the announcement. Somehow, I was finally face-to-face with what I had written about for so many years.

"Now do you understand how we felt?!!," asked a participant in the now famous 1968 rebellion at Columbia University in the City of New York when he reached me by phone that night as I drove away. In terms of scholarship, I thought I had done a decent job researching material for my book, *Harlem vs. Columbia University*; I mean I spoke with many of the right people and read the documents and papers, but I could only imagine the frenzy of the moment and try to write about it as best I could. The night of the nonindictment, when the Columbia alumnus called, I felt the anxiety and fear and anger that so many others felt a half century ago when demonstrations and rebellions were more commonplace—when if young people had a problem with a system or a president or a war, they took to the streets or took over a building or just made noise to voice their displeasure. The Columbia alumnus told me to be careful but more important not to expend all my energy because there would be plenty more nights to demonstrate and many more issues to protest. He said that I should prepare for a protracted struggle for freedom and justice in addition to the emotionally charged battles that the people were waging. That was sage advice. Many of those black and progressive students who attended Ivy League institutions took advantage of the zeitgeist of the moment and protested what they considered injustice, but they also set the stage for future generations' freedom of access. Those students who activated in the decades after World War II should be recognized.

I never attended an Ivy institution, but, like so many others, I wanted to do so. With that said, I have not written this book to manifest personal bitterness or malice for these revered educational centers, but because I believe strongly that black change agents need to be inserted into the American narrative. Furthermore, I have taken to heart the encouragement of the scholarly role model and Harvard alumnus John Hope Franklin to confront America's past and to "see it for what it was and is." In terms of the Ivy League, that means delving into the experience of black people. As is the case with larger American history, going beyond the popular narrative involves accepting the ugliness of discrimination and wrong turns regarding race. This is, in many ways, a story of racial progress, but it reveals the sacrifices black people had to make to enhance elite predominantly white institutions.

As an Ivy outsider, there are a few things that I have noticed in preparing this book. First, these schools keep excellent records of activity, which is quite helpful to researchers. Along those lines, I also noticed that officials of these institutions (like nearly every other American institution) are conscious of self-presentation and public perception. Many of the affiliates at these schools realize that they are "insiders," and as one fellow explained to me when I tried to enter an Ivy library to complete research for the book, "we don't just let outsiders in." That, in itself, was revelatory. Thankfully, the vast majority of librarians, archivists, and special collections staff at each of the Ivy institutions and at the Schomburg Center for Research in Black Culture were extremely helpful along the way. I find what those facilitators of knowledge do to be magical, and I owe them an immense debt of gratitude. I am particularly thankful for the Friends of Princeton University Library Grant that I received. The staff at Princeton was quintessentially hospitable.

Writing this book has taught me a great deal. I learned soberly about the implications of change. The institutions of the Ivy League have existed for centuries by both adapting to and resisting change. These schools were higher education innovators, but they were reliant, perhaps too reliant, upon the policies, traditions, and culture of the past. Change, at least as it regards racial advancement, is difficult—even messy—but necessary. The American university provides a good place to implement that kind of change. As the first black administrator at Princeton noted, "If *total democracy* is to be translated from theory into practice, it will be done first in our *educational institutions* rather than in our *political system*. The college or university, in particular, must bear the burden of this task."[1]

In my years as a student and as a scholar, I have also learned that those who work at universities or colleges are experts in the arena of discussion. They talk about ideas of fairness and liberalism and equality, but implementing justice in the academy is much more difficult for officials to do. That has become ever more apparent as students at dozens of universities and colleges throughout the nation have activated to question the commitment of their institution to equity and fairness. The current demands of the young agitators are similar to those of their predecessors. In fact, some student activists have even resubmitted the demands of protesters from the sixties. That is, in part, why the countless young and progressive people who nudged these institutions toward openness and access during the period between World War II and 1975 should be acknowledged. Their presence in itself symbolized a sea change in higher education and especially the Ivy League, but their protest also provided a way for progress.

When putting together the book, I also realized it would be impossible to name all of the actors in these stories of survival, struggle, and striving. I am bound to leave out the names of thousands who made change possible, and for that I am deeply regretful. Undoubtedly, some important events have not made the pages of the book as well. To those whose names do not appear, please know that I, along with the thousands of others in the generations that followed you into higher education, greatly appreciate your efforts. You were intruders, pioneers, and soldiers, when all you wanted to be was educated. As one scholar explained, you were a "part of and apart" from the institutions you attended.[2] Unfortunately, that meant "being in a school where you couldn't fully participate," remembered the first black woman graduate of Princeton.[3] Perhaps, she thought, the most courageous thing that she and other black students in the Ivy League did was to "keep forging through" to graduation. That courage extended to challenging their own privilege as part of the black intelligentsia to make a way for those they would never meet. Most did not realize that they were making opportunity or history; they were just trying to survive the moment. That is the testament of many a soldier. For that, I personally thank them all for their service.

I wrote the bulk of this book with uprisings of Ferguson, St. Louis, Baltimore, Charlotte, and Baton Rouge in the background. In historiography courses in graduate school (which I then considered boring), my professors droned on about how everything is written in a moment and how that moment informs the writing of history. Of course, that meant nothing to me as I tried to pretend as though I understood the theories of Michel Foucault and Jacques Derrida. I did not get it then, but I comprehended clearly after trying to outrun police atop armored personnel vehicles, breathing in teargas, feeling the heat of burning buildings, and hearing the moans of grieving mothers in Ferguson. The Movement for Black Lives matured before my eyes, and I got a sense of what young people lived through fifty years ago.

Introduction

> With its wealth, power and prestige, the University has the
> capability to correct the injustices under which Black people
> have suffered over the centuries.
> —Association of Black Faculty Members, Fellows, and
> Administrators, 1969

To many, Ivy League institutions, sometimes known as the Ancient Eight, represent the best and highest ideals of American education.[1] They have provided and continue to provide the nation's and world's leaders. In 2008 and 2012, the United States celebrated the election and reelection of its first black president, Barack Hussein Obama. It was not surprising that he had graduated from both Columbia University and Harvard University; nor was it shocking that he had married Michelle Robinson who (along with her brother) graduated from Princeton University; she is also an alumna of Harvard Law. The Obamas' eldest daughter, Malia, joined the Harvard class of 2021. Of President Obama's cabinet in the first and second term, more than 50 percent had received degrees from Ivy institutions. Of the cabinet members of color, more than 50 percent received an Ivy education, and of the black members, more than 70 percent held degrees from the Ancient Eight. The percentage of Ivy degree holders on the U.S. Supreme Court is not much different. All but one attended an Ivy institution.[2] In total, fifteen U.S. presidents have attained degrees from Ivy schools. Of the presidents to hold office since 1944, nine have received a degree from or presided over an Ivy League school. Undoubtedly, America and the world places value on Ivy League education. In terms of achieving the highest levels of access regarding American decision making, policy, and industry, an Ivy League education has proven to be invaluable.

During President Obama's elections in 2008 and 2012, two controversies arose surrounding the experience of the black students attending

Ivy League universities. The first concerned the thesis that then Michelle Robinson wrote at Princeton in 1985; the other involved President Obama hugging and praising the so-called radical Derrick Bell. In 1985, Michelle Robinson's thesis "Princeton-Educated Blacks and the Black Community," attempted to study attitudes of black alumni in their interaction with black and white people after graduating. Additionally, the sociology major investigated whether the alumni wanted to "benefit the Black community in comparison to other entities" and if they had feelings of "obligation" to improve the lives of the "Black poor."[3]

The future attorney and first lady's study shed light on several important themes regarding the black experience with the Ivy League. Her choice of topics displayed an affinity that so many black students had with topics that related to black life. She showed a clear awareness of the fact that black students who attended and graduated from Princeton were unique and that they would be interacting with white people of similar educational pedigree. Also, Robinson and her topic illustrated a deep concern with the formula of the Ivy alumni that maintained their black identity while continuing to help the community even as they entered the professional world. For black alumni of the Ivy League there was the additional burden of race representation as they sought success in their educations and careers. In the run-up to the 2008 election, critics of candidate Obama claimed that Michelle Obama was a militant racist.[4]

The second incident that drew controversy in the 2012 election involved a video clip of President Obama and Derrick Bell, the "father" of Critical Race Theory, which argues that racism has been integral to the fabric of American institutions and society in general. Alongside Critical Race Theory, Bell advanced his interest-convergence theory, which cogently contended that white gatekeeper institutions offer concessions in the way of black freedom and access when those concessions benefit white institutions. Bell's appointment at Harvard was a result of student protest that demanded black professors in the law school. Upon agreeing to join the faculty, Bell stipulated that he would only stay if the law school committed to hiring more professors of color. By 1991, Bell, dissatisfied and disillusioned with the law school's effort, walked away from his tenured position, vowing not to return until the law school kept its promise to diversify the faculty. In 1991, Barack Obama, then a student of Bell's at Harvard Law and editor of the law review, complimented his mentor at a rally for Bell's personal stands against racial discrimination and for his penetrating scholarship. Once the video surfaced in 2012, the conservative right media exploded with charges that Obama was a radical who had been trained by reverse racists.[5]

In the cases of President and First Lady Obama, the access of black people to the Ivy League and the ability of black Ivy Leaguers to positively affect life chances in their communities on and off campus were central. The Obamas benefited from the resilience and activist work of earlier generations of black students who grappled with the challenges of race and rigor while searching for their rightful place in a nation that supposedly valued education, intelligence, and conviction. The black students who preceded the Obamas had to prove that they were worthy of access to the real and implied benefits of the Ivy League while also not abandoning their blackness as students and alumni. Many of those students, like the white graduates of Ivy institutions, navigated their way into the leadership class of America.

In terms of American nationalism, these institutions were in the vanguard. They upheld high academic standards, attracted the most talented faculty members, and sought to mold the noble character of the students. The Ivy League also projected neglect and outright discrimination regarding black people. The white students who graduated from those schools propagated the views of their alma maters when they took leadership of the country. As seven of the eight Ivy schools in this country existed before the founding fathers drafted the U.S. Constitution, these schools may be more American than the nation itself with respect to culture and history. Ivy alumni and officials helped draft the Declaration of Independence and the U.S. Constitution. In the twentieth century, they advanced American ideals in the world. A good example is Woodrow Wilson. Before orchestrating the League of Nations, Woodrow Wilson was in the "nation's service and in the service of all nations" at Princeton first as a student, then as a faculty member, and then as president of the institution. As was the case with the ideal of democracy that he and others propagated in the United States and abroad, the fairness and democracy that he espoused as Princeton's president extended to white people only. The white leaders of Ivy institutions later won American wars and helped to create the United Nations Charter, all while racism raged in the United States and at their alma maters.

Like the nation in the twentieth century, these elite colleges and universities boasted an egalitarian spirit in their missions but struggled with the manifestation of the freedom to which both the nation and the schools aspired. Indeed, the Ivy League reflected the conflicted relationship of traditionally white America with black progress.[6] They attempted to instill a sense of integrity in students while excluding some students entirely and admitting others only by way of quotas. The Ivy students, administrators, and alumni could, with no sense of irony, work to bring freedom and democracy to some while shutting out others. For them, America typically referred to white people, and it was with that in mind they proceeded to direct the institutions and the nation.

Institutions do not exist in vacuums; instead, they operate in a historical context. The Ivy League, in the decades after World War II, confronted the Cold War, Vietnam War protests, the Civil Right Movement and Black Power Movement, the women's movement, student demands for power, and poverty's encroachment. Before World War II, Ivy officials made it clear that they believed their institutions could and should shut out troubles and undesirables with the Ivy-covered walls. As one Princeton alumnus from the class of 1920 remembered of his time at the university, "While at Princeton one is somewhat insulated from outside irrelevant forces."[7] For the alumnus, some of those outside forces included the push for racial equality and access to education.

After World War II, these institutions' officials, in observing the impediments to freedom that black people navigated, realized that they could not close the iron gates to the desires of young people to change their educational experiences and spaces.[8] Along with the legislative and judicial gains that black people made in interstate travel, housing, and education, the postwar years helped some white people to more clearly see the value of black citizens. James A. Perkins, the president of Cornell, suggested that the Ivy League was moving slowly with regard to racial progress. He noted that during much of the postwar era "universities like the Ivy League and like Cornell really lived in a world that did not see the inevitable implication of this basic drift towards concerns for the equality of opportunity."[9] The Ivy League was living in a "dream world," he said. Black students, faculty, and administrators unquestionably awakened the ancient American institutions.

By first arriving at these schools; demanding higher numbers of black students and faculty; pushing for the enrichment of their traditional college curricula with the study of black people; and finally, creating a welcoming environment for black people on and off campus, these students became activists for the black freedom movement. Their efforts to advance the cause of black liberation forever changed those leading American institutions. The cases of these elite colleges have added to what scholar Ibram Rogers (now Ibram Kendi) referred to as the black campus movement and the racial reconstitution of higher education. The accounts of the campus campaigns at the elite schools explain how students blackened the Ivy League with respect to admissions, curriculum, and culture.

In the 1960s and 1970s, there were significant student protests and demonstrations that occurred at public universities. The 1964 Berkeley Free Speech Movement and the 1968 push for Ethnic and Black Studies departments at San Francisco State University were both monumental in their brashness and influential on the Ivy League in their methodologies.[10] Equally significant were lesser known protests that took place in the late 1960s at institutions like City University of New York, Rutgers University, and the University of Wisconsin–Madison. Until recently, the traditional history of the student movement has done little to include campaigns at historically black colleges and universities such as publicly funded South Carolina State College, Southern University, and Howard University. Scholars such as Kendi, Joy Ann Williamson, Jelani Favors, Martha Biondi, Jeffrey Turner, and Robert Cohen have worked to fill that particular historical gap.

Unlike public higher education institutions, the members of the Ivy League were private, elite, and unabashedly exclusive. Scholars of Ivy institutions such as Marcia Synnott, Jerome Karable, Wayne Glasker, Donald Downs, James Axtell, and most recently Craig Wilder, have shown that these colleges and universities did not have to answer directly to state legislatures and executives who controlled much of the funding for public institutions. Instead, Ivy institutions had to report to large donor alumni, whose contributions often determined the fate of their alma maters. Further, the board of trustees at Ivy institutions had considerable influence on the overall operation of the schools and society. The board members' status and affinity for the cultures and traditions of their beloved institutions often put them in direct opposition to the proponents of the bourgeoning Civil Rights Movement and Black Power Movement.[11] Where some scholars have focused mostly on black presence and admissions in the Ivy League, *Upending the Ivory Tower* delves into the activities and activism of black students.

Civil rights and Black Power activity did not just exist in the streets and within the headquarters of traditional organizations like the National Association for the Advancement of Colored People, Congress of Racial Equality, Student Nonviolent Coordinating Committee, and Revolutionary Action Movement. Scholars like Peniel Joseph, Rhonda Williams, Hasan Jeffries, and Jeffrey Ogbar in their respective works have shown that the conceptions of space—in terms of regions, landscapes, and infrastructure—that scholars typically have for these movements must expand. *Upending the Ivory Tower* takes a similar tack by showing how the black freedom movement invaded the racially and economically exclusive Ivy League. It follows the path created by scholars like Komozi Woodard, Jeanne Theoharis, Matthew Delmont, and Matthew Countryman, who argue that the narrative of the black freedom movement must include northern struggles. Although these Ivy institutions were squarely in the North, the isolation, embarrassment, mistreatment, benign neglect, and outright segregation that black students experienced at some of these schools was as bad as that experienced in many southern institutions.[12]

Institutional white racism lived within the policies and cultures of those elite institutions. It propagated and accommodated segregation in housing and social activities and in some cases even admission. Harvard, historically known as one of the most liberal of the Ivies in terms of admissions, struggled to resolve issues of housing for black students when it became a requirement in the early twentieth century that all freshmen stay on campus. That meant that black students would ostensibly have to stay in the dormitories with white students. That was not practicable for Harvard's leadership, which asked black students to lodge elsewhere so as not to cause problems for, what university president Abbott Lawrence Lowell described as, the other "99½% of the students."[13] That was the practice at Harvard as well as several other Ivies. In *The*

Half-Opened Door, scholar Marcia Synnott highlighted the offenses that the fledgling members of the black bourgeoisie had to endure. Even the most exceptional black students coming from the most esteemed families could not live among their peers because of the belief that black people would innately invite problems for white students and officials. In spite of the fact that his grandfather became the first black person to serve a full term as a U.S. senator and that his father was an alumnus of Harvard himself, Roscoe Conkling Bruce, Jr. was denied housing at Harvard in 1922.[14]

Iterations of the Bruce scenario unfurled at each of the Ivies throughout the twentieth century, as it did not matter how high one was able to go outside the ivy walls and gates of the universities; while inside, one's race still mattered. Carl A. Fields, the first black administrator at Princeton, best summed up the coping mechanisms of black students at Ivy institutions before the mid-1960s. The first was to "forget that he was a Negro"; the second was to "be quietly but militantly Negro"; and, the third was to keep to himself [or herself]."[15] Although there were minor adjustments made to admissions policies, not much changed for black people until the mid-1960s. By 1963, according to Synnott, "the new elite was still overwhelmingly white (about 98 percent)."[16] Elite universities did much to open themselves to diverse white ethnicities and religions, but still lagged in terms of the admission of black students.

In the late 1960s, after cities burned and the streets filled with distraught citizens fighting oppression, white administrators finally believed it was important to fully integrate black students with respect to admissions, housing, and other aspects of college life. Having witnessed the deaths of citizens fighting for civil and human rights as well as the local and national reactions to the urban rebellions that occurred in the nation's northern and western cities, a contingent of black students turned the tables on white administrators by demanding black curricula, residences, and spaces on campus. After generations of dejection, some members of the Black Power generation decided to extend the coping mechanisms that Fields had described earlier. They raised the levels of their voices and militancy and some even decided that it was better to live among black people so that they could live without the stress of constantly educating their white peers and "masters" of the residence houses. Those pushing for separation were not always in the majority of black students, but their campaign was a direct response to the ills of institutional racism and a departure from the methods of earlier generations of black students.

Just as the Civil Rights Movement and Black Power Movement did not manifest themselves the same way in the different regions of the United States, the black student movement took on varied shapes on different campuses. The students at San Francisco State College, Merritt College, or Howard University did not have the immediate need to protest for a higher number of black students in the same way that Princeton and Brown black students did. Although all institutions of higher education stake claim to the advancement of knowledge, part of the identity of Ivy League schools is the awareness that in addition to the advancement of knowledge, they produce the world's leadership class. *Upending the Ivory Tower* covers what happened when black people joined that class in larger numbers. In response to the arrival and agitation of young black learners, Ivy institutions worked to respond to their separate emergent needs but also, in ways, banded together to envision outcomes that could satisfy protesting students and the institutions' desires to remain elite.[17] As they competed for black students and professionals, the officials at Ivy schools maintained communication to ensure the league maintained some cohesiveness.

By analyzing civil rights and Black Power in the Ivy League, *Upending the Ivory Tower* attempts to add nuance to the movements. Scholars have for years painted Black Power as part of the "bad 1960s," where violence and destruction reigned, whereas the "good 1960s" featured integrationist leaders like Martin Luther King, Jr., and Whitney Young, Jr. Using this model, those who challenged the white power structure outside of the bounds of traditional marches and boycotts—leaders like Huey Newton and H. Rap Brown—were demonized as narcissistic militants. That rendering is, of course, skewed and simple. With that in mind, it is easy for some to see the Black Panthers, who had a chapter in New Haven, Connecticut, as representatives of Black Power. It is more difficult, however, for some to view the erudite black college students on Yale's campus in New Haven as Black Power agents.

Upending the Ivory Tower argues that what the students did on campus in the name of black freedom was just as significant as what advocates for black liberation did off campus. The struggle for black people existed wherever they found themselves—even in historic, castlelike buildings. Indeed, Black Power, as with all other social movements, had varying elements and people that attempted to attain liberation by employing different tactics. By considering the diversity within the Black Power Movement, which included campus movements, *Upending the Ivory Tower* will help to complicate (and complete) the narrative. While some black students at schools like Cornell, Columbia, Penn, Yale, and Princeton took over campus buildings and even flirted with violence to achieve their goals, students at schools like Dartmouth and Brown were much less dramatic in their demonstrations but equally successful at winning their demands on behalf of black people. Depending on their schools' responses to their demands, black students at each of the eight Ivies employed various aspects of the language, rhetoric, and tactics of the movement.

The question is why. Why would these mostly undergraduate black students and professionals risk their own chances at individual freedom? Some of the students came from the black elite, while the majority in the 1960s came from the urban black working class, and fewer from lower economic circumstances. The mix of working class and middle- to upper-middle-class black people created interesting interactions, but a student's class background was not always easy to determine by the student's actions. As one multigenerational college graduate of Harvard recalled: "Some of the people who were Black Power to the max had parents who were physicians."[18] Regardless of the higher socioeconomic statuses of some students, if they were black they were likely not that far removed from the lower class in terms of familial, friendship, and social ties. The militancy of the moment crossed class dimensions, which for black people were often fluid. Subsequently, young people, regardless of their backgrounds, worked together to change their institutions to better accommodate their blackness. In spite of all else, they shared their race and what came along with it.

One answer as to why they would risk their opportunities involved the call to collective action that so many young people made during the period. Members of the generation, even today, reflect on the times that "we" stopped the war or when "we" faced down the Ku Klux Klan or when "we" brought Black Studies onto campus. Individual progress was important, but at a time when their entire racial group faced threats, acting in coalition with other black people was both logical and practical. Thomas W. Jones, of Cornell's class of 1970, explained that "it was in a spirit of self-sacrifice that we were determined to fight for beliefs and principles greater than ourselves."[19] If necessary, he said, they were ready "to meet our destiny in a struggle that was much bigger than any one of us, and even bigger than all of us," said Jones.

Another reason was the pressure they felt from others. Students described feeling guilty, in some ways, for being at the prestigious institutions knowing that so many black people faced oppression. As more students came from areas and cities where the Civil Rights Movement and Black Power Movement had taken hold, they felt almost beholden to their blackness. This was a point of contention among students, who may have sympathized with the postwar black freedom movement but who did not want to actually demonstrate and protest. Those students felt pressure from some of the urban black working and lower-income students who came during the late 1960s, who believed more militant action was necessary. Moderation and liberalism became targets in much the same way as conservatism and bigotry. That led some black students to relent to what today is called "peer pressure" in the struggle. To compensate for the self-imposed pressure they felt for "making it" to the Ivy League and from the more militant factions on campuses, some black students became activists. These conflicts of ideologies manifested in terms of gender convention, class identities, neighborhood backgrounds, and political agendas.

The few black students who made it to the Ivy League were in a precarious position because of privilege. Ernest Wilson III, Harvard class of 1970, was able to articulate the awkwardness of his situation: "I was born at the top of the bottom and on the inside of the outside of society."[20] His depiction of his life circumstances shed light on the experiences of other black students similarly situated. Ivy Leaguer Eric Holder of Columbia University's class of 1973 bolstered Wilson's point about the educational experiences of black students who attended elite institutions: "I had this dual existence."[21] Although he was in a mostly white environment at school, Holder felt the need to prove he "was still one of those guys" from the neighborhood. He attempted to convince his peers from his Queens neighborhood that he "was still cool." At Columbia that meant he had to stay engaged with the black community through his activism and through service in his black fraternity. As the 1960s ended, larger numbers of black undergraduate students enrolled in Ivy League schools from working class and lower socioeconomic backgrounds. In spite of their paucity of resources, they, too, were part of their communities' and the nation's elite once they arrived on campus.

The members of that minority of black people in colleges confronted double marginalization. They were different than the masses—black or otherwise—because of their opportunities to attend college and especially Ivy schools. Concurrently, they were manifestly distinct from the mostly white, well-to-do students at the top universities and colleges. According to Henry Rosovsky, a white economic historian who headed the committee to design Harvard's Afro-American Studies program, the students, "more or less consciously," felt "something of a dislocation from the black community" while on campus.[22] He argued that they needed to "legitimize, inwardly as well as publicly, their presence at Harvard [or other Ivies] while other blacks remain in the ghetto." The battleground for this war within themselves, then, became the pristine campuses.

In the eyes of the students, little in the Ivy League indicated that black people had been there before or had done anything that mattered to the world. Had they not struggled for Afro-American Studies and to increase black admissions and to create welcoming spaces, they would have been vulnerable to the criticisms of those from the black underclass who labeled the students as materialistic agents of the bourgeoisie who sought no advancement but their own. The students also felt a need to prove to other black students that they were committed to the cause. Ivy students were aware that their peers at state colleges and universities saw them as the most privileged. If activists at South Carolina State College were dying and agitators at San Francisco State College and Howard University were demonstrating on behalf of Black Power, then there was pressure for students in the Ancient Eight to do so as well. The intention of Black Power was to empower black people even if that meant using the wealth and tools of white institutions to do so. The Ivy activists believed they were obligated to create access to their schools and more beneficial structures for those who followed. That is why they activated.

It is reasonable to expect that Black Power would take hold in black neighborhoods and in predominantly black spaces, but *Upending the Ivory Tower* shows how young black people became a conduit of Black

Power in white spaces. Along those lines, it attempts to point out that the Black Power Movement, which was born out of an effort to edify the most disfranchised of the black masses, also took root in the hallowed halls of America's most esteemed institutions of higher education—spaces that few people in the world could hope to occupy. Writing during the moment that black learners were activating en masse on white campuses, founding director of Cornell University's Africana Studies and Research Center James Turner said: "Black students have begun to take a leading role in challenging and changing the status of higher education."[23] By penetrating what was traditionally the "exclusive domain of White America," he wrote, they joined the movement for black liberation. Black students "feel a keen sense of themselves as an extension of the Black community," Turner observed of the period. They were "going through a period unlike any their parents experienced—it is a renaissance and rebirth" of black resistance and rebellion.[24] In this way, members of the black community's intelligentsia took up the trope of Black Power to bring the interests of the black powerless onto campus. In the past two decades the literature surrounding black student protest has bourgeoned as scholars have recognized that the story of student agents of change is worth telling.[25] *Upending the Ivory Tower* is the examination of those few students, professors, staff, and administrators who pushed for change at the peril of losing what privilege they had.

Change was not reserved solely for the elite institutions. The students underwent transformations themselves during their scholastic journey. The moment and the movements that black learners observed in their time spent in the boldly white environment of the Ivy League made an impression on them. Discussing and participating in protest actions and negotiations with officials helped to develop the students' black identities. Some students, particularly those who came in the early 1960s and graduated in 1967 and 1968, witnessed within themselves the rise of black consciousness. Scholar William Cross referred to the phenomenon as Nigrescence, which is the process of actualizing blackness that occurs within Americans of African descent. For many students, that included self-identifying as black and not Negro, changing their style of dress and hair to reflect the Afrocentric trends, and choosing to associate with mostly black people whenever possible. If some students questioned their blackness before arriving, they established a racial identity that linked them to what historian Vincent Harding referred to as the river of black liberation and created an ancestral bind between black people who rebelled against slavery and those who fought to advance opportunities at the collegiate level in the postwar era.[26] That process informed the remainder of their experiences in the Ivy League and also in life.

In wrestling with their own black development, they looked to the now sacred but then recently released Black Power texts. In addition to Frantz Fanon's *The Wretched of the Earth* (1961), they read the searing criticisms of institutional racism and economic deprivation in *The Autobiography of Malcolm X* (1965), Stokely Carmichael and Charles Hamilton's *Black Power: The Politics of Liberation* (1967), Harold Cruse's *The Crisis of the Negro Intellectual* (1967), and Martin Luther King, Jr.'s *Where Do We Go from Here?* (1967). By January 1968, Nathan Wright, Jr.'s *Black Power and Urban Unrest* was available and socially conscious and intellectually curious students read books like *The Black Power Revolt: A Collection of Essays*, edited by Floyd Barbour. In an attempt to extend their international political understanding, some students were reading Karl Marx's *Das Kapital* (1867) and Mao Tse-tung's *Quotations from Chairman Mao Zedong* (Little Red Book, 1964), a favorite of the Black Panthers. Through their reading, students attempted to grasp the meaning of revolution and sought to apply revolutionary principles to their own struggles.[27] In viewing themselves as victims of colonialism, some black students even identified themselves as part of the third world.

In considering the sometimes traumatic experiences the students endured, a logical question is why would they stay? Why would they not leave and attend historically black colleges or universities if education was the sole goal? A few students, like Alford Dempsey (who would have been in Columbia's class of 1969), decided to transfer to historically black colleges and universities.[28] The majority of black students, however, agreed that they had the right to be black and human in any space in the nation and they advanced that concept through their demonstrations. The social movements of the time helped them to see what was possible and they applied the rhetoric and methods used in human rights struggles on campus.

It is clear that the black students who attended Ivy League universities between the close of World War II and 1975 greatly influenced black America and the nation in general. The list of black figures who graduated during the period is impressive by any measure. They became high level politicians, captains of industries, health care officials, and thought leaders. A representative example of those black leaders and figures who took degrees from Ivy institutions was the Haverford Group, which met in the late 1960s and early 1970s to advocate racial integration in a moment when young people of the race proposed Black Nationalism and racial separation. Kenneth and Mamie Clark, William Hastie, John Hope Franklin, J. Saunders Redding, M. Carl Holman, Anne Cooke Reid, Phyllis Wallace, and Robert Weaver, who represented nine of fourteen group members, all attended Ivy universities or colleges before the World War II era. They represented a segment of the civil rights generation and the older guard of the movement that contrasted with the newer guard, which cried Black Power and campaigned for Black Studies.[29] Black Ivy alumni's advocacy in the nonprofit sector (including education) is equally as notable as that in the academy, industry, and politics. In addition to achieving in their careers and in society, black graduates continued to push their alma maters to create access for black students who followed them by joining alumni associations.

It bears noting that there has always been within the ranks of Ivy-educated black people a great diversity regarding values, political allegiances, and beliefs about the best course of action for the larger community. For instance, conservative politician and political commentator Alan Keyes opposed the efforts of black student activists at Cornell in 1969 when he was an undergraduate.[30] He left Cornell for Harvard, where he continued his opposition to the antiwar and black campus movements. Coming from a military household, he supported the conflict in Vietnam. Thomas Sowell attended Harvard for his undergraduate degree, Columbia University for graduate school, and was a professor at Cornell. Like Keyes, he opposed the actions of black demonstrators at Cornell and resigned his post to leave in personal protest.[31] Keyes and Sowell represented the conservative contingent of black students in the postwar era, but there were large numbers of students who were more liberal and an even smaller contingent who were militant enough to demonstrate. They all experienced their time at Ivy League institutions differently. For the most part, *Upending the Ivory Tower* follows the actions of those willing to join in collective agitation on particular issues affecting black people.

Although the black students who attended Ivy institutions, particularly before the late 1960s, mostly came from middle-income communities, by and large they could not fathom the lives that some of their economically advantaged white peers lived. One black student insightfully noted: "You have to have an awareness of how big the world is in order to really take advantage" of an Ivy education.[32] Many of the black students who arrived on the campuses of the Ancient Eight had the opportunity to see intimately how the "haves" lived. Even though most of the black students did not represent the "have-nots" per se, economically they were different than the nation's most wealthy white children.

By the 1960s, there was a new brand of student attending the elite schools. Scholar Marcia Synnott revealed that "before World War II, children of middle-and upper-class families, predominantly Anglo-Saxon Protestant, had found it relatively easy, if they possessed minimum academic qualifications, to be admitted to the elite colleges."[33] That did not necessarily change in the period after the war, but there was a notable shift in admissions, with fewer of the traditional prep school students attending. Black students were just a part of the shift. In general, more students from public high schools and fewer from private and boarding schools attended Ivy universities and colleges. There were more working-class students taking advantage of the G.I. Bill benefits. Then, according to Synnott, when considering the "Big Three" (Harvard, Yale, and Princeton) before the 1960s, nearly all-white secondary schools and preparatory academies like Groton, St. Paul's School, Phillips Exeter Academy, and Phillips Academy Andover sent 50 to 70 percent of students in their graduating classes to those universities.[34]

Private boarding and day school graduates made up the grand majority of the student body at Harvard, Yale, and Princeton, and so the Ivy universities focused their attention on recruiting at those few preparatory schools where all but the slightest percentage of pupils were white Anglo-Saxon protestants. There were exceptions, of course, but the student bodies at the preparatory schools mirrored those at the Big Three. That is why the push for and arrival of black students jarred the sensibilities of alumni who clung to notions of tradition, culture, and "standards." Such reasoning during an earlier period gave way to official and unofficial quotas regarding religion and race. Alumni of these elite institutions created and judged the standards that young applicants needed to meet with college board examinations and personal interviews. Often, potential interviewees got to that point in the application process by way of referral from an alumnus. The alumni of each of the Ancient Eight in the postwar period were also nearly all white. With the shift, the elite institutions still cornered the market on the highest achieving students, as they were ranked among the top 5 to 10 percent of U.S. college students in terms of intellectual abilities.[35] Perhaps as much as academic achievement, one's family name, socioeconomic status, pedigree, and *race* were all extremely important in terms of Ivy admissions before the 1960s.

When university students pushed Ivy admissions offices to recruit black students later in the 1960s, administrators at elite preparatory academies, ironically, suggested that the universities were discriminating against them. In consequence, the move to recruit more racially diverse students at the university/college level indirectly influenced elite secondary academies to review their admissions practices. Still, the Ivies, in spite of some alterations, were exclusive. As one Ivy admissions official indicated in a 1968 report, the son (seven of the Ancient Eight were still male-only then) of an alumnus stood between a 40 and 50 percent chance of admissions; whereas all other applying students had less than a 20 percent chance of admission.[36] That meant that for centuries, the culture of these institutions maintained itself by way of strict homogeneity. Black students, staff, and faculty disrupted that culture.

Some observers recognized that the changes in demographics and culture on college campuses were long in coming. A *New York Times* editorial suggested that the institutions themselves were, in part, to blame for the uprisings on campuses that occurred in the 1960s. The unwillingness to accommodate the more progressive social climate off campus and to lessen the hold on power that administrations maintained on campus left some students little choice but to press their issues. The editorial opined: "Too many university administrators have waited until students—some genuinely idealistic . . . press their demands." The "lack of initiative of school officials" led to "unsatisfactory 'settlements' under pressure," stated the editorial.[37]

The black freedom movement and activism of black youth had immense effects on the Ancient Eight. The stakes, with respect to their traditional existence, were high. Agents of change off campus and from within were able to pop the bubble of whiteness, security, and exclusivity that the Ivy institutions had created. No matter the school's geographical setting, history, or leadership, the social movements of the postwar era dictated that change was coming. In lashing out at the war, young people pushed ROTC programs and defense recruiters off campus. In the same way, by 1975, each of the Ivies had revised its admissions policies to better accommodate black candidates. All but one of the eight Ivies had Black Studies programs, departments, or centers by then as well.

By the end of the period that *Upending the Ivory Tower* covers (1975), women enrolled in and graduated from some of the Ivies for the first time in their histories; black women were among those pioneers. Because most of the eight Ivies did not admit a substantial number of women until the 1970s, the bulk of this narrative will focus on male students, staff, and administrators, while engaging in some discussion of how gender affected the approaches taken to campus life and decision making. Historians Stephanie Evans and Linda Perkins have done fascinating work on black women in higher education institutions. Both covered female collegians before Brown v. Board of Education (1954). Perkins focused specifically on those who attended what are called the Seven Sister colleges (Barnard, Smith, Mount Holyoke, Vassar, Bryn Mawr, Wellesley, and Radcliffe). *Upending the Ivory Tower*, therefore, explores in a somewhat limited way the participation of black students from Barnard (then associated with Columbia), Radcliffe (then associated with Harvard), and Pembroke College (formerly Women's College of Brown University) in the 1960s.

Given the historical context of the institutions themselves, particularly their exclusively male student bodies and staffs, the discussion of black presence in the Ivy League is necessarily male-centric. Recent scholarship has effectively demonstrated that there was no area of social advancement with regard to black life that black women did not influence during the period, and that was true of life in elite colleges.[38] The scholarship regarding the presence and activism of black women at the Seven Sisters during the postwar era and at the eight Ivies in the subsequent period will be useful in filling the scholastic gaps.

The arrival of women was a change for the Ivy League, and so too was the challenge to leaders. By 1975, six of the eight Ivy presidents who served in the 1960s had resigned. The presidents of Harvard, Columbia, Cornell, Brown, Dartmouth, and Penn all stepped down during the period of protest. The nation's most exclusive educational centers could not escape change. From the most conservative to the most liberal, the presidents could not satisfy protesting students. The unity that characterized the nation during World War II had unraveled to the point of disjunction.

The presidents of the elite universities were aware of the moment as they struggled to keep their institutions together. In 1969, at a conference hosted by Cornell University, three Ivy presidents discussed the implications of uprisings on their campuses. They spoke of the "crisis" that was occurring. The president of Harvard, Nathan M. Pusey, suggested that the sentiment of the nation was turning against universities because of the student "militants."[39] Cities and state officials were attempting to take legislative action against campus demonstrators if university administrators could not control the problem. Cornell's leader, James A. Perkins, asserted that if the nonmilitants (whom he claimed formed the majority on campus) maintained their "deafening silence," the university faced grave danger. Only if students operated within the "bounds of checks and balances" could the university function effectively.[40] The Cornell president did concede, however, that the educations that the students were receiving needed to be "relevant" to life after school. That was the language that militants inserted into the lexicon of the period. Harvard's leader warned against altering the well-established curricula and policies of the staid universities because young adults were not wholly satisfied. No need to sacrifice all that "precious and good" for the minority of dissidents, said the head of the nation's oldest university; doing so might threaten academic freedom and lead top scholars to search for work elsewhere. Perhaps, as scholar Ula Taylor indicated in an article about a black Ivy League student-activist, the presidents "longed for the good old days of political conservatism and elitist privilege."[41]

When asked how to keep the militants away from the cherished institutions, Brown University's president remarked that it would require rejecting the most academically talented and reflective students. Scholars Milton Mankoff and Richard Flacks, in their study on the social base of the American student movement, found the Brown leader to be correct.[42] Many of the white campus radicals did well academically, usually majoring in the liberal arts or social sciences. They typically came from politically liberal homes and were financially comfortable. Black students in the late 1960s largely came from working-class homes and public schools and performed well academically. At Ivy institutions, however, there was a sizeable minority of black students who were the second or third in their families to attend a university, but many by the late 1960s and early 1970s were first generation students. The methods of change depended somewhat on each president's style of leadership. Some were more liberal and outgoing, such as Perkins and Yale's Kingman Brewster; while others were more reserved and conservative like Pusey and Columbia's Grayson Kirk.[43] Students and community activists used whatever tactics best suited their situations to achieve their goals.

Upending the Ivory Tower is organized along four major themes, although every effort was made to maintain chronological context. The first is the admission of black students and the various steps the Ivies took to circumvent traditional methods of relying upon prep schools and alumni in an effort attract and keep matriculants from different backgrounds. A second theme concerns students who arrived during the mid-1960s and sought not to assimilate. As urban uprisings stunned white America, black students took inspiration from the Civil Rights Movement and Black Power Movement and applied the rhetoric and methods of outside activism on campus. Seeking to avoid the destruction they observed off campus, administrators of Ivy schools relented to changes. The power to control space and place is the basis of the third theme. The Ivies were at the forefront of the corporatization of the "university" after World War II, and their stance on progress stirred great controversy among black residents and student activists. The final theme delves into the birth of Black Studies in the Ivy League. The struggle for the curricular inclusion of people from African descent was remarkably tense, but Black Studies is one of the most enduring legacies of not just campus activism but the black freedom movement in general. These four themes help provide context for the wave of black youth activism that has arisen since the 2013 death of Trayvon Martin.

Chapter 1 explores the lives of black desegregators in the Ivy League from the early twentieth century through WWII. Rather than analyze the number of black students present in the Ivy League, which other works have capably done, the chapter attempts to reveal the lived experiences of the students as outliers. Although they could matriculate at some Ivy schools, they faced what could only be described as Jim Crow and innovated ways to survive their sometimes-hostile environments. Next, chapter 2 examines the postwar era racial evolution of what some have called the northernmost of the southern universities, Princeton University. Princeton openly Jim Crowed black students before World War II. Even though some scholarship has focused on the growth of Princeton in the postwar era, none focuses specifically on what black students did to evolve the institution toward freedom. That freedom included a push to advance the black struggle internationally in an early anti-apartheid campaign. Brown University's complex relationship to black freedom and education is the topic of chapter 3. Without great fanfare, students pressured the university to allocate substantial resources to achieve racial parity with the population of black people in the United States. This chapter also breaks new ground as there has been little written on the Brown campaigns. Although Dartmouth College's president, John Sloan Dickey, helped to construct a nationally recognized civil rights document, chapter 4 illustrates the conflict between simply accepting black students and creating a welcoming and inclusive environment. The chapter discusses some of the more extreme recruiting efforts that Ivy institutions made to attract black students. There is no scholarship at present covering the influence of civil rights and Black Power at Dartmouth.

The final chapters of the book continue to focus on the role of students, faculty, and administrators as agents of change in the way of admission policies and curriculum offerings, but they also incorporate the role of outside residents and intellectuals who played a part in shaping the Ivy League during the period. Urban Ivy institutions occupy space in contested terrains. The push and pull between schools like Columbia University in New York City and the University of Pennsylvania and the surrounding neighborhoods in Philadelphia is the subject of chapters 5 and 6, which seek to expand the scholarly conversation about the obligations and motivations of white institutions in black and brown poor spaces. They attempt to understand the meaning of the "greater good" as these extremely well-endowed universities attempted to create future leaders among those who had the least. Chapter 7 explores the role that black students and faculty members at Yale played in shaping the field of Black Studies and how black militants off campus influenced university developments. It features in-depth discussions and debates of the early proponents and opponents of Black Studies. The final two chapters delve into the more militant struggles for Black Studies that took place at Harvard and Cornell. The campus battles resulted in the premier programs and centers that exist today. It highlights just how far students were willing to go in the Ivy League to change the culture to accommodate black life.

From their communities and the struggles that arose within them, black students who attended Ivy League institutions in the postwar era carried a history of resistance to racism and a spirit of advancement regarding education that sustained them. Not all of the students sought to fight for the "cause" and still others just wanted to pass their classes. Many black learners, however, became agents of the Civil Rights Movement and Black Power Movement. They employed their Black Student Power by using their privileged status as students and alumni, as well as their race, to win victories for the larger black freedom movement. Because they did, the Ivy League remained in the vanguard of higher education. Those black Ivy students, by way of their will, endurance, and ability to see beyond themselves further opened institutional white America to justice and racial progress.

1

Surviving Solitude

The Travails of Ivy Desegregators

At but not of Harvard.
—W.E.B. Du Bois

Very few black students enrolled in Ivy institutions before World War II. They took up the burden of racially desegregating America's most elite white organizations. As members of the desegregation generation, they had to perform under the intense white gaze of Ivy League students and officials. The new students did so with the hopes of the black masses. There was a small black population in higher education in general, but the number of black learners in the Ancient Eight in the early part of the century was miniscule. To protect themselves, they banded together to create bonds. When life for them on campus turned cold, they sometimes found warm welcomes in the homes of black people in neighboring communities. Many black students in the Ivy League before World War II enrolled in the elite graduate and professional schools, but there were those few who enrolled as undergraduates.

Life for all of them, undergraduate or otherwise, was lonely and remarkably challenging as they confronted what Jeanne Theoharis and Komozi Woodard have termed Jim Crow North; however, they endured. They used tactics of survival and assimilation in their attempts to live a normal college life. They resisted racism, in part, by remaining enrolled, but they did not always directly confront institutional racial bias at the collegiate level in the way that later generations would. Many believed it was their duty to take up the charge of racial uplift after they graduated. This chapter seeks to discuss the experiences of students who went on to comprise the black upper class in the decades before World War II. For as heeled and refined as the black Ivy students were, they were not nearly as exclusive and discriminating as their wealthy and privileged white peers in the elite white universities and colleges of the Ivy League.

The majority of the nation's black students who pursued education beyond elementary school attended agricultural and industrial training institutions in the South. Henry Arthur Callis, who was in Cornell University's class of 1909, noted correctly that at the time "the conflict raged between industrial and 'higher' education." Although some learning institutions were available to African American students, the quality of resources at those black schools did not yet rank with white institutions. As such, Callis continued, "in 1906, for a colored student to be enrolled in an accredited high school was a mark of distinction"; however, "for such a student to enter a reputable university set him apart as 'unusual.'"[1] The black students' distinctiveness at Ivy schools was ostensibly positive in nature. Historian Kevin Gaines, however, wrote about the potential flaws of the upwardly mobile students: "many black elites sought status, moral authority, and recognition of their humanity by distinguishing themselves, as bourgeois agents of civilization, from the presumably undeveloped black majority."[2] Being unusual did not free the young members of the black bourgeoisie from obligations to the larger community and from the pitfalls of their own success.

Black students had been attending Ivy institutions in small measure since the nineteenth century. Edward Mitchell graduated from Dartmouth College in 1828. In 1850, the year that America was compromising legislatively over the freedom of black people, free Black Nationalist Martin Delaney was the first black student admitted to Harvard (medical school), but Boston's George Lewis Ruffin was the first to graduate Harvard with a law degree; another Bostonian, Richard Greener, was the first undergraduate student to graduate in 1870. New Haven's own Cortlandt Van Rensselaer Creed graduated from Yale with a medical degree in 1857, the year of the U.S. Supreme Court's Dred Scott decision. Four years later, Edward Bouchet earned Phi Beta Kappa honors as an undergraduate and then attained a PhD at Yale. In 1877, Inman Page at Brown University became the first to earn a degree. Five years later, the University of Pennsylvania graduated its first black student, James Brister, with a degree in dentistry; that same year Nathan Francis Mossell graduated with a medical degree. William Adger was the first black undergraduate to receive a degree from Penn in 1883. At Cornell University (which was not founded until 1865), George Washington Fields earned a law degree and Charles Chauveau Cook and Jane Eleanor Datcher obtained their bachelor of arts degrees in 1890. The year of the Plessy v. Ferguson (1896) decision, James Dickinson Carr received a law degree at Columbia University, becoming one its first graduates. Princeton graduated its first black student in 1947.

Perhaps the most famous black Ivy alumnus was W.E.B. Du Bois. After graduating Fisk Institute, "Willie" Du Bois continued his scholastic trek to the educational jewel of the nation, Harvard. As would be the case at other Ivy League institutions, black students coming with degrees from historically black colleges and universities (HBCUs) needed to prove themselves by taking undergraduate courses at Harvard. Du Bois entered the college in 1887 with another black student, Clement G. Morgan. They grew close to each other while attempting to navigate the world of snobbery and exclusiveness that was Harvard. Du Bois was rejected membership to the glee club and made few white friends; however, his intellectual acumen caught the attention of white professors who took care to train him.[3] Although he regaled his education, Du Bois always felt that he was "at but not of Harvard."[4] He would not be the last black Ivy student to feel that way.

In the early part of the new century, not much in the way of admissions to higher education institutions changed. On the whole, during the period between 1900 and 1945, college was not an option for most Americans. This was especially true for black citizens. The majority of black people lived in rural areas of the South, and many still worked as sharecroppers or other capacities in agriculture. That period saw high rates of lynching and other forms of racial violence, but it also observed the solidification of a black middle and elite class.[5] In some ways, members of the black elite had the opportunity to enjoy the privileges of their white peers that included taking advantage of higher education. In other ways, even the black elite could not be fully human. By that time, the institutions most available to black learners were the HBCUs: Howard, Hampton, Fisk, Morehouse, Spelman, Tuskegee, Wilberforce, Lincoln (Pennsylvania), and Florida A&M were among the top choices for the black college bound. What today are called predominantly white institutions (PWIs) comprised less of an option to black students, particularly those not from elite socioeconomic backgrounds. As historian Robert

Harris Jr. observed, by 1910, only fifty-four black students (men and women) graduated with their bachelor's degrees from elite PWIs, which included universities such as Columbia, Yale, the University of Chicago, Harvard, Stanford University, University of Michigan, Penn, and Cornell. Black graduate and professional students by and large looked to the Ivy League for their degree options. As of 1939, thirty-five black students graduated from Columbia, twenty-eight from Penn, twenty-five from Cornell, twenty-five from Harvard, and ten from Yale.[6]

At that historical moment, considering the educational options at the secondary level for most black people, even fifty-four black undergraduate degree earners in 1910 was miraculous. In terms of public secondary options there were a finite number of schools that prepared black students for work at elite higher education institutions. Of those secondary schools, the M Street School (later renamed Paul Laurence Dunbar High School) in Washington, D.C., is one of the most (if not the most) acclaimed. With its faculty holding an impressive number of advanced degrees, the black prep school in D.C. trained some of the most influential black figures in the history of the nation. Of its early graduates, 80 percent earned degrees at the collegiate level.[7] Many went from the M Street School to the Ivy League. Famous black educators such as Carter G. Woodson (alumnus of Harvard), Anna Julia Cooper (alumna of Oberlin), and Mary Church Terrell (alumna of Oberlin) worked as teachers or administrators at the prep school.[8]

Although Dartmouth and Harvard had accepted black students earlier, Cornell became an attractive educational home for black college students. Unlike the other Ivies, Cornell did not get its start until the nineteenth century, at the close of the Civil War. When founded as a land grant institution, Cornell's founder and the new president indicated that the university should provide educational opportunities to all students regardless of religion, gender, and race. That was a departure from most of the Ivy institutions that started with religious underpinnings in the seventeenth and eighteenth centuries. Where informal quotas for black students existed at places like Harvard and Yale, there were seemingly none at Cornell. Black students who could afford it attended at will. Between 1904 and 1943, nearly 150 black students matriculated at Cornell.[9] For Cornell's short history, the number of black matriculants was notable in contrast to other institutions in the Ivy League.

Aside from the fact that the institutional mission was more liberal than those of its peers, Cornell featured other qualities that made it alluring to black students. That it was in the North was a positive attribute. Before the Civil War, enslaved people running for their freedom to Canada used Ithaca, New York, as a stopping point. Despite the cold winters and remote geographic location in the Finger Lakes Region, a free black community developed. Ithaca's location gave the town an appeal that New York City or Philadelphia did not have: very few distractions. That was an advantage for serious black students who could use the off-campus community for support and the quietude to study.

Cornell and its affiliates were not always welcoming. In 1900, a white student from West Virginia withdrew from the university in protest of two black students who were enrolled in his agriculture class. His southern sensibilities and rearing, he said, made him uncomfortable with black people being in the classroom. He knew his parents would not appreciate the fact that he sat in the same learning space and swam in the same pool with black students.[10] The white student who withdrew was not typical of all Cornell students, but his behavior represented an aspect of life that black learners had to endure at elite PWIs.

Segregation, as restrictive and insidious as it was, forced black people to innovate in many ways. In 1905, men could not live on campus at Cornell. Most white homeowners would not board black renters so housing became an issue for black students. Black families like the Nelsons, Cannons, Newtons, and Singletons worked service jobs in town and on campus while supplementing their income in other ways. Edward Newton and William Cannon worked in fraternity houses on Cornell's campus. Archie Singleton worked as a butler for a prominent white businessman in Ithaca and Singleton and his wife owned a business.[11] These families opened their homes to black student boarders. The situation provided additional income for the black homeowners but also a secure place for the students to live.

Since enslavement, people in black communities revered formal education and they attempted to assist black learners who sought it. As historian Kevin Gaines put it, "African Americans have, with almost religious fervor, regarded education as the key to liberation."[12] In that way, those homes became more than support centers that allowed students to be human; they were incubators for black civil rights and intellectual leadership. The students appreciated the hospitality their hosts showed. "The social life among our group was carried on in the many comfortable homes of the Negroes [in Ithaca]. Nearly every Friday night, we were welcomed at the home of Mr. and Mrs. Wm. Cannon where we could meet their charming daughter and the other young women of the community. We were allowed to dance and good eats were always served us," remembered Cornell alumnus George Kelley (class of 1908).[13]

While black students dealt with social isolation on campus in Ithaca, further north black leaders convened to address the rights of black people in general. Racial violence and political disfranchisement threatened African Americans wherever they resided. In Niagara Falls, Canada, black Harvard alumni Du Bois and William Monroe Trotter (Du Bois PhD and Trotter BA in 1895) organized a group of nearly thirty other progressive activists. By the end of the 1905 meeting, the group declared that their race deserved total freedom, which included the right to participate in the democracy and to be treated as social equals in all realms of society. Many scholars agree that the Niagara Movement was in many ways a precursor to one of the most influential civil rights organizations in the twentieth century: the National Association for the Advancement of Colored People (NAACP).

Students with a desire to attend Cornell and other Ivy institutions were well aware of the glacial pace of racial progress and understood that by achieving education they helped uplift the community. They also instinctively knew that they would not be able to depend on the liberal notions of white administrators to succeed. Even though some elite universities allowed excelling black students to attend, those places were often all but welcoming. In the early twentieth century, Harvard's president Abbott Lowell provided insight regarding the position of many liberal elite administrators: "We owe to the colored man the same opportunities for education that we do to the white man; but we don't owe to him to force him and the white man into social relations that are not, or may not be, mutually congenial."[14] Some race leaders (particularly those who participated in the Niagara conference in 1905) agitated against that attitude. Booker T. Washington, who received an honorary master's degree from Harvard in 1896, bolstered the opinion of the president with his famous Atlanta Cotton States Exposition speech of the same year, in which he accommodated racial discrimination by explaining that social segregation should be acceptable as long as mutual progress was respected. Thought leaders like Du Bois and Trotter vehemently opposed this viewpoint. Black students who attended the Ivies in the early twentieth century attempted to push the envelope beyond the accommodation of racist treatment.

The activities of black Cornellians best exemplified the more assertive campaign for racial equality that students made in the new century. Keeping in mind that at least five black students had not returned to Cornell from the previous semester, in the fall of 1905 some remaining students took the initiative to create their own support network. In addition to socializing, the early group members worked to improve their academic opportunities by studying together. The students borrowed a study technique from the members of white fraternities on campus. They banked the tests they took so that black students who took the courses in the future would know how and what to study.[15] Current institutions of higher education expend millions of dollars to recreate the academic and student affairs retention models that these isolated black students conceived of for their own survival in 1905–1906.

Soon afterward, some of the men in the social/study group suggested that it become a literary society that surveyed and discussed the works of black intellectuals. The idea of a literary society was profound in the sense that so many Americans were either illiterate or had little or no time for leisure reading.[16] That these black collegians enjoyed such a luxury is telling. Although the members of the group were amenable to adding literary discourse to their meetings, they could not agree on what to name the society. Some members of the group who had been working in white fraternity houses to support themselves wanted to use Greek letters. One group member, a graduate student, disapproved of the idea, claiming that there were no Greek signifiers that could be used for African Americans. After some debate and research, the leading members of the society came up with the name Alpha Phi Alpha.[17]

Within months of naming the literary society, at the home of the Singletons on December 4, 1906, seven members established Alpha Phi Alpha as the first collegiate fraternity for black men.[18] With the help of members of the African Methodist Episcopal Zion church, students held their first fraternity ritual in an Odd Fellows masonic lodge. The fraternity followed the trail that the founders of Sigma Pi Phi Fraternity, Inc., also known as the Boulé, had blazed in Philadelphia.[19] The founders of the Boulé represented the black elite in the professions, with members having attained education at Phillips Exeter, Penn, Harvard, Columbia, and other elite institutions. After their college and academic training, they entered professions in medicine and dentistry while using their status to create more freedoms for people like them. At the collegiate level, the founding members of Alpha Phi Alpha organized around principles of scholarship, uplift, and service to the black community.

To be sure, the founders of Alpha were the sons of relatively established families, but the students were still only one generation removed from slavery. Various members of their families had served in the Civil War, attended college, taught at the collegiate level, were ministers, and owned businesses.[20] The founding members included Henry A. Callis, Charles H. Chapman, Eugene K. Jones, George B. Kelley, Nathaniel A. Murray, Robert H. Ogle, and Vertner W. Tandy. Two were from the South, and the remaining five were from either northern states or the nation's capital. Of the seven founders, the parents or another close family member attended college at institutions like Hampton, Howard, and Harvard. Two of the founders had attended the M Street School, and two others had attended HBCUs before arriving at Cornell.[21] In making the fraternity's motto "first of all; servants of all; we shall transcend all," the students were quite aware of their elite status in officially creating a brotherhood for black college men.

The fraternity also expressed the need to establish networks of fictive kinship on university campuses. Fictive kinship was a survival tool that black people employed for generations. Although universities claimed to adhere to the concept of in loco parentis, black students had to engineer their own family models while on campus—often without the help of their schools' institutional parenting. When the Cornell administration recognized the fraternity, the members made it a resource for black intellectualism and community progress within and outside of the university. The fraternity quickly expanded to other institutions, creating another chapter on the campus of Howard University and then another at the University of Toronto, making Alpha the first national and international black collegiate fraternity. By the 1920s, the fraternity established chapters at six of the eight American Ivies. In spite of declarations of uplift and service to the community, the founding members wanted to remain somewhat exclusive. Famous historian, Sigma Pi Phi member, and Alpha Phi Alpha member Charles H. Wesley explained that "it was only natural" the founders would turn the fraternity "toward other colleges and universities of the first rank."[22] Additionally, it was important to the fraternity not to admit what one founder called "undesirables."[23] The founders and members of Alpha did not escape notions of elitism even in their good works for the race. Their sentiments echoed those of many from their socioeconomic class during the period. After the founding of Alpha Phi Alpha, students founded other black Greek letter organizations at Howard, the University of Indiana, and Butler University.

When the founders of Alpha Phi Alpha graduated, they took their place among the race's leaders and in the professions. Callis, training under the prominent surgeon Daniel Hale Williams, became a physician and charter member of the National Medical Association, which allowed black medical doctors to share information and best practices.[24] He had a brief marriage with fellow Cornellian, club woman, and activist Alice Dunbar Nelson, who was formerly married to Paul Laurence Dunbar.[25] Chapman became an award winning agriculture professor at Florida A&M, inspiring students and colleagues alike.[26] Jones became an executive of a new organization called the National Urban League and a leading figure in the struggle for black rights in New York.[27] His son, Eugene Kinkle Jones Jr. graduated Cornell Law School in 1933. George Kelley became the first registered civil engineer in New York and worked on the Barge Canal system.[28] He also achieved the rank of second lieutenant in the U.S. Army during World War I. Murray taught at Dunbar High School (formerly the M Street School) and Armstrong High School in Washington, D.C.[29] Ogle moved to the nation's capital, where he worked as an assistant for Republican U.S. Senator Frances E. Warren who headed the Senate Appropriations Committee.[30] Tandy became the first recognized registered architect in the State of New York. Also a prominent member of black New York society, he designed the historic St. Philip's Protestant Episcopal church in Harlem and the palatial homes of black millionaire and mogul Madame C. J. Walker.[31] Black Cornell graduates achieved in spite of Jim Crow.

Back on campus, fraternity members became student leaders. The fraternity put together a "Committee on Student Affairs" to address black student needs. The fraternity's and committee's duty was to "promote the scholarship of all the colored students of the university and to promote a sympathetic relationship between the townspeople and the students." As part of the desegregation generation, black students at Ivy schools believed they had something to prove to their institutions and other observers. In performing at a high level, they understood they were paving the way for other black students to attend and for potential social acceptance at PWIs. Aware that they were on a metaphoric stage, Alpha members offered programs and services "in order that the colored student body may get some recognition in the eyes of the university." It was vital to modify their behavior and to be as respectable as possible, "for outsiders are quick to criticize and [are] severe in their judgments." That was why they looked to each other to uphold a standard of decorum that was irreproachable.[32] Scholars have argued that artists of the Harlem Renaissance took a similar tack in trying to present to the world the best of black people in the hope that white America may accept black people as being as refined as any other American. For members of the desegregation generation in the Ivy League, the burden of respectability and representation was all but light.

Cornell women especially shouldered the burden of respectability while overcoming other circumstances that called into question their status as ladies. For the black female students of the university, the issue of housing came to the fore. Between 1911 and 1914 black students at Sage College (Cornell's school for women) faced issues because of the requirement that female students stay on campus. The earliest black students at Sage, including Harlem Renaissance luminary Jessie Fauset, stayed on campus without major event. But by 1905 the college had stopped housing black women.[33] The fact that it was compulsory for women (white) to stay on campus when it was not for men spoke to the period's flawed notions of female fragility and the need to monitor women for their own sake. Ladies (white) deserved a certain amount of accommodation, according to the ideas of the period. The regulation revealed the desire of men (white) to protect women (white) from the dangers of the outside world. Those noble men's desires to shield women from undue burdens did not, apparently, extend to black women. That a school that professed openness to all students would have a conflict over whether to allow black women to be housed in the same fashion as their white peers illustrates the contradictory nature of the informal and formal policies that black people had to navigate in institutional white America during that period and later. It also illustrates the devaluation of black womanhood that was common at the time; black ladies did not receive the same respect as white women in the eyes of administrators.

In the minds of some, there was much at stake if black and white students lived together in such close quarters at Ivy schools. According to a white Mississippian who graduated Harvard in 1898, race mingling led to dire consequences. Commenting on the controversy over black freshmen rooming with white peers that was occurring during the same period as that at Cornell, he said, "social equality—marriageability, if you will—is implied in sharing 'bed and board' with another."[34] He based his statement on the premise that black and white people were not equal to begin with, and that merely sleeping near white men would entice black men to take on white wives. Aside from being racist, the statement was irrationally illogical. At the root of his and others' concerns about living in close proximity to black people was the strange fixation that white America had on the prospects of miscegenation. In following the Harvard alumnus's line of reasoning, racial equality under any circumstances meant a loss of power in terms of reproduction. Perhaps eating separately under the same roof in a dining hall or restaurant was permissible and even inevitable, conceded the Harvard educated southerner, but to "'sleep with a nigger'—is a horse of another color" and unacceptable.

As scholars like Komozi Woodard, Jeanne Theoharis, Matt Delmont, and Mathew Countryman have convincingly demonstrated in their works, racial bigotry was not reserved for men of the South and southern locations. When Oswald Garrison Villard, grandson of famous white abolitionist William Lloyd Garrison, Harvard alumnus (class of 1893), and founding member of the NAACP weighed in on the issue, compelling Harvard to be as fair as its reputation on the issue of black housing, white northerners raised their voices in opposition as well. A Connecticut alumnus from the class of 1901, in a revelatory statement, called for Harvard's administrators to be forthright about the issue. He criticized "overseers" for not having the intelligence to innovate creative ways to keep black and Jewish men out of the university. The alumnus asked, "does the possible flare-up of such men as Villard" scare administrators such that they will not return Harvard to being a "white man's college?"[35] Finally, he queried, "why not come out into the open and take the . . . criticism for a year or so and save our University for our sons, grandsons and for our posterity?" Of course, "our sons and grandsons," meant future white men.

The concern about living arrangements continued with the women of Cornell as well. In 1911, two black women, juniors Pauline Angeline Ray and Rosa Vassar, attempted to register for housing on campus, pointing out that accommodating racism had become too expensive. It cost them extra to get to campus by streetcar; their rent was more than what white women paid at the dormitory; and they were at a disadvantage when attempting to attain materials in the library because the on-campus students pilfered them first. When the dean of Sage College met with the students and heard their appeal, a controversy ensued, as the dean suggested that it was not her but the white female students who would have a problem with living with black women.[36] Of course administrators, not students, made policy, but the dean was correct in her prediction that white women would protest black residents. Two hundred students of Sage College signed a petition stating that they could not tolerate living with black women and gave it to the trustees of Cornell.[37] The New York chapter of the NAACP took up the issue. Subsequently, black women begrudgingly but not consistently were permitted to live on campus. Administrators at Cornell and the other Ivies often valued the comfort of white segregationists more than the human dignity of black learners.

Unfortunately, the controversy regarding housing continued in 1914 and beyond. When white women in the dormitory confronted first-year student Adelaide Cook, the daughter of a black alumnus, wanting her to leave, the mother and daughter made their displeasure public. Again, the NAACP joined the conversation to keep equality of opportunity and access a priority. As the controversy became public, the university president had to, once again, reaffirm the institution's commitment to its mission. The trustees and administration had to confront the reality of racism on campus in the face of their liberal mission of educating everyone.[38] By 1939, black women were again having difficulty accessing Sage College with little support from the administration. It should be noted that these students who struggled to find housing still had to attend their courses and compete in the classroom. Ultimately, students who happened to be black shouldered undue burdens while trying to excel in their studies. They learned that racism made education at an elite PWI an expensive endeavor.

That same racism, however, cost the university as well. Evie Carpenter, who graduated in 1918, dissuaded her daughter, Emily Spencer, from going to Cornell. Spencer was a second-generation college woman who received a bachelor's degree from Virginia State College and was considering Cornell for graduate school. Carpenter believed her daughter was "too young to be isolated in Ithaca," where she would have to endure some of the same problems surrounding housing that Carpenter had faced.[39] The isolation of Cornell combined with the negative experiences with discrimination caused some black families to rethink sending their children to the university. In future decades, housing issues would again plague black women in the Ivy League and particularly Cornell.

The decision to place one's self in such trying circumstances spoke to the value that black students placed on an Ivy League education and the invasiveness of racism in the culture of these leading institutions. As historian Genna Rae McNeil insightfully noted in her seminal biography of eminent civil rights attorney Charles Hamilton Houston, "One did not come to Harvard and forget one's racial heritage."[40] That went for both black and white affiliates of the university. McNeil referred to the experience of Houston as a law student, who had completed his undergraduate work at Amherst College.

During what scholars refer to as the Red Summer of 1919, when white mobs attacked black citizens in forty cities and counties, Houston enrolled at the Harvard Law School. During the turmoil of the race riots, black people, some of whom were veterans of World War I, assertively defended themselves and their property. Houston and his fellow veterans understood their rights as citizens, and he especially believed it his duty to make the law work for the most oppressed Americans. That is why he chose one of the most, if not the most, renowned law schools in the nation. Houston's father was an attorney and Houston himself was already a member of black elite society, having been an officer in the war and a college graduate. He was also a member of Alpha Phi Alpha Fraternity, Inc. Like the founders of the fraternity in Cornell, he recognized racial divisions at Harvard. Just as the Cornell students could not join white fraternities, Houston and other black students could not join the law clubs and societies at Harvard. That sort of rejection led to the creation of the Nile Club on campus, which brought together black students much the same way as the study group at Cornell in 1905 did. The racial rejection also inspired the establishment of the National Bar Association for black attorneys, over which Houston's law school friend and fraternity brother Raymond Pace Alexander (the first black graduate of the University of Pennsylvania's Wharton School of Business) eventually presided.[41]

Again, members of the black elite banded together to establish parallel organizations to advance their own opportunities but also to deflect white racism. Great Black Nationalist Marcus Garvey personified that effort with the Universal Negro Improvement Association's *Negro World* weekly and the Black Star steamship line. Houston and his classmates admired Garvey's vision to establish a black economy that spanned the world while rebuilding pride in black culture. At a moment when black life was so fragile, young leaders like Houston invited Garvey to campus to meet with the small group of black students and Cambridge residents. If they were to remain mentally and emotionally fit, they had to craft a social and cultural life for themselves.[42]

Like so many early black Ivy students, Houston, feeling that he had to represent the race well, excelled in his studies, which earned him a place on the prestigious *Harvard Law Review* editorial team. Not surprisingly, he was the first of his race to serve in that capacity.[43] As an attorney, he revived Howard University's law school and went on to engineer the desegregation of public education as head of the NAACP's Legal Defense Fund. Fellow fraternity brother and protégé Thurgood Marshall, who succeeded Houston, credited the Harvard-trained lawyer with providing the blueprint for the 1954 U.S. Supreme Court decision in Brown v. Board of Education. Incidentally, Houston's law school friend Alexander used his training to bring social, educational, and economic justice to Philadelphia as part of the NAACP.

Houston and Alexander were in league with Ralph Bunche, who started his graduate studies at Harvard in 1928. Having attended the University of California, Los Angeles, he had some conception of life at a PWI, but Bunche was still solitary in the political science department and one of few at the prestigious university. He studied colonial Africa and upon graduation enjoyed academic fellowships at the London School of Economics and Capetown University in South Africa. Bunche became arguably the most well-known black man in the world. During World War II, he worked for the Office of Strategic Services, which was the precursor to the U.S. Central Intelligence Agency and eventually for the State Department. At the close of the war, he was among those (including eventual Ivy presidents Grayson Kirk and John Dickey), who helped to plan the United Nations and construct its charter. Bunche, as an UN mediator, achieved what has not been possible since, a signed armistice between Israel and Palestine. His efforts earned him a Nobel peace prize and world acclaim. Between 1960 and 1965, Bunche became a member of Harvard's Board of Overseers.[44]

As Houston, Alexander, and Bunche took the fight for racial equity to the courts and world stage, back at Cornell, black women took the lead in organizing efforts during the Great Depression. In addition to the arrival of black fraternities and later a black sorority (Alpha Kappa Alpha Sorority, Inc.), students organized the Booker T. Washington Club at Cornell. The group delved into conversations and debates regarding segregation and invited speakers to campus to inform their discussions. In 1935, the same year as the Italian invasion of Ethiopia, Margaret Morgan took over as president of the club.[45] The group did not survive for long, but the seriousness of the students in their approach to the oppression that black people faced on and off campus is noteworthy. So, too, is the leadership of black women in these matters.

Students at other Ivy institutions shared the travails of the black men and women at Harvard and Cornell. J. Saunders Redding poignantly provided a glimpse into the solitary life of an Ivy desegregator. Redding, who eventually became a prominent literary scholar, arrived at Brown University as an undergraduate student in 1924. He was the second in his family to graduate from the Ivy League university. His brother, Louis, achieved his BA at Brown before receiving his JD from Harvard. Of his time as an undergraduate at the university, Redding remembered there being only four other black students—if that; two of them graduated after his first year. Although he and the remaining student shared what he called a "consciousness," Redding said: "we took elaborate precautions against the appearance of clannishness."[46] Claiming to emulate the behavior of the black students who graduated before him, on campus and in the presence of white students he attempted not to give off the impression that he was only interested in matters of blackness. This led him to avoid eating with and fraternizing with the other black student in public but only "in the secret of our rooms at night with the shades down," he revealed. Redding admitted an awareness of himself and his actions: "We were lost."[47] To find solace, Redding and his fellow black Brunonian left campus to engage other black students who were attending New England colleges.

Even with those cultural outlets off campus, Redding's schoolmate could not adjust to always guarding his speech and measuring his movements on campus. The other black student, Redding remembered, exclaimed: "There's something wrong with this" in reference to the way they felt constantly on alert.[48] The unsettled student wondered aloud: "There must be some place better than this. God damn it, there must be!" Declaring his desire to leave, the student shared his feelings: "I feel like everybody's staring at me, all these white guys, waiting for me to make a bad break." The student suffered from what modern scholars have termed "racial battle fatigue"—experiencing intense stress as a result of the small racialized slights (called microaggressions today) and behaviors of the dominant (white) race.[49] Unable to withstand the pressure further, Redding's school friend exited Brown and shortly afterward committed suicide. That left Redding to feel as though he was "fighting alone against the whole white world."[50] In 1928, he graduated, earning Phi Beta Kappa honors, and shortly afterward entered the MA program in English. He finished his master's degree in 1932. Later he took courses toward a PhD at Columbia University without completion.

During the Depression, the experience of black graduate and professional students at Harvard in some ways mirrored that of Redding. A graduate of Dunbar High School in Washington, D.C., William H. Hastie, like his cousin Charles Hamilton Houston, came to Harvard from Amherst College. He earned a Bachelor of Law degree at Harvard followed by a Doctorate of Juridical Science in 1933. He, like Houston, became editor of the *Harvard Law Review*. After working with Houston, Hastie took an appointment as governor of the Virgin Islands and eventually became the first black federal court judge under the Harry S. Truman administration.[51] Shortly after Hastie graduated, premier historian and activist John Hope Franklin enrolled in the graduate school of

Harvard to study in the Department of History. In his memoir, *Mirror to America*, Franklin described taking a loan from his white Fisk University advisor Ted Currier to afford tuition. The son of an attorney in the Tulsa area, Franklin had the advantage that many black students in the Ivy League enjoyed: educated, supportive, and active parents. They worked to ensure he believed he was intelligent and capable of achieving. The value of that singular notion can never be underestimated when students are thrust into racist and racially oppressive environments. Those qualities and beliefs are what Franklin, and so many other Ivy League students, claimed sustained him when he found himself in a space filled with rich whiteness.

Franklin's memory of his time in Cambridge represented that of other black students trying to make the best for themselves via education. He remembered: "A day, and often an hour, didn't go by without my feeling the color of my skin—in the reactions of white Cambridge, the behavior of my fellow students, the attitudes real and imagined struck by my professors."[52] Growing up witnessing the destruction of "Black Wall Street" in Tulsa during the riot of 1918, he was fully aware of his blackness; however, the constant reminders of others grew irksome. "Race precluded my enjoying the self-assurance to which most of my colleagues, along with the affluence and influence, were born," he said. That which had worked in his favor for most of his life, "being ambitious and black," also attracted the often unwanted gaze of white observers, recalled Franklin.

Unlike his peers of affluence and influence, the only thing he remembered having was his "determination and a corresponding work ethic to fall back on." He needed both when his professor told a "darky" joke while Franklin sat embarrassed in class.[53] The joke was based on ignorance regarding black people, but the entire curriculum at Harvard and throughout the Ivy League glorified white civilization and supremacy. In part, that is what made those institutions elite. Harvard and its peers perpetuated racial dominance and racist ideology while simultaneously establishing themselves as American stalwarts. Unfortunately for Franklin, life in Cambridge was at times not much better. He told the story of an outing with a black lady friend. The couple waited in a restaurant in the northern city for more than hour without so much as being recognized by the wait staff.[54] The North and elite universities were not sheltered from racism.

Life for Franklin was not all bad, and he had positive interactions with white peers and professors. He always had to be cognizant, though, of the potential for situations to sour because of his race and the racism of others. For many black students in Franklin's generation, unrelenting determination and work ethic motivated them to succeed academically and professionally. Franklin became the premier scholar of black history while assisting his fraternity brother Thurgood Marshall with research for the Brown v. Board case. Nearly forty years later, Franklin took an appointment to head a presidential commission on American race relations.

In the pre-World War II period, black students often found a modicum of acceptance at Ivy League universities and colleges as athletes. In higher education in general and the Ivy League especially, athletics translated to privilege in terms of one's mobility on campus. There is a long history of black athletes entertaining predominantly white audiences in the United States. William Rhoden, author of *Forty Million Dollar Slave: The Rise, Fall, and Redemption of the Black Athlete* (2007), described black sportsmen in the period of enslavement having to perform to meet the expectations of their masters. If good enough, those chosen few athletes received elevated treatment. During the period of Jim Crow, white Americans loved black sportsmen—as long as they performed their duties on the field or court. Once back in society, however, black athletes faced the same kind of racism that nonathletic citizens confronted. Scholars have called this the "key functionary theory."[55] When applied to race and sports, as long as black people performed their roles in entertaining and amusing white people, they could be applauded and even admired. In the early twentieth century, this was true for athletes racing horses and bicycles as well as boxing and playing football. Perhaps a clear example of the key functionary theory was Jesse Owens. White Americans cheered the gold medal winning Olympian, but he could not stay on campus at his northern predominantly white university.

The Ancient Eight got the name "Ivy League" because of football. During the early part of the twentieth century, some of the Ivy institutions were more renowned for their sports wins than their academic rigor. For some time, the Ivy League led the way in football competition.[56] The names of black players could be found on rosters at most of the Ivies, but Princeton, which did not enroll black students, often refused to even play against teams fielding black athletes. Historian Charles Martin, in *Benching Jim Crow: The Rise and Fall of the Color Line in Southern College Sports*, relayed a story of a Dartmouth black player who took the field against Princeton only to have his collar bone broken within the first minutes of the game, effectively ending his season. After the incident, a Princeton player said, "We'll teach you to bring colored men down here. You must take us for a gang of servants."[57] The animosity that the Dartmouth player experienced was not unusual for black athletes, especially when playing teams throughout the South. Princeton was not in the South geographically, but it was well known as a haven for southerners who had a predilection for oppressing black people.[58]

In most of the Ivy League, however, black players had a chance to display their talents on the field and court. In the early 1890s, William H. Lewis became the first black football player in the league. Lewis has the distinction of being the first in a number of other categories as well. He was the first black player selected for Walter Camp's All-Time All-America team. Enrolled in the law school, he played center for Harvard University. There, he also became the first black player to be named captain of the Harvard team. His leadership on the field portended his career as the first black coach in the Ivy League, when he spent eleven years on the coaching staff of the Harvard team. As if his football exploits were not enough to fill a lifetime for Lewis, President William Howard Taft appointed him U.S. assistant attorney general in 1910.[59] After his term as a federal appointee, he spent his life fighting against lynching and other forms of racism.

Joining Lewis in the Ivy League were footballers like the Pollard brothers. Leslie and Frederick "Fritz" Pollard represented Dartmouth and Brown respectively. Fritz Pollard was also a Walter Camp All-American, graduating Brown with a degree in chemistry in 1919. While on the field he met with hardnosed players and racist taunts from the crowd. At one game against Yale, the white students in the crowd sang the tune "Bye Bye, Blackbird."[60] Despite the jibes, Pollard had a successful college career and went on to play and coach professionally. Incidentally, Fritz Pollard also pledged Alpha Phi Alpha while at Brown. While the athletes played football and joined fraternities, black people throughout the United States tried daily to escape racial violence. In spite of their acclaim, black athletes had to keep in mind the threat of lynching and the blatant disrespect of racism in the same way that other black men and women did.

Cornell University was competitive in football during the depression years. In the 1930s at Cornell, the students, staff, and administration adored Jerome "Brude" Holland, who was the first black varsity football player there. Born in upstate New York, he played offense and defense, with his presence affecting much of the game. Off the field he was a member of black Greek organization Omega Psi Phi Fraternity, Inc., and the Booker T. Washington Club, which students started on campus to debate the utility of Washington's philosophy. Holland also mentored black youth at a newly established community center in Ithaca founded by the Francis Harper Society. Although he was black, because he was a beloved football player he enjoyed a Cornell experience that was not available to students who were not standout athletes. For instance, Holland was selected to a very exclusive honor society, Aleph Samach. White people at Cornell were generous in granting Holland the distinction of the honor society, but at the very same time black women, who did not play football, faced rejection for the housing that was supposed to be compulsory for women. Ater graduating, Holland earned a doctorate from the University of Pennsylvania and eventually became the president of two HBCUs and an ambassador to Sweden during President Richard M. Nixon's administration.[61] He also accepted an appointment as trustee of Cornell University.

Black students also excelled in other sports in the Ivy League. At Columbia, George Gregory received national commendations for his play on the basketball court from 1929 to 1931. He was the first black player at Columbia and he remained in New York City after graduating, taking posts in civil service leadership roles.[62] On the lacrosse field, Lucien Alexis of Harvard gained acclaim in 1941. That year, he and his white teammates played against the University of Maryland in College Park, making that the first integrated athletic competition of the twentieth century in the state. Harvard coaches were egalitarian enough to field a black player, but they were not above accommodating other teams' racist culture. That was the case when, in 1941, Harvard was set to play the U.S. Naval Academy in Annapolis. The academy maintained a rule that its teams would not host black players. Rather than cause controversy, the Harvard coaches benched Alexis and played the game. Black athletes at Ivy institutions may have been revered on their campuses, but when they traveled, the sportsmen met with traumatic circumstances.

The concession of Harvard in 1941 was especially hurtful because, in 1916, the university had righteously canceled a track meet with the naval academy because it would not allow a black long jumper to participate. The wavering on principles that Harvard displayed was the source of a great deal of embarrassment, disillusionment, and frustration for Alexis and black onlookers. The rights of black people to participate fully in society or to be fully human largely depended on the unpredictable integrity of even the most well-intending white people. Fortunately, fair-minded students pressured Harvard to establish a policy of competition regarding race, and the university responded with a statement indicating that it would not reenact the Alexis scenario.[63]

The spirit of a "unified" nation and the observation of black men sacrificing themselves in defense of the country influenced some Ivy officials to put black athletes in play. The estranged relationship between the Soviet Union and the United States that led to the Cold War helped to called into question ideas of race and American democracy within institutions. Additionally, the re-desegregation of the National Football League in 1946 and of Major League Baseball in 1947 may have provided some outside societal pressure for the elite colleges to allow black students to play as well. At Yale, a black basketball player, Jay Swift, graced the court, helping the team to win. Soon after, Levi Jackson became the first black football player at Yale; the team selected Jackson to be the captain, making history again.[64] In addition to being chosen to lead the team on the field, he was selected to join the secretive Skull and Bones society. The military and the Ivy League's athletic teams found utility in black men, as long as they could help the institutions win.

World War II and the Cold War made it possible for an evolution in race relations to take place at Ivy League institutions. The V-12 Navy College Training Program that called on universities to provide education to sailors so that the navy could increase its pool of officers did not restrict itself to white servicemen.[65] That made it possible for black men to attend an institution like Princeton, which had traditionally rejected black applicants. There, Arthur Wilson, one of the first black students to attend the university, played basketball for three years and even became captain of the team. At the Yale School of Nursing, a question arose regarding the admission of black women because they would necessarily have to make skin contact with white patients. When a prominent white Yale alumnus wrote to point out the irony of "opposing Nazi ideas of race" while still rejecting American students because of their race, Yale's president responded that from that point forward the nursing school would admit or reject candidates based solely on their student qualifications.[66] Here, again, the school's leadership had to be steered toward morality and justice.

At midcentury, there were still few black students at Brown, but the university did, at least, have a course that covered the black experience. J. Saunders Redding, who by then had established himself as a scholar, returned to his alma mater as a visiting professor and taught a literature course on the Negro in American literature in the fall of 1949, making him one of the first (if not the first) black professors in the Ivy League. Inasmuch, his course was one of the first of its kind offered at Brown and its peer institutions. Interestingly, a fellow Brown alumnus, Morehouse president John Hope, gave Redding his first opportunity in the professoriate at the historically black college in Atlanta. After a brief unsettling stay at the institution, Redding resigned his position to seek other opportunities. That led him back north to Brown. As a student and as a professor, Redding was one of very few black people on campus.[67] In spite of his and his brother's presence at Brown, Harvard, and Columbia, the early generation of black Ivy Leaguers faced extreme isolation. Redding was able to help other black students ease their transition to elite college life when he took an endowed chairmanship at Cornell University in 1970. He was the first black professor to do so at Cornell.

A great scholar-athlete, who could not attend the Ivy League university of his choice as an undergraduate, found redemption in the fact that his son could attend the school he selected. Paul Robeson was an All-American star football player at Rutgers University where he earned varsity letters in four sports. He pledged Alpha Phi Alpha and graduated valedictorian of his class at Rutgers; however, he originally wanted to attend Princeton University, which is in Robeson's hometown. When his brother, William Drew Robeson Jr., was denied acceptance, Paul Robeson made the decision to stay in New Jersey but to attend Rutgers. Robeson graduated at the head of his class and then took a law degree at Columbia University while acting on Broadway. Rather than even consider Princeton (which had very few black students enrolled just after World War II), Robeson sent his son, Paul Robeson Jr. to Cornell, where he graduated in 1949.

From the nineteenth to the twentieth century, black students in the Ivy League pushed through difficult circumstances to achieve. When given the opportunity, they excelled in all categories. Not surprisingly there was a high number of black students who received Phi Beta Kappa honors and many of the student athletes achieved national and university recognition for their work on the fields and courts. Many of these students were "firsts." With the exception of few, black firsts, in nearly every category, have always known they had to carry themselves in a manner that exuded confidence but not arrogance in the face of white competition. Working within the system, black Ivy students during the desegregation period strove to shine scholastically and athletically through diligence and excellence. That would not change in the period after World War II, but black learners, following the lead of black agitators off campus, began to critique the system and move away from the idea of assimilation as a survival mechanism. The small number of black students attending the Ivies before World War II, however, did whatever they could to maintain their dignity while striving for excellence.

2

Unsettling Ol' Nassau

Princeton University from Jim Crow Admissions
to Anti-Apartheid Protests

We knew we were intruders in the white country club.
—Shearwood McClelland, 1998

At the beginning of the twentieth century, the brother of famed black
Renaissance man and the town of Princeton's own Paul Robeson
attempted to make an application at Princeton University. The university president at the time, Woodrow Wilson, refused his application even
after the town of Princeton's most popular black minister, William Drew
Robeson (Paul Robeson's father) of Witherspoon Street Presbyterian
Church, appealed to Wilson personally. Historically, black ministers
acted as liaisons between black and white communities, which had typically been the case in the town of Princeton. With regard to the Reverend
Robeson's son's application for admission, however, the tacit relationship
between the black clergy and white institutional power meant nothing.
Paul Robeson resented Princeton University's treatment of his brother
and father for the rest of his life.

Princeton, as a northern town and an elite university, was as segregated as any place below the Mason-Dixon Line for much of its
history. Although black students met with cold receptions when they
arrived at the seven other American Ivy League universities, they
could at least attend those schools. Unlike those fortunate students
who attended the seven other Ivies, African American students could
not attend Princeton in earnest until the middle of the twentieth
century. For that reason, Princeton University earned the unique
reputation of being what one might describe as southern-most Ivy as
it took on the culture of the Old South.[1] One can understand how
engulfing racism was in this nation's history by studying the experi-

ence of black people at Princeton University—a premiere institution
of education.

Those associated with Princeton University and other elite Ivy
League schools can proudly say that their students, faculty, and administrators go on to literally lead the nation in terms of politics, culture,
and economics. For instance, presidents of Princeton University signed
the Declaration of Independence and created the Fourteen Points Plan
and one need not look any further than recent American presidents
and U.S. Supreme Court justices for the contemporary influence of the
Ivy League.[2] With that in mind, Princeton affiliates boast that their university is "in the nation's service and in the service of all nations."[3] In
essence, Ivy League universities represent at times the best and most
powerful aspects of America. The standards that these universities use to
select students and the curricula that the Ivy institutions establish trickle
down in various forms to institutions of higher education throughout
the nation and the world.[4] Although Princeton University and its peers
are among the oldest and most prestigious American universities, in
some ways these institutions had to be led into a new era of freedom
for black people and social justice. In the twentieth century, students
and progressive-minded school officials, as well as social movements
led to Princeton's acceptance of black students, the establishment of
its Black Studies curriculum, and the school's stand against apartheid
South Africa.

Although there is rich scholarly literature surrounding Princeton
University in general, surprisingly little has been written about Princeton and its historic relationship with black people. Carl A. Fields, who
came to Princeton as an administrator in 1964, published his memoirs of his tenure at Princeton. Recently, Melvin McCray, a black alumnus, produced a documentary titled *Looking Back: Reflections of Black
Princeton Alumni* that covers the topic. Jerome Karabel, in *The Chosen*
(2005), discussed Princeton's struggle to attract a certain type of student
that did not include African Americans and even Jews at one point.[5]
Marcia Synnott and Geoffrey Kabaservice wrote about admissions and
the leadership at Princeton. Then, James Axtell constructed a history of
the New Jersey Ivy institution. Comprehensive in many aspects, Axtell's
history neglects the role of black people in shaping Princeton. Several
articles in university publications have focused on the arrival of black

students to campus, but the evolution from black admissions to the campus activism of black students remains generally absent.

When scholars of the Civil Rights Movement and Black Power Movement discuss the protests and demonstrations that took place in the state of New Jersey, they typically mention the unrest that occurred in Newark during the urban uprisings of 1967.[6] Some remember the student protests that occurred at Rutgers University during the period.[7] But less attention has been paid to the student demonstrations that took place on the beautifully landscaped campus of Princeton University in the late 1960s. Although there were no snipers atop buildings and no tanks maneuvering through campus, as was the case during the Newark uprising, students on Princeton's campus took up the cause of the black freedom movement in their own way. This chapter seeks to illuminate the role that students, particularly African American students, played in transforming Princeton University using agitation that was inspired in part by the activism off campus. Black students and administrators as well as white university officials were keenly aware of what occurred in the nearby townships. By the end of the 1960s, black students, with the assistance of liberal university officials, were able to improve Princeton University's relationship with black people domestically and abroad with their campus campaigns. The progress that black students made at Princeton was squarely in the context of the urban uprisings in the Northeast as well as the organizing efforts of the Black Power Movement that was underway.

Of its Ivy League counterparts, Princeton, in terms of culture, was certainly closest to the American Old South that fostered strict racial separation and blatant stereotypes. Several of the university's early trustees owned slaves, and during the antebellum period nearly half of the student body consisted of southerners, which was more than other Ivy League institutions at the time. One of the university's presidents, John MacLean, held membership with the American Colonization Society, which encouraged the deportation of black people for the sake of the nation. In that sense, the school had a long, entangled history with black people and Jim Crow policies.[8]

As did many of the Ivy League institutions, Princeton originated with unofficial ties to religious groups. The Presbyterian Church helped to establish the College of New Jersey, which later became Princeton

University.[9] Adhering to the mission of Christianity, the college trained men (Princeton University did not become coeducational until 1969) to enter the Presbyterian ministry. By 1774, two African students attended Princeton Theological Seminary (which was technically separate from the university) for "preparatory work" preceding a trip to Africa for missionary work.[10] Although enrolled for several years, the aforementioned students, Bristol Yamma and John Quamine, left without graduating. The September 25, 1792, minutes of Princeton's Board of Trustees reveals a recommendation that a free black man, John Chavis, study with the president of the university, John Witherspoon.[11] After studying with Witherspoon, Chavis later became a Presbyterian minister in North Carolina. Incidentally, two centuries later John Chavis's descendant Benjamin Chavis became the executive director of the National Association for the Advancement of Colored People (NAACP) and eventually a minister with the Nation of Islam.[12]

Princeton as a town allowed slavery, and enslaved people were present on Princeton University's campus. One Princeton student turned in a black man he recognized in the town of Princeton for violating the Fugitive Slave Act of 1793.[13] A relative of former university president John Witherspoon eventually paid to manumit the escaped slave, but the culture of the university permitted those who favored the peculiar institution. As one observer noted about its relationship to black people, "she [Princeton] has not measured up to the Christian standard in her attitude." The observer claimed that this owed largely "to the proslavery spirit . . . caused by Southern slave holders, who settled in and about the place."[14]

In the years after slavery ended, Princeton continued to confront challenges regarding the presence of black people on campus. During Reconstruction black men came to campus not as enslaved servants but as potential students. By 1876, four black men were attending Princeton's Theological Seminary. As was custom, the university permitted seminary students to attend courses. When one of the black students, Daniel Culp, entered a psychology course on Princeton's campus, some of the white students rebelled. A southern newspaper reported the presence of this black student upset "some representatives from the 'Sunny South'" so much that the southerners chose to exit the lectures.[15] Subsequently, several of those southern white students left the university in protest of the black student's presence. The rebelling students later requested to be readmitted when the university president refused to expel the black student.[16] Twenty years later, Alexander Dumas Watkins, a black man, was an informal instructor for several years in the department of histology at Princeton where he assisted geology professor William Libbey.

At the turn of the century, Princeton president Woodrow Wilson (in a foreshadowing act to his time in the White House) ensured that the institution would remain exclusively white. Reared as a southerner in a family that once enslaved Africans, Wilson frequently embraced racial stereotypes associated with black people and disregarded them as innately inferior beings. A fellow Princeton alumnus remembered Wilson's great ability to tell "darky" jokes.[17] Like many southerners of the period, Wilson strongly opposed the mixing of races on the grounds that it would taint the pure white race. In 1904, Wilson discussed the potential presence of black students at Princeton: "While there is nothing in the law of the University to prevent a negro's entering, the whole temper and tradition of the place are such that no negro has ever applied for admission, and it seems extremely unlikely that the question will ever assume a practical form."[18] Wilson's words were not encouraging.

Five years later, a black student from the Virginia Theological Seminary and College wrote to Wilson, stating "I want so much to come to your school at Princeton."[19] Wilson quickly referred the letter to his secretary, who replied on the president's behalf that the aspiring student should either attend a university in the South or apply to universities like Harvard, Dartmouth, or Brown, where he would be more welcome.[20] It came as no surprise to many when Wilson, who in 1912 was elected president of the United States, resegregated all government offices or when he endorsed the glorification of the Ku Klux Klan in D. W. Griffith's *Birth of a Nation*. Furthermore, Wilson, who had received a doctorate in government and history from Johns Hopkins University, claimed that the movie, which demeaned black citizens, was like history written in lightning. The irony of the matter was that Wilson, while president of Princeton and the nation, pushed to advance democracy. He waged a campaign to change Princeton's class caste system by attempting to abolish the exclusive eating clubs. The clubs provided many of the social activities on campus, but they also denied students of lower economic ranks. Wilson believed it was wrong to turn away students because of their economic class, but did not go a step further by removing de facto Jim Crow barriers to the admission of black students.

Wilson had support from his fellow alumni. As one alumnus put it, "Princeton must remain the shining citadel of white supremacy and set an example for all of the world to see of the tolerance and intelligence of the white man."[21] Indeed, to state that there were no African Americans on Princeton's campus during the first part of the twentieth century would be fallacious. There were black cooks who prepared food for the exclusive eating clubs (which was characteristic of eating facilities at nearly all the Ivy institutions) and, in at least one case, a black man acted as a servant for one of Princeton's premiere constitutional scholars.[22] Until the 1940s, those were some of the only black people Princetonians saw at the university. In some ways the auspicious presence of black people almost exclusively in the role of cooks and servants was reminiscent of images from the institutions of the Old South. A Dartmouth College president in the 1920s claimed that at Brown, Penn, Cornell, Dartmouth, and Harvard, few black students were admitted but those who did attend could participate in the bulk of college life. At Yale, he explained, black students were admitted but did not have the opportunity to socialize with their white classmates. The Dartmouth president observed that with regard to Princeton University and black students, however, "the color line is drawn with the utmost rigidity and the [black] man [is] not even given access to the curriculum."[23]

In 1939, Princeton town resident Bruce M. Wright applied and won a scholarship to attend the university. Although he was talented as a high school student, he happened to be black. Wright had not seen any reason to share his race with the admissions office and no officials thought to ask. The underpinnings of the sacred white institution nearly came loose when the stand-out student arrived to register for courses. The white registration officials, using their innate powers of racial perception, immediately recognized Wright as black. They mobilized to protect the sanctity of Princeton by refusing to enroll the scholarship-winning teenager in any courses and by expeditiously shooing him off the yard.[24]

Crestfallen, Wright knew why he could not attend, but he wanted the Princeton officials to explain their broken logic. In response to a letter Wright wrote, the dean of admissions reasoned that as someone who had "very pleasant relations with" the "colored race," about which he was "particularly interested," he believed that Princeton would be too lonely a place for a black student and that such a student would not be "happy in this environment." He further explained that there were a great number of southern white students there who held close to their "tradition." Overall, he concluded, it would be best for a black student to not challenge the culture.[25] His letter did not read any differently from those of the noble white men who had previously denied black applicants. If anything, it provided a superb example of white paternalism and racism wrapped into one document. Further it made clear the position of those who had the power to make decisions on behalf of the institution.

World War II forced officials at American institutions to reflect on their policies of excluding citizens. The U.S. military is as steeped in tradition as any American institution; yet, the military in some ways outpaced the rest of American society as it concerned racial progress. In the case of Princeton, the actions of the military helped to change the admission practices of the Ivy League institution. The U.S. Navy, in partnership with Princeton University, instituted the V-12 Navy College Training Program on campus. The program allowed naval cadets to take college courses in the hope of increasing the number of eligible officers for service during war time.[26] In 1945, the partnership resulted in admission of four black naval cadets. The efforts of northern civilian activists of the NAACP, who waged the "Double V(ictory)" campaign during World War II, also had some influence on Princeton's policies of allowing black students as undergraduates. Those activists sought to defeat fascism abroad and to dismantle racism at home.[27] With black serviceman attending Princeton, they achieved both goals.

In the midst of World War II, some Princeton alumni could not justify making the world safe for democracy and rescuing Jewish victims from Nazi concentration camps while their university rejected American citizens who wanted to attend an American university. Norman Thomas, member of the class of 1905, explained that Princeton men claim that their alma mater "is for the nation's service" and is "dedicated to 'democracy,' . . . to 'the liberal spirit'—in complete opposition to fascist standards. Yet Princeton maintains a racial intolerance almost worthy of Hitler."[28] Thomas decried the fact that "a race which is furnishing an increasing number of artists, musicians, scientists, can send no man be he as versatile as Paul Robeson . . . to the fourth oldest American institution of learning." Thomas chided that "Negroes may go to, and make good in Harvard, Yale, Columbia . . . indeed all leading American colleges and universities except Princeton."[29] Between 1928 and 1948, Thomas ran as a Socialist candidate for president of the United States. He also received an honorary Doctor of Laws degree from Princeton.[30] Another alumnus echoed Thomas's sentiment. Ralph J. Reiman, from the class of 1935, stated that "Negro students have much to offer Princeton and Princeton has much to offer Negro students."[31] Reiman eventually graduated Harvard Law and served as a U.S. Army intelligence officer during World War II.[32]

Two students from the class of 1945, W. F. Weaver and J. L. Webb, exclaimed that "to make democracy come true we must begin at home."[33] For Weaver and Webb, manifesting democracy at home meant allowing black students to matriculate at the university. Another student hoped for racial progress at the institution: "Princeton, a leading university with a strong Southern tradition, could seize this opportunity to take the lead in working out the only alternative to eventual revolution—that alternative is [racial] cooperation. . . . Lest we forget, Princeton is the last of the leading institutions outside the deep South which still adheres to this faith in racial superiority."[34] Although few in number, there was a contingent of concerned Princeton affiliates pressuring the university to evolve.

In some areas of post–World War II American society, the race problem tempered. Jackie Robinson signed a contract with the Brooklyn Dodgers, President Harry Truman issued Executive Order 9981, which desegregated the U.S. military, and the Supreme Court ruled against the segregation of public interstate transportation and restrictive covenants. Robinson's entry into the major leagues, the desegregation of the armed forces, and the rulings of the Supreme Court occurred because of the constant efforts of black citizens who wanted to ensure their nation lived out its creed.[35]

As U.S. officials and heroic American citizens made history, so too did one of the four naval cadets whom Princeton admitted in 1945. While on campus, these black student-sailors did not join the exclusive eating clubs and rarely socialized outside of class with their fellow white students. Despite the social isolation, in 1947 John L. Howard became

Figure 2.1. In the nation's service, James E. Ward (left) and Arthur J. Wilson, both class of 1947, took advantage of the U.S. Navy's V-12 officers training program to become two of Princeton University's first black graduates. Courtesy of the Seeley G. Mudd Manuscript Library, Princeton University.

the first African American to receive a bachelor's degree from the university.[36] Howard, who had attended integrated schools in New York, noted that his was a "very mellow experience." He explained that he was not attending "traditional" Princeton University but rather a "wartime Princeton" that catered to students from the military.[37] Howard eventually became an orthopedic surgeon. By 1948, another black cadet, James E. Ward, also received a bachelor's degree. Ward eventually worked for the Texas Commission on Human Rights as an investigator and legal counsel. Another of the cadets, Melvin Murchison, became the first black athlete to play a varsity sport (football) at Princeton. Along those lines, the fourth black cadet, Arthur "Pete" Wilson played two seasons of varsity basketball, and even acted as the team captain.[38] Interestingly, high-achieving black students who were admitted literally had to be "in the nation's service" to attend Princeton.

White veterans, who witnessed the service of black men during the war, moved to alter Princeton's racial policies of admission. In 1946, several white soldier-students in coalition with several civilian-students formed an organization called the Liberal Union. In an attempt to enlighten the campus with respect to the abilities and equality of black people in general, the Liberal Union brought NAACP Executive Director Walter White (who had Caucasian physical characteristics) to campus to speak to the general student body. Sixty-two years later, Robert Rivers, a black observer from the town of Princeton, remembered the shameful treatment the executive director received upon arriving at campus. Rivers, who eventually attended and graduated from the university (and became its first black trustee), recalled "the scene where Princeton [University] students taunted and threw snowballs at the NAACP executive director." The Walter White scene is notable on at least two levels. On the one hand, if Princeton were a place that pledged to forge the leaders of the future, it appeared that those future leaders had not yet matured. Indeed, heaving snowballs at an actual societal leader could be characterized as nothing more than juvenile. On the other hand, the fact that a dogged advocate of integration who happened to be black could speak on campus marked a shift in Princeton's history.[39]

Even if slow and incremental, Princeton's culture changed with the times. The first black undergraduate student that Princeton University admitted without impetus or assistance from the military was Joseph

Ralph Moss. A resident of the town of Princeton, Moss arrived at the university in the fall of 1947. While he did not participate wholly in campus events, he did eventually join a campus eating club and even lived on campus at one point. The admissions officer who interviewed Moss noted that the student had a light complexion and a mother of "very high-grade." The officer further observed that Moss's brother, Simeon, had attended the graduate school as part of the G.I. Bill. Joseph Moss graduated with a bachelor's degree in 1951.[40]

Although Princeton desegregated in the immediate post–World War II era, it may not have done so out of sheer goodwill. An article in the *Princeton Alumni Weekly* pointed out that in 1947 state legislators rewrote the state's constitution to explicitly prohibit racial discrimination.[41] In doing so, state-funded institutions were required to adhere to the new policy regarding discrimination. Although Princeton was a private university, it did receive some funds from the state of New Jersey. Subsequently, Princeton more freely admitted black undergraduates.

One of those new black students was Robert Rivers (class of 1953). Like Robeson and Moss, Rivers grew up in Princeton. He, however, actually enrolled in the university. Rivers's father worked at an eating club for decades and his mother was the maid for a professor for years; so the Rivers family understood full well what white students and faculty were capable of and what the very few black students who attended the university had to endure.[42] Rivers arrived at the university embracing the spirit of pioneers like Jackie Robinson, Ralph Bunche, and Charles Drew. There was little comfort for him on campus, but his home in Princeton became one of the spaces where black students felt welcome for years to come. He watched as the members of the exclusively white eating clubs rejected his black peers. There were few exceptions for black students looking to be part of the clubs.

Eating clubs were not officially part of the university and it did not regulate them. As fraternity life was not available to Princeton students on campus, eating clubs provided much of the fun and extracurricular activity for students in the way that fraternities would. They also provided housing for upperclassmen. By rule, they were exclusionary, as the clubs used an interview and "bickering" processes to select members. Black students during the period, who numbered few, rarely showed interest in joining and were selected infrequently when they did. Arthur

Wilson recollected being initially accepted by the occupants of Tiger Inn but then rejected because of the overriding will of the eating club's all-white alumni, who did not want him to join. Tiger Inn members, apparently, did not have anything against black people in general because a black man (Rivers's father) was a servant in the house for decades. It was the possibility that a black student who would not be acting in a service capacity might join the club that threatened the status quo. Wilson, although dejected, did gain membership to the Prospect Club, which welcomed him and Jewish students alike.

Black students, according to a 1995 *Daily Princetonian* article, lived in systematic isolation. The article claimed that black freshmen, even if they requested a roommate (which would have likely have been a white student), had to stay in single rooms. The policy changed during the 1960s, but in the eyes of Royce Vaughn, who graduated in 1953, the campus officials were clueless about his experience. Nearly four decades later, Vaughn said: "a counseling program was sorely missing in those days." Considering the anxiety associated with being one of the few black students of campus, counseling would have benefited Vaughn and his predecessors. Charlie Shorter, who graduated nine years after Vaughn, stated: "some consideration by the university officials at some level as to the expectations for African Americans would have been nice." Shorter noted that "there was nobody who really understood what it was about." He recognized that he was in the midst of some of the best and brightest students in America, but he emphasized that the group "included a number of people who were bigots and racists and [who] made my life at Princeton in some respects miserable."[43] To achieve their goal of attaining a Princeton degree, the early black students, Vaughn said, "went through an experience that was painful and prolonged."

As the university accepted more black undergraduates, it also observed changes regarding faculty demographics. Princeton hired its first black tenure-seeking faculty member during this period. On July 30, 1955, the black newspaper the *Newark Herald* proclaimed that "one of the most glorious chapters in the history of Princeton was written . . . when Dr. Charles T. Davis, a Negro, was appointed a member of the faculty of this famous University."[44] Davis, thirty-nine years old, had graduated from Dartmouth College and received a PhD from New York University. A Walt Whitman scholar and former army officer, he arrived at Princeton to teach English. His arrival was indeed historic, but it seemed to cause less friction than the arrival of black students.

During the 1940s and 1950s, few black students (undergraduate or otherwise) attended Princeton. The situation changed, however, in the 1960s. By then, Princeton alumnus and faculty member Robert Goheen had become president of the university. Born in India the son of American Presbyterian missionaries, during World War II Goheen rose to the rank of lieutenant colonel in the U.S. Army.[45] Goheen's worldview was somewhat more liberal than that of his predecessors. In terms of the university's relationship to black students, Goheen attempted to change the university's racially exclusionary image. In a moment of clarity he stated: "For the past decade, we have been terribly concerned with what we could do for students from underdeveloped countries. It took a shock (the civil rights crisis) to make us realize our problems at home."[46] President Goheen authorized a tutorial program for mostly black youth in the nearby city of Trenton, which had a significant black poor and working-class population, as a long-term approach to admitting more black students.[47]

The early 1960s saw further tentative admission of black students. One *Daily Princetonian* article noted that of the 1,202 applicants who were accepted for the 1963–1964 academic year, only ten were black. Although the number of accepted African Americans was small, the article claimed that no black student had been accepted in 1953, 1954, and 1959. The article blamed the unfriendly nature of the town of Princeton and the university itself, as well as the "scarcity of qualified Negroes, which is slowly being corrected."[48] To be sure, the town of Princeton had a history of segregation and discrimination against its black residents. The town's treatment of African Americans, however, did not mean that the university had to be unwelcoming. Incidentally, the article also noted that of the class entering the 1963–1964 school year, 20 percent were the sons of alumni. The article did not mention the qualifications of the legacy students.

Years later, the Association of Black Princeton Alumni (ABPA) commissioned a survey of black Princeton alumni that revealed several interesting things about the experiences of students. The number of black students who attended Princeton did not increase significantly until after 1963, so the bulk of the respondents were still relatively young in their careers and not too far removed from life at Princeton. Because black students did not attend any of the Ivies in great numbers until after the mid-1960s, the ABPA survey is somewhat useful in assessing the experience of black students at peer institutions.[49]

The survey reported that most (78 percent of the respondents) of the black graduates came to Princeton from the East Coast. After graduating they "principally" lived in the Mid-Atlantic states of New York, New Jersey, Pennsylvania, and Connecticut. Two-thirds of the respondents disclosed that they came from predominantly black neighborhoods and that their communities could have been characterized as low and middle income. When asked why they chose Princeton University, the answer was predictable. Fifty-seven percent said they were "attracted because of Princeton's prestige and because of what the university could do for them." Likely, the grand majority of students—irrespective of race—would have answered similarly. Black students coming from low to middle income neighborhoods and families, however, were well acquainted with what attending an Ivy League school could do to alter their life chances.[50]

The opportunity to attend Princeton came with significant emotional and mental costs, according to the survey. More than 90 percent of those surveyed remembered "observing at least a few separate instances of racial discrimination"; 46 percent remembered seeing more than five instances. Unfortunately for the students, it only takes one experience with racial discrimination to induce trauma and set into motion negative reactions. Students considered having to observe Confederate flags flying outside the windows of dormitories and eating clubs on their way to class racial discrimination. One student regretfully recalled having to confront "Southern attitudes" on campus.[51] Charlie Shorter, in the class of 1962, called Princeton the "Northernmost of the Southern schools," referring to its stance toward black people.

Following the lead of Goheen, who recognized the significance of the Civil Rights Movement, Princeton's admissions office targeted black applicants. The director of admissions sent letters to 4,000 public and private high schools, notifying the school counselors of Princeton's "search for Negro applicants."[52] The university also attempted to cultivate potential black students through the Trenton Tutorial Project, which involved university students and faculty members tutoring mostly underprivileged and black students at the nearby high schools. In 1963, over 140 Princeton students assisted the more than 200 Trenton students (a significant number of whom were black) who signed up for the project.

Although university officials encouraged the effort to racially diversify Princeton's campus, there were students who still outwardly opposed integration. In March 1964, several university students created an organization called the Princeton Committee for Racial Reconciliation. Apparently, the members of the all-white group believed that the best way for the races to reconcile was to remain segregated. The group's president, Marshall Smith, claimed the group represented the opinions of a third of the student population (in fact there were only fifteen members of the groups). "We just want to show that in the midst of all this sympathy for the Negro there exists some opposition on campus," Smith explained, "Segregationists are not going to give up by default."[53] Hoping to contradict the "integrationist propaganda" to which Princeton students had been exposed, Smith's group pointed to the controversial book by Carleton Putnam, *Race and Reason,* that attempted to confirm racial stereotypes regarding black people and to make the argument for segregation. The segregationist group claimed that Putnam's work provided evidence of the ineffectiveness of social integration.

Taking advantage of the 1965 Higher Education Act, Princeton used a federal grant to reestablish a cooperative program with the nation's first college established for black students, Lincoln College in Pennsylvania. Like Princeton, Lincoln had early ties to the Presbyterian Church, and Lincoln's first president supported colonization as did several early Princeton trustees. In 1854, Princeton alumni helped to found the institution to educate black men, and the universities maintained a relationship throughout the years with Princeton men serving on Lincoln's faculty and the board of trustees. In 1965, the $113,000 Higher Education Act grant allowed for a faculty and student exchange. Lincoln faculty came to Princeton to take graduate courses and teach specialized courses while Princeton graduate students had the opportunity to teach at Lincoln. Moreover, Princeton students and faculty members would have access to Lincoln's African Studies collection. While select Lincoln faculty members had the chance to take advanced courses from Princeton, a critic of the exchange might have observed that the white Princeton students, acting as instructors, were able to "practice" on black Lincoln students and to exploit Lincoln's special collections for the advancement of their own research agendas, which would allow the white Ivy League students (who would benefit from Princeton's reputation) the chance to be in the forefront of a relatively new field of study. Critics may have charged that the exchange was hardly equal. Still, the president of Lincoln explained: "The benefits . . . to both faculty and students through [the] cooperative relationship between a great university such as Princeton and a small liberal arts college will be of incalculable" value.[54]

The Princeton-Lincoln exchange was one way to expose black students to Princeton, but there were others. Another source of exposure to the university was the Princeton Summer Cooperative Program (PSCP), which began in 1963 as an attempt to draw secondary students from the surrounding urban centers to Princeton to bridge the cultural and racial gap that existed. Officials believed that if the mostly black lower-income students spent time on campus they might learn what was necessary to eventually matriculate at Princeton or another higher education institution. In that way, Princeton was attempting to solve the problem of the ghetto by providing young people with potential options for their futures. There were similar programs at Ivy institutions, including Dartmouth's A Better Chance and Columbia's Project Double Discovery. The PSCP marked another step toward racial progress for the Ivy institution that had only desegregated less than twenty years earlier.

Historian Komozi Woodard, who participated in the PCSP at Princeton University in the summer of 1965, believed that it and similar programs were mostly positive, but they had drawbacks. He viewed the summer program at Princeton as an experiment to see if ghetto children could make themselves culturally worthy of elite universities and colleges.[55] As a memo from the news office at Columbia explained about its program, "the premise is that a deprived youth with a college education will become a productive citizen, able to pull himself out of the environment from which he comes."[56] Other than a reference to an improvement in "lifestyle" that teachers observed in program participants, there was no explanation of what exactly the memo's author meant by a "productive citizen." The sentiment and language of the document, however, smacks of the Horatio Alger narrative, protestant work ethic, and Christian missionary zeal rolled into one. The programs were, indeed, missionary in nature, as representatives of predominantly white institutions of higher education went into the foreign lands of the ghetto to seek converts to the college way of life.

The officials, students, and administrators who applied for and funded the programs viewed the potential young participants as those who might not otherwise become productive citizens without their assistance. That is not to discredit the important work and efforts that the programs coordinated, but it does illustrate the way that even when couched within good intentions, public and private policies "othered" black and brown children from low-income households. By bringing them into the environment in which the nation's wealthiest and whitest children dwelled, perhaps the children from the ghetto could eventually hope to be respectable, read the tone of the document.

Woodard, after completing the program at Princeton, eventually graduated from Dickinson College and earned a doctorate at the University of Pennsylvania in history. Reflecting on his experience with the Princeton Cooperative Schools Program a half century later, he said: "It was a life changing experience for me because I thought I was an all-American boy, and that everyone in America lived like I did in the ghetto of Newark." When he went to Princeton, however, he discovered he was wrong, and that "inequality was real." Reading Michael Harrington's *The Other America: Poverty in the United States* (1962) while in the program bolstered his conclusion about the unevenness of life for him as a young black person from Newark and the majority of the white students who attended the Ivy League school in New Jersey. Woodard, who concluded he was not typical, was wrong to an extent. He was, in fact, an all-American boy, just not in the way the print and electronic media depicted Americans. Millions of citizens faced slum circumstances and toiled in the working class to make a living; he and his family were certainly not alone. Class differences—more than race—impressed him initially, Woodard recalled.[57]

As part of the Princeton program, Woodard also found out that some of the instructors were researching and tracking the participants. He remembered leaving campus without permission on a mission to meet girls with the other participants in the all-male program. When he returned, a white counselor exclaimed: "you ruined the experiment!" Woodard was confused by the statement. Upon investigation, Woodard believed he learned that both Princeton University and Dartmouth

College were trying to use the summer program to test the assimilation model that had been used on Native Americans centuries before
on black youth. Dartmouth, according to its charter, started as an institution whose mission it was to educate and assimilate Native peoples.
Woodard sensed that the idea behind the "experiment" was to get black
children away from what the designers of the program would have considered "pathological black culture" and bring them to the more reasonable and liberating campus of Princeton. Back then, Woodard admitted
decades later, he felt like a guinea pig in the War on Poverty. Acting on
his feelings, he and several other students rebelled with their behavior.
The prospect of being experimented on caused him to question the purpose of education. In spite of his feelings then and decades later, the
program, working in combination with his abilities, helped to advance
his life chances.

One of Woodard's inspirations in the PCSP was senior Robert "Bob"
Engs, one of the two black student-counselors attending Princeton for
the PCSP in the early 1960s. Engs's upbringing was atypical, in that he
grew up in Germany as part of a military family. He graduated from
Princeton in 1965 and earned a PhD in history from Yale in 1972. He,
like so many other black alumni of the Ivy League, went on to mentor
younger generations of black scholars, who paid the favor forward to the
generations of black learners that followed.[58] Engs began doing so in the
Princeton summer program, where he taught Woodard. It helped to
have someone with whom Woodard and other black participants would
relate racially.

With the Princeton administration continuing its desegregation effort
at the high school level, university students dealt with the implications
of the movement. Although a higher number of black students than ever
before were attending Princeton, they did not always feel welcome. Harvard Bell, who was a sophomore in 1968, remembered Princeton as a
"lonely" place, and he recalled feeling at times "unwelcome" and "under
attack."[59] As it was, the arrival of black students set into motion a cultural experiment on Princeton's campus that was ultimately positive but
at times troublesome.

Princeton, said 1969 graduate Nathaniel Mackey, had a "southern
gentleman" stereotype. By that, he meant southern white gentleman.[60]
Mackey claimed that many people associated with the university accepted

the stereotype. The negative behavior that black students withstood included antagonistic attitudes and gestures toward the prospect of racial integration. Segregation and racism were widespread throughout the nation. The southern culture that celebrated slavery and the Confederacy was, however, particularly prevalent at Princeton as a member of the Ivy League, according to black alumni and white officials. One black alumnus remembered that when he arrived in 1965, Princeton boasted that "half of its [Princeton's] students who died during the Civil War fought on behalf of the South."[61] In spite of the fact that officials walked the same paths and took in the same views as the black students, the flag of the nation that attacked the United States flew proudly in the Princeton sky. Black students saw that as an "affront" to their personhood.

It was not just the Confederate flag but the open hostility that black students faced from white students and professors that damaged their impression of Princeton. John Caldwell, class of 1968, remembered urine and garbage being thrown on black students walking beneath Rock Suite dormitory.[62] In response, black students approached the white residents in the dormitory ready for a physical confrontation if necessary. Perhaps the white students who participated in the reprehensible acts were merely inebriated, or maybe they understood that it would be difficult for black students to compete scholastically if they had to concern themselves with getting to the classrooms without being dumped upon. In any event, it was left to the black students to "get over" the incident.

Then, there was still the issue of eating clubs. The ABPA survey indicated that 83 percent of the graduates refused to join an eating club at all. With the eating clubs as a very narrow option, socializing became difficult for black students. "There was essentially no social life," remembered Shearwood McClellan who graduated in 1969, "you [black Princetonians] were really on your own."[63] Although most of the clubs, according to the survey were "cliquish," McClellan's classmate Brent Henry recalled that some "were more tolerant than others on issues of race and politics." Henry said that he and his peers occasionally attended events at the Dial Lodge and the Campus Club on Prospect Avenue. In terms of the suffering that black people without an education experienced outside of Princeton, not being able to join or feel welcome at exclusionary eating clubs was seemingly insignificant, but having the liberty to be human everywhere black people existed was still important.[64]

By most accounts, 1968 was a year that stood out as both eventful and traumatic for the nation and the world. Popular leaders Martin Luther King Jr. and Robert Kennedy were assassinated, while students and other activists railed against the escalated war effort in Vietnam and for youth empowerment. Some Ivy League university campuses, like Columbia University, shut down because students rebelled against the university's ties to the Vietnam War as well as what the students viewed as racist policies concerning Columbia's expansion. At Cornell, black students took over offices to protest for Black Studies. Princeton students opposed similar ties to the university's relationship with the Department of Defense. Indeed, Ivy League universities were not immune to the social unrest and uprisings that affected the rest of the nation. The Black Power Movement had reached college campuses along with a more militant cadre of black students.

In 1968, Princeton University offered courses that focused on black history and culture. That year, Henry Drewry, a black educator, became the director of the university's office of teacher placement and preparation.[65] Drewry, who had taught in the town of Princeton's school district for fourteen years and as a lecturer on the university's campus, made history at Princeton by teaching the university's first black studies courses. He and his wife Cecelia offered two seminars, one covering Black American Writers and another dealing with Afro-American History. Considering Princeton's past with regard to race relations, there was little surprise when news outlets noted that the courses were the first of their kind in Princeton's then 222-year history. It should also be noted, though, that Henry Drewry was teaching a seminar in addition to his teacher placement duties with the university. The dean of Princeton's college of arts and sciences stated that the introduction of the two courses would help the college in "establishing a more formal, comprehensive program relating to black culture."[66]

Princeton was benefitting from the largesse of black faculty and staff. The Drewrys, a black couple, along with one of Princeton's first administrators, Carl A. Fields, became default mentors to many of the black students who were experiencing homesickness and racism at Princeton. Fields was first hired in financial aid and then became the university's first black dean. As is still the case with black education professionals, he became the advocate, confidante, surrogate parent, and champion of many black students who had no one else to whom they could turn. Fields, along with the Drewry family, helped to improve the experience of many students.

The homes of Fields and the Drewrys, like that of the Rivers family, became shelters. Realizing the importance of those connections, Fields formalized the mentoring relationships and provided safe zones for the students by creating a network of family homes in Princeton. As one student remembered, those families were there to provide "good meals" and a "sympathetic ear."[67] The families provided them with the same kind of hospitality that black families offered black students at Cornell University in Ithaca at the turn of the twentieth century.

Despite the progress that the university made, Princeton still faced racial problems. In October 1968, black and white students confronted each other in a campus dormitory. Upset about the volume at which white students played music at a mixer, several black students who lived in the dormitory first complained to the dormitory director and then met the white residents in their room. The white residents, according to a university investigation, made several "racially offensive remarks" to the black students, who left and returned to the room with several more of their fellow black students. While in the white students' room, one of the black students used a knife to slash the stereo speakers. As the situation escalated, nearly fifty students altogether participated in the controversy, but there is no record of violence. While race may not have been at the root of the conflict, certainly race became an issue when the white residents, who hosted the party, used epithets to address the black students. Race may also have been a factor in the dormitory director's refusal to reprimand the noisemakers or neglect of the situation altogether. To be sure, noise complaints are common in residential settings, but in this instance the race of the residents added a new dimension to the conflict. None of the students faced criminal charges.[68]

From the 1940s to the early 1960s black students struggled to even matriculate at Princeton; by the late 1960s, however, Princeton's black students had established a unique identity for themselves. Because of isolation on campus and a growing black consciousness, black students bonded.[69] Out of that bond, in 1967 black students established the Association of Black Collegians (ABC) as a local campus organization. With university funding, the new group attempted to aid in the social and academic acclimation of black students and to initiate dialogue with the surrounding black communities of Princeton and Trenton. The group's founders viewed ABC "as a bloc, effecting policy both now and in the future." Taking on the cadence of Black Power rhetoric, an early coordinator explained that "when something is going to be done, we are the ones who are going to have to do it."[70] With regard to the abysmal number of black students enrolled at Princeton, the members of the organization took up that ethic. ABC subsequently visited predominantly black high schools around the country during the winter breaks to recruit for the university.[71]

In addition to their high school visitation program, the members of ABC acted as on-campus hosts to potential black students. In February 1968, Princeton, in conjunction with ABC and Jim Brown's Negro Industrial and Economic Union, sponsored twenty urban youth who visited Princeton. ABC members brought the potential students to the admissions office, where they underwent interviews. One of the most important aspects of ABC's approach to recruitment was the fact that the members of the college group provided examples of black students who readily navigated what many black youth called the "system." One of the only black admissions officials explained: "[the visiting young people] learned that 'they could have higher education without losing their own black identity.'"[72]

Because the members of ABC took it upon themselves to ensure that Princeton became an option for other black students, in 1968, President Goheen and the elite institution saw the fruits of the black student group's efforts. That school year, Princeton admitted seventy-six new black students while ninety-seven black men altogether attended Princeton, which marked a high for the university.[73] Sociologist Jerome Karabel has argued that even more than the Civil Rights Movement of the South, the urban uprisings and Black Power Movement of the North influenced the decision of Ivy League universities to admit black students. The universities, Karabel asserted, were concerned that the rage of the urban poor might be waged on the elite white institutions of higher education if they did not attempt to improve ghetto circumstances by admitting students.[74] As a result, black students, some of whom had witnessed violent rebellions in their neighborhoods and were sympathetic to the tenets of Black Power, arrived on Princeton's campus.

Figure 2.2. One of the first black administrators in the Ivy League, Carl A. Fields (center) of Princeton University, attended the inaugural banquet of the Association of Black Collegians in May 1968. Fields is with the association's president Paul C. Williams (left) and member Alan D. Buchanan. Courtesy of the Seeley G. Mudd Manuscript Library, Princeton University.

Although very able as recruiters, ABC's larger agenda extended further. The group saw itself as part of the tradition of black students and youth who changed society for the better. With that in mind, ABC, with the help of Carl A. Fields, organized a national conference that involved students from over forty universities and colleges.[75] Under Fields's tutelage, the members of ABC focused on the future of the "Negro undergraduate" with seminars concerning education, economics, politics, and community organization.

When Martin Luther King Jr. was assassinated on April 4, 1968, ABC members led students in a boycott of classes.[76] In an emotional letter to the school newspaper, the ABC expressed its sorrow and anger with the civil rights leader's murder: "It is not one man, however guilty he may be, that murdered Dr. King. Rather, it is the society as a whole that we indict." The group lamented that because of the "injustice of this society, black America is under no constraints to obey white America's hypocritical laws. It is in America's best interests that the black man revolts."[77] The ABC declared that "No black student will attend classes! No black student will work any job!" In order to avoid controversy, President Goheen provided his endorsement of the group's actions.[78]

Members of the ABC looked beyond themselves toward the larger black freedom movement and fell in line with other student activists. Following the lead of Malcolm X, the Student Nonviolent Coordinating Committee (SNCC) in the late 1960s sought to tie the struggle of black people in the United States to that of black people abroad.[79] In taking a Pan-Africanist approach to the struggle, SNCC eventually called for an end to European colonization of African countries. As it was, black South Africans dealt daily with the impacts of colonization under apartheid—a racial caste system of governing that not coincidentally mirrored America's Jim Crow laws and culture.

In the 1960s many African Americans who battled poverty and racism domestically also chose to denounce South Africa's racist policies. As the United States officially desegregated, South Africa further entrenched its racial caste system. Organizations like the American Committee on Africa, which enjoyed the support of black fraternal and sorority groups, the National Council of Negro Women, the Brotherhood of Sleeping Car Porters, the Congress of Racial Equality, the NAACP, the National Urban League, and the Southern Christian Leadership Conference, registered their objections to apartheid. In 1962, the committee issued a resolution calling for black Americans to protest the mistreatment of Africans abroad, and three years later made recommendations to the federal government regarding apartheid.[80] The United Nations general assembly also brought apartheid to the forefront in the early 1960s. Black politicians like Congressman Charles Diggs brought up the issue of apartheid to U.S. political officials who had previously turned a blind eye to South African policies.[81] Tennis star Arthur Ashe was another who loudly protested against apartheid, as did the scholars John Henrik Clarke and C.L.R. James. Abroad, scholars in Britain opposed apartheid in a boycott of South Africa.[82] Other anti-apartheid activists included the American student/athlete members of the Olympic Project for Human Rights (OPHR), which was led by former athlete and educator Harry Edwards.[83]

The members of the OPHR were not the only students to oppose what they viewed as immoral policy in South Africa. In 1968, black Princeton students, in alliance with white radical students, protested against Princeton University's investment policy with regard to South Africa. In doing so, the student activists preceded the American collegiate anti-apartheid movement by nearly two decades.[84] Furthermore, they set the stage for what would become a major battle for justice within the U.S. Congress in the 1970s and 1980s. Princeton students envisioned their anti-apartheid campaign as part of the international struggle for black freedom and the Pan-Africanist movement.

In April 1968, students at Princeton proposed that the university not invest any future funds into companies associated with the apartheid-sanctioning governments of South Africa and Mozambique. While students at Yale demanded a Black Studies program, and those at Columbia demanded that their university show more respect to its black neighbors in Harlem, students at Princeton insisted that the university divest $127 million from its financial portfolio.[85] The students recognized that they had peers from nations like Tanzania and Kenya where Africans had won their independence from European colonists. Those African students interacted with black students born and reared in the United States and informed them of the human rights struggle that was occurring in southern African nations.[86]

Armed with the knowledge of history concerning segregation and apartheid, the students took action. ABC members and other anti-apartheid student demonstrators marched at the Woodrow Wilson School of Public and International Affairs—a school named for a man who reinstituted the American version of apartheid in the civil services—and caught the attention of university officials. Princeton authorities, aware of protests elsewhere that escalated to violence and destruction, attempted to defuse the rising controversy.

University officials formed a committee that included administrators, faculty members, and students to study the impacts of the school's investments and the efficacy of divestment. In January 1969, the committee issued a report that claimed that the university had no investments in companies that "directly support the governments of southern Africa, or that have substantial operation in the region."[87] Furthermore, the committee reported, "the designated companies [that the students had identified] derive an average less than one per cent of their sales and profits from southern Africa."

The student members of the committee refused to endorse the report, which explained that divesting might cause the university to lose the equivalent of 10 percent of its educational budget. Doing so, according the committee report, would necessitate the curtailment of programs such as urban studies and "important programs that make a direct contribution to the cause of racial justice such as the active recruitment and granting of scholarship aid to more black students, the establishment of closer working relationships with organizations in New Jersey concerned with racial problems, and other programs such as the summer program for the disadvantaged youth." Asserting that divestment would be mostly a "symbolic gesture" anyway, the report suggested that such a gesture "would be a heavy price to pay."[88] What did a university creating leaders in the land of the free continuing to do business with apartheid-supporting nations symbolize?

The report placed the student opponents of apartheid in a moral conundrum. If they chose to push forward with their protests, then they might have won a victory for the image of the university and against what they perceived as evil. At the same time, by continuing their efforts they risked losing funding that was used to attract and cultivate potential black students. If the students abandoned their push against the university's financial ties to apartheid South Africa and Mozambique, then they became implicated in a relationship they believed was immoral. Then, if the university acceded to the students' requests, it risked the financial stability of the institution. Essentially, the authors of the report constructed a scenario in which only black people abroad or black people domestically could be helped, but not both at the same time.

Presenting a potential slippery slope regarding the negative impacts of divesting, the report speculated about what type of precedent divesting might set. It stated: "If a policy of using moral, social, or political criteria in investment in a number of different instances, including 'munitions makers,' companies with 'unfair' labor practices, companies dealing with discriminatory unions, companies with investments in Portugal, companies doing business with communist countries, etc. . . . No company is completely free of connections that might be morally-politically-socially objectionable to a significant part of the University community."[89] Such a burden would be too much for an educational institution, argued the report. The problem with the argument was that Princeton was not just an educational institution but also a mill for the nation's future leadership. What lessons were those leaders to learn from the report's stance on the university's tie to apartheid?

On the anniversary of Malcolm X's assassination, the ABC led a boycott of classes and held an action. To point out the death that occurred because of white imperialism and antiblack racism, ABC members carried a coffin with a red, black, and green flag draped around it to the center of campus and held a silent vigil. They were growing tired of negotiating freedom with white decision makers.

By March 1969, the Princeton students (mostly black), who formed the group United Front, wondered if their university could *afford* to be a moral institution with regard to racism. President Goheen attempted to address the concerns of the students. As a matter of policy, he stated that Princeton "will not hold securities in companies which do a *primary* amount of their economic activity in South Africa."[90] Goheen noted that doing so constituted an "unusual commitment on the part of this, or indeed any, university." The president also acknowledged the important contribution of the black graduate students, who sat on the committee to study the apartheid issue. He then pointed to the fact that the faculty voted overwhelmingly to reject gifts to the university from companies "doing a *primary* amount of their business in southern Africa," and that he would recommend that the trustees adopt the policy. In addition, he pledged that Princeton would work with other educational institutions that stood against apartheid and followed through on Goheen's pledge.

Finally, the president reassured the students who worried about the original report's suggestion that changes in the university's investment policies could lead to cuts in funding for the recruitment of black students. He expressed great respect for the "depth, intensity, and nature of concerns which moved the United Front" and the other black students who pushed the issue. "We can and will do more to enable all our students—black and white—to study and learn from the Afro-American experience. We can and will extend our current efforts to add more black faculty, students, and staff to the University community. We can and will support and encourage the efforts of students, faculty, and staff to work with local community groups on problems of mutual concern."[91]

To bolster the president's proclamations, in early March 1969 the Princeton faculty voted to approve an Afro-American Studies program for the university.[92] As the story about the university's ties to apartheid became national news, Goheen's approach to the stirring controversy was open to scrutiny.[93]

Although positive in tone, the president's message did not provide the anti-apartheid students with solace. For the members of the Unified Front, divesting was a clear issue of morality and societal values. To emphasize that point, black students disrupted a service at the university chapel. A representative highlighted a passage from the Bible: "what does it profit a man to gain the whole world but lose is soul?" (Mark 8:36).[94] Strategically, they chose a space where contemplation and reflection were requisite. They had tried meetings and committee work; the next step was to employ moral suasion in a sacred place.

Days later, on the morning of March 11, 1969, the ABC launched what it would later call a "symbolic gesture" by staging a demonstration on Princeton's campus. Moving beyond moral suasion, fifty-five black student members of the ABC and five white members of the campus chapter of the national New Left organization Students for a Democratic Society (SDS) entered the New South building that housed some of the university's administrative offices and chained the doors shut. They decided not to just sit in but to take over the building, making the demonstration that much more serious. In the cold early morning hours, the agitators approached the janitor, who was also black. It must have been interesting for the janitor to see students that early in the morning. They informed the custodian that they were commandeering New South and that he did not have to perform his duties that day. According to Brent Henry, the janitor said "cool" and left the edifice.[95]

Although not adversarial, ABC and SDS had not worked closely on any projects before the demonstration. In addition to ABC and SDS, the Pan-African Student Association and the New Jersey Committee for South Africa assisted in organizing the protest. As the sixty students demonstrated inside the buildings, fifty others (mostly SDS members) marched outside the hall. In a move similar to that of black student protesters at Columbia in 1968, ABC leadership asked the few white students who were in New South to leave so that the black students alone could express their disdain with the university's decision not to completely

Whether he knew or not, the undergraduates knew differently. PATH, voice's splinter offspring, placed six representatives in the undergraduate assembly, effectively leaving Kaminsky in office but not in power. United behind the ambiguous banner of "moderation," the UGA representatives moved to table any measure that might have looked ahead, vote in favor of any bill that confirmed sentiments long since accepted by the rest of the undergraduates. The action passed to the SDS, the ABC, the United Front, and, oddly, the student departmental advisory committees. The first tentative gropings toward revision of thesis and comprehensives requirements blossomed into the refusal by the radical, highly mobile philosophy department to sign its examinations until the "pernicious" shackles of grades were lifted from the hands with which they signed their names. Like the UGA, the department responded by tabling the problem until the spring. There were other events that stretched out through the year, events occuring in month-long acts on the inside pages of the Prince, circumstantial muttering that occasionally rose to a shout. Beer or bigotry? What started the fight between the blacks and the green tees?

328

Figure 2.3. Off-campus activists support the United Front's campaign against Princeton University's investment in apartheid southern Africa. Courtesy of the Seeley G. Mudd Manuscript Library, Princeton University.

Figure 2.3. (*continued*)

divest.[96] In this way, these young activists employed Black Student Power by strategically using their race as a lever for power in negotiation with the university. The black demonstrators still enjoyed the support of SDS and the Third World Liberation Front, which was another group of students that opposed Princeton's ties to the apartheid governments. If the ABC members believed that the university maintained racist ties to oppressive governments of predominantly black nations, then they wanted to be at the forefront of the movement to illuminate and break those ties. The sentiment mirrored that of black youth who demanded Black Power around the nation. For those black youth and Princeton's black demonstrators, it was necessary for black people to take the lead on issues that directly affected black people.

SDS and other supporters of the ABC held rallies throughout the day. At one rally a banner read in capped bold letters: "CRY, BELOVED PRINCETON."[97] Surrounding the refrain were the words apartheid, murder, fascism, oppression, suffering, racism, and misery.

The black students were alone in the building. ABC leader Jerome Davis stated to the growing crowd of onlookers: "We have taken this action to demonstrate our disgust as black people and as human beings."[98] The protesters pointed to what they believed was "outright and admitted moral inconsistency of the university's commitment to mankind and the Government of South Africa." The university committee that studied Princeton's ties to apartheid explained that to divest would be financially prohibitive. To that notion ABC declared: "Morality has no price" and refused to leave the building until it decided to do so.[99] The occupiers did not allow many people to enter the building; they had to be wary of undercover police and counter-protesters. Hoping to have their story told accurately, they allowed reporters from WNJR (a black operated radio station based in Newark) to enter, but insisted that other journalists conduct interviews from outside. When a reporter asked when they planned to end the demonstration, an ABC representative replied: "When we leave, you'll know."[100]

As was the case with the black students who occupied buildings at Columbia, Cornell, Howard, City College of New York, Rutgers, and so many other universities, the students at Princeton did well to make provisions for their demonstration. Princeton demonstrator Gerald Horne, who was among those in New South, observed firsthand the methods

In the Princetonian in September: ". . . the pre-
vailing mood here this fall is an ugly, brooding
one." They were wrong, the mood of the campus
then was as sullen as the late-summer days; but if
the phrase were prophecy instead of description
. . . No one listened to anyone else. The campus
was filled with the ghosts of misconceptions, crowding out the inhabitants of the place. There was what
President Goheen did, what he said he did, and
above those images, there was the SDS' interpretation of what he did, the double exposure of
circumstances. Or take out Goheen's name, substitute: trustees, faculty, dean, Kelley-Malkiel; and
for SDS, read: UGA, Kaminsky, Butler, Scott-Spight,
The Princetonian, the ABC, the United Front—the
deafening sound of political challenge. If the administration creates a committee to study restructure
of the university, who can tell where the emphasis
falls: on "restructure," with its implications of needed
reform; on "study," with its implications of delay,
obstructionism; or on "committee," with its implications of compromise? And who could tell,
when the Kelley Committee issued its interim report,
calling for "changes," whether their keen perception
of the obvious were a stall or a genuine revelation
they had achieved after months of deliberation?
Could Peter Kaminsky tell when he announced that
he would stay on the Committee until it had had
a chance to disprove itself? Or did he learn the
answer in the six-day interval between that announcement and his resignation?

327

Figure 2.4. A member of the Princeton Association of Black Collegians holds a sign during the group's protest to end the university's ties to apartheid southern Africa in March
1969. Courtesy of the Seeley G. Mudd Manuscript Library, Princeton University.

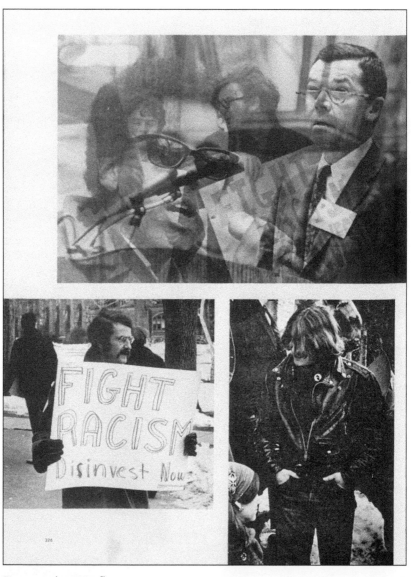

Figure 2.4. (*continued*)

and tactics that students had used during the uprising at Columbia University the previous year.[101] He knew that having a successful campaign required preparation for arrest, meals, lodging, and other practical matters. The student agitators who took over buildings elsewhere had community members to bring in food and supplies, but the Princeton students planned for such provisions. The leadership of the ABC chose New South for their demonstration in part because there was a cafeteria, but there were other reasons. There were no classrooms, so the takeover would not hinder instruction and learning; it was, after all, midterms. Also, the building only had three points of entry, making it easier to secure the place. An important step for the demonstrators was to not unnecessarily destroy anything or to create a mess that would create more work for the black custodian. As they reflected on what they had just done, the demonstrators contemplated next steps.

In spite of the students' resolve to stand for black freedom, President Goheen pressured them to leave by pointing to the university's policy against taking over campus buildings.[102] The president observed: "Many members of the university, members of the staff no less than students and faculty, are deeply troubled by this incident." The demonstration, he suggested, had "the potentiality of kindling latent antagonisms and provoking unconsidered counteraction."[103] If the university did not divest, it also risked antagonisms and counteraction. Goheen declared: "The university cannot tolerate this seizure. . . . The students face penalties up to and including dismissal." He added, "I don't believe in offering amnesty." The black student protesters had not asked for it.

Deliberate in their disobedience, the demonstrators operated on the first and seventh floors of the New South building. Those floors housed the university's comptroller's office as well as the university's payroll offices. The comptroller oversaw stock transactions, which included those with the companies that maintained relationships with apartheid-sanctioned governments, and the payroll offices issued checks to university employees.[104] ABC members understood well that if the university was making the potential loss of money a main issue with regard to divestment, then black students would attempt to gain control of the issue by denying the university's access to money and the building. To that effect, the demonstrators succeeded in stopping business in the building. In addition to halting the operations of the comptroller and payroll offices,

Figure 2.5. Association of Black Collegians members outside New South building, where they protested Princeton University's investment in apartheid southern Africa in March 1969. Courtesy of the Seeley G. Mudd Manuscript Library, Princeton University.

And the raw material: the events, laid out on the pages of the Princetonian. But the events, for all their impact, are only the insignia of thoughts, emotions, beliefs; facts are just the medium meaning exists in. You call it "the tension of change." But from what, to what? If you were writing your novel in June, instead of a yearbook article in March, you might be able to put the nostalgic seal of the graduating senior on the bound volume of the year's memories. But in the midst of it, at the moment of it, it's just a three-demensional collage, a linking together of existential ambiguities.

Figure 2.5. (*continued*)

the student activists impeded the progression of admissions applications as well.[105] This was significant in the sense that Princeton was competing against the rest of the institutions in the Ivy League for students. The demonstration, by delaying the admissions process, could have potentially made Princeton less attractive to prospective students.

The goals of the ABC were threefold. First, the members of ABC wanted to express their dismay with what they viewed as the president's inaction on the issue of South African divestment. Second, they wanted to highlight their commitment to raising the issue to the larger student body and all those who would listen. Third, ABC wanted to "sensitize as many individuals as possible to the need for serious moral commitment against racism throughout the world."[106] When the internationally acclaimed *New York Times* picked up the story, it brought light to the students' struggle to sensitize the masses.[107]

At one point, there were hundreds of students and some faculty members outside the building observing the demonstration. Some disagreed with the tactics of the protesters but sympathized with their cause. One observing student said: "It's just not pragmatic" to take over buildings, and suggested that the ABC "had to do something to keep the issue going." Another student opined: "Just in itself, it's tremendous. . . . It was great to see something like that happening here, seeing this place break out of its complacent attitude." Regarding the ABC and SDS's efforts, one student commented to a reporter that "the ABC guys are really concerned and committed on this issue. . . . The SDS seems to be more of a bandwagon-type group." Still other students, frustrated with the disruption, unsuccessfully attempted to physically remove the demonstrators by attempting to open the doors.[108] Under the leadership of student Rod Hamilton, who was in charge of security, the ABC protected their position and rebuffed the would-be intruders.

ABC evacuated New South twelve hours after the initial takeover. The group's leaders claimed that the demonstrators did not leave for fear of punishment or arrest but rather because "the administration has already began to shift the emphasis on our protest away from [the] moral issues of South Africa to the legitimacy of our tactics."[109] Such a statement not only pointed up the seriousness of the students, but it also illustrated a strategy in black student activity whose origins dated back to the earliest parts of the modern Civil Rights Movement. That strategy was for demonstrators to focus onlookers' attention on the issue without making the methods a distraction.

Interestingly, years later, Henry revealed an often overlooked facet of protesting: boredom. Drama did not fill every moment of the demonstration (and most actions). He and the other students realized that after having made the statement against apartheid and refusing to leave when the administration ordered them to, there was not much to do inside the building besides study. If the intention was to draw attention to immorality of apartheid and the collusion of the university with the racist system, then they accomplished that goal, reasoned ABC leaders. With that in mind, they decided to leave that night, after twelve hours, making the demonstration "a tidy event," as Henry recalled.[110]

ABC leadership asserted that the takeover was only part of their larger movement. Although the students faced disciplinary consequences, they refused to recognize any punishment that the university imposed. "We cannot accept in good faith any so-called moral judgments made by such an immoral institution," Rod Hamilton of the ABC stated.[111] Realizing that a single takeover was not enough to change policy, the student activists explained: "The battle for disinvestment will not be won quickly, but it will be won."

In a bold act, the white student members of the joint student-faculty disciplinary committee refused to participate in proceedings that would punish the demonstrators. Eventually, five black demonstrators were punished just as the spring break began and therefore did not miss any classes or activities. Perhaps more students would have been punished, but the disciplinary committee claimed that it could not identify any others. Although the black student demonstrators did not receive amnesty, they faced little to no punishment for their act of rebellion.[112] Inasmuch, the university averted a potential crisis like those that occurred at universities around the nation.

Princeton, unlike some of the other universities that featured student disruptions, had voted—without the impetus of demonstrations—to not give academic credit for Reserved Officer Training Corps courses and to establish an Afro-American Studies program. With respect to the anti-apartheid protests, the administration wisely did not call police onto campus, which may have hastened or even provoked violence. Finally, the administration, particular President Goheen, *reasoned* with students regarding their demands that Princeton become a more "moral" institution. At some institutions, administrators refused to reason or negotiate with respect to any university policy.[113]

While disruptive, the activity of the black students who demonstrated improved the university. Gerald Horne, a demonstrator at Princeton in the late 1960s, believed that black students had to act "to put the elites [powerful white institutional officials] on alert that we [students] were not inert."[114] Indeed, in the twentieth century, black students moved from matriculation to activism at Princeton. Horne has noted that "activism is one of the best teachers." His fellow activist, Henry, agreed: "When you come to a place like Princeton, your world vision expands,"[115] which ideally should happen to all college students. In the case of Henry, Horne, Hamilton, and the other activists in ABC, their ideas of blackness expanded beyond the borders of the United States as Pan-Africanism gripped the progressive black activist community. In this case, activism taught students that their presence was not an end goal and that they should think outside of themselves. Activism also taught an elite white institution to improve its relationship with black people domestically and abroad.

The student activists did not get all they wanted but they made progress for black people on and off campus. In 1969, after graduating, ABC leader Brent Henry campaigned for and won a position as trustee of Princeton. Black students were infiltrating every level of the university. Henry commented on the liberal nature of some of the board members when he joined the body after graduating in 1969.[116] Surely, some of the board members had been in their positions for years and had been aware of the experience of black students. Nearly all of the board members were alumni, so they saw the travails of the few black students during their time in school. The late 1960s must have been the moment that captured the officials' desire to act.

Princeton did not observe the constant demonstrations that other institutions did during the period. The protesting black students at Princeton did not go as far in their actions as other students, in part because of the presence and advice of Carl A. Fields. Henry explained that Fields acted primarily as a mentor to the students but also as a liaison to the administration, which allowed for a certain amount of understanding between officials and students that was not always available at other institutions.[117] About the small number of confrontations on campus, Fields said that one of his objectives was to "change the nature of confrontation" regarding black students and administrators. He pointed out that "there are a hell of a lot ways to be militant," and that building takeovers, strikes, and physical displays were only a few methods.[118] Noting that students at Princeton were not necessarily less militant than their peers at Northwestern University or San Francisco State College, he commented that "one of the reasons we haven't had any more confrontations than we've had is not because our guys (black men on Princeton's campus) are any more passive" than other campus activists "but because the University has created mechanisms that make confrontation unnecessary." That served both Princeton administrators and students well because they could work toward agreement on issues in a less dramatic way than was common elsewhere.

By 1970, the president of Princeton and all other school officials had an awareness of the experience of black students and felt pressure to improve the situations of the students on campus. Goheen remarked in his annual report of 1968–1969 that "differences in [the] previous experience and background between white and black students are likely to produce suspicions, hostility, and forms of intolerance."[119] Speaking to the behavior of white students, the liberal president wrote: "Too few white students, I think, have an adequate conception of the black students' situation on campus." He could have said the same about white officials. Without an adequate conception, white students, the president surmised, could "scarcely predict their behavior on the blacks." As a result, Goheen explained, "The opportunities and scope for misunderstanding and mutual distrust in such a situation are very great."

The president was correct; black students suffered from the misunderstanding. So much so that one student said this about Princeton, misunderstanding, and mistakes: "Education is the opportunity to make mistakes. The bigger the error made, the better the education received. So essentially," he wrote, "Princeton has been one the biggest mistakes of my life."[120] The characterization of his choice to attend the Ivy school was likely not typical of most black students, but it did represent the thoughts of some. The ultimate question for them at the beginning and end of their time at Princeton was: What were they willing to bear to be a Princetonian?

The relative peace at Princeton regarding black activism carried into the 1970s. Henry also theorized that higher numbers of black students and socioeconomic class played a role in the peace that resumed on campus in the 1970s. In Henry's graduating class (1969), there were fourteen black men. The number of black students rose exponentially in the years following 1965. During the late 1960s and early 1970s Princeton pursued black students from lower socioeconomic backgrounds. Henry speculated that with more black students enrolled there was a looser bond than when there were fewer students, who could remain tighter as a group. The students who came before 1965 were also mostly black middle and working class, which allowed them to initially relate to each other better than when a more economically diverse body of black students arrived on campus, he thought. Henry did not mean that students from lower socioeconomic backgrounds did not get along with those from higher socioeconomic backgrounds, but rather that their economic class status played a part in how they approached life at Princeton. Framing his thoughts as conjecture, he supposed that students from working class and poorer families were perhaps less likely to engage in protest to protect their student status. They might have thought, "I can't afford not to be here" because they knew that finishing at Princeton would present opportunities to improve life for their families.

Ralph Austin, from the class of 1973, represented one of the students from a lower-income household. He grew up in Trenton, where he had observed ghetto life. He described the environment at home and at Princeton as like "night and day" and recalled it was almost as if he had gone from "the ghetto to utopia as far as the surroundings."[121] This was not, though, his first experience with Princeton as a town or university. He had family members who made deliveries to the eating clubs and Austin had also participated in the summer program that brought inner-city black youth to campus to take courses. This was the same program in which historian Komozi Woodard participated as a boy. Knowing something about the campus helped ease his mind when he finally enrolled. Still, he had to confront the history of the school, when he lived in a dormitory that at one point in history, Austin claimed, housed enslaved people. In spite of being relatively acquainted with the campus, much of the scene was new to him.

The stark whiteness of the institution was obvious and Austin also took notice of the nuances in the socioeconomic class status of black students. He said that some of the black students "had some money," which made them different from the black people he knew in Trenton, who were "poor." Austin admitted to being a little intimidated by the prep school students, some of whom were black. He used their background in contrast to his as motivation and inspiration. "My whole attitude was hey, I came from an inner city high school and I can compete with you guys and you come from prep school, so I think I'm doing better than you are." Other students from his background, he claimed, shared that attitude. To make money, he worked as a waiter in an eating club. The presence of the ABC, which included black students from all backgrounds, reassured him that there was a network of support. In his mind, the network of ABC and "being in the midst of the black revolution" were enough to assuage some of his anxiety of being different racially and socioeconomically.

Henry had a final thought about the number of demonstrations in the 1970s. Injecting a bit of humor, he suggested that a lot of the demonstrating and protesting that the young men did at Princeton in the 1960s was just "pent up whatever," and that when Princeton finally invited women to enroll, the university relieved some of that tension.[122] The entrance of women certainly changed the dynamics of campus life, but whether they helped with the "pent up whatever" is debatable. Women Princetonians faced unique circumstances and resisted in their own ways and with others. Black women in the Ivy League and the "Seven Sister" schools were often participatory and in the leading roles of student actions. In the late 1960s and early 1970s, however, survival was a priority for most women in the Ivy League.

At Princeton, women did not enroll until 1969 and the transition was not always smooth for them. Mistreatment, rejection, and discomfort were not reserved for black male students. Women had been able to attend Princeton in the past, but they could not officially graduate. The idea to become coeducational was not always popular among the male Princetonians. One alumnus from the class of 1920, E. S. Hubbell, who represented the Denver Committee for the Preservation of Princeton, was upset when he learned of the decision. He remarked that "Princeton

Tradition" was important and "precious."[123] Princeton, he emphatically stated, "has been a male domain; it must remain so." At stake was the manhood of the "traditional" students, Hubbell claimed. College should be a place where a boy is allowed to develop his manhood because after his time at the university, "he is forever lost in a feminine world," according to the alumnus. Hubbell clarified, though, that he was not a "woman hater" because he was married with two daughters.

Hubbell was not alone in his opinions. George Hammond Jr. in the class of 1940, concurred, stating: "Male isolation is the big, contributing aspect to the success of his education."[124] It seemed as though Hammond believed that men would not be able to control themselves with women present. He said the Princeton man had a reputation for being a "dashing, undisciplined fellow" in his time. Hubbell and Hammond's voices were two of a number of diverse voices on the issue of coeducation, but the notion of gender equality in admissions prevailed. The one-time bastion for white men was crumbling, and Princeton welcomed its first official class of women in the fall of 1969. Black women were part of that class, and they experienced multiple levels of bigotry.

Vera Marcus from Birmingham, Alabama, was the first black woman to enroll, attend, and graduate from the university. Her family lived modestly as her father was a minister, janitor, and street sweeper; her mother was a beautician. Prior to enrolling at Princeton, Marcus was one of the first black students to attend a newly desegregated high school in Birmingham, so the distinct feeling of isolation and being the "other" was familiar to her.[125] Because of her forced solitude, she focused on her academic achievement. Marcus's performance, she believed, was the reason that Princeton recruited her with a scholarship. She had not thought to apply to Princeton initially, but once she received an offer letter, she was New Jersey bound. Being the first black woman to graduate from the Ivy League institution never occurred to Marcus before she actually came to campus.

As she was part of the first class of women officially enrolled as Princetonians, she regularly confronted sexism. The eating clubs, which were historically problematic for black students, did not allow women to join either. The entire lifestyle that some of her white peers maintained was completely outside of her worldview. She commented that at Princeton, she experienced "first-hand what life could be like if you were among the haves" in contrast to the have-nots.[126] Those who joined eating clubs had a privilege that others did not. Marcus, who came from a city where black girls were murdered in a church a mile away from her home in 1963, recollected that in high school and college she was not trying to be a hero, but rather she just wanted to "stay alive." Looking back on her academic career, she explained that the last time she had felt normal was when she was eleven years old and attending her all-black elementary school. There, she was merely another student. That was not the case at Princeton for Marcus. As one scholar described the experience of early black Cornell University students, black students in the Ivy League were "part and apart" from their institutions. Sadly, Marcus stated, her college career was "colored by that loneliness," and it was intensified by the fact that there were only two other black women in her class.

Another black Princeton alumna, Caroline Upshaw, who graduated a year after Marcus, discussed the modern concept of intersectionality when she recalled her time at Princeton. It was difficult for her to face the reaction of not only a majority of white people but also a majority of men to her as a "minority, not only as a woman, but as a black" person.[127] This difficulty manifested in the ignorance of her peers and slights with which she had to cope. "I have been confronted by people who have asked me to let them watch me wash my hair . . . to watch me comb it, even touch it," she said of her interaction with white Princeton students. Again, in light of the high rates of poverty and death that black people endured in the urban sections of Trenton, Patterson, and Newark, the rude and discriminatory behavior that Upshaw tolerated may have seemed minor, but her white peers questioned and challenged her intimate humanity. Aside from being annoying, the suggestion to watch the student do her hair was voyeuristic, objectifying, and dehumanizing. It was quite possible that the white students who made such requests had never been around black women before coming to Princeton. That was a result of the systematic subjugation of black people that legal and de facto segregation cultivated. Having grown up accustomed to American apartheid, white students could not help but view black students and especially black women as foreign objects.

White students, according to Marcus, were not the only ones that caused some black women to feel different. Marcus claimed to observe a recognizable distance between black men and women at Princeton in the first years of coeducation. "The black men were more like the white men than they were like us," she asserted.[128] In clarification, she noted that the "division at Princeton was more distinctly along gender lines than racial ones." She suggested that at least black men somewhat fit the centuries-old male template of Princeton, but black women were nearly the antithesis of what Princeton had always been. As someone who had fought in the black freedom struggle in the South, she had not foreseen having to fight battles over gender in the North. That was an additional stressor for black women like her.

There were few people at the institution who could empathize with black students when they experienced or observed racism. The 1977 ABPA survey showed that most black students had one or no black professors throughout their college years. The presence of black professors and administrators has proven effective in the retention rates of students and their presence was no less essential then. In that regard, the culture and history of the university was clearly not accommodating to black students.[129]

The long-standing tradition and culture of Princeton affected black students in the postwar era. The struggle to change the university brought them together to confront issues of racism and isolation, and that created a special bond for them. The intense college experience, however, also disaffected many of the black students. The feelings the black alumni had about their alma mater had implications. For many, their relationship to Princeton paid off in terms of mutual benefits. Princeton officials could boast that the university had evolved, and black alumni could tout their Ivy League credentials when embarking on new life endeavors.

Life for many black students was complicated at Ol' Nassau. They could distinctively remember their travails; however, those memories did not prevent some from giving back to the university. Remarkably, 28 percent who responded to the 1977 ABPA survey said that they participated in annual giving to the university. The survey suggested that the students who remembered having a more positive experience at the university were more inclined to donate money, while those who merely "survived" the university gave less or not all. Perhaps one of the best indicators of the relationship of Princeton University to black people came in the response to the question of whether the respondents would

you send their children to the university. Almost two-thirds (62 percent) said that they would encourage their children to attend Princeton.
Only 7 percent stated outright that they would not send their children to
the university. Those in the remaining percentage were not sure if they
would or would not.[130] Vera Marcus articulated one sentiment among
the graduates: "I'm very proud to have gone to Princeton. . . . But it could
have been so much more."[131]

As it is, Princeton University is still an elite and exclusive primarily
white institution. The institution that was once the southern-most Ivy,
however, now touts diversity as one of its main values. It took the efforts
of students—particularly black students—to improve Princeton's reputation with regard to race and to move the institution closer to morality. In
this case, morality meant admitting American citizens who happened to
be black, including the experience of African Americans in the curriculum, and reconsidering the institution's financial support of apartheid.
When they made a stand for international black rights, those who came
in the postwar period followed in the footsteps of intellectual and activist Paul Robeson, who lived in the town of Princeton but did not have
the opportunity to attend the university. Undoubtedly, black students
helped Princeton University to be "in the nation's service and in the service of all nations."

3

Bourgeois Black Activism

Brown University and Black Freedom

Racism at Brown University and other citadels of higher learning is so entrenched and pervasive that it becomes blatantly
visible.
—*Black Studies: An Educational Imperative*, 1971

When many consider the words "Brown" and "education," their
minds quickly race to the famous 1954 Brown v. Board of Education
Supreme Court decision. Others may remember the recent revelation
about Brown University, the exclusive Ivy League institution, and its
ties to slavery. The university oversaw the work of a study group that
researched the amount of revenue that the founders of the institution
garnered from the trade of human chattel. Others might think of the
notable fact Brown recently featured not only a woman as president but
an African American woman, Ruth Simmons. In that way, Brown has
hurdled past many of the racial barriers that still exist at other institutions of higher education. It is conceivable, though, that much of the
racial progress that Brown has made would not have been possible were
it not for the activism of concerned black students in past decades. During the decades following World War II, young black people—like their
nonblack peers—came to the elite institution situated in Providence,
Rhode Island, to achieve degrees. In the process, however, these black
Brunonians sought to advance the larger black freedom movement by
agitating their university to create further opportunities for African
Americans on and off campus.

At Brown University and Pembroke College (Brown's women's college) in Rhode Island, African American students made up a small but
significant segment of the generation of students who sought to effect
change on their exclusive campuses. While students, they provoked a

renaissance of ideas about black life that sometimes stirred controversy. The discourse that resulted from the renewal of perceptions and concepts eventually improved the university.

In localizing the story, it must be noted that although many young African Americans admired the courage and leadership of figures like King, Malcolm X, and Stokely Carmichael (Kwame Ture), the few black Ivy students could only look to themselves (and potentially their surrounding communities) to advance change. In essence, these students had to become their own versions of freedom fighters. This chapter concludes that this small but effective minority of youth practiced Black Student Power: African American students used their racial status in conjunction with their ties to institutions of higher education to win victories for the larger black freedom movement. Brown students' peaceful display of Black Power advanced the freedom movement and indirectly aided the effort to appoint the Ivy League's first (and so far only) black president.

To contextualize the role of black people in determining post-World War II policies, it is important to understand the relationship of Brown to black people in earlier periods. Brown University began as the College of the English Colony Rhode Island and Providence Plantations in 1764. As one of the oldest universities in the nation, it has long stood as a pioneer of education. According to the official university website, Brown was the first of the Ivies to admit students from religious backgrounds other than Protestant. The school boasts that making the college available to those of all religious affiliations was a "testament to the spirit of openness" that existed at Brown then and now.[1]

Although Brown was open to the various religious affiliations of its oncoming students, the elite university has a storied past concerning people of African descent in this nation. The university is named after the Brown family, who had profited from the American and international slave trade. With the Browns acting as original signatories on the college's charter and as benefactors, the university directly and indirectly benefited from the trafficking of humans. Enslaved people even built some edifices on campus.[2]

Brown, in that way, is one of the most conflicted of all the Ivy institutions with regard to its history of black freedom. Although the university got its start, in part, from the enslavement of black people, Brown had an important impact on black educational advancement in the nineteenth century. In 1877, Inman Page and George Washington Milford Brown became the first two black students to graduate from the Ivy institution in Rhode Island. Impressively, Page served as president of Lincoln College and Western Baptist College in Missouri, Agriculture and Normal University in Oklahoma (later Langston University), and Roger Williams University in Tennessee.[3] At the turn of the twentieth century, black Brunonians John Hope and John William Beverly affected the educational opportunities of other black students by taking posts as president of historically black colleges and universities like Morehouse College and Alabama State Normal School.[4] John Brown Watson, who graduated in 1904, founded a college and eventually acted as president of Arkansas Agricultural and Mechanical Institute. Another black alumnus, William Dinkins, was president of Selma University from 1935 to 1950. Ethel Robinson, a student at Women's College in Brown University, graduated in 1904 and then began teaching at Howard University. While there, she acted as an advisor to a group of women who established the world's first college sorority for black women, Alpha Kappa Alpha Sorority, Inc.[5] The university was also the alma mater of alumni like Frederick Douglass "Fritz" Pollard, a 1919 graduate and the first black professional football coach. Pollard, while at Brown, was a standout running back who made the prestigious Walter Camp All-America First Team.[6] Those Brown and Pembroke alumni returned to the black community to uplift and create more opportunities for others.

* * *

In the 1960s, life for black students at Brown was still, unfortunately, an isolating experience. "Don't stand together like this, man. If a bomb drops, they've got all of us," went the joke that black students at Brown in the early 1960s told each other.[7] Speaking to the psychological effects of desegregating and trailblazing in an *Esquire* magazine article, alumnus Barry Beckham (class of 1966) wrote: "It wasn't difficult to reach the ego-building deduction that we were the only talented negroes in the country who could pass the stringent admissions policy of Brunoversity."[8] Shortly after his arrival to campus, he wondered if that were the case or if he had been "chosen only to add some color."[9] There was a fear, he revealed, that "perhaps we [black students] weren't equal, or at least *they* [white people] thought it."[10] That particular line of thought was erroneous. University officials later admitted that the institution had not searched for all of the qualified black students it could, which meant that Beckham and his early 1960s black schoolmates were well qualified (and equal to their white peers) but certainly not exclusively talented.[11]

As the number of black students remained relatively small in the early 1960s, the number of white "legacy" students remained steady. Beckham made note of that fact: "every university in the county maintains separate admissions standards for different groups," he charged. "Sons and daughters of alumni and alumnae are almost always given preference over other applicants in colleges."[12] Beckham, to some extent, was correct. In the 1963–1964 school year at Princeton University, which was similar to other institutions in the Ivy League, 20 percent of the entering class were sons of alumni.[13] The Princeton alumni were all white. The same was virtually true of Brown.

By 1965, black students made up 316 of the 14,125 students accepted to universities/colleges in the Ivy League.[14] Harvard's dean of admissions explained that the forty black students (up from thirty the year before) they accepted for the 1965–1966 school year was double the number accepted to the nation's oldest university a decade earlier. Harvard accepted 1,370 for the 1965–1966 school year. As Ivy schools accepted higher numbers of black students, an admissions official at the University of Pennsylvania pointed out that the elite schools were competing for a small number of students even though there was an "unprecedented" number of black students applying to Ivy institutions. Applications from students of black middle-class families stood out to the Brown dean of admissions. He was surprised in part by their existence but also by the fact that they had little need for financial assistance. Of course, for decades, the National Urban League's *State of Black America* report had indicated there had always been a professional class that existed in the black community that sought to provide their children with the highest forms of education possible, but that may have escaped the Brown dean's attention.

Black students, apparently, had not been at the forefront of admissions officials' minds, and so those gatekeepers could unknowingly overlook the children of the black middle class. At Columbia University, black students made up 35 (up from 25 the previous year) of the 1,125 students accepted. Cornell University accepted 70 black students (up from 25 the previous year) and 3,925 students in general. There were an estimated 30 black students (up from 14 the previous year) out of a total 1,220 students admitted to Dartmouth College. At the University of Pennsylvania 2,750 total students were admitted, of which 46 were black students (up from 30 the previous year). Of the 1,210 students admitted to Princeton University, black admitted students comprised 30 (up from 20 the previous year) and Yale admitted 35 black students (up from 25 the previous year) and 1,425 students total. Brown's dean of admissions estimated that the university was admitting 1,100 total students and 30 black students (up from 15 previous year) into the oncoming class. Each of the universities/colleges saw an increase in total applications, reflecting the effects of the baby boom. Black students, irrespective of their economic status, still made up a lonely minority (2 percent) of Ivy admits by 1965.[15] Even though more students than ever before attended four-year institutions, black students only made up 5 to 6 percent nationwide. Along those lines by the end of the decade, half of the students at universities/colleges came from the top 25 percent in terms of family income; only 7 percent came from the lowest family incomes.[16] Black high school students were more likely than their white peers to come from the lowest family incomes.

The numbers of black admits was bleak, but the sense of otherness black students felt was profound. In discussing his experience, Barry Beckham pointed out ways that he tried to avoid loneliness and stave off isolation. "It was only natural that we [few black students] stuck together," he explained. In 1966, he counted approximately eight enrolled black students "out of a class of 659." Many of his white schoolmates had come from the extremely exclusive Exeter, Lawrenceville, and Groton preparatory schools and had families in the banking industry, stock exchange, and medical field. Even though Beckham and other black students may have come from the black middle class, they stood out from their white peers. When asked why the black students sat together at campus locales, his answer was not dissimilar to those of black students at Ivy League schools at the turn of the century: "the common ground between black student and white student is so uncommon, the possibility of a badly needed entente is so slight, that it shouldn't seem so unusual for black students to spend that perfect opportunity to mix and talk—at mealtime—with other blacks." The tradition of black students sitting together continued at Brown, with the students even claiming an informal "Black Table."[17] That is precisely what the black Cornell students who founded the first black collegiate fraternity, Alpha Phi Alpha, did to survive their Ivy League experience.[18]

Out of a need to socialize and to feel secure, black students in the Ivy League throughout the century felt an obligation to come together. Of the natural coalescence, Beckham claimed that "it was elementary, my dear Watson," riffing on the Sherlock Holmes line.[19] In a circumstance where there were so few black students, professors, staff, and administrators, the social life of young black people was difficult, said Beckham. "Socially we were castrated," referring to the fact that black students at Brown (and Pembroke) did not have the same options as their peers in terms of dating, housing, and socializing. Beckham concluded: "The white student can date anytime he wants with anyone he pleases. . . . He has friends who rent off-campus apartments. He has a car." In essence, Beckham exclaimed: "The white student is white. He belongs here."[20] The nagging question for Beckham and others like him was whether black students did.

As the decade progressed, black students at Brown and Pembroke envisioned themselves as representatives of the larger black community, and they made sure Brown officials understood they belonged at the Ivy League institution and society in general. By 1968, black students only made up 2 percent of the university's total student population of 3,780 students; at Pembroke, black female students made up 3 percent of the nearly 1,200 students.[21] Although the black students at Brown and Pembroke were few in number, they, like previous generations of black students, made the most of their opportunity to attend an elite institution of higher education. Furthermore, the black students of the late 1960s were extremely effective in their bids to improve life for black people on campus. They began their protests with campaigns to increase black admissions, which was the typical course of action for black student activists at Ivy League and other predominantly white institutions (PWIs) during the period.[22]

The members of the Afro-American Society (AAS), which included members from Brown and Pembroke, led the way in the campaign to increase black enrollments. In 1968, the director of admissions, Charles

Doebler, admitted that "We [Brown admissions officials] have had the most marvelous cooperation from our Afro-American Society."[23] Brown needed the efforts of those black students to advance its enrollment campaign. As Doebler explained, "In the years I have been at Brown, all the people who have been involved in getting Negroes to come here have been white. Now it is the Negroes themselves who are involved in it."[24] Doebler could have very well added that those white people who had been involved in getting black people to come to the elite institution could not boast of a record of high achievement.

By referring to the fact that black students were involved in recruitment, Doebler made a crucial point that marked the arrival of a new era for both elite universities and the black freedom movement. With the advent of Black Power throughout the nation, black people (and black students) sought to do for themselves what white America had been unable to do. In this case, an almost exclusively white institution had been incapable (or perhaps unwilling) to recruit a significant number of black students. To remedy the situation, black students at Brown and other Ivy institutions took it upon themselves to recruit fellow students from their race. As leaders and scholars like Malcolm X, Stokely Carmichael, and Charles V. Hamilton taught, members of the black community needed to use their collective power to support efforts to advance opportunities. Sometimes that meant voting as a bloc; at others, using the collective power meant demonstrating against racism; and in still other instances, supporting the efforts to advance opportunities meant using the resources offered at white institutions to gain knowledge that would assist in the creation of black institutions.

The black students at Brown and Pembroke, who devoured the words and ideas of their leaders, believed their role in the struggle for freedom was to create opportunities for black advancement by making their Ivy institution more accessible to the members of the black community. Taking the initiative and responsibility to recruit black high school students placed AAS squarely in the movement. The initial phase of their version of the movement involved the creation of a larger black presence on their campus. Scholars have explained that in the larger Black Power Movement, leaders pushed for the entrance of black people into positions of power and spaces they had not previously occupied.[25] The next step required those black students to use the powerful white institutions to acquire skills and knowledge that could benefit the masses in the black community. "You're going to fight institutionalized racism" Student Nonviolent Coordinating Committee (SNCC) leader Stokely Carmichael told students.[26] He was hopeful about the young people who were to take up this battle: "One of the most promising developments in the nation today is the new mood among black college students, who have long formed a conservative group . . . imitating white America at its worst." Now, he boasted, "humble appeal is gone; a powerful mood has developed based on a black consciousness."[27] Rather than humble, students entering universities in the late 1960s were determined to make a place for themselves and those who followed.

For Brown University, there were different phases in the creation of its new identity as an institution that welcomed black people. The first phase required the institution to get beyond its liberal rhetoric and actually increase the number of black people on campus. The next phase involved making resources available to a group of people (black students) who were essentially strangers to institutional white America. The resources came in the form of funding for student organizations, curricular enhancement, and space for the students. In addition, that second phase necessitated changes in the university's human resources practices. While higher numbers of black students was a coup for the institution, more students without higher numbers of black faculty and administrators might cause them to lose the newly admitted black students.

As a result of their spring recruitment efforts, Brown students were able to point to the fifty black students admitted in the fall of 1968. Brown's admission of black students, while impressive by its own standards, was somewhat lower than its peer institutions. For instance, Princeton admitted 76, Columbia and Cornell admitted 80 to 85, Penn admitted 125, Yale admitted 70, and Harvard admitted more than 80.[28]

Although Brown and its peers were admitting black students at a higher rate than ever before, the actual matriculation of black students did not grow as quickly. Part of the reason for this was the fact that the accepted black students had made applications to several of the Ivy schools but could only attend one. Also, in spite of efforts from groups like AAS and progressive-minded white administrators, the pool of black students that would matriculate was still relatively small. To that effect, Princeton's director of admissions revealed: "We're [Princeton and other Ivy League schools] pretty much admitting guys who are getting lots of good college offers."[29] That was the case with Brown student Spencer Crew, who originally planned to stay in his home state of Ohio. Upon meeting with a forward-thinking guidance counselor and consulting with his cousin who attended Yale, Crew applied to and was accepted at Brown, Cornell, and Penn. He chose Brown, in part, because a representative from Brown came to meet with him.[30]

The Princeton admissions director's statement about competing for the same students pointed to the prospect that the students that Brown and the other schools admitted would have potentially been admitted anyway—that the institution was not in fact extending its search for black students much farther than it had been in the past. Noting this possibility, the director explained that "what we're doing for the disadvantaged is not enough."[31] That was precisely the point that black students on Brown's (and Princeton's) campus had been making since the mid-1960s and why they demonstrated in the latter part of the decade.

Black students at Brown and Pembroke began the transition to the second phase of their movement (getting black support staff hired). In November 1968, members of the Afro-American Society at Pembroke brought a list of demands to the president of the college that included calls for a black admissions officer to be hired by January and for the matriculation of at least thirty black students by the fall of the next year. This is an important aspect of black student activism during this period because the role of black male activists has been heavily highlighted in the majority of scholarly works, but it is noteworthy that black women like those at Radcliffe or the members of the Barnard Organization of Soul Sisters (BOSS) at Columbia pushed the envelope with regard to the black freedom movement on campus.[32] The women of BOSS led the way in the push for a Black Studies program at Barnard College, which had a great influence on the efforts to create one at Columbia University.

As did consciously black women elsewhere, the Pembroke students took action. On November 18, 1968, they declared: "We, the black women of Pembroke, are concerned about the lackadaisical attitude of the Pembroke Admissions Office towards the case of the black woman applying to Pembroke."[33] They wanted a system put into place that would more pointedly focus on black recruitment. Without the serious commitment, they said, "We will refuse to help in finding black students." Perhaps foreshadowing, the black Pembrokers also noted that if the college did not put forth an immediate and more concerted effort, then "we will do what we can to make known this lack of interest" in black people.

Via a series of position papers, activists at Pembroke demanded that the overall enrollment of black students at the women's college at least match the overall percentage of black people in the United States, which was 11 percent. The black men of Brown University supported the female activists' cause. In response to the demand, Brown University president Raymond Heffner (who presided over Pembroke as well) wrote a letter that began "Dear Black Students" and explained that the university would not automatically agree to admit any percentage of students, but that it would "endeavor" to enroll thirty-five black students into the incoming class at Pembroke (which would make up nearly 12 percent of the class).[34]

The Pembroke women also demanded a black admissions officer for the college that could act in the same capacity as Richard Nurse, the newly hired admissions officer for Brown. Nurse came to the university after Brown's AAS took its grievances regarding the need for a black recruiter to President Heffner.[35] These student-activists on the Brown and Pembroke campuses knew the benefits of attaining an education and a degree from such a prestigious institution, and they attempted to make it possible for more black people to enjoy those benefits. In doing so, these young members of the black intelligentsia were extending the movement for black freedom to campus, like many other students across the nation had done. In their minds, black students could not afford to be just students. They had to be freedom fighters as well. In their push for freedom, they were maneuvering white university officials into areas of thought and action that the officials had never contemplated.

It is true that after the advent of the Civil Rights Movement Ivy League institutions attempted to admit higher numbers of black students, but it took black students themselves to intensify the tenacity with which these universities approached the effort (this happened, in part, because students and professors at these universities were participating in the Civil Rights Movement).[36] In doing so, black students helped their universities and colleges live up to their own proclamations of fairness and liberalism. For those student demonstrators, however, the goal of admitting thirty-five black students into Pembroke that Heffner suggested for the fall 1969 semester was not enough to assure them of the institutional commitment to black advancement. The protesters explained that while that number might have been a good goal for the time being, the president did not take into account the fact that Pembroke's (and more broadly Brown's) population might increase in the future and thirty-five black students per class would be less significant.

Their rebuff of the president's suggestion launched a debate in which Heffner publicly refused to employ any "quotas" to admit students. The black student activists reacted quickly by clarifying that they did not seek a quota. "A quota is an upper limit. We are seeking a minimal goal," explained Pembroke sophomore Sheryl Grooms, who came to the college from nearly all-black Roxbury, Massachusetts.[37] As the term "affirmative action" was just coming into the lexicon of the nation, the debate regarding black college admissions and employment raged at Brown and Pembroke.

Dissatisfied with the progress of the negotiations, Brown and Pembroke students took further and more militant action. The *New York Times* reported that on December 5 (incidentally the thirteenth anniversary of the start of the 1955 Montgomery bus boycott), sixty-five black students from Pembroke and Brown, with suitcases and sleeping bags in hand, organized outside the student center on Brown's campus and then marched to the nearby Congdon Street Baptist Church, where they intended to stay. Because there was so little in the way of black life on campus, students had previously established connections with the members and pastor of the church. The relationships the students established made it possible for the Congdon Street congregation to welcome them as they boycotted the university.[38] The actions of the church members mirrored those of black community members around the nation who provided solace and help to black students seeking to advance their causes on and off campus. In the South in particular, the black church became the staging ground for the movement in the 1960s. In Providence, the black church also provided the space for black freedom visions. In a similar vein, black community members who lived nearby and observed institutions like Brown, Yale, Columbia, Penn, and even Cornell, understood the difficulty black students had in navigating the starkly white environments. The residents sympathized with the actions of the students who were attempting to increase access to a white institution, and in doing so improve the community.

The black student activists pledged to boycott classes and stay in the basement of the church until their demands were met. The *New York Times* reported that the students claimed they were "disassociating" from their institutions because of the schools' inability to meet the needs of black people and particularly the students.

As was the case in other demonstrations involving black students and demands, white students and professors showed up in solidarity with the black activists. Nearly 800 mostly white supporters met at University Hall, one of the oldest buildings on campus—and one that enslaved black people helped to build—to discuss the black student demonstrators' demands.[39] Before showing up, white supporters issued a statement that read, "We support our black brothers in the Afro-American Society in their attempt to achieve their goals."[40] The statement called for progressive white people to "Come to the Speak-Out" at "noon on the green" to discuss ways to augment the black protesting students' efforts. In a message sent to "White Brothers and Sisters," student Marc Sacardy outlined the philosophical conflict facing his racial peers. "Because black students have taken the initiative to test the university's policies and its sincerity," he wrote, "it is our [white students'] responsibility to take sides: part of the problem or part of the solution," Sacardy said. "I hope we, as white students, can learn to understand blacks on their terms" and in a way that allows white students to at least attempt to "think black."[41]

Other students reinforced Sacardy's message: "We white students of Brown support completely the twelve demands of the Afro-American Society and their right to determine the terms on which they will remain as members of the university community," wrote Paul Rosenburg.[42] Then, a group explained that they were inclined to support AAS's demands for two reasons. The first involved black students having the ability to "determine for themselves decisions affecting their position"; the second was in regard to "the racist policies of the University" and "how they affect the entire educational environment."[43]

AAS member Kenneth McDaniel, who was graduating in the spring of 1969, revealed that the black activists had not asked for the support of the white students but that they were grateful for the white students' efforts.[44] He said AAS members wanted to "extend our thanks to the white students on campus who have given us support." Progressive white students around the nation took the initiative to bolster the campaigns of black campus agitators. The interaction between the black and white demonstrators did not always resemble the participatory democracy kind of relationships that developed in organizations like SNCC and the Congress of Racial Equality in the southern movement in the early 1960s and Students for a Democratic Society in the late 1960s. Integration was not a priority for many black student activists in 1968, and white students had to accommodate the need for them to close ranks in terms of decision making. Regarding the demonstration at Brown and the Congdon Street Baptist church, black students did not inform white students of what was happening until just before the action. In doing so, AAS attempted to maintain control of communication to the press. Additionally, as McDaniel pointed out, AAS only wanted "direct communication" with the administration. Such communication did not require checking in with white students. Understanding this, white students and Brown affiliates organized on behalf of the campaign, showing solidarity with the cause. The organization of the activists resulted in a petition that 2,878 Brown and Pembroke affiliates signed in support of the black students' demands.[45]

White students and university affiliates were not the only backers of the AAS action. In a news conference on December 9, AAS leaders explained that they benefited from external support.[46] The wanted to "express gratitude" to the local black community "not only because of their support in giving us money and food but most important of all they gave us moral support." The black members of the surrounding community may not have been able to attend Brown or Pembroke, but they wanted to make it possible for their children or others' children to have the opportunity. Community members in urban areas offered help to protesting black students and youth throughout the Civil Rights Movement and Black Power Movement and certainly throughout the black campus movement. Historically, the black church, in particular, was supportive of activist movements, and the Congdon Street Baptist church acted in that tradition.

Black Power, and thus Black Student Power, meant foregoing class distinctions to unify along racial lines for the advancement of black

life chances. The students and church members succeeded in that measure. "They [the church members] have done something tremendous
in bridging the gap between the community and the students," the AAS
spokesman said. Linking campus and community was imperative to
many of the black Ivy League students whose institutions resided within
urban areas. That connection was also crucial to achieving Black Power,
according to H. Rap Brown. The SNCC leader told students there is a
danger that befalls some young people who are fortunate enough to
make it to a university: "Black students begin to assume they're different
from the people on the other side of the track," when in fact, "the [white]
man stratifies the [black] community" by creating a distance between
the campus and the people in the neighborhoods.[47] The off-campus
community members and the students hoped to benefit the larger black
community from the coalition and shorten the distance to which Rap
Brown referred.

In light of that coalition and the support that white Brown and Pembroke affiliates offered, the increased number of demonstrators supporting AAS demands gave administrators that much more cause for
concern. Negotiating early was essential if officials did not want the
demonstration to reach the proportions of uprisings at Columbia University, Northwestern University, and San Francisco State College.

Indeed, what occurred at institutions like Columbia shaped the
outcomes of the Brown campaign. Black students, in a letter written to
President Heffner in May, explained that in light of King's assassination and the student rebellions of the spring, they observed that "the
white university in America inherently reflects" racism. Black activist on
campuses, the students claimed, were reacting to a "pseudo-egalitarian
racist environment" and "Brown University is no exception to this characteristic white, educational institution." The students warned that "The
condition which precipitated the Black student rebellions at Columbia
and Boston exist here." According to the letter, "Brown is a stifling, frus-
trating, and degrading place for black students." The students critiqued
the university as a "bulwark of American liberalism" and questioned
whether they were admitted in "order to maintain its image as a non-
discriminatory liberal university." Years earlier, other black students
asked the same question of themselves. The black student agitators in
1968 stated that "it is our hope that the removal of these conditions is

carried out without the need of an insurrection here." In a tone that indicated impending action, the students exclaimed: "The university has been laboring under the misguided impression that we are happy because we have been quiet."[48] Believing that the president was taking the relative peace on campus for granted, the letter explained that Heffner and the university were "sure that we would blend right in and be silently grateful that we were here at all" even as tokens. "We are tired of being tokens and nothing else," the students said.

Black students clarified their stance on life at the university and college. Suggesting that they had been "refined enough, timid enough, and conservative enough to be Brownmen," they were at the point where they knew "something must be done" and "racism, in all its diverse forms, must be eradicated" from the university (and Pembroke) to make life better for black students.[49] Black Brunonians and Pembrokers in 1968 went beyond surviving at the university, which was what Redding and Beckham focused on, to demanding "a right to a complete, educational experience" that allowed them to not only feel as though they belonged but also gave them knowledge of themselves. Although they were willing to give the university time to "prove its sincerity," with regard to its relationship to black people, the students wrote in the letter that "if the University tries to pacify us with excuses or stop-gap measures, we will have to think of the University as an enemy of black people and take appropriate action." With their enhanced black consciousness and the letter they wrote, the young activists made the turn from mere presence to protest and sought to use their Black Student Power.

The *New York Times* also reported that President Heffner did not plan to levy any disciplinary measures on the demonstrating black students. The point seemed moot as the students had not technically done anything to garner such action. They left campus during the day, which was entirely permissible; further, they took their protest off campus, which should have satisfied any restrictions against on-campus demonstrations. By disassociating themselves, these black students illustrated the power that young people had to draw attention to their issues without seeking permission from authorities. As black students disassociating themselves, they used their race and status as students to advance goals for the larger black freedom movement. Recognizing that they could affect black life in their own space, the students acted accordingly.

As Sheryl Grooms put it, "The walkout is essentially to get a reaction, to force them [university and college officials] to do something" about life for black students and people in general.[50]

The decision to walk off campus and boycott rather than take over a building was also deliberate. At about the same time that Brown students boycotted, black students throughout the nation took over buildings and flirted with violence in their demonstrations.[51] Brown students moved peacefully—yet forcefully—to the church. Decades after the boycott, Spencer Crew explained that the black student activists understood that there was a "Brown Way." The Brown Way, Crew indicated, did not involve raucous and potentially acrimonious confrontations. While students may have been concerned about punitive repercussions, they believed that it was more tactical not to provoke a bad reaction with a violent or disruptive campaign. As AAS coordinator Phil Lord remembered later, "we were very conscious of the role that peaceful agitation and nonviolence could play" in the demonstration.[52]

This proved effective at that moment because Brown officials did not have to look far to see campuses shutting down when students chose to disrupt the normal operations of university business, which was the method used by black students at Columbia and Penn months earlier. Crew explained that before walking off campus there was a discussion about strategy. During the conversation, the students asked: "Do we want that kind of confrontational approach [like that at Columbia University] or do we want to try something different?" The demonstrators, according to Crew, "decided that the position to walk off was different and it might highlight issues without imitating what people had done earlier." Brown junior and AAS coordinator Phil Lord was excited to be in a position where he could put into practice the "black consciousness" he had gained.[53]

The Brown students' discussion was a perfect example of the nuances of the movement for Black Power. Recent scholarship has highlighted the misleading way that traditional narratives about Black Power have inferred that violence or violent rhetoric was inherent to every action. This was clearly not the case with the Brown activists, who sought innovative ways to make their point but who also sought to create opportunities for black freedom. Nonviolent militant action proved effective in advancing the ideals of Black Power.

The situation at Brown caused a problem in terms of publicity and undesirable attention for the university, but officials understood that the scenario could have been worse. University officials saw young black people participating in the urban uprisings in cities across the nation the previous spring, when a white supremacist assassinated Martin Luther King Jr. So, working with black students, who took such a measured approach, was much easier for Brown officials than having to call police onto campus as Columbia University officials did in April and May. Further, it was less expensive with regard to money, time, and energy to respectfully discuss issues with the student protesters than it was to face the fires that blazed in several cities as a result of violent rebellions.[54] In that way, Brown protesting students benefited from the actions of demonstrating students at other institutions and young people in urban centers around the nation.

Although their demonstration was peaceful, Grooms, Crew, and the other black student activists undoubtedly drew a reaction with their boycott. When Phil Lord's mother found out he had walked off campus and settled in the church basement, she exclaimed, in her Barbadian accent: "Get out of there!"[55] By the next day, representatives of the university delivered a proposal essentially accepting the Pembroke demonstrators' demands, saying, "The university pledges as a continuing policy to at the least reflect in each class entering Pembroke the black representation in the general populace."[56] The New York Times reported that the proposal established a five-year timeline. For the fall of 1969, the goal that the university proposed for Pembroke was that black students represent 11.3 percent of the prospective class of 310. By the fall of 1973, Brown and Pembroke officials expected to make black students at least 12.5 percent of the incoming class at Pembroke and to hire a black admissions officer.

For the protesting black women of Pembroke, the proposal was satisfactory enough to end their campaign against the women's college, leave the church, and return to campus.[57] When asked in a news conference why the Pembroke activists left, an AAS spokesman stated that it was a "show of good faith in that their concessions had been met." Such a move on behalf of the campaign made officials aware that all was not well with black students at the elite institution, but also it gave officials at the university and college a sense that they could reason with the student activists. This potentially helped to advance the continued efforts of the

Brown men's demonstration and demonstrations elsewhere. Certainly the black men of Brown were inspired by the black Pembrokers' action.

The Brown men were not the only ones Pembrokers influenced. In the adjacent state of Massachusetts, black women activists calling themselves the Ad-Hoc Committee of Black Students at Radcliffe College held a sit-in and delivered eight demands to the college president.[58] Like the Pembroke women, the agitators at the women's college in Cambridge sought the admission of at least thirty black students and a black recruiter. In New York, black women at Barnard waged similar struggles. As had been the case throughout the movement for black freedom, women spearheaded the cause for educational access. Indeed, black women led the charge for increased opportunities on their elite campuses.

The proposal, which also had goals for black admissions at the all-male Brown, did not go far enough to convince the black men to stop protesting. Although the university proposal estimated the admission of 5.6 percent black men in the fall of 1969 and a continual increase until black men made up 11.1 percent of the Brown student population in 1973, the male members of AAS maintained their demonstration. Conceding that the admission goals appeared to be positive, the students showed great insight in refocusing the attention of their protest on the commitment of the university. As an AAS representative explained, "A commitment cannot be considered valid until the resources have been allocated to bring about that commitment."[59] By resources, the representative clarified, AAS meant funding.

To finally end the demonstrations against the university, Brown officials issued a statement that the university was willing to devote upwards of $1.1 million toward the recruitment and admission of black students for the three school years from fall 1969 to 1972.[60] President Heffner made clear, however, that the agreement to increase black admissions and to devote the funds to development was contingent on the potential black students being "fully qualified for Brown University." Perhaps the president believed that all of the white students admitted to Brown at the time must have been fully qualified for the Ivy institution. Demonstrating black students argued cogently that part of being qualified, until that point, meant being upper middle-class and white. The *Providence Journal* reported that $239,000 would be allocated for the 1969–1970 school year, $386,000 for 1970–1971, and $554,000 for 1971–1972.[61]

AAS issued a statement in response to the university's claim that its membership was not satisfied, but that it would end the demonstration. Reflecting the hard-edged rhetorical resistance of organized laborers and Black Power activists who found themselves in negotiations with powerful institutions, AAS stated that the offer was "racist in nature" and that it was not a complete resolution to the problems they faced. In spite of their dissatisfaction, to advance the movement for black freedom and to create opportunities for black students who came after them, the members of AAS acceded to the offer "because to refuse would be a disservice to black people," they said.[62] With that in mind, after four days, the forty black men of Brown left the Congdon Street Baptist Church victorious and reassociated themselves with their university.

The agreement then had to meet the approval of the Brown University Corporation (board of trustees). After a four-hour meeting that ended just before midnight on December 10, the corporation members conceded to the proposal of the university that grew out of the black students' demands.[63] In making their decision, the members of the corporation took into consideration the petition of the students and the fact that 300 members of the faculty unanimously and "wholeheartedly" supported the agreement. In addition to the faculty endorsement and the petition, various student groups backed the proposal. Those included the Cammararian Club (student government body); the student councils of 1969 and 1970; the interfraternity council, the Pembroke Council (student governing body), and the class council of 1972.[64] Each of the endorsing groups, from the student organizations to trustees, understood that making the recruitment and retention of black students a priority likely required a different way of disbursing funds and, moreover, a different way of envisioning the Brown experience.

There were various reactions to the boycott. "We really woke up," said the chaplain of the university. The challenge, he believed, was to "not go back to sleep."[65] Another Brown official stated that as a result of the demonstrations, a "real education was taking place" at the university and college. President Heffner admitted that he and his administration "looked within themselves . . . [and] re-examined their thinking."[66] He seemed relieved and reflective, but the president made it clear in a local paper that "there is a moral commitment [on behalf of the university] and there are specific targets. But there is no 'quota' for next year or any year."[67] Pointing out there would be no quotas sent an overt message to the alumni and other Brown and Pembroke affiliates. To the idea that they wanted a quota, AAS members responded that they were "not asking the university directly to give us bodies," but rather to ensure that achieving black students received enough support to enroll and graduate from the university and college.[68] A dean at Brown, F. Donald Eckelmann, believed that the agreement between the black student activists and administrators was "a compromise born of genius," reported the *Pembroke Record*.[69] The administrator had an interesting vantage point, as he considered the behavior of the student demonstrators ideal, a reference, no doubt, to the more raucous actions occurring on other campuses. Eckelmann claimed to admire the way that concerned black students confronted the issues and also the manner in which white students supported their black peers from "the sidelines." He believed that the demands and grievances of the black students were legitimate and that the institution had to address them because "the university was overdue." In that way, he observed, the elite school was in line with the nation, which was also overdue. One local periodical framed the university president as a man of action, stating "he is a man ready and eager to defend the course he has set for the nation's seventh oldest institution of higher education."[70] As it was, Heffner and his administration *reacted* positively to the demands and suggestions of students; there was not a previous plan for such an aggressive course of action. The black activists of Brown and Pembroke, not white administrators, sounded the clarion call for change. As the leader of the institution, Heffner responded to the students' action.

Brown, like so many other universities and colleges across the nation, espoused liberal goals of creating a fair society and of uplifting mankind, but it took Black Student Power to help the exclusive institution in Providence to solidify those goals. Brown had existed since the colonial period without matriculating a substantial number of black students, but in a matter of five years, black students changed the admission policies of the university. Although Brown officials (as well as officials at other institutions) were uneasy about the nature of the demonstrations that black students rendered, they appreciated the efforts of groups like AAS, which provided their institutions with pivotal moments of change. Regarding the activism of the students, a university administrator stated clearly: "Brown is now and will continue to be a better place because of it."[71]

As Joy Ann Williamson, Ibram Rogers (now Ibram Kendi), and other scholars have explained, the issue of admissions was one that became complicated for black students and university officials alike. Part of the complications resulted from the ideological viewpoints of the black students on campus. Some of the consciously black students at Brown were concerned as to what type of black student the university would admit in the future. In the postwar period through the early 1960s, many of the black students that Brown and other Ivy League institutions admitted came from middle-class black families and had not endeavored to transform university policies through demonstrations and nonsystematic means. Black students in the latter part of the 1960s, however, demanded that students who cultivated their blackness be admitted so that when they arrived they could take up the struggle for black freedom.

Pembroke student Sheryl Grooms, who was a sophomore during the boycott, made her desire for the recruitment of black and not "Negro" students clear.[72] Further, the young leader expressed the need for the college to look beyond its typical socioeconomic pool of admissions to find the new black students. That, she claimed, would require a black admissions officer who could go where white admissions officers had not gone or perhaps would not be welcomed. Grooms stated: "They [college and university officials] are looking for middle-class bourgeois students, but most black students aren't that."

Perhaps black students who attended Pembroke in the late 1960s were not from wealthy or even economically middling black families, but surely they were some of the most academically talented representatives of the larger black community. Their struggle to open doors educationally placed them in the black intelligentsia. Southern Christian Leadership Conference leader Hosea Williams had hopes and ideas for the black intelligentsia. Speaking on a panel at Brown several months after the boycott, he said: "it is the intelligentsia that sparked the changes" in revolutions of the past.[73] Like Grooms, though, he worried that the black intelligentsia would not remain true to the needs of their communities. "The black intelligentsia are coming to institutions like Brown and Pembroke and turning away from their race," Williams asserted. He warned that "you come here to be trained like an animal and get that degree," and the experience will turn "about 99 per cent" of those black students into "Uncle Toms on the side of the white power structure." Williams was frustrated: "I hate to see a nigger get a little education and become a part of the power structure and not look at his own mother and father," he said.

Grooms and Williams were on the same accord with respect to the dangers facing the black middle class and particularly students who might attend Brown. Although the scope of institutional admissions widened to include more working-class and economically lower-class black students, those young people who made it from middle-class homes or impoverished ghettoes represented the most privileged of their race. They embodied the hopes and dreams of those black people who could only imagine the possibility of black youth having access to the most exclusive white institutions. Even as students made the conscious choice to embrace blackness in opposition to their notions of the "old Negro" they could not escape—and in fact struggled with—their status as part of the black bourgeoisie. Attending Brown (or nearly any institution of higher education) during this period marked these black students as nothing less than privileged in the realm of American society and especially in the black community.

The students faced double marginalization: although they were black, they were more privileged than most in their community; although they were academically capable, they were not allowed complete access to institutional white America. Being in a state of double marginalization had emotional and psychological implications. John Wideman, who attended Penn in the 1960s, explained: "Away from school I worked hard at being the same old home boy everybody remembered . . . because I didn't want you all [family and neighborhood friends] to discover I was a traitor."[74] By traitor, Wideman inferred that by donning a "mask" of survival at his predominantly white institution, he was not remaining true to his "authentic core." Then, at his Ivy League school, he revealed, "I was losing contact with the truth of my own feelings . . . learning to mistrust and deny my own responses left me no solid ground, nowhere to turn." Wideman's sentiments could have been those of the dozens of black Ivy Leaguers during the period who struggled to maintain a sense of self at school and in the home community.

Black Brown students reinforced Wideman's sentiment in describing relationships to the white students they encountered on campus. Monte Bailey believed that "the average white Brunonian found it difficult to react to me as a person. I seemed to be a victim, a national problem, or a statistic. . . . I wasn't an individual," he said.[75] Similarly, Brown student and football player Spencer Crew remembered that, with the attention that came along with being one of the few racially different students, he and other black students felt as though they "had to be the experts on all things black."[76] Some black students were growing weary of explaining their presence and existence. Like her male counterparts, Grooms at Pembroke experienced double marginalization while making her push for freedom as a woman. Her gender, in this case, did not impede her leadership, but the fact she was female added greatly to the uniqueness of this campaign. By virtue of her student status, Grooms was privileged; however, the time and circumstances in which she operated were undoubtedly challenging because of her race and gender.

The social support of black students did not always keep up with rising admission rates. Some black students and their faculty allies were disturbed to learn that not everyone was as invested in the scholastic and cultural achievement of the new students. According to one document, a white professor turned away a black student who had reached out for "individual tutorial help." Although anecdotal, the story was telling. The professor's treatment of the student was an incidental reaction to some of the changes that occurred at Brown. Unfortunately, such a response to the student's request was problematic because, aside from the fact that the new learners needed assistance acclimating culturally, reaching out for help academically was difficult for students who were already different from their peers. It was not as if the new students were incapable of scholastic success, but they needed access to help. For as responsible as the new black students were in seeking assistance, the university—especially the faculty—was equally responsible for making help available.[77]

Although privileged, the double marginalization and other challenges surrounding race, class, and gender made some of the black students uncomfortable. This, according to civil rights leader Hosea Williams, was the problem with which people in the black middle class struggled regularly. Not kind in his assessment of the members of the black bourgeoisie,

Williams opined: "Middle-class blacks are the sickest persons in our society."[78] He claimed that "They [middle-class black people] try to be white but white folks won't let them and they don't have the sense to be black." Harsh in his criticism, Williams touched on the inner turmoil that earlier black students experienced. The members of the generation that attended universities/colleges in the late 1960s were determined not to allow their privileged status to distance them from what they perceived as authentic blackness, and that is why they boycotted the university. Williams commended the students for their act of resistance.

When referring to his experiences as a Brown student, Kennard McDuffie spoke to the discomfort that some students felt in a university recruitment booklet that black Brown students designed for black high school students. The recruitment booklet was a result of the agreement that student activists and administrators made to end black students' boycott of the university.[79] A university document responding to student demands stated that the admissions office would "finance a booklet written by and addressed to black students. It is understood that students will decide the content of the booklet." In the booklet, McDuffie revealed that "the term 'black bourgeoisie' takes on embarrassing import" for him.[80] The knowledge that he was part of the larger black community's struggle for freedom could not overshadow the reality that he was enjoying a lifestyle not typical of the black masses. McDuffie reflected: "By seeing what the white establishment thinks of him [at Brown], the black student is finally given a chance to know his true social identity."[81] That identity entailed both privilege with regard to access and thoughts of otherness because of race and gender. The significance of these young people's struggle with their identities and status both in and outside of the black community is notable in that they used their privilege (even if they did not feel privileged) to fight what they perceived as institutional racism. The embarrassment to which McDuffie referred, in part, motivated black students to act on behalf of their brethren who did not and would not have the access to power that Brown graduates would be afforded.

By the mid-1960s officials at Ivy institutions explained that there just were not enough "qualified" black students coming out of high school that could meet their institutions' exclusive standards. One article about the subject claimed that on the college board review examination only

10 to 15 percent of black students in the nation received an average 400 or higher on the verbal part of the assessment, when the average Brown student received a score of 644 and Pembroke students 698.[82] The article posited the disparity in scores as a point of contention that could impede the new path that Brown was taking in terms of attracting and graduating black students. Although the exams were not sole determinants of college success, many officials believed that the exams were primary indicators of student ability. The exams were, of course, constructed and evaluated by white assessors and featured biases toward white middle-class culture—particularly in the verbal section.[83] Alumni worried about the university's loss of prestige as an academically exclusive institution. Other concerned Brown affiliates worried about the "devastating" effect that bringing unqualified students to campus would have on the students themselves, as they would struggle to keep up once they arrived. Students who could not achieve scholastically served neither themselves nor the university well, they argued. Perhaps the apprehension was altruistic, but it also reflected a measure of white paternalism. Equality of access meant the opportunity for people to succeed and fail. The U.S. commissioner of education and segregation opponent Harold Howe II (who also was the grandson of Samuel Chapman Armstrong, founder of historically black Hampton Institute) explained to officials at PWIs throughout the nation that they should stop confusing "admissions standards with academic standards." Another issue was the fact that Brown was not alone in seeking out black students. As the article put it, regarding black recruitment, "the pressures are increasing throughout the nation from riot-torn San Francisco State College, to a recent demand to step up the effort at Radcliffe."

Part of an explanation for why it would appear there was a shortage of black students to recruit was that in the places where admissions officers had traditionally looked for black students, which was the same high schools they found white students, there were few black students from whom to choose. Grooms pointed out that there were indeed more qualified black students in the places where the Ivy institutions had not gone. "They've [Pembroke and Brown officials] got to have a black admissions officer to go into the ghettos and compete for the students," Grooms implored. Speaking to the type of students for which Brown and Pembroke should seek, she emphasized that "they've got to get off this thing about getting girls who will 'profit from a Pembroke experience.'" According to Grooms, many black students in other than middle-class circumstances could benefit greatly from the "Pembroke experience."[84]

The *New York Times* reported that most of the black students attending Brown by the fall of 1968 came from families with incomes of $6,000 to $7,000 a year, which was atypical of most Brown students.[85] Spencer Crew, who entered Brown in 1967, recalled that "there was a [socioeconomic] spectrum of black students," but that "most of our parents were working; there weren't a lot of professional people," he remembered. Crew's father worked as a chemist in a paint company and his mother as a nurse, placing his family in the American working class, but his family would have been considered part of the black middle class.[86] As an admissions counselor from Princeton indicated, the students entering Ivy universities in the late 1960s included many from working class and disadvantaged backgrounds. Students like Grooms understood that by adding students from different economic brackets to the pool of admitted students, the college and university offers more than scholastic training but also social education. Black students coming from areas like Roxbury and from families making less than the average Brown or Pembroke student changed the culture of those institutions by their sheer presence and eventually by their will. They understood what Brown officials who followed traditional protocol did not know: how to relate to young black people well enough to encourage and convince potential students to apply and matriculate if accepted.

Both the enrolled black student recruiters, who volunteered their time, and the institutions benefited from the black students' efforts. The university benefited by having access to a new pool of applicants and from being able to claim that it was doing its part to help with civil rights. In addition, the university further retained the student recruiters by tying them even closer to the institution, and in effect making them responsible for its success. According to some student affairs literature, such high impact engagement in diversifying the campus is a key factor in a student's sense of usefulness in solving a problem and belonging at the institution.[87] The collective experience of working to recruit potential students provided black Brown students with a unique cocurricular learning opportunity. They were motivated to stay at the university to monitor the success of their recruitment work. Because they were adding new elements and techniques to traditional recruitment, the university benefited from their efforts long after the student recruiters graduated.

Black students, of course, benefited from having more students to whom they could relate and they believed they had a responsibility to stay and graduate to show others that it was possible. In finishing their studies and graduating, many of the students grew an affinity for the institution and continued to participate in recruiting efforts after they had left. The benefits that those concerned black students in the late 1960s and early 1970s provided were invaluable to the university.

Yale University dean of admissions, R. Inslee Clark, was one of the key players in Yale's movement to attract and accept more black students. Nonwhite students had not been a major part of the Ivy League's recruitment strategy before the late 1960s, but in 1969, Clark noted that a change in recruitment strategy meant that "a large number of young men and women [came from] both inner city and rural areas" and gave "balance to the matriculants from the suburban backgrounds." Presumably, Clark coded black and other nonwhite students in the inner city and rural category and the traditional white matriculants in the suburban category. Of the students attending Yale in the 1969–1970 school year, 65 percent were from public schools.[88]

Brown and Pembroke scrambled to attract black students and to keep their current black students from demonstrating again. To do so, in 1969 Pembroke hired its first black recruiter, Tiajuana Mosby. Acting on a mandate, she quickly worked to get 102 black women admitted in the spring of 1969. That did not happen without controversy. Not used to such aggressive recruitment, some of the deans at the college withheld the notification letters for the 102 black women and wanted to reconsider financial implications of such a high number of black admits. At the same time, the deans allowed the letters of notification to go out to nonblack students. Mosby protested the ad hoc decision making and called on black students to help convince the students who had been notified late to attend Pembroke. Mosby's campaign was effective. Fifty-two black women enrolled at Pembroke for the 1969–1970 school year.[89] The director of financial aid at Brown (and Pembroke) claimed confidently that all the black students at Pembroke who needed financial aid received it.[90] Black professionals and students constantly struggled to expose the college to black freedom.

In September, the *Brown Daily Herald* ran a story entitled "Blacks at Brown: A Cross-Section" that described life for some of Brown's black students.[91] The article pointed out the importance of black admissions officer Richard Nurse and the role of black students, who, in addition to demonstrating for the addition of a black admissions officer, gave generously of their time to actually recruit potential black students to Brown. The same could have been said about Mosby and the black Pembrokers. The paper captured the director of admissions, James Rogers, proudly stating: "Brown has more black applications than any other school in our competition." It is interesting because Brown's black students, not at all trained as admissions officials, did so much to assist admissions offices. The students, along with the consultation that they constantly gave to the admissions office, helped recruit on their vacations and weekends. That black students did so for free should be highlighted because until that point those who recruited white and the few black students who enrolled received remuneration for their efforts (notwithstanding alumni). In that way, black students, on their own initiative, took up the charge of innovating the field of admissions. Today, consultants are paid well to advise on recruitment techniques that best attract students of color. Black students must have pioneered those methods because in 1969 nearly eighty black students arrived at Brown.

One of the concerns of students like Sheryl Grooms at Pembroke was whether in recruiting new black students the university would seek only those who came from traditional Brown and Pembroke student backgrounds: students who had attended elite private, predominantly white high schools on the eastern seaboard. Richard Nurse explained that the class of 1969–1970 was indeed a cross-section of the black community that welcomed students from all regions and socioeconomic classes. He pointed out that some of the changes occurred by recruiting at schools like Hotchkiss and Deerfield, the same schools where Brown had previously recruited. The difference was that those schools had begun to participate in Upward Brown programs that brought in working and lower class black students. Then, of course, Brown recruiters went to schools in urban areas that had not previously been visited. "There are about as many views of black consciousness among the freshmen as there are colors of blackness," Nurse noted.[92]

In particular, a higher number of black students from urban areas like Harlem and Bedford Stuyvesant, Brooklyn, arrived on campus. Because of the work that black students did, James Rogers, the head of admissions admitted: "We have become aware of discrepancies in our criteria" concerning black students.[93] Before, Rogers noted, the admissions office did not take into account everything that students from inner city-schools faced. Black admissions officer Nurse went a bit farther: "maybe our criteria is wrong. . . . College board scores have been shown to be largely irrelevant." To question the traditional criteria on which the university had based its admissions in his first year of employment was a bold act.

Another way of considering the issue involved evaluating the usefulness of standardized test scores. In an earlier period, Ivy League universities altruistically looked to standardized test scores as a way of equalizing admissions. They were some of the first institutions to implement the tests as part of their admissions process. Since then, scholars have presented cogent arguments of the cultural biases that exist in the examinations. From those who wrote the test questions to those who graded the exams, standardized testing was very much a white endeavor. Nurse's suggestion that the use of the tests as one of the sole gatekeepers to entrance was and indirect challenge to white supremacy. These exams, claimed many scholars, have been used to uphold white dominance in society. The idea of measurable standards of assessment appealed to admissions officers who could use the scores to quickly determine a student's aptitude for college success. If by chance that measurement had notable flaws, then those like Nurse contended different assessment tools needed to be employed. Alumni donors worried, however, that if the university stopped relying on college review board examinations, then Brown might admit and enroll students who could not manage the rigor of college life. One of the students who worked with Brown's admissions office, Ernie Nedd, predicted that students admitted in fall 1969 were "obviously well qualified for Brown. They're not going to have any kind of trouble here."[94]

The new class of black students came mostly from New York, New Jersey, and Washington, D.C., and they took advantage of financial aid more than their traditional Ivy peers. When they came to the Providence campus, unless they explicitly stated that they would like to live with a white roommate, black students lived with other black students, which was the decision of the dean of freshmen. While students often pushed for black housing spaces, some black students at Brown did not agree with the imposed rooming situation. As explained by AAS leader Phil Lord, "There is a serious difference between placing oneself in a black community and being forced into one by a white institution. . . . It's not that we don't feel that a black student would feel more comfortable with other blacks, but it must be a voluntary decision."[95] Even though some students desired entering black freshmen to be at least sympathetic to and at best involved in the black freedom movement, admission officer Nurse did not totally agree. Through discussions with some potential students, he found their opinions of the movement varied. With a larger black population, there was a possibility of black students not joining AAS, which could be a positive or negative phenomenon depending on the current students' points of view.

The new cohorts of black students were able to ride the tide of the Civil Rights Movement and Black Power Movement that changed the nation. In an article in *Esquire* magazine, Brown alumnus Barry Beckham drew out some of the differences he observed between the generation of black students who came to the university in the early 1960s and those arriving later in the decade. "In contradistinction to today's blacks," Beckham wrote in 1969, "a piece of the action is what we [students from the early 1960s] failed to claim."[96] There was a lure, he explained, to take "for granted that the university had searched the countryside for qualified blacks." Black students at Brown in the late 1960s took a piece of the action by protesting policies and pushing the university toward black freedom. Beckham accurately observed a change in dynamics and opinions about admissions when university officials created broader guidelines for admitting students. Not surprisingly, Beckham stated, "Now that some more forward-thinking colleges are using guidelines for nonwhites [and especially black students] instead of against them, the administrations are being accused of unconsciously dispensing preferential treatment." That line of reasoning became the basis for the argument against affirmative action in the upcoming decades. Beckham made the point that "universities—being no less American than other institutions—have always used discriminating admissions standards for different groups."[97] He was correct.

President Heffner and other administrators understood the place the university occupied in higher education. A December 1968 statement outlined a proposal for a new approach to recruitment: "Brown University, in recognition of its role in education and social responsibility, commits its resources, both financial and human, to that achievement of certain goals of admissions of black students" at Brown and Pembroke.[98] The statement was a response to the position paper issued by the black protesting students at the beginning of the demonstrations. It indicated that the institution committed to hiring black counselors in "admissions, financial aid, and resource development."[99] Interestingly, the hires, according to the document, had to be "acceptable to both the administration and the black students at Brown." This point was significant because in their position paper, the black protesting students of Pembroke explained that the university and college needed to recruit "not only the obvious candidates that will fit into the Ivy League mold and whom other 'superior' colleges are consequently also recruiting" but also black women who had been overlooked because of the "ignorance and insensitivity of white recruitment officers."[100] The language of the position paper clearly indicates that black women activists were at the vanguard of the demonstration. According to the document responding to the position paper, black students were finally able to receive remuneration for the recruitment that they did on behalf of the university. Additionally, the university pledged to fund and intensify efforts to implement the Transitional Year Program and to fund the recruitment booklet.

In terms of the admissions process and in response to Pembrokers' and Brunonians' demands, the university greatly modified its approach to black students. The document noted that "each application sent expressly to a black student will be stamped with the statement that the application fee is waived."[101] The university no longer required admitted black students to interview, and if a student chose to interview, he or she would meet with a black admissions officer "unless the student desires otherwise." If the student were from elsewhere, the new option greatly reduced the financial burden associated with traveling to Rhode Island. The university, however, took a risk in not spending the extra time to interview all students. Taking that point into account, the members of

AAS emphasized that traditional procedures had not worked thus far and they welcomed new techniques.

Retention efforts also became a priority. Typically, scholarship students had to have a job during the semester, but that was no longer necessary for black students who could ostensibly concentrate solely on their studies, as most of their white peers had done for centuries. The hours spent studying instead of working could have been the crucial difference between excelling and failing at the elite institution. Of course, if a student wanted to work, the option was still available. In addition, black scholarship recipients would no longer be "rigidly bound by academic requirements for the continuation of his scholarship," and no black scholarship recipient could be placed on "academic probation before the end of the second semester."[102] Instead, black scholarship holders were to be issued a warning and then given a semester's notice before being placed on academic probation. The concessions made in the university's statement astound on multiple levels. In contrast to today's push for "diversity," Brown University, in 1968, unabashedly pursued black students to attend the university and Pembroke. In the same moment, black students at Brown, by employing their protest methods and communicating the issues that the university needed to address to allow them to succeed, actually created access for their peers and students to follow. Based on its prior history, the university was not going to be able to achieve its goal of enrolling 12.9 percent black students at Pembroke by 1970 using typical recruitment and retention techniques. In working with the students, the university innovated.[103]

At the university level, some officials worried about the financial and cultural stability of Brown as it accommodated some of calls for change that black students made. In contrast to many of its peers in the period, donations at Brown seemed to be up according to an article in the university paper.[104] At Penn, after students took over buildings and waged protests, the president of the university received numerous letters from alumni decrying the fact that he would tolerate what they considered to be insolent and bratty behavior from students. Further, they wrote they would be cancelling their donations. At Brown, the situation was different. In the fall of 1969, alumni donations to the development fund increased by 25 percent, totaling nearly $2.5 million for the year.[105] Although donations increased, the number of donors decreased from 42.6

to 39 percent. According to the article in the *Brown Daily Herald*, Penn only received donations from a quarter of its alumni. At Brown, the alumni who wrote letters to the university came down on several sides of the issues students had raised in the months and years before 1969. In particular, the black student walkout at Brown the previous year became a major point of concern for many alumni. They worried about the school's academic standing, according to the editor of Brown's alumni magazine.

In 1969, Brown University experienced a tidal shift in curriculum by moving away from a required core set of courses. The shift allowed students the option of not specializing in particular disciplines. That unique move set the university apart from its peer institutions and most other American colleges and universities. Observers and scholars of the shift attribute the bold step to the cultural changes that occurred internationally, nationally, and locally.[106] The "gentlemen under the elms" that Brown University chronicler Jay Barry described began to look different in race and style by the late 1960s.[107] Inasmuch, so too did the curriculum. One of the additions to the culture and curriculum of Brown was Black Studies.

The black freedom movement that captured the nation began to etch away at the traditional culture of the nation's oldest universities and colleges. Not surprisingly, the culture and curriculum at Brown contrasted starkly with the mostly black environs from which some new-generation black students came. Regarding the curriculum, one student, Phil Williams, observed the very noticeable absence of studies surrounding people of African descent. "The contributions of Black Americans and peoples have been literally left out of the 'Brown Experience.'"[108] He questioned "whether or not this liberal educational institution is just a mirroring of the racist society in which we live." Although Williams came to the conclusion that Brown was indeed reflective of dominant society, he held out hope. He believed that "the enrollment of more black students will, perhaps, make a difference in the curricula's structure and priorities."

Williams could have added that in addition to enhancing the structure and priorities of the curriculum, the augmentation of courses regarding the black experience would have made the curriculum more relevant to the experience of students in general. The issue of relevant coursework was important to Black Nationalists and those interested in Black Power. To achieve such power, Williams noted correctly that it would take more student advocates to effect change to the curriculum that white men had written and overseen for centuries. Williams's fellow student, Spencer Crew, agreed: "We wanted black and relevant courses in an ever-evolving world."[109] In the new age of agitation, young people at Brown were learning many important life lessons. A document entitled "Black Studies: An Educational Imperative," noted that they "learned to find their exclusion intolerable."[110] That was a vital lesson and the basis of the campaign for Black Studies at Brown.

To be sure, there was at least one course dealing directly with the black experience. Shortly after the boycott ended in December 1968, an article in the *Pembroke Record* announced that Brown professor John Thomas, who happened to be white, was teaching a history course.[111] The article indicated that another seminar titled "Black Assertion" would be offered in the spring semester as well. With his course, Thomas wanted to "get inside the black mind" and to delve into the way that history and historians have treated the black experience. By focusing on the past works of Du Bois and the recent works of Malcolm X and Charles Hamilton, he hoped to shore up the knowledge gap. Thomas explained candidly that the course was an effort at "pure discovery" into blackness, which he admitted "I've just begun." That Thomas was offering such a course at that moment was timely and well-intentioned, but the fact that there were black educators who had moved past discovery to analysis and research into different facets of the black experience rankled students who wanted experts to teach courses on the subject in the same way that professors did with all other topics. That meant that the university would have to hire black instructors who were cognizant of the most recent and the seminal literature and affairs of black life. Perhaps assigning Thomas, a very well-respected scholar of white abolitionist William Lloyd Garrison, to teach African American history was a reasonable stop-gap measure, but that appointment sent a message about the piecemeal approach that the university took to issues affecting black people.[112]

AAS, whose numbers had swollen as a result of the new university recruitment efforts, ensured that Brown's curriculum evolved to not just mirror the "racist society" to which Williams referred. In 1969, the faculty of Brown, with the assistance of AAS, took steps to construct a Black Studies program. By that time, Brown's peer institutions Yale and Cornell had already established programs as had San Francisco State College after an embattled five-month boycott. Nationally, black intellectuals, like those associated with the Institute of the Black World in Atlanta, attempted to provide the ideological and theoretical framework for Black Studies, while students and faculty members on campus saw to the actual creation of academic units.[113]

In light of the student activism on campus the previous year, Brown officials worked to stay abreast of the movement. On March 3, 1969, Dean F. Donald Eckelmann wrote to President Heffner about Black Studies.[114] Noting that, nationally, Black Studies was a "hot issue" and that "our [Brown University] black students could make it one for us," Eckelmann entreated the president to forgo further disruption by hiring and appointing renowned scholar Charles Nichols as the head of the new program or the committee that would eventually lead to the institutionalization of the program. After receiving his doctorate in English from Brown University, Nichols enjoyed professorships, fellowships, and academic appointments throughout the United States and Europe.[115] Eckelmann made it clear that he and others believed Nichols was the right choice to help Brown create its program.

Initially, Brown faculty and officials struggled with two issues concerning the Black Studies program: a name for the unit and whether it would maintain program or department status. These issues were not dissimilar to those that other institutions faced. During the period, the term "black" had taken on new meanings for young people who had grown up being called "Negro." As so many scholars have noted, the evolution from Negro to black was crucial to young people in their development of race consciousness. Grooms and her fellow students pointed out that up until this period, Brown and other Ivy institutions recruited students who classified themselves as Negro. When the campaign to increase black consciousness bourgeoned, a different type of student arrived on college campuses and Brown in particular: the black student. With that in mind, Black Studies almost became a default term for the propagation and investigation of people of African descent.[116]

Early in the program's existence at Brown, some referred to the potential unit as the Afro-American program (due perhaps to the presence of the Afro-American Society or because Yale had an Afro-American Studies program); however, the students and faculty associated with the unit called it the Black Studies Program.[117] The decision on what the program was to be called is important in the sense that as black people sought power and control over their lives, naming became a crucial step. As Ture and Hamilton later explained, black people had to "redefine themselves, and only *they* can do that."[118] If black people could not exert their agency over anything else, they could do so regarding the way to which they referred to themselves. Although a minor point, the significance of naming was not lost on this group of young people whose enslaved ancestors did not have the freedom to name themselves. Therefore, with care, they named the new unit the Afro-American Studies Program, and the student-faculty committee set off to formally insert black history and culture into the curriculum.

On March 24, 1969, Brown Provost Merton Stoltz sent a letter seeking to clarify the steps to fortify the program.[119] It confirmed the topics discussed with President Heffner in a meeting the week before. The upper administration understood that the university would create a program for all students, and that it would be "a program of merit which might well serve as an example." In typical Ivy fashion, a main concern for the provost and president was the institution's place in the vanguard. The letter indicated that the chairman of the program would report directly to the president. That, on its own, spoke to the significance of Black Studies. Most academic units reported to a dean, and some units like that at Cornell reported to the provost. So Brown's structure was unique.

While curricular reforms typically moved slowly in universities, the advent of Black Studies developed rather quickly, which led to some difficulties as the programs and departments grew.[120] Needing to stabilize the Brown program's progress, a committee of administrators, faculty, and students met to create a formal proposal to be submitted to the president and curriculum committee of the university. Michael C. Beaubien and newly recruited Charles Nichols acted as co-chairs of the Black Studies committee (also referred to as the Committee on Afro-American Studies), which had faculty and planning components. The faculty contingent consisted of those who taught classes germane to Black Studies and the faculty members provided counsel for the chairperson regarding matters of personnel and course scheduling. The planning component included students, who helped with ideas regarding programming and courses. The students in the planning contingent also provided their opinions relating to faculty candidates. Regarding new hires, the letter from the provost indicated that that in the 1969–1970 school year the university would hire two faculty members that would hold appointments in both Afro-American Studies and traditional disciplines. The program could also hire two faculty members in the 1970–1971 school year. The provost understood, however, that some of those lines might be visiting rather than tenure-track professorships. The hiring plans drew some attention to the fact that the perhaps traditional disciplines had produced a negligible number of tenure-track candidates for a black-centered program of study.

Resources did not seem to be an issue with the Ivy institution, but finding candidates with doctorates to teach Afro-American Studies became a problem early in the program's existence. Also important to Brown was its ability to compete with its peers. If Yale had an Afro-American Studies program, then to be on par, Brown and the remaining seven Ivy institutions had to work toward acquiring similar and even more vibrant programs. As the Princeton admissions officials stated, students who got into Harvard likely got into another Ivy university, which meant that the potential student would base the decision to attend an institution on what the school had to offer in the way of academic and other resources. This had historically been the case for certain populations of white students, but after the mid-1960s it also became true for some black students, who finally garnered notice from the admissions professionals at elite colleges. The Brown program of courses, like that at Yale, was to emphasize particular disciplines or tracks. According to the committee, one of the goals of the Black Studies unit at Brown was "to humanize the total university community."[121] The Brown program was to consist of ten courses spread across the humanities and social sciences.

It should be noted that half of the thirty-four committee members were women. Additionally, the committee included student members who went on to become influential in various fields. Bill Perkins became a New York State Senator. Ann Holmes Redding became an Episcopal priest (only to be defrocked after announcing that she was also a Muslim). Juaryln Gaiter became a senior behavioral scientist a center for disease control in Atlanta. Seymour James Jr. became president of the New York State Bar Association and Ernest Nedd graduated from Arizona State Law School in 1975.[122]

The Afro-American Studies program benefited black and other Brown University students. Three hundred students enrolled in the first two courses taught in the program. Considering the small number of black students, the enrollment list meant the classes consisted of a majority of white students. This bode well for the program, as the high enrollment numbers clearly indicated student interest. The program director, Charles Nichols, observed that "other areas of the college are much more aware of the role of the Negro in American life as a result of the program."[123] The new director noticed that white students were curious about the program but not all black students demonstrated interest. Although, to some, it may have seemed that all 225 of the black students at Brown should have had a desire to enroll in the Afro-American Studies program, such an assumption would have denied black students the diversity of opinion and perspective. As it were, the program met its first challenge of successfully populating courses.

In spite of the fact that every black student did not enroll in the Afro-American Studies courses, Nichols was proud of the black student agitators who brought the program to life and made the university aware of the problems affecting black students. Pointing up the generational differences, Nichols, who received a doctorate in English from Brown, remembered struggling with racial challenges when he was young, but choosing to endure rather than address the issue with institutions. He resented being dictated to, but, he claimed, "I didn't do anything about it."[124] Black students at Brown in the late 1960s, Nichols stated, "had the political astuteness to dramatize the problem without disrupting the campus." In a different interview, Nichols conceded that he may not always agree with the methods of young people who were demonstrating on college campuses, but he believed they were "morally alive."[125] Furthermore, Nichols revealed, he was "in sympathy with the goals of young people today." It took a coalition of the older and younger generation of black intellectuals to advance the freedom struggle.

Nichols and the members of AAS worked to establish an Afro-American Research Center. The program director and administrators sought to construct an elaborate plan that would lead to the establishment of the center. The five-year projected budget for the proposed center was $1.75 million, which included personnel and overhead costs. The proposal outlined plans for postdoctoral fellows, senior faculty members, and a cataloguer for the materials in the John Carter Brown Library that were relevant to the black experience. The university was to cover part of the expense for the center, while a private foundation would cover the remaining costs. Brown officials submitted a proposal for funding to the Ford Foundation, but unfortunately the philanthropic organization denied the request.[126] The Ford Foundation program officer indicated that the foundation had done a great deal to provide base funding for Black Studies programs at other universities and that the foundation intended to focus more on the graduate education of black students and move away from programs concentrating on undergraduates. In spite of the detailed plans, the Afro-American Research Center never came to fruition at Brown.

Another issue at stake was whether the Afro-American Studies Program would become a department. For some observers inside and outside the academy, Black Studies as a discipline was not respected. Nichols's successor, Jesse McDade, proposed making the program a department in 1971: "There are those persons who are not too comfortable with Black Studies as a program, but who are traumatized by the idea that it might become a department."[127] McDade spoke to the anxiety that there was no academic merit to the new field of studies. To that notion, he responded: "if Black Studies doesn't have 'academic legitimacy,' it shouldn't exist as a program" in the first place. White and black critics of Black Studies in general wondered the same thing. If, however, it is illegitimate and yet it still exists, then "it is a pacification strategy by the university's administrators." That, explained McDade, would be a "cruel hoax, an inexcusable insult" to black people. On a university campus, the director emphasized, departments generally have a gravitas that is not available to most programs. For instance, in terms of hiring, the Afro-American Studies program had to depend upon the willingness or unwillingness of traditional departments to make joint or affiliated appointments. That placed his unit "at the mercy of another department." Situating Afro-American Studies as a department at Brown would add respectability as a discipline and as an academic unit.

When McDade and the AAS made their concern about the status of Afro-American Studies known to the president and other top administrators, the officials undertook a brief study to observe the similarities and differences between programs at other Ivies and Brown. The study noted the structure, faculty, curriculum, and atmosphere on campus at Harvard, Princeton, and Yale. In 1971, Harvard had a program, but the university intended to create a department. Unlike Brown, Harvard's chairperson was tenured in Afro-American Studies. The program in Cambridge featured ten faculty members, of whom two were senior professors and the rest "term." The dean of the college of arts and sciences at Harvard explained that students played a significant role in the recruitment and hiring of professors for the program but that students would not be involved in tenure decisions, which was the case with all other faculty members at the university. Along with the role they played in recruitment and hiring, students at Harvard also participated in making suggestions for course offerings. Regarding the atmosphere, the dean at Harvard pointed out that ninety students had been admitted each school year (1969–1970 and 1970–1971), insinuating that with a larger black population the atmosphere was less tense. Dean of Faculty Richard Lester reported for Princeton University. There, the dean had initiated a target of opportunity program to recruit faculty of color and helped to established an Equal Employment Opportunity Committee at the Ivy institution in Princeton.[128] According to Lester, the Black Studies program at Princeton, which started in 1969–1970, was struggling. According to the document, Lester revealed that the first director of the program was an alcoholic and could not continue in his duties. By 1971, Princeton employed an assistant professor from Rutgers as part-time director with Rutgers University, and the program was not in a position to become a department. Unlike students at Brown and elsewhere, Princeton students had not been prioritizing Black Studies in their campus campaigns. In its early stages, Brown modeled its Afro-American Studies program after that at Yale. Although students at Yale conceived of and assisted in designing their Afro-American Studies program, no students were on the advisory committee. Also, different than at Harvard, the faculty for the Afro-American Studies program all came from other units and split their time with the new program. Among students, the program was relatively popular, with eighteen students concentrating in the Afro-American Studies at Yale. Brown's fledgling program was in a position to improve and compete with those at peer institutions. To ensure that the Afro-American Studies program could keep pace with others, President Hornig agreed to allocate $100,000.[129]

Although the center was never established (at least until the Center for the Study of Slavery and Justice came into existence decades later), black students were able to make progress in other arenas. By 1972, the AAS had amassed enough members and resources to publish a monthly newsletter, *Uwezo*. This allowed the students to describe life at Brown from their perspective. An article in November of that year discussed a particular point of advancement for the black students and the university in general, when two black students won seats in the general student government.[130] Black students pursued the seats to increase black representation on university committees. They sought ways to incorporate themselves into campus life on their terms. In that way, they believed, they could retain their blackness while influencing the affairs of the institutions. Additionally, black student activist efforts brought forth the Rites and Reason Theatre program that was part of the Afro-American Studies program. Starting in 1970, the program called for community members to participate in the creation and production of plays that students and local residents could attend. Rites and Reason welcomed major playwrights and artists to the campus to share their expertise with the public in Providence. In 1970, as part of the Afro-American Studies "black arts festival" that reflected the rise of the flourishing black arts movement, acclaimed poet Sonia Sanchez visited to the delight of students and community members alike. Sanchez spoke to the ability of the Ivy League institution to garner resources that could benefit the black community and how conscious the students were to invite a popular figure among the people. The theatre and program added a great deal of black culture to Brown.[131]

With the help of black students, by 1972, Brown had its own black-centered house. Space was one of the last phases of the campaign of black Brunonians and Pembrokers. The university had acquired the edifice in 1970, and throughout 1971 AAS members engaged in private and public negotiations with university officials in an effort to occupy the house. The house was to house ten students, a classroom space, and a space for events.[132] In 1972, the Afro-American Studies program and the AAS moved into the house. At that time, the new director of the Afro-American Studies program, Jesse McDade, worked to make sure the building suited the needs of the program and students. McDade, who had completed his graduate work at Boston University, made it clear in a letter to the university registrar that the program had to have priority in scheduling courses and programming in the building. Reminding the registrar of the agreement the institution had made when Afro-American Studies was conceived, McDade wrote: "I am sure it is in the interest of Brown University to honor its commitment to the Afro-American Studies Program and the black undergraduate and graduate students."[133] That statement alone hinted at the volatility of the moment in terms of protest and activism.

National Black Power advocates emphasized the concept of self-determination, and McDade, who was a representative of the movement, believed that the registrar threatened the ability of the program and society to control the space it occupied. "To say your office [that of the registrar] will determine whether a given Afro-American Studies class will or will not meet in Churchill House is to say too much," McDade stressed.[134] That, he argued, was the business of the program. He noted that the agreement was to create a space that was suitable for black students to convene in a formal or informal fashion. Such spaces were crucial to the experience and development of many students not just on Brown's campus but at institutions throughout the nation. Just as the role of women activists has been understated in the literature of student activism, so too has the significant part that black administrators—at every level—have played in maintaining and advancing goals on behalf of their students.

In making the space viable for the students, faculty, and staff of the program and society, the building needed $40,000 worth of renovations. When some administrators questioned whether spending that much on overhaul and repairs was practicable, McDade pointed out that in previous discussions with the university president Donald Hornig and other administrators, renovations costing less than $100,000 seemed reasonable. In a letter to the acting president Jacquelyn Mattfeld (who eventually became president of Barnard College), McDade attempted to garrison the advances of the students: "40,000.00 to rehabilitate . . . is, in our opinion, not excessive."[135] He kindly explained that "we do not wish to cite the costs expended for other buildings and/or renovations for which we have knowledge." Having to remind and convince the administration of a deal already brokered led McDade to feel that the brewing controversy "undermines any trust that had been fostered during our deliberations." To be sure, $40,000 was a great deal of money at that moment, but in the context of student uprisings that occurred around the country, the amount was a small price to pay with respect to the maintenance of trust between black students and the institution. As a result of the black students' and administrators' vigilance, the Churchill House is still home to the Afro-American (now Africana) Studies unit.

Gains that the students and university made with regard to black admissions came with some setbacks. For instance, although a higher number of black students enrolled at Brown, the percentage of black students who faced dismissal because of their poor performance increased as well. In jumping from just over thirty black students in 1968 to more than 300 in 1971–1972, the university displayed evidence of widening the pool of applicants to include more students from urban and segregated environments. This was not problematic in itself, but the students had to contend with the pace of academic life at Brown and the cultural factors. In an open letter to university president Donald Hornig, AAS members noted that some of the new black students were experiencing "calamitous academic difficulties."[136] The group estimated that 13 percent of the black undergraduate population faced some sort of academic sanction, including warnings, probation, and dismissals. Part of the trouble concerned new students taking and failing advanced level courses. AAS charged the problem to poor advisement.

Pleased with the growth in admissions, AAS members recognized the need for more support. They observed that there were "few friendly black faces" to greet the first- and second-year students. A sophomore reported that when he had trouble with his coursework, "there's no one to turn to."[137] With such a small number of black upperclassmen available for advice, the newer students missed out on informal advising. AAS also raised the issue of a lack of black professional counselors. Well aware that they needed to make strides in spite of their minority status, having professional counselors who looked like them would have been helpful, they believed.

The letter referred to the fact that some students did not feel comfortable admitting to white people that they were struggling. Doing so would have exposed the students' vulnerability. Additionally, black students then and now suffered from what psychologists refer to as "imposter syndrome."[138] In spite of the university's recruitment efforts, imposter syndrome caused some black students to question whether they belonged and were good enough to be at Brown and similar institutions. This affected their confidence in their own abilities and restricted their desire to seek help. Those issues were compounded by the fact that the students, who sometimes came from lower economic backgrounds, had difficulty covering the cost of books and other fees. The result was subpar performance.

The arrival of activist black students, the institutionalization of Afro-American Studies, the employment of black faculty, and the establishment of a black space in the late 1960s and early 1970s marked the waning of an era of white exclusivity and the beginning of another for Brown (and Pembroke). Of the 1,020 black and Latino male and female students who applied (Pembroke merged with Brown in 1971) to be part of the class of 1975, the university accepted 262. Most were from urban areas and had attended public schools. Of those who enrolled, 84 percent received financial aid. They were the children of parents who, by and large, did not attend college. More than thirty of the black and Latino students had participated in Brown's newly created Transitional Summer Project. The group of black and Latino matriculants contrasted with sons of alumni. There were 218 alumni children who applied to be a part of the class of 1975. Of those, 77 eventually matriculated. The admissions culture and practices at Brown had shifted to allow for more racial and socioeconomic diversity but still accommodated traditional legacy admits.[139] Black students in the class of 1976 made up 20.1 percent of all financial aid award recipients.[140] Black students whose families earned from $5,000 to $14,999 per year represented the largest percentage of those who received financial aid. In contrast, white students whose families earned from $10,000 to $19,999 represented the largest percentage of those taking financial aid.

University officials were aware of the need to stay vigilant. In a letter to "All Deans," the associate dean of student affairs William Brown, the assistant dean of student affairs Anderson Kurtz, and, the assistant dean of academic affairs Nanette Reynolds (all of whom were black) stated that the black admissions numbers at the undergraduate and graduate level were "abysmal" in 1972.[141] They implored their fellow deans to look back and take inspiration from the 1968 agreement when approaching black undergraduate and graduate candidates. The black administrators charged that "it is critically important at this point in Brown University's history to intensify, rather than diminish, its stated goal of equality of educational opportunity." The pressure to continue the recruitment and retention effort came from outside and inside the administration. Additionally, the black administrators who likely owed their jobs to the students' campaigns, brought the struggle with them in their professional lives.

The black students arriving in the 1970s were ardently intent on maintaining the gains that earlier generations of students had won. They called on the university to reassess its commitment. To measure and maintain progress, in March 1973 President Hornig authorized a document entitled "Recommendations for the Reaffirmation of Brown University's Commitment to Its Black Community Based upon the December 1968 Agreements with Its Black Students."[142] The document, marked confidential, took note of recruitment statistics as well as the allocation of resources that had been provided for the success of black students up to that point. Because the university hired black recruitment officers, it did not rely as heavily on current black students to do the recruiting themselves. The classes of 1973 and 1974 met or nearly met the demand that black students make up 11 percent of the class population. There was a dip in the class of 1975 and 1976.

Just as the rise of Black Studies lent itself to the creation of Chicano and Latino as well as women's and gender studies, the focus on black admissions assisted other groups as well. The university accepted nonblack "disadvantaged" applicants at a higher rate because of the new policy on black admits. In that way, black students were once again creating access for those whom the university had regularly overlooked. Although that was positive in nature, admitting the nonblack minority and disadvantaged students was not part of the 1968 agreement to prioritize black recruitment. Officials recognized that in order to honor the agreement and to halt the slip in enrollment, the university needed to renew its focus on black students and to clarify that monies designated for black recruitment were not to be used for other students. As a result, the admissions office established a new policy to admit nonblack minority students that used similar criteria.[143]

To address the issue of black academic retention and support, the document indicated that funding should be expanded to cover the hiring of new counselors and tutors, which was a demand of the AAS in 1973. In addition to money for hires, the document suggested that faculty and staff undergo training and development to better identify and deal with the academic transition of black students. AAS had requested black faculty and staff to assist with the student transition. By 1973, there were twenty-one black faculty members, which made up 4.1 percent of the total faculty. Of that population, the largest percentage of black faculty members were classified instructors and lecturers. The document stated that the university should focus on tenuring junior faculty to promote stability. At the administrative level, beyond the black admissions officers whom the university hired, there were two black deans.[144] The pressure that students placed on Brown officials was bearing fruit.

To maintain the pressure on the institution, in 1975 black students who were part of the newly formed Third World Coalition took over University Hall. In spite of the 1973 report that the administrators submitted, the students protested the slowness of some Brown officials to maintain the resources agreed to during the 1968 boycott and subsequent demonstrations. The takeover lasted less than two days but it was significant in that the Brown officials agreed to maintain the financial resources and arrangements made seven years earlier. If figures like Fritz Pollard, J. Saunders Redding, and Ethel Robinson opened doors in the early part of the twentieth century, students like Beckham, Lord, and Grooms as part of the AAS helped many black students enter through Brown's door of opportunity in the 1960s and 1970s.

Presently, black students make up nearly 9 percent of the total student population and Brown's Africana Studies Department features some of the top scholars in the world. Life at Brown, however, can still be troublesome for black students. In 2014, Armani Madison, then president of the college chapter of the National Association for the Advancement of Colored People, explained that "Brown paints a picture of diversity," but that the number of black faculty members was not in line with the population of African American students.[145] This was problematic because, according to Madison, students look to faculty members of color as mentors who afford African American students a deeper connection than may be available with white faculty members. In this way, the Afro-American (now Africana) Studies department is still incredibly important to students. The president of the Black Student Union (formerly Afro-American Society) described his Africana Studies course taught by a black woman as an "eye-opening experience."[146]

Although Brown University's student population is still largely white and socioeconomically elite, the university can at least point to a notable presence of black students and scholars. That was not the case before black students arrived on campus in the late 1960s. Brown, which has been known for its willingness to shirk tradition, needed black students and professionals to establish a new tradition of inclusivity. When discussing the legacy that his generation of black students left, Phil Lord (class of 1970) expressed pride in knowing that he helped to break "barriers about stereotypes of Ivy League students being a certain race or class."[147] Lord pointed out that before he and his peers arrived there was no affirmative action, but through agitation they "challenged" the university to open its doors wider to black students and professionals, which "broke ground for future efforts." Young black people and their mentors, in bringing Black Power to campus, created a culture that could eventually welcome a black woman as president. Ruth Simmons's appointment as the eighteenth president of Brown seemed fitting, as it took black women in the 1960s to lead the campaign for access and inclusivity at Brown. Incidentally, Spencer Crew, who walked off campus in 1968, was a member of the Brown Corporation (board of trustees) and on the search committee that called for Simmons's appointment. Proud of what he was able to accomplish at Brown, Crew sent both of his children to the university and they, too, joined the ranks of black Brunonians that helped to advance opportunities for the community.[148] After the boycott of 1968, a Providence newspaper rightly stated that "Brown never will be quite the same."[149] Indeed, black people, who shared the same hue as those enslaved people who built the institution, brought their university into an era of freedom.

4

Black Power and the Big Green

Dartmouth College and the Challenges of Isolation

We must dedicate ourselves to Black freedom and Black peace
of mind, no matter what the obstacles, no matter what the
barriers.
—Wallace L. Ford II, Commencement Address, Dartmouth
College, 1970

Dartmouth College in the last quarter century has earned a reputation
as one of the more conservative institutions in the nation when it comes
to race. In part this claim stems from its periodical, the *Dartmouth
Review*, which has lambasted affirmative action in higher education as
reverse racism. Jim Yong Kim, who in 2009 took the helm of the college
to become the Ivy League's first Asian American president, was often
portrayed in viciously stereotypical terms, including in a student-created
periodical. This and many other more recent events reflect a decades-
long struggle by nonwhite students, particularly African Americans,
sometimes with the help of progressive Dartmouth affiliates, to fight
against the school's predilection toward being exclusively white and rich.
In the midst of the Civil Rights Movement and Black Power Movement, Dartmouth students, officials, and alumni waged a tenacious
and relatively successful campaign to increase black admissions to the
college, a fight that was also rooted in larger national developments.[1]
   Dartmouth College experienced a taste of what historian Ibram
Kendi (formerly Ibram Rogers) has termed the "Black Campus Movement," but, like Princeton, Dartmouth did not experience the highly
dramatic rebellions that its peer institutions witnessed. Unlike Cornell, there were no black student activists parading with rifles to defend
themselves at Dartmouth and students did not attempt to take a dean
hostage, as some had at Columbia. They did not invite world-renowned

black militants onto campus to join their demonstrations, as some did at Yale; nor did they walk off campus in a boycott, as did young learners at Brown. Black students at Dartmouth acted on their own behalf and were able to alter the traditional policies of higher education while advancing the black freedom movement on and off campus via small but effective campaigns.[2] The students and officials took advantage of the activism elsewhere to advance their causes on campus. This chapter depicts how the black freedom movement managed to reach the quiet green of Hanover, Hew Hampshire.

Dartmouth as a case study of the period between 1945 and 1975 is unique for several reasons. The first is that unlike some elite schools in the Midwest and Northeast and most in the Ivy League, there was virtually no black community in the upper valley region of New Hampshire to influence policy making at the governmental or college level. In a racially homogeneous space, black students at Dartmouth acted by themselves as the key catalysts for change. This set them apart from many of their protesting peers in the Ivy League and around the nation who were closer to support networks. Second, although universities looked to public and urban secondary schools in the late 1960s to achieve racial diversity in higher education, Dartmouth College took that effort to another level by actively recruiting black students who were self-identified members of a notorious youth gang in Chicago. Dartmouth's case provided a different view of black student recruitment during the era. It not only recruited economically middle-class black students from elite college preparatory schools in the earlier (and later) period but the college also recruited on the streets of Chicago. This, along with the eventual arrival of black women, faculty, and staff on campus greatly added to the diversity of the student body and partially relieved black students' sense of otherness.

There were other aspects of the Dartmouth campaign that set it apart from other elite non-Ivy institutions. Ivy League students and officials understood their national significance. The Ivy League presidents met periodically to discuss practices and issues affecting their institutions, including race relations. Dartmouth's leadership was wary of the sometimes violent and raucous demonstrations that occurred at high-ranking schools like Northwestern, Amherst, and Berkeley, but it more closely followed the protests at Harvard, Princeton, Yale, Columbia, Penn,

Brown, and Cornell. Officials concluded that if such turmoil could take place at any of the "ancient establishments," then it would only be a matter of time before it erupted at Dartmouth. In addition to detailing the efforts of students to diversify Dartmouth on their own terms, this chapter compares and contrasts black student protest at several Ivy League schools.

College and university presidents were key figures in the student protests, and several white Ivy League heads responded relatively progressively to the times. Princeton's Robert Goheen, the son of a Presbyterian minister, opened Princeton to black students and faculty members after pressure from students and community members. Cornell's James Perkins, who was reared a Quaker and was a former Ford Foundation administrator, believed that integration on campus was one of the "only hopes for future understanding between black and white" people.[3] His liberalism notwithstanding, Perkins's campus, too, faced the threat of violence when black students shouldered arms to defend themselves. Cornell, like Dartmouth, was in a rural location. Ithaca, New York, was not near any major cities and had a small black population. At Yale, which was led by the socially liberal Kingman Brewster, black students worked with the local Black Panther Party to advance dual agendas on campus and in the community of New Haven, Connecticut. Brown University students, after a brief boycott, were able to negotiate with the sympathetic Raymond Heffner to increase black admissions and to add a Black Studies program.

More conservative and removed from student affairs were Columbia's Grayson Kirk and Harvard's Nathan Pusey. Both pushed back against radical and militant students in an attempt to maintain law and order. Both called police onto campus to clear student demonstrators from buildings and spaces that they had commandeered. Kirk's and Pusey's actions resulted in strikes that became international symbols of youth rebellion.[4] Students in France, Germany, Mexico, and elsewhere admired these demonstrations.

Dartmouth College, under the leadership of John Sloan Dickey, had no internationally famous student strikes or demonstrations, yet it achieved many of the same goals that activists fought for at peer institutions. Between 1945 and 1975, Dartmouth avoided much of the era's tumult and turmoil by both acceding to the demands of its black students and taking proactive steps toward improving race relations on and off campus. It made an institutional effort to become a place where black students felt welcomed. Dartmouth officials learned from what happened elsewhere and thus escaped the more dramatic showdowns that rocked other campuses. By the early 1970s, Dartmouth had a Black Studies program, a black culture center and residence hall, an admissions strategy to recruit and matriculate a higher number of black students, and seasonal and year-round programs that assisted urban black youth who hoped to attend college. What happened at Dartmouth highlights how a movement that originated with a push to empower the poorest and most disenfranchised members of black America found its way to one of the most exclusive spaces in the country, an Ivy League college. Those black students who could and did attend Dartmouth were usually their communities' elite, yet they chose to propagate a campaign that intended to bring freedom to the black masses. Indeed, by the 1960s, Black Power had invaded the Big Green.

Established in 1769, Dartmouth has had a long relationship with black people and civil rights. Resting in the beautiful green hills of Hanover, Dartmouth College began ostensibly as an institution to educate Native Americans and English youth, although few Native people attended the college in its early years.[5] Within fifty years of its existence, however, some African Americans had the opportunity to attend. The college graduated Edward Mitchell in 1828, the first black student to earn a degree from an Ivy League institution and only the fourth African American graduate of a U.S. college or university.[6] Nearly 120 people of African descent had matriculated at Dartmouth by 1945.[7]

Dartmouth's twelfth president, John Sloan Dickey, an alumnus of the class of 1929, was one of the fifteen luminaries who served on President Harry Truman's prestigious Committee on Civil Rights.[8] After learning in great detail the issues that challenged black America on a national level, Dickey and his administration attempted to bring civil rights to his own institution by helping to significantly increase the population of black students.[9] His hope (and that of black people throughout the country) was for education to lead to racial equality. Even with Dickey's civil rights committee experience, the movement to establish black rights and freedoms at Dartmouth did not always go smoothly. In spite of their liberal intentions, institutions do not always achieve without agitation of their stated goals of uplift. Black students at Dartmouth provided the vigor necessary to transform mere talk about freedom into reality.

Born in 1907 and originally from Pennsylvania, Dickey was the first in his family to attend college, which may have explained his sympathy for first-generation college students. Before joining the professoriate, he had a varied career that involved working for the Massachusetts Department of Corrections. Dickey eventually took up a life in politics and worked with future New York Governor and U.S. Vice President Nelson Rockefeller (a Dartmouth alumnus) as well as statesman Dean Acheson (graduate of Yale and Harvard) to establish a blacklist of suspected traitors and people who sympathized with the Axis powers.[10] Similar to Columbia University President Grayson Kirk, Dickey focused his pre-academy life on international relations. The two men, in different capacities, helped to facilitate the United Nations Charter.[11] Dickey put his negotiating skills to good use as he proposed to diversify Dartmouth's elite, exclusive, and isolated racial climate for what he saw as the greater good of society.

During Dickey's tenure, for example, a black student from Jersey City named Julian Robinson who had previously flunked out was readmitted and began to turn around his life.[12] Robinson was one of the privileged and had a unique story, but his case also provides some representation of what life was like for a black student at Dartmouth in the postwar era. Enjoying the new experiences in college, he recalled that Robert Frost taught his freshman English course, but Robinson soon strayed from his studies. "I ran into a couple of guys who were playboys, and I played right along with them," he admitted. Sponsored by a wealthy white New Jersey family, Robinson said, "I was at Dartmouth with a checking account . . . but I never saw statements." Robinson failed his classes, left school, and joined the war effort in Korea. While abroad, he successfully appealed to the college to readmit him. This time, Robinson graduated and then worked for the National Scholarship and Service Fund for Negro Students (NSSFNS).[13] Established in 1947, the NSSFNS was a private recruitment and development agency designed to funnel black students into predominately white universities. Before the advent of the NSSFNS, Ivy institutions typically recruited from the same preparatory

schools, including Exeter, Phillips Academy at Andover, and Choate—
all in the Northeast. With the help of the scholarship and service fund,
the schools could cast wider nets for good students.[14]

Julian Robinson's work eventually affected the lives of others. R. Harcourt Dodds, a black student, attended Dartmouth during the Dickey
administration as well. Dodds came to the college from Harlem in New
York City and graduated in 1958. He was one of a growing number of
black matriculants on campus during the dawn of the modern Civil
Rights Movement. Taking advantage of the NSSFNS, for which Julian
Robinson worked, Dodds applied to Dartmouth to study engineering.
Like the few other black students there, Dodds witnessed the nation's
struggle with its conscience and went to Hanover in search of personal
growth and advancement for not only himself but also his race.[15]

Dodds enjoyed the amenities of campus life. Unlike black students
who had arrived in the previous decades, Dodds lived with white roommates in a dormitory. Also unlike most of the black students before him
and many after, he pledged a fraternity—Chi Phi. Historian Geoffrey
Kabaservice has noted that Dartmouth and other Ivy League institutions
had not immediately welcomed black or Jewish students, and also had
imposed admission quotas on them.[16] Even as the quotas faded, there
still existed problems with fraternities at Dartmouth excluding black
and Jewish pledges even as the nation fought to rescue Jewish victims
of the Holocaust. President Dickey had observed anti-Semitism in the
Greek system when he was a student.[17] During the 1950s there were still
remnants of racial and religious discrimination in fraternities. By the
time of Dodds's arrival, however, most fraternities had given ground
with regard to racial and religious restrictions.[18] With Jewish and Asian
members already in the fellowship, Dodds claimed that his fraternity
accepted him as a brother without regard to his race and helped advance his social life immensely. After graduating Dartmouth and then
Yale Law School, Dodds took up a career that included employment
with the Ford Foundation. Two decades after graduating Dartmouth
magna cum laude, Dodds became a trustee in 1973, one of the first black
people to achieve that status at an Ivy League institution and the first at
Dartmouth.[19]

Not all Dartmouth black men received such hospitality. As had been
the case at Harvard and Cornell in earlier periods, there was controversy

in 1963 over the rejection of black students from a fraternity because of their race. Sigma Epsilon Chi fraternity, eventually known as the Brotherhood of the Tabard, refused to allow a black student to rush because it claimed his character did not meet the standards of the organization. But he had only been to the fraternity house once and had not met most of the members.[20] The fraternity claimed that it was not "house policy" to exclude black members, but rather a small but powerful minority of members blocked the progress of black candidates by threatening to leave the fraternity if they were admitted.

This dichotomy shines an interesting light on Dartmouth. Like many of the northern institutions and most of the Ivy League universities, the college itself did not overtly discriminate on the basis of race. In fact, its policies suggested some respect for the black freedom struggle. Not only did it admit black students, but in 1954 Dartmouth passed a referendum outlawing several other forms of discrimination in the Greek system: "By April 1, 1960, any fraternity, which as a result of a nationally imposed written or unwritten discrimination clause restricts, or can be interpreted to restrict membership because of race, religion, or national origin, shall be barred from all interfraternity participation."[21] Although most northern universities celebrated the idea that they, unlike their southern counterparts, admitted black students, once those students arrived they were not welcomed by certain segments of these institutions. After the denial of the black student by Sigma Epsilon Chi in 1963, the school's Interfraternity Council pledged to make every attempt to "eliminate discrimination at Dartmouth."[22]

Students weighed in on the fraternity's and Dartmouth's actions. Terry Lee wrote to the student newspaper, "I think that to alter fraternity procedure enough to prevent discrimination on racial and religious grounds" would mean that the "right of private association would be abrogated." Another student, David Johnston, countered that the fraternities on campus were not private and that they were a part of the larger college. He explained, "If those fraternities could exist as separate entities, without affecting anyone else with their personal prejudices, I would say fine. . . . [B]y discriminating against a person because of his ascribed status, the fraternities are violating the civil rights of every Dartmouth man."[23] The debate about fraternity admissions on campus mirrored that concerning civil rights in larger American life. In other arenas, it took sit-ins and boycotts to change policy; at Dartmouth College, the change happened much less dramatically but no less significantly.

Around the same time, Dartmouth faced another race-based controversy. Like many universities across the nation, Dartmouth sometimes hosted notorious and divisive figures. Two speakers who caused student uproars were Alabama Governor George Wallace and racial theorist William Shockley. Wallace's home state was at the forefront of the civil rights struggle. With school-aged youth and older activists like Fred Shuttlesworth and Martin Luther King Jr., leading the fight to end segregation, Governor Wallace and Birmingham Commissioner of Public Safety Eugene "Bull" Connor used their authority to maintain the "southern way of life." The world watched as Birmingham city authorities assaulted black American citizens who demonstrated for their rights.[24]

By the time of Wallace's first visit to Dartmouth in November 1963, he had observed the deaths of four black girls who were killed in a church bombing in Birmingham, closed public schools to prevent desegregation, allowed "Bull" Connor to mobilize the fire and police departments against peaceful youth activists during the Children's Crusade, and stood in the doorway of a University of Alabama building to intercept enrolling black students. When he arrived at Dartmouth, students and faculty met him with varying reactions. One group of students, which included people who had participated in the Civil Rights Movement in the South, planned interracial pro-integration marches before and after the speech.[25]

Though a number of Dartmouth students supported the idea of picketing Wallace, one thought the idea was immature and departed from the local culture by encouraging students to close their minds to new ideas. Another astutely brought up the irony of students on Dartmouth's campus wanting to picket the southern segregationist but not taking the same measures to attack northern segregationists, like the fraternities that segregated—on campus![26] A student from Alabama praised the work Wallace had done with regard to internal improvements for the state and decried the reaction of Northerners.[27] A second Alabaman believed that black people in his home state should have the right to vote—eventually. He stated that black people are "easily corruptible . . . and prone to not use their votes wisely."[28] Although Dartmouth seemingly supported the Civil Rights Movement, Dartmouth students still had to confront segregationist sympathizers on their own campus. Campus groups like the Political Action Committee and the Dartmouth Christian Union attempted to counter segregationist ideology by donating money to the Student Nonviolent Coordinating Committee and by traveling to Mississippi to work with the organization.[29]

Members of the faculty also made arrangements for Wallace's arrival. A contingent of professors planned to demonstrate their disapproval of Wallace's views by donning black armbands and protesting silently, a method that organizations such as labor unions and the National Association for the Advancement of Colored People had used for decades.[30] Like those who attended the monumental March on Washington earlier in the year, the nearly twenty faculty members and hundreds of students, most of whom were white, marched through campus and around the field house, singing "We Shall Overcome" and carrying "Freedom Now" signs. On the day of the event, the school newspaper reported that there had been possibly more applause than jeers for the governor. A spokesman for the politician said that Wallace believed that Dartmouth students were better representatives of an educational institution than those at Harvard, whose interruptions had prevented him from carrying forth with his speech the day before. One Dartmouth student speculated that there would have been more disruptions than cheers, but that students had decided to remain respectfully silent.[31] Martin Luther King Jr. argued in his *Letter from a Birmingham Jail*, "we will have to repent in this generation not merely for the hateful words and actions of the bad people but for the appalling silence of the good people." If the men who left Dartmouth went on to become world leaders, they would have to take a stand on the issues that affected their own nations and institutions. They would not always be able to remain "respectfully silent."

Wallace visited Dartmouth again in 1967, and found that much had changed. The approaches to the movement for black freedom began to shift from boycotts, sit-ins, and marches to more militant tactics and rhetoric. Because of its geographic isolation and the relatively small number of black people—less than one-half of 1 percent of the state population—the arrival of Black Power in nonurban Hanover was noteworthy.[32]

Dartmouth and the other Ivy League schools had to confront these shifting expectations. Scholars have argued persuasively that Ivy institutions admitted more black students at the end of the 1960s because of the manifestation of the movement in the North. In New York City, Columbia University observed members of the Harlem community organizing against its expansion efforts. Ivy League schools in Cambridge, New Haven, and Philadelphia faced similar problems.[33] As one scholar explained in his work on the University of Pennsylvania, when black students arrived on these campuses, they took up the rhetoric and attitudes they observed in urban centers. A plank of their platform became the demand for increased black admissions. In doing so, they extended the struggle for survival of earlier black Ivy students. The hope was for African American graduates to advance the freedom struggle.[34]

In addition to the students' demands, officials from the institutions felt the pressure of the times. President of the Ford Foundation McGeorge Bundy (a Yale alumnus), who had acted as President John F. Kennedy's (Harvard alumnus) and Lyndon B. Johnson's National Security Advisor, explained: "Black demand, white awareness, [and] riots in the cities" as well as "a fundamental contradiction between an asserted opposition to racism" and the low numbers of black students on campus, pushed these institutions into action.[35] A black student from Columbia commented on the increase in admissions, "We [black students] know that we are admitted to Ivy Colleges . . . because black people engaged in demonstrations, rioted, and otherwise pressured the white establishment."[36] This was true at Columbia and, to a degree, at Dartmouth as well. During the late 1960s, Dartmouth admitted more black students than ever. To encourage such enrollments, Dartmouth looked for promising candidates from poorer neighborhoods. While many of the students of Robinson's and Dodds's generations had come from the black middle class and more exclusive high schools like Brooklyn Tech and Stuyvesant, Dartmouth, as did its peer institutions, broadened its search to include less prestigious public schools.[37]

To assist in the search, Dartmouth employed the use of several programs, including the NSSFNS, Outward Bound, an exchange program with Alabama's historically black Talladega College, and a program started on Dartmouth's campus to create a pipeline for future black students.[38] Similarly, Princeton established a relationship with historically black Lincoln University of Pennsylvania and Brown University created an exchange program with the historically black Tougaloo College in

Figure 4.1. Dartmouth student Paul Robinson (third from left on bottom row) surrounded by Jersey City youth participants in the A Better Chance program. Courtesy of Rauner Special Collections Library, Dartmouth College.

Mississippi. Cornell partnered with historically black Hampton University of Virginia.[39] Other Ivy League institutions also established pipelines, but few were as wide as Dartmouth's. The college's isolation, in contrast to its peer competitors, forced its officials to be more intentional and work harder to recruit black students.

To cultivate potential students, Dartmouth authorized the establishment of its "A Better Chance" program in 1963. Dartmouth, along with twenty preparatory schools in the Northeast, launched the project to groom high school students for college. Funded in part by the Ford Foundation and private corporations, the program ran in the summers, and (along with the Ulysses S. Grant Foundation at Yale) was one of the first of its kind in the Ivy League.[40] With the guidance of municipal officials like Jersey City Director of Health and Welfare Julian Robinson, Dartmouth students went to surrounding urban areas to tutor disadvantaged black youth, hoping that these students might one day enroll. The college even brought to campus two leaders of a notorious Chicago gang, the Conservative Vice Lords, to improve their academic preparedness. The two men, Tiny Evans and Henry Jordan, eventually matriculated as degree-seeking students. Dartmouth officials, who were obviously proud of the program, noted one participant's comment: "ABC has put many doors in front of me. The doors are not yet open but for the first time in my life, the door knobs are within reach."[41] By encouraging students with such different backgrounds from those of its typical students, Dartmouth helped create opportunities for black youth. Fortunately, the college had valuable alumni like Robinson and R. Harcourt Dodds working to move Dartmouth toward black freedom in a new era.

With help from the Black Alumni Association, Dartmouth later established the Foundation Years project, which was a transitional program for young black men. In an effort to address the inadequate schooling and preparation that many urban black people suffered, Foundation Years offered students the opportunity to work their way up to college-level courses. Those who finished the two-year program and were able to pass the college's entrance requirements could enroll immediately at Dartmouth.[42] Conservative Vice Lords founder Edward "Pepilow" Marlon Perry, after spending time with David Dawley, a white Dartmouth alumnus who participated in a two-year embedded study with the gang, took advantage of the Foundation Years program.[43] When asked about the prospects of succeeding in college life, Perry explained that white people "taught me to believe I was second-rate. I believed it for a long time but I don't now." His indictment of white people must have excluded Dawley, who became a friend. "My two friends from the Lords . . . went up there and they were just dynamite. . . . I know I can do just as well," Perry predicted. Coming from Lawndale, a predominantly black and impoverished neighborhood in Chicago, Perry wanted better for himself and his family. "I want that degree. I've seen what it can get," he said. Perry was one of eighteen black students who participated in Foundation Years. Of those eighteen, all but one came from Chicago.[44] In an effort to assist the community where they claimed President Lyndon Johnson's Great Society had failed, the Conservative Vice Lords even provided financial assistance to local students who left the city to attend Dartmouth.[45]

The Foundation Years and A Better Chance programs set the college apart from many of its peers and showed what was possible when institutional commitment met the individual desire for advancement.[46] By inviting members of a youth organization with a reputation for violence, Dartmouth risked its reputation of exclusivity and isolation, not to mention the possibility of campus unrest. Surely college officials had doubts, but they took the mission to heart by offering opportunities to young people who would be ignored by most programs. In this way, Dartmouth positively influenced the life chances of individual African Americans as well as the larger black freedom movement.

Many of these new students were unlike their black and white predecessors in that they did not come from preparatory schools or the middle class; many arrived from working-class neighborhoods in urban metropolises like Chicago, Boston, Newark, and New York. The Higher Education Act of 1965 that made federal loans and financial aid available partly aided this shift in admissions.[47] Although they may have had alumni acting as advocates from afar and legislation working in their favor, once on campus these students had to brave a new world alone. Their militancy and radicalism contrasted with the entrenched cultures of Ivy League schools.

With the advent of Black Power, there were changes in the demeanor of Dartmouth's African American students. Martin Kilson, a professor at Harvard and an advisor of Harvard's Association of African and Afro-American Students, noted that black college students in white institutions had been "much influenced by the ghetto riots" and Black Power in general. He asserted, "no issue, not even the Vietnam War, has dominated their attention more than these violent outbursts."[48] This militancy, combined with rising black consciousness and pride, led these students to reject the assimilationist efforts of their black predecessors. As one such militant claimed, "the Negro who previously enrolled in white institutions . . . was convinced that his path to success was . . . through an adherence to middle-class values of the white society."[49] The student suggested that, "he [the black student of previous generations] compromised his own integrity as a black man" and became in the eyes of white America nothing more than a "genteel nigger—a showcase coon." This new generation of black Dartmouth students wanted to ensure that they would be considered neither.

Although the student's rhetoric reflected the militancy of the times, he wrongly characterized black alumni who endured the racial trials that came with desegregating white institutions of higher education. It took as much courage to be one of the few black students on campus before the mid-1960s as it did after that period. As a result of the shift in attitudes, however, black students in the latter part of the decade found themselves more likely to physically or verbally confront their white counterparts than those who came before. Dartmouth officials, like those at peer institutions, needed to accommodate this new age of students.

Rather than trying to fit in and integrate, many in this new group of black students sought to establish new identities by creating the Afro-American Society (AAS) in 1966. They were inspired by the creation of the Students' Afro-American Society (SAS) at Columbia University, established by Hilton Clark, son of the famed psychologists Kenneth and Mamie Clark, two years earlier.[50] Clark's rationale for the group's creation was that "there is a great deal of apathy among educated or so-called Ivy League Negroes to our race's continuing struggle." He wanted the members of the society to think "about their identity with other Negroes." A member of Dartmouth's AAS explained, "we were hurt because we felt like we had given in to apathy and isolation. We wanted to follow their [SAS members'] example."[51]

By 1966, the forty-five members of Dartmouth's AAS wanted to "be assimilated into those things of our choice, without loss of the things important in the heritage of the American Negro," stated AAS president Woody Lee.[52] Although he had been reared in a suburban New Jersey town as part of what sociologist E. Franklin Frazier might have considered the black bourgeoisie, Lee asserted his black identity more than ever at Dartmouth, as he desired to join the movement.[53] Historians have argued recently that it is necessary to reconsider the geography of the Black Freedom movement to include spaces like college campuses.[54] Joy Ann Williamson, William Exum, and Ibram Rogers (now Ibram Kendi) have all explained that black students across the nation took to heart the advice of Black Power advocates and created organizations to express their identity and desires.[55] Dartmouth accepted and funded its black students' manifestation of the movement by recognizing the AAS.

Like Columbia's SAS, which in the late 1960s took up the cause of the nearby Harlem community, members of the AAS at Dartmouth demonstrated on behalf of the larger black population of the Northeast. The AAS, similar to peer organizations at other Ivy League schools, worked tentatively with the campus's chapter of Students for a Democratic Society (SDS), which was a national New Left organization created in 1960[56] with a chapter at Dartmouth that emerged in 1966. In the late 1960s, SDS protested on campuses across the nation to end the war in Vietnam, fight racism, increase opportunities for the poor, and achieve power for young people.[57]

While their nonstudent peers battled the Vietcong and North Vietnamese Army thousands of miles away, students at Dartmouth waged a different kind of war at home. SDS members teamed up with AAS members to demonstrate against Dartmouth's $400,000 investment in Eastman Kodak, Inc. Dartmouth students decided to act in April 1967 after discovering that the Kodak plant in Rochester, New York, refused to hire black employees. They joined ranks to support the Rochester black advocacy group Freedom Integration God Honor Today (FIGHT), which was partly inspired by radical white organizer Saul Alinsky. Dartmouth student activists brought to college officials a demand to remove the college proxy from the Kodak board, in addition to appealing to the company itself.[58]

The treasurer and vice president of Dartmouth, John F. Meck, upon meeting with representatives of the AAS, SDS, and the Dartmouth Christian Union, first suggested that Kodak had good leadership and that the company was capable of making fair decisions with respect to hiring. Then, in predictable institutional fashion, the vice president suggested that a campus committee be formed to study the college's investment policies. The students were wary of such tactics. "I'm highly doubtful of how effective it [a committee to study investment policy] will be," stated AAS leader Woody Lee. Using the rhetoric of the Civil Rights Movement, he continued, "We have to face the issue—the students can't wait for the administration to do anything." An SDS leader concurred, observing, "the administration always needs more facts."

Confronting what students for decades had battled, the activists met with entrenched university bureaucracy.[59] To overcome it, they forced the issue by occupying the office of President Dickey, while allowing business to continue. Dartmouth students did not grind university operations to a halt as did militant students at peer institutions like Princeton. The brief demonstration at Dartmouth ended a few hours after it had begun, but the students had proved their point and acted on behalf of the black community.[60] Their efforts marked the variance in the methods of Black Power.

Although the college never removed its proxy from the Kodak board, the company subsequently hired black workers. In this instance, black students in collaboration with their white allies at one of the most elite institutions in the nation went beyond campus to advocate the progress of the black working class. This was a significant alliance that resulted in a small victory for the larger freedom struggle.[61]

On a different front, when campaigning presidential candidate George Wallace returned in May 1967 at the invitation of the school newspaper, *The Dartmouth*, he met a student body with a new and more militant attitude. Whereas before students and faculty members had met Wallace with a march and silent protest that mirrored some of the civil disobedience methods in practice at the time, *The Dartmouth* reported that students in 1967, some from the AAS, jeered during the speech and led a walkout. Then, in one of the most militant acts of the decade, some students, including members of the AAS, attempted to turn over the former governor's car and banged on the top of the vehicle as he left campus following the speech. By interrupting Wallace and disrupting his exit, the students violated one of the college's most sacred ideals: academic freedom. Although college officials were sympathetic to the AAS's position regarding Wallace, they felt that in advancing its own ideas, the AAS had impeded the rights of others to hear different viewpoints.

Embarrassed by the students' behavior, the administration sent a letter of apology to Wallace. In news reports, Wallace claimed that he was not hurt but noted that many of those who wanted peace in Vietnam could not act peacefully on their own college campus.[62] Wallace did not discuss his role in maintaining racial segregation and violence. The Hanover police chief called the event a riot, but such terminology was hyperbole in contrast to the deadly urban rebellions in Detroit and

Newark. In exercising more militant methods to advance black freedom, Dartmouth students made it clear that they would no longer tolerate Wallace's message of segregation, one that some students had welcomed (or at least tolerated) in the early 1960s.

In response to the demonstrations, the administration condemned the black and white student participants and brought many before the judiciary board. Eventually, Dartmouth called for the suspension of those students who "overtly" participated in the acts. The suspension would not affect the demonstrators' draft eligibility, but those suspended would have to reapply for admission. The AAS called a conference to discuss the demonstrations. The 400 attending students, mostly white, claimed to "affirm" their responsibility for the unruly behavior as a "community." No one, however, chose to identify himself individually as an overt participant.[63] Rejecting whatever punishment the judiciary board levied, AAS members demanded that the university recognize a "Black Judiciary Committee." Consisting of four black students, two black professors, and two white professors, the Judiciary Advisory Committee for Black Students was formed to oversee cases dealing with black students.[64] The AAS's refusal to be judged by the traditional judiciary committee was not a new response for black student activists, but Dartmouth's response in recognizing a black judiciary committee was unique to the Ivy League.

While Dartmouth students, faculty, and administrators debated the racial issues on campus, the nation reeled after the April 4, 1968, murder of Martin Luther King Jr. Distraught and disillusioned citizens across the country rebelled in a hundred cities, illustrating their frustration with racism. After black students took over the campus radio station to express their anger and disappointment with the assassination, the trustees of Dartmouth could not help but recognize the crucial nature of poor race relations in the post-King era and predictably established a committee to investigate the racial climate on campus. With former acting college president and retired trustee John R. McLane chairing the committee, the Trustees' Committee on Equal Opportunity delivered its report, called the McLane Report, in December 1968. It is notable that these observations did not come exclusively from students but also from those who were in charge of the college. As the report stated, "we as a committee have tried to envision what Dartmouth should do for the disadvantaged student, particularly the black" student.[65] Although the trustees of other Ivy institutions were concerned with "disadvantaged students," none submitted a report as extensive as that the Dartmouth trustees created regarding African Americans. That the trustees, who were the elite of college officials, took the initiative to research and address the issues of black students, was quite significant in that it brought the Black Power agenda to the white boardroom and got results.

The McLane Report noted the broader troubles surrounding race relations in the decades after World War II. Citing the revelations of the Kerner Commission (which analyzed the causes of the race rebellions of the decade) and the philanthropic Ford Foundation, the McLane Report indicated that discrimination in jobs, housing, and education were all impediments to the progress of black people.[66] Then, the report moved the discussion to Dartmouth and described the unpleasant experiences of black students. After revealing that campus life for many was a struggle because of their isolation and the shock of such a new experience, the McLane Report proposed suggestions to improve campus life.

By even forming the committee, Dartmouth officials placed the institution well ahead of some of its Ivy peers. At Columbia, one was not formed until after students took over campus buildings and initiated strikes. The Dartmouth study contended that elite institutions like Dartmouth thrived from tradition, but that "tradition alone is a vacuum." Using that as a point of departure, the committee suggested that all those affiliated with Dartmouth "must be exposed to a greater understanding of the black, his culture, his history, his goals, his problems, and his frustrations" in order to defeat racism on campus and in the nation.[67] This, of course, had been the suggestion of the AAS.

The report revealed much. It noted that the challenges to enrollment were the small number of "qualified" student applicants, the isolation that Hanover presented for black students from urban areas, the competition with other schools for top black students, and the fact that there was no black administrator to help recruit African American high school students.[68] The McLane Report suggested how to eradicate those impediments to enrollment, and it is notable that it was the trustees and not administrators who came to these conclusions. At institutions like Cornell and Princeton, administrators ranging from presidents down were usually charged with solving such problems.[69] The trustees of elite colleges and universities were often captains of industry and influential in larger American society. Having access to such figures gave the black Dartmouth students an advantage in negotiating.

A particularly enlightening observation of the committee was that there were few black women in Hanover and none at Dartmouth (the college did not become coeducational until 1972).[70] This situation presented a special problem for the social lives of black men at the institution. College regulations stipulated that students receiving scholarship aid could not have cars on campus. In following that rule, many of the black students lost the mobility necessary to meet women off campus. R. Harcourt Dodds of the class of 1958, remembered that while his white roommate maintained a healthy dating schedule, he had far fewer opportunities to court. "The black students had discovered that there was, in fact, a black family in Hanover and there was a teenage daughter in that family who, as one might imagine, became enormously popular," Dodds recalled.[71] The isolation of Dartmouth made the experience of black students different than that of their peers at other Ivy schools that either had higher numbers of black students or were set in cities that had large black communities. Dating may have seemed normal to white heterosexual college men, but at Dartmouth such an act was out of the reach of their black classmates.

If black men wanted to date within their race, they typically had to go to Boston or wait for black women from other schools to visit Dartmouth. Such bleak prospects could dissuade many a young man from attending school in Hanover. To shore up the local gender disparity, the report suggested an on-the-job training program be established at the college and any other local institutions that could attract black women. With the number of open secretarial, nursing, and service positions available in Hanover and on campus, the committee believed that it could help the larger problem of black employment by providing jobs. In addition, the committee suggested "an incidental advantage . . . would be that a number of black girls would be brought for 1 to 2 year periods."[72] This was not a problem that black men confronted at other Ivy institutions.

AAS members took the remarkable step of directly recruiting other African American students to come to Dartmouth. With the arrival of Black Power, black students saw such work as an opportunity to advance the race and assist the movement. Black Power used white institutions to gain knowledge that would help the race establish black ones. Although the message of Black Power was directed toward the masses, students attending an Ivy League institution could greatly aid the effort to use white institutions for the benefit of black people. While students at Penn and Columbia took over campus buildings to highlight the need for increased black admissions, Dartmouth's AAS took a more subtle approach by designing a pamphlet that it sent to prospective students.[73]

Apparently, the efforts of the AAS and the college were fruitful. An article in the *Bay State Banner* reported in the fall of 1968 that "a record 29" black freshmen enrolled at Dartmouth. That brought the number of black students at the college to 89.[74] This number was lower than that at Dartmouth's peer institutions, but the total number of students at Dartmouth was also lower. For instance, Columbia had accepted 58 black freshmen (in Columbia College), Penn enrolled 62 black freshmen, Yale enrolled 43 freshmen in the college, Harvard enrolled 51 freshmen, and Cornell had more than 200 black students enrolled that school year.[75] But as Dartmouth AAS leader Bill McCurine pointed out, "In terms of action, more has been done here in the last three years than on any other campus that I know." Praising his school, McCurine said that Dartmouth was "a very exciting place for a black student to be."[76] The AAS leader, originally from the South Side of Chicago, served on the Trustee's Committee on Equal Opportunity and became a Rhodes scholar after graduating.[77] With the boost in black student population, the membership and activity of the AAS also increased. At one point, the AAS even put on the Leroi Jones (Amiri Baraka) play *Dutchman*, which was representative of the burgeoning Black Arts Movement. Dartmouth also was home to a black arts festival organized by the AAS.[78] None of those achievements required the types of demonstrations that were occurring at San Francisco State, Columbia, and Harvard, where students participated in strikes, or at South Carolina State College where student demonstrators were shot dead in the streets.

As the AAS ascended, Dartmouth officials attempted to understand the students' methods in order to prevent the troubles that occurred elsewhere. Charles Widmayer, biographer of John Sloan Dickey, explained that after observing the week-long building occupations at Columbia in 1968, both the radical students and the Dartmouth administration

had learned lessons: "It (the Columbia crisis) alerted college administrators to be prepared to handle this new development in the protest
movement."[79] Widmayer claimed that because of this awareness, Dickey
and Dartmouth "were ready to handle . . . [disruptions and demands]
promptly, firmly, and humanely." That did not, however, mean that the
president agreed with the students' movement for Black Power. The
liberal Dickey noted, "Having been in the cause of Negro 'liberation'
twenty years ago as a member of Truman's historic Committee on Civil
Rights . . . and having won a few battle stars since then," he added, "I
have no reason to be hesitant about saying that this kind of 'political
bluster' (the call and demonstrations for Black Power) is a tragically ill-
advised disservice to the cause of righting the worst wrong of America's
proud history."[80] Dartmouth's black students contended that their approach had changed in the two decades since Dickey's turn on Truman's
committee. They also stressed that they did not need advice from white
administrators regarding black concerns, they needed action.[81]

The trustees' committee hoped that "the effect of the Black Power
Movement in encouraging the black students to associate exclusively
with one another may be only temporary." By assisting the students with
resources and by recruiting more African Americans, the trustees and
other college officials tried to steer them toward eventually integrating
and interacting more with white students. "Once the black students are
more significant in numbers and are able to lead from strength, meeting white students as equals, more genuine integration may occur,"
the committee noted.[82] That the trustees acknowledged the presence
of Black Power illustrated both the officials' awareness of the period's
cultural environment as well as a sign of the students' new identity as
representatives of the movement. Further, by making the issues clear
to the school officials, Dartmouth student activists accomplished what
at other schools took takeovers and occupations. Dartmouth's trustees
and administrators learned from the communication gaps that existed
between other institutions and their students.[83]

By 1969, Dartmouth's bicentennial year, black students had come
under national scrutiny. An article in *Ebony* featured song lyrics, written
by Gregory Young, that used rhetoric to call Dartmouth black men to
action. Entitled "Song to My Brother at Dartmouth," several lines went
"Don't git caught up in the enemy's camp, eatin' his food, thinkin' his

Figure 4.2. Dartmouth College students George C. Riley III (second from left) and Derek J. Rice (second from right) speaking to classmates in 1969. Courtesy of Rauner Special Collections Library, Dartmouth College.

thoughts."[84] Encouraging the AAS to take a more militant stance, the song exclaimed: "chump! . . . ya brothers at home, poisoned, dyin' in the streets. . . . Niggers up at Dartmouth 'being cool.' Acting 'ra-tion-al,' playin' the role-Nothin's a game my brother! . . . Dyin's for real!" The song indicated that those outside of Dartmouth counted on privileged black youth within the institution to use their Black Student Power to improve the lives of all black people—especially those in the ghetto. Considering their location and cultural environment, the college's black students acted militantly in their own ways to meet these challenges.

Perhaps inspired by the *Ebony* piece, in 1969 representatives of the AAS sent a letter to President Dickey that identified the need for urgent change with regard to the college's relationship to black people on and off campus. It listed a number of proposals that included increased black admissions and a Black Studies program. "As black students, one of our uppermost concerns is the College's social commitment to the black community," the letter read. The AAS believed that this commitment could be "manifested in its (Dartmouth's) recruitment and admissions policies and in the living circumstances of the black student on campus."[85] AAS members did not barricade themselves in buildings as did black student groups at Penn, Cornell, and Columbia, but the society still emphasized the need for urgency. Fully cognizant of the events unfolding at peer institutions, Dartmouth officials responded accordingly.

Although Dartmouth avoided some of the more dramatic rebellions that other schools witnessed that year, its black students still waged smaller-scale demonstrations, such as in 1969 when Nobel prize-winning physicist William Shockley visited the campus. Shockley had moved from physicist to inventor to racial theorist in an effort to prove that black people were genetically inferior to white people. Propagating eugenics, Shockley claimed that the less intelligent black race was breeding quickly and weakening American civilization. He brought that message to Dartmouth at the National Academy of the Sciences Conference that the college hosted. But every time Shockley attempted to read his speech, an interracial group of students clapped loudly, interrupting him and drowning out his voice. Consequently, Shockley was unable to share his paper. When the Dartmouth Committee on Standing and Conduct placed seventeen black students (along with white students) who had participated in the disruption on college probation, the eight-member Judicial Advisory Committee for Black Students that had been created and recognized in 1968 resigned in protest. It was clear that students (and faculty) in the late 1960s were reacting much differently to white supremacists than they had earlier in the decade.[86] The students completed their probation without any further incidents.

Dartmouth experienced protests from other student groups as well. Native American students demonstrated during the university's bicentennial celebration against the stereotypical imagery that appeared around campus in the form of murals and the "Dartmouth Indian" mascots. Throughout its history, the picture of a Native man donning feathers followed the sports teams to every venue. Irrespective of its founding as an institute for Native American education, fewer than twenty Native students had actually graduated from the college in its 200 years of existence. The few who attended in the late 1960s and early 1970s, along with black and white allies, checked the college's indiscriminate use of the imagery and called for a Native American Studies program. By 1970, fifteen Native students enrolled in the freshmen class. Like black students, they wanted the curriculum to accurately depict their place in history and society. With that in mind, they protested and eventually worked with officials to agree upon a program of study. In 1972, the college made the Native American Studies program official, and by 1974 Dartmouth formally abandoned use of the "Indian" mascot and began referring to its athletic teams as the "Big Green."[87] Black and Native students took advantage of the moment to change the culture of the college so that it did not remain as racially exclusive in the student body or curriculum as it had in the previous two centuries.

Due to the activity of the new generation of students, Dartmouth officials made policy changes regarding college life and the curriculum. In 1975, Dartmouth revisited its commitment to equal opportunity by forming another Trustees' Committee on Equal Opportunity. That the college made the decision to form the committee shed a positive light on the institution for its ability to self-evaluate. The new committee consisted of trustees, faculty members, alumni, and students. It attempted to measure the college's progress with respect to black admissions and campus life in the years since the release of the McLane Report (1968). The members of the new committee commended the college for increasing the number of black students on campus.[88] A good deal of the credit for the increase should have gone to the African Americans who assisted in the recruitment effort and strategies. Convincing urban black youth to spend four years in starkly white Hanover indeed took cooperation.

By 1975, Dartmouth had employed an action strategy to admit more black learners and women. With black students making an internal push at the college, the plan included hiring black admissions officers and making use of the Black Alumni Association. After implementing the strategy, the overall enrollment of black students shot up to 376. Of that number, approximately fifty had participated in the A Better Chance program. Consequently, black students made up 7.8 percent of the class of 1979, which according to the committee meant that Dartmouth had "the second highest percentage of black freshman among Ivy League colleges."[89] The work of concerned black students and progressive-minded college officials markedly improved the racial diversity of the student body. Part of the population increase was a result of Dartmouth's move toward coeducation, which led to the admission of black women, who made up 30 percent of the black student population in 1975. The black female students' presence addressed one of the problems that the McLane report identified as an impediment to retention.

Black students addressed other aspects of college life as well. As a result of previous efforts, they could rush campus fraternities and sororities freely, but many chose not to. Those who did pledge a fraternity often chose to enter Alpha Phi Alpha Fraternity, Inc., which was chartered on campus in 1973. Along with being the first black collegiate fraternity that Dartmouth recognized, in 1906 (at Cornell University) Alpha Phi Alpha became the first black college fraternity. The brotherhood included members such as Supreme Court Justice Thurgood Marshall and Nobel peace prize winner Martin Luther King Jr.[90] Dartmouth aspirants of the fraternity hoped to join the ranks of such esteemed figures. With regard to college life, the fraternity allowed black students the opportunity to socialize among themselves while living in a predominantly white setting. It is significant that Dartmouth had finally amassed enough black students to offer the option of a black Greek-letter fraternity to its college men.

By the late 1960s and early 1970s, black students at Dartmouth and on campuses across the nation had established new identities and began the push for spaces to express themselves. The Dartmouth administration allowed students to use a building on campus as a center for black culture and residential space. With communication lines increasingly open, the college's trustees allocated $10,000 toward the arrangement of the center, which was situated in Cutter Hall.[91] The hall, where Malcolm X spoke in 1965 (weeks before his assassination), also acted as a de facto black dormitory for a time. Later, under pressure from black students, the college renamed the Afro-American Center the El Hajj Malik El Shabazz Center.[92]

The establishment of a black cultural center was not particularly unique for a university or college; however, naming a center after Malcolm X was outstanding for the times. Although he clearly annunciated a love for blackness and a push for black empowerment, in much of

America (particularly white America) Malcolm X represented black hate to white people. Furthermore, to many, he certainly did not represent a figure after whom an Ivy League institution should name a student center. When at Dartmouth, though, Malcolm X's message was anything but hateful. In an interview with the campus radio station he explained, "when humanity looks upon itself not as black men, white men, brown men . . . but as human beings, then they will sit down and live together in peace. . . . The only time you'll have a society on this earth when all men will live as brothers will be when all men *respect* each other and *treat* each other as brothers."[93] By naming a building the Shabazz Center, Dartmouth recognized Malcolm's personal transformation after his *hajj* to Mecca as well as his significance to American history.[94] The Shabazz Center also symbolized that black students expected acceptance on their own terms.

While Dartmouth made advancements in admissions and the campus climate, the establishment of the college's Black Studies program was also significant. In the late 1960s, black students across the nation and at Dartmouth called for recognition of Black Studies and took drastic measures to institute programs and departments. In heeding the call at Dartmouth, the McLane Report suggested the establishment of a program as soon as possible. To be sure, Dartmouth was not the first of its Ivy peers to establish a program, but it is noteworthy that one of the smallest Ivy institutions (in a starkly white town and state) saw the need to augment its traditional curriculum to include a regimen of courses regarding black history and culture.[95] Dartmouth established its Black Studies program in 1970, with Professor of Errol G. Hill as the director. Between the time of the 1968 McLane Report and the 1975 report by the Committee on Equal Opportunity, the Dartmouth faculty had created or modified nearly thirty courses that dealt with the black or Third World experience. The Black Studies program itself listed six new courses, which added to the potential body of knowledge for all Dartmouth students. Additionally, the establishment of the program at Dartmouth and elsewhere led to the recruitment of black faculty, which likely aided in retention. Dartmouth's Black Studies program, however, came about without the campus rebellions that took place at San Francisco State, Harvard, and Yale.

As part of the institution's affirmative action plan, the trustees set an employment goal of 10 percent minority faculty hires in the years between 1972 and 1982. The college succeeded in that effort due in large part to the Black Studies program.[96] Such a goal could not have been achieved without the assistance of black students who, with their deliberate agitation and relatively peaceful approach, communicated the need for Dartmouth to participate in the black freedom movement.

Undeniably, Dartmouth affiliates are among society's most influential powerbrokers. Just as President Harry Truman once selected John Sloan Dickey to participate on the Committee on Civil Rights, President Barack Obama (himself an alumnus of Columbia and Harvard) tapped then-current Dartmouth President Jim Yong Kim to lead the World Bank. The college, like its peers, has been and continues to be an exclusive enclave for America's (and the world's) elite. Further, in some circles, Dartmouth is considered to be culturally conservative. During the 1960s, in direct challenge to its reputation as an exclusive and essentially white fortress, Dartmouth experienced the invasiveness of social movements in much the same way as its Ivy League peers. Students like Julian Robinson, R. Harcourt Dodds, and the members of the AAS advanced the causes of civil rights and Black Power and made the movements tangible in the isolated hills of Hanover. The students influenced the elite college to evaluate its role in creating equal opportunities on campus and in society. That so few students were able to change a conservative colonial institution is remarkable.

Black students, whose numbers had grown between 1945 and 1975, came together in spite of their economic class differences to push the college to implement changes that improved life for black people on and off campus. Those policy changes benefited the institution in several ways. First, they led to an intensified recruitment effort of black students, faculty, administration, and staff. Second, the changes brought Dartmouth a Black Studies program that allowed the college to be competitive in its course offerings with peer institutions. Third, white and other nonblack college affiliates benefited from the presence of the black culture center, people, and subjects.

If one believes in the skewed view that Black Power necessarily meant violence in rhetoric and action, then Dartmouth black students were not representative. If, however, one takes the more nuanced view that Black Power was an ideology used to achieve tangible goals on behalf of black people, then Dartmouth students succeeded in their movement for Black *Student* Power. The case of black freedom at Dartmouth illustrates how traditionally white liberal institutions had to change if they were to manifest their goals of fairness. The changes that Dartmouth made prevented the college from having to experience the building takeovers, violence, and disruption that other Ivy League universities witnessed. With President Richard Nixon's "law and order" providing context to the period, Dartmouth was able to maintain peace and relative tranquility. A 1969 article about the potentiality of violence at Dartmouth claimed that one of the reasons for peace until then was "the quality of student leadership. . . . One must credit Dartmouth's Afro-American Society which, with confident and consummate diplomacy, has set an effective precedent of non-violent action."[97] Nearly four decades later, former AAS leader Wallace Ford II (class of 1970) explained: "I was not a militant. . . . I was very vocal, very committed to the things I believed in." To be sure, though, Ford and his fellow student activists were relatively militant, considering the space they occupied, and it helped them to negotiate, demand, and effect "some major institutional changes at Dartmouth," as Ford later recalled.[98]

Dartmouth officials learned from observing peer institutions and succeeded in maintaining the safety of Dartmouth's campus by cooperating and communicating effectively with black students. Fully aware of the relative peace, civility, and understanding that black and white college affiliates exhibited, the AAS noted in 1969 that, "Dartmouth [was] a model to which other institutions can turn for guidance."[99] Indeed, Dartmouth College provided an example of how black youth helped an elite white institution effectively deal with the racial instability and changes of society in the decades after World War II.

5

Space Invader

Columbia University Enters Harlem World

No matter how much fun a youngster might get out of a good
sports facility, it isn't worth sending them in the back door of
a segregated gym.
—West Harlem community member, 1968

Housing and education have always provided the arena in which advocates and opponents of black freedom battled. The advocates of black freedom knew their life chances were tethered to their ability to live safely and to improve themselves with education. Opponents of black freedom, who often did not conceive of themselves as racist, understood that black people living near and attending schools with white people posed a threat. That threat included lower property values and the potential for lower social status if black children had the same access to educational resources.[1] Then, of course, there was the ever-looming potential for miscegenation. Not all opponents of black people's ability to live where they desired and attend the schools they wanted to practiced individual racism; however, the opponents benefited from institutional racism, which is the brand of racism that segregated neighborhoods and schools, allowed white officials to declare homes blight, and encouraged government-private alliances that disadvantaged the black working and underclass.

Despite the fact that officials at universities like Columbia and Penn were relatively liberal and personally sympathetic to the cause of civil rights, their universities played a part in stymying opportunities for black people. As institutions, Columbia and Penn engaged in skirmishes over housing and education by implementing their expansion plans. The influence and means of the Ivy schools stunted the ability of some black people to achieve power or wealth in the same spaces. Essentially, the black residents in the surrounding neighborhoods struggled to live. To that point, the cases of Columbia and Penn in the 1960s highlight the movement of seemingly powerless black residents to organize and co-alesce with allies in an effort to check institutional racism.

This chapter falls in line with the contemporary research regarding higher education and urban development undertaken by scholars such as Davarian Baldwin. In his concept of "UniverCities," Baldwin noted that universities and their facilities "have played an increasingly critical role in urban change since at least World War II."[2] In focusing on the University of Chicago's expansion into the neighborhoods of Woodlawn and Bronzeville, Baldwin insightfully stated that "as colleges and universities are given the keys to 'save the city,' the black and Latino communities that largely surround urban campuses are left especially vulnerable to the for-profit ambitions of higher education."[3] More than just centers for knowledge, these exclusive places are tax shelters for donors and social engineers of neighborhoods.

When the University of Pennsylvania and Columbia University implemented institutional expansion plans during the second half of the twentieth century, the Ivy League institutions confronted resistance from local residents who stood little chance of ever attending the elite schools. During that period, federal, state, and municipal governments encouraged individuals and private institutions to replace urban "blight" with developed properties to improve neighborhoods. Urban renewal, although popular with governmental entities and private beneficiaries, caused consternation among neighborhood residents who lived in blighted areas. Penn in West Philadelphia and Columbia on the Upper West Side of Manhattan were situated in areas where poor and working class people resided. Class tensions in those areas arose alongside the always pervasive issues of race and residential segregation that plagued the United States. Then, the element of a full-blown conflict in Vietnam added to the dangerous mix of problems that waited to explode on or near college campuses. Employing the collective agitation methods of the Civil Rights Movement and Black Power Movement, neighbors of Ivy League universities—often in coalition with students—fought back against institutions that they viewed as space invaders.

The town-gown relationships between colleges and neighborhoods are not new, but they are indicative of the complexities of urban life.

Colonial colleges, and particularly those categorized as Ivy League universities, were not immune to the issues of the metropolis. As the cities crowded and different ethnic and racial groups encountered each other, conflict occurred over real or imagined territorial lines. With that in mind, this and the next chapter seek to engage several questions: Can black and working class neighborhoods coexist with Ivy League neighbors? Who deserves urban space? Can elite institutions of higher education value their missions of educating above the need for residents to live without fear of displacement? And how are disputes of space settled?

The cases of Columbia and Penn debunk the notions that Black Power gains only manifested from "riots" and violence. If reframed and reconceived, violence can also be viewed as a tool of the police and universities. The concept of "structural violence" can apply to the expansion the institutions undertook and the way that the State protected the private property of those elites. Who protected the property and respect of those who were not at Columbia or Penn? Those not fortunate enough to affiliate with the universities had to protect themselves, and in the late 1960s, some did so in coalition with college students.

Columbia University came under intense scrutiny in the late 1960s for its asset acquisition and construction projects. The plans for those projects began in the 1940s but manifested in the 1960s in the form of tenant evictions, the leveling of buildings, and the construction of new edifices. The expansion fueled the resentment of the neighboring black neighborhoods while also giving students another issue to add to their protest platform. On campus, black students, as they did elsewhere, pushed the university to admit higher numbers of their racial peers and to provide cultural as well as curricular accommodations for their blackness. At the same time, white students, as members of groups like the Columbia Citizenship Council, as well as the campus chapters of the Congress of Racial Equality (CORE) and Students for a Democratic Society (SDS), attempted to help residents organize around housing issues. Surrounding the battles of race and space that raged between the university and the adjacent neighborhoods was the Vietnam conflict. As a member institution of the Institute for Defense Analyses, Columbia had at least indirect ties to the military research and the war. In 1968–1969, those conflicts made the university famous as an institution that would impose its will on those who could seemingly not defend themselves.

Today, those who casually glance at New York–based daily and weekly periodicals, know of Columbia University's expansion into various parts of the island of Manhattan.[4] No one is more aware of the higher education institution's presence than the neighbors around the university and those in the areas in which the university is expanding. The neighborhoods around the medical school in Washington Heights, parts of Manhattanville, and other enclaves have observed Columbia's creep. As the university attempts to create future leaders, businesses and homes have been displaced. Although it continues to be a pressing issue for residents and owners today, the school planted the seeds of the expansion plan more than a half century earlier in Morningside Heights and Harlem.[5]

Black and brown freedom fighters were not the only ones organizing in the postwar era; so too were institutions. Just after World War II, Columbia joined with fourteen other institutions to form Morningside Heights, Inc. (MHI): Barnard College, Cathedral Church of St. John the Divine, Corpus Christi Church, Home for Old Men and Aged Couples, International House, Jewish Theological Seminary, Julliard School of Music, St. Hilda's and St. Hugh's School, St. Luke's Home of Morningside House, St. Luke's Hospital Center, Teachers College, the Interchurch Center, Riverside Church, and Union Theological Seminary.[6] It was telling that Columbia, an educational institution, and the Cathedral Church of St. John the Divine, a religious institution, were the two largest landholders in the group. MHI resolved to become a "confidential clearinghouse for the development plans of the several institutions."[7]

The coalition represented a commitment to "improve" and "secure" the neighborhood of Morningside Heights for the students and patrons of the institutions. Multiple institutions offered initial start-up funds in 1947. Columbia offered the most with $31,000. From 1947 to 1949, each institutional member of the coalition contributed monetarily to MHI to fund an initial study of area residences and amenities. Larger institutions like Columbia University paid $2,750 "plus one-tenth of one percent of the assessed valuation of tax exempt property." Small institutions like Corpus Christi Church paid a reduced fee of 0.1 percent of total tax exempt property to associate with MHI.[8] Columbia, incidentally, held $28 million in tax exempt properties at the time.[9] Later, the representatives' dues went toward expansion assistance. The coalition quietly worked to socially engineer and "protect" Morningside Heights. Community and

SPACE INVADER | 171

student organizers, in contradistinction, worked to check the strong organizational efforts of MHI and Columbia University specifically.

In 1947, the year that the first black student graduated from Princeton and the year that Dartmouth president John Sloan Dickey helped craft the "To Secure These Rights" document and the year that Jackie Robinson re-desegregated major league baseball in New York City, representatives from the various entities of the Upper West Side enclave came together to advance their spatial and cultural interests in the neighborhood. By that time, the neighborhood of Morningside Heights was undergoing significant demographic shifts. As a result of the second Great Migration of black people from the South, Harlem grew and Morningside Heights became blacker and economically poorer than it had been in previous decades. At the same time that black people were arriving in Manhattan in droves, so too were Puerto Ricans who were moving to a new island for opportunity. Both groups found housing in Morningside Heights.

The leadership and board of MHI was, by any measure, impressive. David Rockefeller acted as the first president of MHI. A Harvard alumnus, Rockefeller was a grandson of Standard Oil magnate John D. Rockefeller and educator Laura Spelman (after whom historically black Spelman College in Atlanta was named) and the son of real estate titan and financier John D. Rockefeller Jr. (Brown University alumnus). As a child, David Rockefeller attended an experimental school that Teachers College of Columbia University operated on 123rd Street in the heart of Harlem. At the time that he took the helm of MHI in 1947, Rockefeller was an executive at Chase National Bank, which eventually became Chase Manhattan Bank. Cornell graduate Lawrence M. Orton, who was MHI's vice president, was an original member of the New York City Planning Commission.[10] Another member of the MHI board of directors, Princeton alumnus Cleveland E. Dodge, helped establish the Phelps-Dodge Corporation. He headed multiple well-endowed organizations, including the Charles H. Dodge Foundation, the Laura Spelman Rockefeller Memorial Fund, and the Protestant Council of the City of New York. He was also a trustee of the American Museum of Natural History and Teachers College.[11] Columbia University alumnus Frank D. Fackenthal was also on the board of directors for MHI. He had been provost at the university and was acting president of Columbia at the time that MHI started. MHI's leadership was undeniably part of America's privileged class. Their personal ties to powerful New York real estate, finance, and political power brokers were extensive and provided immense access to resources. Symbolically and practically, their place at the head of MHI was notable and directly benefited institutions like Columbia.

Rockefeller indicated in a 1948 letter to a potential member of MHI that "crowding and obsolescence have taken their toll" on the neighborhood of Morningside Heights.[12] Columbia University had moved to the area to avoid similar circumstances in lower Manhattan. "The housing and living conditions are no longer attractive to the staffs and patrons of these [MHI] institutions," Rockefeller noted. Another document stated that "the community is clearly on the downgrade and its deterioration may be expected to continue at an accelerated rate, unless effective steps are taken to combat these trends."[13] With the belief that they could save the neighborhood from itself, the members of the coalition came together to make life more appealing for the owners and users of the educational, spiritual, and cultural centers. The objectives of MHI, according to Rockefeller, were to improve housing as well as "recreational and school facilities for the staffs, students, and clients" of the member institutions and general community.[14] To accomplish those objectives, MHI began a study of the area that later manifested in the displacement of residents.

In its early years, there was a question of whether MHI's efforts were based in racism. Rockefeller claimed that the coalition did not tolerate racism and, in fact, all the participants are keenly sensitive to this issue [the appearance of racism].[15] He pointed specifically to the International House, whose motto was "that brotherhood may prevail," as an example of the antiracist nature of MHI. Perhaps in a most revealing statement, Rockefeller said, "you can readily see how embarrassing it would be to us to have any part in our organization that had the slightest taint of racial discrimination." Perhaps more than being racist, the potential appearance of being racist was a threat to MHI's progress. On all matters, Rockefeller emphasized, it was important to display a united effort "from the moral and public relations point of view."

Even though representatives from the coalition expressed their disdain for racism, the effects of their actions led to racial discrimination.

That was precisely the nature of institutional racism. Rockefeller stated in his own words that the primary purpose for the confederacy was to cater to the needs of the institutions' clients. The institutions themselves were nearly all white, operated by nearly all white men, and patronized by nearly all white people. In the case of Columbia University there were a handful of black students enrolled but no black professors or administrators were employed there. Columbia, and the remaining institutions in MHI, found themselves in an increasingly black and brown neighborhood. What seemed innocuous—revising zone ordinances, creating "better housing," and developing positive programs to "improve the neighborhood"—had a less than positive effect on black and brown people who lived in the area.[16] In the years coming, improving the neighborhood essentially meant whitening the blocks. To some, the working class and poor people, with their crime and lowly living habits, became problems for the privileged white people who needed the space to advance their own goals.

As the presidency of Columbia passed from Fackenthal to General Dwight Eisenhower (1948–1953) to Grayson Kirk (1954–1969), the university remained the keystone of MHI. The school continued to grow outward and earn a reputation as an encroaching neighbor among the people who lived on the Upper West Side. The institutional members worked with the assistance of the municipal government. In 1951, Corpus Christi pastor and Columbia University chaplain George Ford, on behalf of MHI, wrote to the highly controversial and powerful city political appointee Robert Moses. A graduate of Yale, Oxford, and Columbia, Moses was the head of the New York City Committee on Slum Clearance Plans. The Rev. Ford explained MHI's offer to develop housing complexes in Morningside Heights and Manhattanville. Moses, known for his unrelenting effort to clear land for large housing complexes, approved the Morningside Committee on Cooperative Housing's plan, which included 1,000 units that would go for $23 a month after the initial down payment.[17]

Moses considered several factors, including the passage of the American Housing Act of 1949, which provided funds for development, and the findings from the survey that MHI completed in 1950. Public policy and influence worked in favor of Columbia and MHI. For those who could not afford to buy into the cooperative or move, the city and MHI were supposed to arrange relocation funds. Although the media publicized the development as potential low-income housing, an MHI report stated: "This is the sort of housing that is greatly needed by the staffs and faculties of our institutions"—the nearly all-white staffs and faculties.[18]

To construct the complex, the institutions needed to clear the "slum," which consisted of turn-of-the-century tenements on two blocks between Amsterdam Avenue and La Salle Street on one side and Broadway and 123rd Street on the other. The *New York Times* celebrated the fact that MHI and the Manhattanville Neighborhood Center would be clearing those and more blocks of slums. "We may see a congested, slum-infected area of about five blocks replaced with modern, clean housing."[19] Another article from the *New York Herald* characterized the neighborhoods as having physically fallen "on evil times."[20] The article further suggested, however, that evil had invaded the neighborhoods' "social life." The arrival of evil beckoned the need for, what the paper called, "corrective action" by taking on the joint slum clearance project, which was "the first of its kind in the history of the city." The paper hoped that the project was "the beginning of a new era in making New York a better place for all who live here." It must have meant better for all who did not lose their homes to the progress of a few institutions. Like Penn in Philadelphia, Columbia was taking advantage of the wave of federal, state, and municipal supported urban renewal in New York City.

Although there were components of MHI that focused on the educational and recreational activities of local youth, the main concern of MHI was to secure and protect the investments of the cooperating institutions. Inasmuch, MHI established its own police force as part of the MHI security council that worked in conjunction with the New York City Police Department. The private MHI police patrolled the neighborhoods of Morningside Heights and especially Morningside Park, the home of a great controversy in the late 1960s. Before students, community members, and others clashed over the use of the park, MHI tried to police it. Drugs, particularly heroin, had infiltrated the neighborhoods of Harlem and Morningside Heights, and the park sometimes hosted illicit activity. To feed habits, addicts snatched purses and mugged people in and around Morningside Park. That made life unsafe for those who worked at, attended, or benefited from the institutions that made up MHI. To combat the crimes, MHI police stationed themselves at the entrances of the park and posted plainclothes officers in strategic areas on the outskirts of the park.[21]

MHI was not alone in its campaign to police the effects of the drug epidemic. For a short period, politicians emphasized the need for rehabilitation, but as the scourge of drugs showed no signs of abating, the political will gave way to criminalization and harsher punitive measures for users and dealers.[22] Harlem politicians like Percy Sutton and others tried to walk the line between increased policing and the desire of residents not to live in an authoritarian state that stigmatized their low-income neighborhoods as hopelessly lost in crime. In the 1960s, conservative, moderate, and liberal politicians found common cause in legislating stricter drug laws. The enforcement of those laws had implications for West Harlem and for Columbia.

To keep the institutions aware of policing efforts, the MHI council circulated a weekly briefing aptly titled *Security*. In it, the council reported on crimes that had taken place and the responses of the police force. The security council called on correctional experts to advise MHI on how to improve coverage and patrolling. Along those lines, to be identifiable, the street patrollers wore arm badges that made others aware of their presence. The private police officers walked thoroughfares such as Amsterdam Avenue and Morningside Drive to prevent and fight crime. In addition to the uniformed officers, the MHI security council employed a tactical patrol force that regularly used "stakeouts" to intervene in muggings and chase down perpetrators.[23] Crime occurred at all times of day and night, according to the bulletin, which reported that members of an NBC camera crew had been mugged when getting footage of Morningside Park and Columbia University. Then, when a hit-and-run accident killed a pedestrian, whom the *Security* reported was walking in the middle of the street to avoid muggers, the patrols increased. Members of the security council also met with local residents to discuss safety.

The MHI council was very thorough in its approach to crime fighting, and kept records of muggings, car break-ins, and other minor violations. By far, the highest number of incidents took place in the form of police contacts for "disorderly youths."[24] That there were so many cases of disorderly youth is interesting because if the police department had kept records of disorderly youths on college campuses the numbers would have skyrocketed. This illustrates what scholar Rashad Shabazz recently highlighted: that urban planning, architecture, and policing create pathways to incarceration for young black people.[25]

In addition to its council on security, MHI had a committee on education in 1966. MHI encouraged the member institutions (many of which were academic entities) to share resources to provide opportunities for school-aged children in the area. One such resource was the Stone Gym Youth Center, a recreation center for local young people. Nearly two years before the Columbia students took over Hamilton Hall to protest against gym construction in Morningside Park (among other things), MHI hosted an event at the center. Four hundred young people took advantage of the chance to meet famed actor Sydney Poitier at the event.[26] That there was a recreational center available to children had some implications regarding Columbia's decision to build a gymnasium in Morningside Park.

The university worked with area youth in different ways to expose them to college life and to provide potential opportunities for educational success. Starting in the 1960s, almost all of the eight Ivies created or made use of programs designed to cultivate black talent either in the summer or during the school year. Some, like the Negro Scholarship Service and Fund for Negro Students (NSSFNS), which got its start in 1947, were national organizations. Universities looked to the NSSFNS to recruit promising black students.[27] The NSSFNS's goal was to improve race relations by helping high-performing black students gain admissions to elite white institutions at the secondary and collegiate level. Many of the students who took advantage of the service came from the South to attend schools in the Northeast. Although the NSSFNS was available to the Ivies as a resource, the number of black students admitted to the elite schools was minimal until the 1960s. At Harvard, for instance, the number of black undergraduate students doubled in the late 1950s and early 1960s to 2 percent of the population.[28]

By the mid to late 1960s, several of the Ivies designed their own development programs. Their mission was to create a larger pool of black candidates for admission by improving the young people's academic skills while also instilling a sense of confidence in the secondary students. There was the A Better Chance and Foundation Years programs at Dartmouth; Project Double Discovery at Columbia; the Transition Year

Program at Brown; and the Princeton Cooperative Schools Program. Some programs were employed as direct pipelines to particular schools while others encouraged general college readiness and awareness.

In 1965, mostly white students in the Columbia Citizenship Council (CCC) and several university officials established Project Double Discovery.[29] Based on a proposal submitted by popular Columbia history professor James Shenton and students, initial funding ($157,000 in the form of a grant) for the program came from the U.S. Office of Economic Opportunity that Yale alumnus and presidential appointee Sargent Shriver headed.[30] Shriver, brother-in-law of Harvard alumni John and Robert Kennedy, founded government programs like the Peace Corps and Upward Bound, which became important in terms of higher education opportunities for black and first generation students. Columbia was one of the first seventeen universities and colleges to receive federal funding. On Columbia's campus, members of the predominantly white CCC, which included Barnard College students, acted as academic success coaches in the subjects of math and English for mostly black and Latino students from ghetto areas of New York City. The project selected participants who had potential but had underperformed in at least one class in high school. That factor differentiated them from those whom the NSSFNS selected.

Although remediation was primary in Project Double Discovery, another part of the program concerned the socialization of students. Many of the high school participants came from the adjacent neighborhoods of Morningside Heights and Harlem. For some of the students, Columbia and the Ivy League were unattainable in terms of cost, culture, and accessibility. The timing of the program's start is notable. As the university pushed forward with its effort to improve circumstances for urban youth with Project Double Discovery, Columbia was also forcing many black and Latino tenants out of their homes via an expansion program that started after World War II. The resentment that the expansion spurred among people in the surrounding neighborhoods bolstered the feeling of distance from the university that the young people had. So, through Project Double Discovery, the participants could experience the city from the point of view of Columbia affiliates. They attended plays, visited museums, learned chess, and engaged in other creative activities. The participants even had the opportunity to attend a service at Riverside

Baptist Church where the Rev. Martin Luther King Jr. preached in 1965. King was at the height of his popularity, as months earlier he and young black activists from the Student Nonviolent Coordinating Committee (SNCC) led a successful campaign in Selma, Alabama, that influenced the U.S. Congress to propose legislation for and eventually pass the Voting Rights Act of 1965.[31]

While Columbia attempted to fight the ravages of ghetto life with the Project Double Discovery program, the institution contributed to the stress of life for those in poor neighborhoods who confronted inadequate housing with high rents (housing they were at risk of losing) because of a powerful expansionist neighbor. With the program, the objective was to remove the young participants from the ghetto and place them in a different environment, but that did not resolve the problems of the challenged neighborhoods. Granted, funding the public schools and cultivating a legal economy in the urban centers, where so many black and Latino young people lived, was a formidable task that no one institution could complete. The university did what it could by drawing out some of the youth from their home environments.[32]

Project Double Discovery acted as bridge of sorts to expose students to the elite college environment. In an attempt to merge public and private interests, by 1968 the project received more than $300,000 in public funds (and more $30,000 from Columbia) annually. Public school teachers joined the Columbia and Barnard College students as instructors. By then, Double Discovery, under the auspices of Upward Bound, was transitioning into a year-round program for secondary students. The program recruited tenth graders who attended after-school and weekend courses along with the residential summer programs until they graduated. In the English courses, the curriculum included works by black authors to help the students culturally identify while addressing more of the technical issues of language.[33] Ten years after the program started, it boasted 762 participants who graduated high school. Of those, 652 enrolled in colleges and universities.[34] The university took pride in its involvement with Double Discovery, one of the largest, and apparently successful, Upward Bound programs in the nation.

In the Columbia University alumni magazine, *Columbia College Today*, participants regaled Double Discovery and what it did for them. One young lady, Clementine Warren, who once lived in Harlem, said that her participation in Double Discovery helped to evolve her thinking about the future. Before enrolling in the program, she thought she would graduate high school to become a factory worker, but after joining she decided she wanted to be a writer to depict the people she best knew and "how they are striving to live."[35] In another article, Mike (no last name indicated) had the opportunity to explore his interests in the program. "This summer I learned something about computers. I'm going to get to college and learn all about the field," he proclaimed. Other students reported that during the summer program they read more books than they ever had. Project Double Discovery participant Ron Johnson noted that he attended a high school that was known for drugs and that was essentially "uninspiring." He claimed that his mother's constant encouragement and the summers he spent honing his study skills in science and other fields in Project Double Discovery turned his "world right side up."[36] It appeared that Project Double Discovery was paying dividends. In 1968, Carlos Sanabria and Tony Ferreria, who were in the first class of 160 participants, enrolled at Columbia University as students.[37] Ron Johnson eventually graduated from Columbia University in 1976.

Another participant, who graduated from John Jay College of Criminal Justice, explained that because of Double Discovery, he was no longer "wild and loud," and learned that he could be "seen and heard without acting like a child." That the Ivy League summer program helped to refine the student is an interesting notion. Officials at the institutions referred to the students as disadvantaged and poor. "Culturally deprived" was another phrase that was part of the parlance of the period. The young people who participated did not want to be known by those terms and did not always feel culturally deprived. The culture with which they were most familiar happened to be different from that of the majority of instructors and college students. According to scholars like psychologist Robert L. Williams, who developed the Black Intelligence Test of Cultural Homogeneity-100 (B.I.T.C.H.-100) test in 1972, pointed out the inability of the standard IQ test to assess the intelligence of the majority of black people. Williams showed that the cultural values most celebrated by those in the Ivy League and other elite white institutions were not necessarily indicative of intelligence but rather environment.[38] Taking Williams's assertions into account, if the black and brown participants were deficient culturally, then so too were the white Ivy League students who sought to tutor children in the ghettoes.

Economically, the participants undoubtedly came from low-income families and were in need of remediation regarding their academic work. Their "disadvantage," however, proved to be advantageous to those mostly white college students who had the opportunity to apply the theories they learned in their education, social work, sociology, and urban issues classes when interacting with the participants. Further, the mostly white students could safely learn firsthand the effects of urban neglect in the city. The partial objective for the program was for the student-counselors to "benefit from the encounter."[39] Essentially, the mostly white counselors became better citizens by spending time with poor black and brown children. Incidentally, the college students received $600 plus room and board for the eight weeks they worked in the summer and participants received a weekly stipend of $10. Graduates of Project Double Discovery took part in an interview with the Columbia University admissions office and, upon completing the program, they were guaranteed admission to one of the colleges in the City University system (including community colleges).[40]

The participants in the summer programs were well aware of the circumstances in which they lived and did not need reminders. Samantha Carter wrote a poem entitled "Harlem" for a Project Double Discovery publication.[41] Throughout the poem she asked her iconic but withered neighborhood: "Why won't you change?" She described Harlem as swinging and filthy and sweet and ugly. She portrayed the people of the neighborhood as hungry, melancholy, black, and beautiful. In the face of prostitution, drugs, and depression, she asked why Harlem would not change. The answer to her question was larger than the enclave itself. It involved the federal, state, and municipal governments and economies. It also involved neglect and underinvestment and impediments to opportunity.

In the late 1960s, as the university intensified its recruitment of black students, it offered the new students summer work as Project Double Discovery counselors. By that time, Columbia University had enough black students to create a chapter of the black Greek-letter organization Omega Psi Phi. Several members of the fraternity became counselors in the program, which altered its relational dynamics. Bill Sales, who was not a member of the black fraternity but was a counselor, explained that he was glad that Project Double Discovery existed, but he had some reservations about it. Sales saw the project as charity, which was not necessarily good. He thought of charity as a form of slavery in which "the giver has no respect for the receiver" and the receivers "begin to hate the giver."[42] Charity, in the end, ruined the receiver, he explained in a Project Double Discovery publication. The program, he believed, was not "planned because people felt sorry" for the youth participants but rather "for their [Columbia affiliates'] own good." Sales, who had graduated from the University of Pennsylvania in 1964 and was a graduate student at Columbia from 1965 to 1969, believed the program was part of the history of white liberals potentially causing further harm to black people by doing good works in their own eyes.

There was some tension between the new black counselors and the veteran white counselors. The mostly white counselors, who were often only a couple of years older than the participants, tried too hard to "out cool" the participants rather than counseling them, some students complained.[43] For the counselors in the early years of Project Double Discovery, relating to the participants was not always easy. Mark Naison, who graduated from Columbia in 1969, was critically aware of his whiteness.[44] He used basketball and athletics, however, as a way to draw out some similarity of interests with the participants. He also had the advantage of having a black girlfriend, who helped him to recognize context clues. Some participants claimed that their counselors seemed to do as little as possible with the participants in the program. Those complaints were not endemic, but for the participants who observed the behavior, the criticisms were valid. Many of the black counselors kept to themselves, choosing to either spend time with the participants or with each other. The program that started as an altruistic effort at integration was reflecting the trends in society of racial segregation and intentional self-separation. But despite their race and cultural differences, the counselors were meaningful in the lives of the program participants.

At the same time that Columbia was coordinating its Project Double Discovery, university representatives still attended MHI meetings to exchange ideas on best practices regarding expansion and how to address pushback from the residents who lost homes to institutional progress. The mood in neighborhoods had shifted along with the movement for black freedom and liberation that had gained steam across the country. When a member of MHI bought residential buildings and began displacing residents, community activists voiced concerns. By 1967, the coalition had established a five-year prospectus on expansion in the neighborhood. In a draft of a report given in a January meeting, MHI revealed that the Bank Street College, whose faculty was helping to create the national Head Start program, sought to expand in Morningside Heights to the west of Columbia on Riverside Drive and 112th Street. That project was set to displace residents. So too was the dormitory that Barnard College was building east of Columbia on 121st Street and Amsterdam Avenue. Barnard also, to meet enrollment needs, was converting an apartment building into a dormitory for students on 116th Street.[45] Teachers College sought to acquire the area between 121st and 122nd Streets and Broadway and Amsterdam Avenues to expand. Jewish Theological Seminary had plans to greatly increase its faculty and student body in a twenty-year period. To do so, it chose the area between 122nd and 123rd Streets, from Broadway to Amsterdam Avenue, to "develop." Then, the Interchuch Center intended to develop 150,000 square feet of the location between 119th Street, Riverside Drive, and Claremont Avenue. The acquisition and construction phase for these institutional plans was set to take place within five years of the report. That meant that the demographics, look, and culture of Morningside Heights was going to change rapidly. Although the public was not wholly aware of the details of the expansion plans, homeowners and renters alike understood what it meant to be essentially evicted from their domiciles.

Columbia, of all the MHI institutions, had always maintained the most ambitious expansion program. The January 1967 MHI report explained that "in order to provide the physical facilities required in the addition of 3,800 students . . . with the resultant per annum increase of 700 employees and a $2 million payroll, Columbia must develop a $144 million construction program."[46] With a growing university, officials believed there was nowhere to go but outward. Acquiring more property in an area with such rigid confines greatly added to that property's value. The prospect of owning more land was then good for the institution but threatening to the residents in the buildings that the school had to commandeer. Columbia, according to the report, intended to "purchase any property at a reasonable price in the Morningside Heights Core Area."

The laws of capitalism promoted and encouraged Columbia's aggressive approach to ownership in neighborhood; indeed, there was nothing legally to stop the institution. There were, however, the distraught residents and citizens who had to live with the university's plans upon implementation.

Columbia concentrated on the blocks between Broadway and Amsterdam Avenue from 111th Street to 114th Street; east of Amsterdam from 115th to 116th Street; and, on 117th Street along Morningside Drive. There were also plans for west of Broadway. The immediate outward expansion caused consternation among the people living around the university, but one of Columbia's plans in 1967 included "the piers or Manhattanville West Area," which was farther north and west of the Morningside Heights area. The report indicated that within five to fifteen years the university would begin acquisitioning land and buildings to create an "an additional 3,000 dwelling units" available mostly to Columbia affiliates. That area of development would be the root of controversy for decades to come.

Regarding the dwelling units that Columbia already owned and was purchasing in the late 1960s, university faculty, staff, and personnel only occupied 33 percent. Non-affiliates of the university lived in the other two-thirds of the units. That meant that other than financial, the university did not have any relationship with the majority of its tenants. The lack of a relationship became clear when the relocation phase took place. According to the "Preliminary Relocation and Institutional Occupancy Estimates" section of the 1967 report, Columbia owned hundreds of traditional dwelling and single-room occupancy units (SROs). This set the university apart from many of the other institutional members of MHI that did not own anywhere near as many housing units.[47] Columbia had become one of the New York City's largest landlords.

Some tenants had problems with the university as a landlord. Over a ten-year period, Columbia moved 10,000 people out of their homes. It relocated nearly 2,400 people, most of whom lived in SROs.[48] To make use of the buildings that the university purchased with the assistance of urban renewal funds and accommodating redevelopment policies, Columbia needed to clear out the residences. There was no city in the nation where it was easy to remove people from their homes, but doing so in Manhattan made for especially difficult and sometimes traumatic situations. Moving to new areas required immediate access to capital, which many working class and poor residents did not have. To assist with that, the university provided relocation funds between $450 and $750 for the forced move, which was commensurate with the city's Rent and Rehabilitation Commission guidelines for private institutions. In that particular housing market, however, the moving stipend was often not sufficient to find similar living arrangements for those who dwelled in spacious rent-controlled apartments. In spite of the fact that Columbia owned the apartments, tenants did not always want to leave their homes. In the years leading up to the campus rebellion, that meant that the university took measures to evict tenants against their will.

By 1968, tenants gained allies in responding to Columbia as a landlord. The members of the racially integrated university chapter of CORE had been working with the community throughout the decade.[49] As early as 1965, the organization attempted to educate its peers about the aggressive moves Columbia was making in the nearby neighborhoods. The student newspaper reported on a panel titled "Urban Renewal: The Community and the Student," that CORE held on campus.[50] Local politician Mary Cox, district leader of the Thirteenth Assembly District, and housing activist Mary Pierce of the Bryn Mawr Tenants Association as well as former director of the Office of Neighborhood Services at Columbia attempted to provide context concerning the effects of institutional expansion.

Along with CORE, the CCC sounded the alarm about expansion. By 1967, in the minds of some, the gymnasium in Morningside Park was becoming a symbol of Columbia's willingness to usurp land at will. The CCC made its opposition to the gym known by releasing a statement, explaining that the university should end its plans to build if for no other reason than to head off "a dangerous clash between Columbia and West Harlem residents."[51] The CCC emphasized that "park land should be sacrosanct" and suggested that the university had been delaying construction "in hopes that all possible community resistance would exhaust itself." If that was the rationale for university planners, then they could not have been more wrong. A likely explanation for the gym, which had been proposed in 1958, was fundraising. By the time of the article, the university had millions of dollars invested in the project. The students and community members were concerned that urban renewal policies had allowed the university to create a monopoly on park land and residential space in the area.

In the Students' Afro-American Society (SAS), the leadership was becoming more militant. What started in the mid-1960s as a group that encouraged the small number of black students to meet and discuss mutual issues evolved into an activist organization by the late 1960s. Like students at other institutions, the society pressed school officials to add Black Studies to the curriculum, but there were also issues particular to Columbia's black students. For instance, black students, particularly men, were constantly asked to produce proof of identification on campus. This was humiliating and annoying when the black students did not see their white peers having to undergo the same scrutiny. There was also a controversy involving the black Greek-letter organization Omega Psi Phi Fraternity, Inc., which had just received a charter at Columbia in the fall of 1968. Perhaps misunderstanding the rituals and culture of black fraternity life, the student newspaper printed an article with demeaning images that showed the drawings of the fraternity men in chains and diminutive postures. Upset about the depiction, fraternity members rallied other black men at Columbia and black women from Barnard College to collect as many of the copies of the issue as possible. Barnard student Thulani Davis remembered that once collected, the students burned the issues in front of the office of the *Daily Spectator*, causing a controversy on campus.[52] Although controversial, the students let it be known that they would not tolerate the paper portraying black people in an undignified manner.

In an effort to be useful to the black community, SAS members offered their support in opposition of the gym and expansion. That was after, it claimed in a statement, the members attempted to help heal relations between the university and its black neighbors. "Black people have repeatedly made suggestions designed to enable the university to more successfully [relate] to black people," the statement read.[53] Because of that, SAS explained that if the university did not accede to the demands of the community to cease gym construction, there would likely be "racial animosity and violence." SAS made that statement on April 8, 1968, four days after university students and officials looked down into Harlem to watch white-owned businesses burn when residents received news of Martin Luther King Jr.'s assassination.

King's death radicalized black students at Columbia and elsewhere. The young learners understood that the beloved leader's peaceful approach to fighting racial bigotry did not work to spare his life. At that moment, for many of them, using love to persuade the enemies of freedom was no longer an option. With that in mind, the members of SAS met with community members in a rally on April 20, where the students and neighborhood activists voiced their plans to stop the gym regardless of the university's plans. Members of the Harlem chapter of CORE, as well as opponents of Columbia's acquisition of Harlem Hospital, joined students on 125th Street and Seventh Avenue. The coalition of students, white and black, with community members was powerful.

When people from and around the neighborhood questioned whether ending the gym project was a good idea, there was a response. Even though having new facilities for the children could be good, one observer noted: "no matter how much fun a youngster might get out of a good sports facility, it isn't worth sending them in the back door of a segregated gym."[54] The statement referred to the fact that, in the designs of the gym, the community entrance was in the basement of the structure, while Columbia affiliates used a different entrance on a different level. Nonuniversity patrons would have been able to use two floors of the facility while an additional eight floors were open to those from the university. The actual floor space allotted to the community part of the gymnasium came to 15 percent while the university portion was 85 percent. Because of these disparities, some community members called the potential edifice Gym Crow. In a moment when black people sought to gain control of the neighborhoods where they lived and the policies that affected them, Columbia represented a white institution that evicted tenants, displaced residents, and had a private police force in the park that arrested black youth regularly. Throughout Harlem and the nation, organizations like the Black Panthers, the Revolutionary Action Movement, the Black United Front, SNCC, and CORE challenged the power of white institutions and demanded power of their own. The university became part of that challenge.

The mostly white SDS chapter at Columbia, led in part by junior Mark Rudd from New Jersey, had worked throughout the school year to radicalize white students on issues of race and the war. In spite of the intense planning the members did and the demonstrations they held, the SDS was largely marginalized as a fringe organization on campus. SDS members argued that apathy regarding politics and racism afflicted Columbia students and that the students needed to be jolted into reality. There was also a contingent in the SDS that wanted to see more revolutionary action. Rudd had visited Cuba that March and believed that perhaps the struggles on campus could be part of a revolution. "Cuba seemed to me a society inspired by a new morality . . . I wandered around Havana in a euphoric haze . . . Cuba's socialism was the moral and political wave of the future. I was stoned on socialism,"[55] he claimed. Rudd could not wait to return to New York and challenge the social status quo via the SDS. The SDS leadership believed that the issue of the gymnasium and university expansion could move the apathetic student body. With that, nearly three weeks after King's death, the SDS organized a rally in the center of Columbia's campus.

On April 23, a diverse group arrived at the sundial on the Columbia campus that included black students from SAS, SDS leaders and followers, student proponents of gym construction who were frustrated with the conditions at the old gym, and curious onlookers. SAS and SDS members had not collaborated much before the rally. Both groups represented what student athletes and others considered to be radical elements on campus.

History graduate student Bill Sales from Philadelphia was a leader in the SAS and he, along with Rudd, captured the attention of the several hundred students present. Sales, who had been active with the Revolutionary Action Movement while an undergraduate student at the University of Pennsylvania, was part of the more militant wing of the SAS. He attempted to tie the world revolutions into what was happening at his university during the fall of 1967 and spring of 1968 when Columbia student activism seemed to epitomize the broader currents at play across American campuses. White student Hilton Obenzinger, who was not a member of the SDS but was sympathetic to its causes, remembered Sales telling the crowd of students that when "you strike a blow at the gym, you strike a blow for the Vietnamese people. You strike a blow at Low Library [where the administration was housed] and you strike a blow for the freedom fighters in Angola, Mozambique, and South Africa."[56] Black students saw themselves as being part of the long continuum of the black freedom movement that featured various approaches

Figure 5.1. Columbia Students Protesting. As part of the famous 1968 student rebellion, Columbia University members of the Students' Afro-American Society protest the institution's expansion into Harlem and Morningside Heights in New York City. Courtesy of Richard Howard.

to struggle: revolution, rebellion, and resistance. Sales, who in addition to checking the university's ambition to build a gymnasium in nearby Morningside Park, also advocated the need to bring Black Studies to Columbia, later acknowledged: "we [SAS leadership] knew this was not the revolution, per se, but that it was part of an ongoing struggle to improve the lives of black students and black people in general."[57] In that vein, the SAS coalesced with not just the neighboring black community but with the mostly white SDS to stop the construction of the new gym.

After an unsuccessful attempt to take over the administration building, some of the students demonstrated at the gym construction site in Morningside Park. Earlier in the year, mostly black community members had staged dramatic protests that included standing down bulldozers and being arrested. When the students arrived, they too dramatized the moment by tearing away a cyclone fence around the site. One white student engaged in a physical altercation with the police. Sales, who had been training in the martial arts, attempted to prevent an officer from physically handling a fellow activist. After the action in the park, the students, high on adrenaline, headed back to campus. There, Rudd and the other leaders of the rally regrouped and led the students in a takeover of Hamilton Hall, a classroom building and home to the office of the acting dean of Columbia's college of arts and sciences, Henry S. Coleman. Hundreds of students poured into Hamilton with the goal of ending gym construction and ceasing the university's ties to the war through the Institute for Defense Analyses (IDA). University president Grayson Kirk represented Columbia as a member of the IDA, which was a non-profit corporation that sought to marry scientific research with national defense. Leaders of elite and flagship universities throughout the nation were members as well.

Before that could happen, the students needed to figure out how to proceed in the building. Coleman, who had at one point been charged with diversifying the student body when he headed the undergraduate admissions office, returned to the building to find the students waiting for him. Knowing that the students had taken over Hamilton, he chose to enter his office anyway to be with his staff. At that point there seemed to be no threat of violence but rather scores of curious students eager to see what would come next. While inside, SDS and SAS leadership along with other campus leaders met to discuss the demands of the university and how to move forward with the action. In addition to cessation of construction on the gym and of ties to the IDA, the students called for amnesty for previous student demonstrations and for the current action. When the SDS proposed that the action become a sit-in, which would allow people to enter and leave the building at will, SAS leadership demurred. Realizing that the entrance of the dean added an increased element of danger to the situation, the black student leaders proposed that the hall be secured and barricaded with little access in or out of the building.

The integrated group agreed on a barricade and decided to stay until the university met its demands. While inside, black community members clashed with white activists over tactics and strategies. Overnight, the trajectory of the protest changed. In a midnight meeting with Rudd and SDS leadership, SAS leaders explained that it would be best if black students occupied the building solely. Upset with the change of plans, but wanting to support the solidarity of black students with the Harlem community, the white demonstrators left with the mission of carrying on the protest with a successful takeover of the administration building.

By mid-morning the demonstrators who had left Hamilton, commandeered four other buildings. They were Low Memorial Library
(the administration building), Fayerweather Hall, Mathematics Hall,
and Philosophy Hall. In each building the atmosphere was different. In
Low, where Rudd stayed, students entered the president's office, reading his papers and drinking his liquor. In Fayerweather, students held
a sit-in. Tom Hayden, author of the famous Port Huron statement and
a seasoned activist from Newark, strategized with the young agitators.
Loose paper and other materials littered the floor in Philosophy Hall.
Effectively, student demonstrators had boldly captured the campus. Not
being able to use five buildings caused disruption in the lives of students, staff, faculty, and administrators. To achieve peace and resume
operations, the administration needed the student activists to leave. A
major concern for Grayson Kirk and his administration, however, was
that black demonstrators alone occupied Hamilton.

In an obvious show of Black Power, the students in Hamilton tightly
controlled the building. They let in allies from Harlem as well as national figures. From Harlem, community leaders like Victor Solomon
of CORE, Sam Anderson of the Revolutionary Action Movement and
the New York Black Panthers, and Charles 37x of the Mau Maus visited.
Some community members brought food and supplies. Community
protesters marched with signs indicting the university and supporting
the students on the sidewalks near the entrances of the university. Hoping to keep the situation calm, city and state officials like State Assem-
blyman Basil Paterson and New York Human Rights Commissioner
William Booth arrived to try to help with negotiations. The administration asked alumnus and nationally renowned psychologist Kenneth
Clark to assist. Incidentally, Clark's son, Hilton, established the SAS at
Columbia in 1964, which was ten years after his father helped win the
Brown v. Board of Education decision. The executive director of the National Urban League, Whitney Young, also spoke with the young people
in Hamilton.

Perhaps the visitors who stood out most to onlookers were the tall
and lean Stokely Carmichael, former leader of the SNCC and minister
in the Black Panther Party for Self Defense, and H. Rap Brown, chairman of the SNCC, who had also been associated with the Panthers. Each
leader was known for his charisma, passion, and rhetoric. Both men had

been arrested while freedom fighting, and both were the subjects of FBI surveillance even while they arrived to support the black students at Columbia. Brown had been charged with inciting a riot in Cambridge, Maryland, and Carmichael was accused of the same in Washington, D.C. Mayor John Lindsay, after witnessing the destruction of the uprising in Harlem weeks earlier, instructed the university president not to call the police to remove the students—particularly the black demonstrators. The mayor sent labor negotiator Theodore Kheel to discuss the possibilities of the black students leaving. All the while, students in Hamilton and the other buildings anxiously strategized ways to address their potential confrontation with police.

After a week of occupation, on April 30 Kirk shut off the power to the buildings and called for the New York City police to remove the students. Representatives of the NAACP stood outside of Hamilton to ensure that the police did not brutalize black student activists when making arrests. Subsequently, the black activists allowed themselves to be arrested without resisting; they had proven their point.

In the other buildings, the police and demonstrators met each other in violence. As Columbia is in New York, the media capital of the world, scenes of police aggressively and brutally arresting students went out in the media. Although some students resisted, the force of the police was undeniable. The New York City police officers seemed to live up to their reputations. In all, police arrested more than 700 people on campus and took them to central booking at 100 Centre Street.

The images of swinging batons and blood were enough to move the sympathies of liberal and moderate students alike. They also caught the attention of community members who gained a new respect for students. The coalition that opposed the gym was growing and momentum had swung in favor of the activists. After another violent clash between police and students in a demonstration in early May, the students launched a strike that lasted six weeks. The university was injured.

Grayson Kirk, among other university officials, worried greatly that the nationally famous protest that took place on campus would dissuade donor and alumni gifts. He appealed to them in June, in "A Message to Alumni, Parents, and Other Friends of Columbia."[58] Messages of that nature from university presidents had become obligatory during the period. Kirk, wanting to remain in communication with those who he believed cared most about Columbia, claimed to offer them a "full and objective account" of what occurred. He began his accounting of the events by explaining that the SAS and SDS had held Dean Coleman hostage for twenty-four hours. (By his own remembrance and that of the student activists, Coleman chose to stay in his office, so he was not technically a hostage.) Kirk's statement explained that when confronted with the choice between granting amnesty to students for their "illegal acts" or calling in the city police, the situation forced him to choose the latter. His administration did not want to reward the students for their behavior.

Kirk had come to the same conclusion in May when students and community members again took over buildings. SDS members and other activists protesting university expansion occupied an apartment building. On campus, students took over Hamilton Hall again to protest the university's disciplinary proceedings. When police arrived to arrest the activists, more violence erupted with students and others breaking windows and doors in the building. The president emphasized in his message that he had told the students they would be reprimanded and disciplined for their acts of rebellion. The tone of law and order was stern, and Kirk assured the readers that the university policies surrounding demonstrations had been enforced.

Befuddled by the pushback against the gymnasium, Kirk emphasized how much money the university invested and the good Columbia was doing for the community. The school spent a quarter of a million dollars to reclaim the land in the park and create softball fields and then poured more money into the Columbia-community athletic program that, he noted, kept 2,500 youth off the streets of Harlem during the "hot summer months."[59] The gym that he proposed to then Parks Commissioner Robert Moses was to be a university and community collaboration, Kirk explained in his "objective" message. He did not, however, mention that the initial designs for the gym did not include accommodations for the non-Columbia community and that upon discovering this fact, community representatives insisted that the private school share the public space—no matter how unwanted and dangerous it was to him and Moses. Troublemakers, including a new parks commissioner and people opposed to the physical expansion of the university, had mounted a unified assault on the gym project and the university in general, the message indicated. Kirk claimed that they had ruined the opportunity for safety and health that the university was offering to the neighborhood children. Kirk seemed inconsolable about the idea that the private entity could not take over public land in spite of the great sums of money and influence the school wielded. He had not accounted for the opposition from civil rights, Black Power, student power, and environmentalist movements that came together in the late 1960s.

"Our struggle has a special relevance to the future of private institutions of higher education," Kirk aptly surmised.[60] It was true that the university's peer institutions were observing Columbia's reactions to the upheaval. Perhaps no other student protest in 1968 was as influential. Around the world, student activists shouted "Two, three, many Columbias!" That was not comforting for university presidents. At Columbia, Kirk concluded that those who were intent on destroying the integrity of the university must not be permitted to prevail. Furthermore, there were many in the majority who did not condone the agitators' acts of disruption and that many would "protect and preserve the kind of Columbia you have known." Perhaps not all of the "you" to whom Kirk referred wanted the university to remain the same institution that had admitted so few black students and hired so few black people. It was also possible that some of the readers would not agree with the aggressive plan of expansion that the school undertook. The student and community activists who protested insisted that, in contradiction to the president's portrayal, they actually sought to preserve the integrity of the elite institution. No matter, Kirk asserted, "If there should be turmoil in the months ahead, it will be dealt with firmly."

As is the case with black uprisings throughout history, there are those who critique the approach the activists took to achieve freedom. Members of the Columbia University Law School in a published statement chastised the students for what the professors and administrators characterized as bullying.[61] Extolling the virtues of civil disobedience, the law school affiliates were "confident that American students will themselves recognize the unwisdom of attempting to gain goals by illegal force." Until community members and students checked Columbia in 1968, the university was able to gain most of its expansion goals by way of capitalism and legal force. The effects of nonviolent legal force and violent force seemed to be similar in the great disruption of life that took place.

The teachers and administrators stated that "no problem that confronts Columbia or other American universities is beyond the capabilities of men who use the tools education has given them." Educated men, using those tools, partially created the circumstances of rebellion. The tools of education allowed men like David Rockefeller, Robert Moses, Frank Fackenthal, and many others to extirpate blocks to further advance the cause of education. It is questionable whether the "unyieldingly lawless intruders" (as they were described by the law school officials) who took over buildings and marched through campus were not nearly as destructive as the law abiding members of MHI, who removed poor people from their homes. One law school professor, Michael Sovern, did not sign the statement because of his commitment on an upper level committee that involved the demonstrations. Sovern, incidentally, became the seventeenth president of the university.

Columbia's position on gym construction and expansion was unsustainable in the tense historical moment. The university could have moved forward with the project, but it would have cost the institution greatly to do so. Consequently, Columbia announced that it was suspending construction and within a year the university abandoned Morningside Park as a site for the gym. The university also took a different approach to expansion, housing, and tenant relations.

Kirk resigned within months of the rebellion and Andrew W. Cordier succeeded him as president. Before coming to Columbia, Cordier, like his predecessor, was an advisor to the U.S. Department of State and helped to organize the United Nations. He also played a role in arbitrating the Congo Crisis. Seeking to cool matters a year after the rebellion on Morningside Heights, he created a new policy that no one would be evicted from university-owned apartments except for those who failed to pay rent. If tenants in the future were to fall victim to university expansion, Columbia would ensure that proper "staging"—the arrangement of adequate and sufficient housing at a similar price—would be covered. It took protest and demonstrations to help the university make the move toward justice with respect to housing.[62]

In a revelatory 1969 announcement, Cordier explained that the university was not going in the direction that had been set in 1963, which involved doing away with SRO buildings and aggressive outward expansion. The 1963 directive, according to Cordier's announcement, was to "guard against either public or SRO housing between 110th and 123rd streets." The Ivy institution was trying financially and geographically to shut out the poor people who lived in public housing and SROs. Doing so would protect the university. The new plan, Cordier said, was to engage in no new construction without first "exhausting all capacity to use existing ground on the present campus."[63] By 1969, non-Columbia affiliates occupied nearly two-thirds of university-administered apartments. Faculty families and graduate students represented most of the other occupants.

When Columbia needed to reconsider its expansion and construction plans, it contracted world-renowned architect I. M. Pei. The architect design expert had attended the University of Pennsylvania for a short period before transferring to the Massachusetts Institute of Technology, where he completed his undergraduate degree. He also earned a degree from Harvard University's Graduate School of Design. During the postwar era, Pei quickly became one of the most influential urban designers in the world. U.S. President Lyndon Johnson appointed him to the National Council on Humanities and he was a member of New York City Mayor John Lindsay's Task Force for Urban Design and the city's design council. Columbia could afford to employ him in its quest to re-envision its campus's physical development projects. The activism of students and community members in the late 1960s forced university officials to exert more effort looking inward for growth. Pei believed that Columbia was "in many respects a microcosm of the city."[64] Just as a city had the responsibility to serve the needs of the people, Columbia, Pei said, had an obligation to address the needs of Columbia affiliates. He also asserted that the university would do well to consider the needs and opinions of those in the surrounding community when planning. Creating a design that minimized "dislocation," he predicted, could lead to an "environment that enhances the quality of life for all." The interim university president, Andrew Cordier, concurred, not wanting the university to become a "colossus," taking up every inch of space in the neighborhood.[65] In spite of Cordier's desires, Pei's designs never materialized.

When the coalition of students and community members brought their issues to the university, they faced a powerful private institution with a great deal of political influence. The confrontations that took place at Columbia pointed up the conflict over institutional power and the courageous collective will of powerless individuals. When the disenfranchised coalesced with young people who believed they were acting on behalf of the Civil Rights Movement and Black Power Movement, the university experienced trauma. As a result, Columbia officials rethought and re-envisioned what growth should look like and what role the university played in its neighborhood.

6

There Goes the Neighborhood

Penn's Postwar Expansion Project

For decades, these institutions have flexed their huge muscles of property ownership and pushed their way into the surrounding areas.
—Judith Rodin

These damn colleges . . . just keep tearing down homes and putting black people out in the street.
—Marvin Alsion, 1969

At nearly the same time that the Columbia crisis unfurled, the University of Pennsylvania endured similar trials in Philadelphia. In the 1960s, Penn sought to be useful to the world by creating a science research center near campus. During the period, the University City Science Center became a lightning rod of conflict. If creating a place that focused on research that could benefit the military industrial complex to which General and then U.S. President Dwight Eisenhower (also former president of Columbia University) referred in the 1950s was not controversial enough, there was the issue of Penn's reputation for displacing poor and working class black residents. Although black people had lived in Philadelphia since the Revolutionary War era, the black population skyrocketed during the first and second Great Migrations that pulled black laborers from the American South to work northern industrial jobs. As scholars have crucially pointed out, when they arrived, many white people, along with a great deal of tax revenue and civil services, fled the city. As the Cold War would have it, universities like Penn applied for and received government funding for research and resources that could benefit the nation in its time of need. In return for research, Penn received funding for the science center and the university hospital. Penn's presence was vast; the university held 300 acres in the city.

Achieving a healthy reciprocal relationship between a university and the surrounding neighborhoods has proven to be difficult if not elusive for institutions like Columbia and Penn. Regarding Penn and its most recent revitalization efforts, scholar Harvey Etienne has noted that "a critical challenge . . . is accessible and mutually agreeable goals, directions, and metrics of progress and impacts."[1] In terms of a university's attempts to improve the neighborhoods it occupies, not all residents' opinions or points of view carry the same amount of weight as those who represent the university. As Etienne observed, "If resource-rich institutions such as Penn are interested in urban revitalization for their own 'enlightened self-interest,' city planners are wise to respond by clearing hurdles."[2] Society expects a great deal from universities like Penn, Columbia, and Harvard because society gives so much to those institutions with respect to tax exemptions and subsidies, Etienne explained. Society does so in exchange for the creation of jobs and knowledge that should ostensibly benefit the whole. These knowledge factories attract retail economy, which may indirectly push people who do not attend or work for the university out of their homes either by eminent domain or extreme spikes in the cost of living and rent. Perhaps the most poignant question Etienne posed was: "for whom [are] urban places rehabilitated and by what methods?"[3]

Judith Rodin, who was president of Penn from 1994 to 2004 tackled similar issues in her book, *The University and Urban Revival.* She explained the need for Penn to rethink its approach to the university's urban presence.[4] Rodin's position regarding Penn is similar to that taken by the other urban Ivies regarding their place in city neighborhoods. Such reflection occurred at Penn after the removal of the Mantua "Black Bottom" neighborhood and the creation of the new "University City" neighborhood in West Philadelphia.[5] In the late 1960s, Mantua was virtually all black and mostly working class with a sizable segment of poverty-stricken inhabitants. Mantua was not economically thriving at the time, but it was culturally rich in the eyes of the residents.

Institutions of higher education in cities have undoubtedly provided services and employment to surrounding neighborhoods, the nation, and the world. The U.S. government turned to several Ivy institutions during World War II and the Cold War to assist with research that informed national defense and public policy.[6] Ivy institutions like Columbia played their part in national defense by allowing research for top-secret programs such as the Manhattan Project. So too did Penn, which had contracts with the U.S. Air Force and whose faculty researched biological and chemical weaponry. The period after the war observed the rise of what University of California at Berkeley president Clark Kerr referred to as the "multiversities" that served multiple roles in society. Some of the roles of played by postwar universities involved educating students (and providing a space for young people to safely mature), researching for national defense, and providing health care in their cities.

The postwar West Philadelphia that historian Matthew Countryman described represented struggle for black people. Deindustrialization challenged the job market while residential segregation plagued neighborhoods and schools. Not unlike other black residents in American cities, black Philadelphians shared a tense relationship with law enforcement. Frank Rizzo, who from the 1950s to the 1970s led Philadelphia's police department and eventually took the reins as mayor, became a symbolic representative of what many black residents viewed as institutional racism. As captain of the police force in the 1950s and 1960s, Rizzo was notorious. Countryman noted that because of "his harassment of black-owned bars and private clubs . . . Rizzo's reputation for racism in the black community grew."[7] Typically the historical narrative has reserved portrayals of abusive, racist law enforcement officials for the likes of southerners Theophilus Eugene "Bull" Connor of Birmingham and Jim Clark of Selma, but figures such as Rizzo illustrate the fact that black citizens faced similar struggles for freedom in the North as they did in the South.[8] Racism was not regionally reserved but was instead widespread throughout the nation—even in the city where American liberty began.

As black residents battled government institutions and agents, they simultaneously pushed back private entities as well. During the period, Penn set about growing its campus and tamping down the "blight" in neighborhoods that surrounded the university. Former president Judith Rodin wrote, "as early as 1948, [Penn's] trustees approved a twenty-year master plan . . . that would ultimately extend the campus west of 40th

Street" in order to create a closed-off campus that allowed pedestrian rather than motor vehicle traffic.[9] That meant closing streets and acquiring more property. Rodin suggested that the new campus and buildings that sprouted in the two decades after the plan's submission presented a "fortresslike appearance to passersby." One might have wondered what the fortress was protecting.

Sydney Martin, who chaired the architecture subcommittee of the larger Trustees Committee on Physical Development, submitted a report for expanding the campus in 1948 that recommended the rehabilitation of surrounding spaces for Penn affiliates. More specifically, increased student housing to accommodate the veterans and a larger number of students enrolling in the university after the war provided the impetus for Penn's desire to clear the area and construct new buildings for campus housing.[10] According to that plan, the campus would stretch east to west from Thirty-Second to Fortieth Street and north to south from Walnut to Spruce Street. Implementing the plan would have required the university to close streets and knock down existing housing structures. The trustees made the development plan part of the university's fundraising program.

The university's development design happened to coincide conveniently with the passage of the American Housing Act of 1949, which was the progenitor of what would be termed "urban renewal."[11] Ostensibly, politicians meant for the act to revitalize cities by encouraging state and municipal collaboration with private entities to create viable and affordable residential housing. To receive funds and subsidies, cities needed to submit redevelopment designs indicating the current use and state of the neighborhoods they wanted to revitalize. Additionally, the cities needed to outline the populations that would be affected by property clearance and reconstruction. Aware that there might be some resistance to the Penn plan, university and city officials anticipated the use of eminent domain, which would allow the government to usurp private properties for the larger public good. The area was overcrowded with low-income people living in row houses where they rented individual rooms and shared bathrooms. The act intended to create public housing that allowed families to live safely. Penn, with the assistance of government subsidies and eminent domain, not to mention the $13.5 million in the fundraising campaign between 1948 and 1953, moved forward with its development.[12]

Scholar John Mollenkopf, in *The Contested City*, pointed out the pro-growth coalition that came together in the postwar era. Using the New Deal as a springboard, Mollenkopf explains that the pro-growth alliance consisted of political, public, and private interests. Politically, the Democratic Party in large urban areas often led the way in terms of development. And urban development, according to Mollenkopf, often favored corporations, banks merchants, and the construction trades. This meant that smaller businesses and individual property owners did not hold as much sway in the decision-making process. The federal government provided base funds to local municipalities while "political" and private entrepreneurs filled the economic gaps. This left political officials, who could claim victory in their cities' development, beholden to private investors. Equally, private interests became staunch political supporters of the politicians who were best able to make federal dollars available.[13]

Regarding the decisions about the future of these neighborhoods, few if any black people participated. Gaylord Harnwell, who had been the chairman of Penn's physics department, assumed the presidency of the university in 1953. Upon taking his post as president, he commented on the need to foster better relations with the neighborhood into which the university extended itself. Harnwell and the admissions officials knew that with the spike in birthrates during and after the war, the population of Penn would balloon in the oncoming decade. Faced with the prospect of denying students the opportunity of a Penn education or of expanding to allow for more students, the new president chose to continue implementing the physical growth plan. Tuition, alumni donations, private industry, and government provided the bulk of funding. With revenue streams coming from those varied sources, the president understood the need to satisfy the interested parties with little concern for the neighbors destined to lose their homes. Even with students engaging in service in the area, progress for the university necessarily meant the displacement of residents.[14]

Another issue that drove the expansion of Penn and other universities was national defense. The Cold War threat loomed over the heads of American officials and politicians who largely agreed that higher education could be a useful tool in fighting communism while defending the United States and national interests. Harnwell, a physicist by training, had served in research capacities for the U.S. Navy during and after World War II. His work had contributed to weapons and defense designs that the navy implemented in the Pacific Theater.[15] Thus, Harnwell was sympathetic to the notion that universities could help with national defense. As scholar Margaret O'Mara has indicated in her book, *Cities of Knowledge*, international developments drove domestic decisions regarding education and defense. This proved fortunate for urban universities that could make use of government subsidies. "A savvy university could undertake most massive construction programs with little or no expenditures of its own," O'Mara explained.[16] Thus, Penn took advantage of the government assistance as well as the political desire for scientific research, making a powerful institution that much more powerful.

In essence, many parties had interests in universities like Penn and the neighborhoods that surrounded them. Those making decisions about those neighborhoods, incidentally, rarely had to live in them on a permanent basis. To be clear, the area surrounding the university at the time was predominantly black, with Penn providing a white oasis to the mostly upper-class students who could afford to attend. According to the U.S. Census, between 1900 and 1950 the black population in Philadelphia increased from 4.8 percent of the total population to 18.2 percent. In the pursuit of work, black southerners left home for the North and West as part of the Great Migrations; many landed in Philadelphia to work in the steel, shipbuilding, and defense industries. This significant boost in black population during the war and interwar periods occurred concurrently with the decline of the white population in the city. Scholars have done well to point to "white flight" as a key phenomenon in the making of the ghetto. This trend became clearer in the years leading to 1960 when the percentage of black people in the city shot to 26.4 of the total, while the white population decreased 13.3 percent from the previous decade.[17] As was the case in cities across the nation, the black population clustered in certain areas of Philadelphia, including the Black Bottom of Mantua. In a relatively short period of time, Penn's neighborhood became predominantly black.

Mantua—named after the Italian city, had a history similar to many currently black neighborhoods. It was located in Philadelphia's Twenty-Fourth Ward. Before 1920, mostly recent European immigrants called Mantua home. The newly built row houses in the neighborhood provided a space for Italian, Irish, German, and Jewish ethnics to become white. In the decades after World War I, black southerners moved from the rural South to places like Mantua. The black population of the neighborhood jumped from just under 4,000 residents in 1910 to almost 18,350 in 1940. At that point, black residents made up more than a third of the Twenty-Fourth Ward's population. Most of the black people who lived in Mantua were working class and were employed in the manufacturing and service sectors.[18]

A great deal of change regarding black progress occurred during and after World War II. Labor leader A. Philip Randolph, educators like Mary McCleod Bethune, and so many other black agitators pushed to defeat Jim Crow and to ensure that black people would have a share of the war industries jobs. Those activists, in the attempt to persuade President Franklin Roosevelt to desegregate the military, got the president to relent on desegregating war industries with Executive Order 8802. The order was a victory for black workers as nearly a million jobs became available. Taking advantage of the opportunity, black people moved in large numbers to neighborhoods like Mantua.

Perhaps in a foreshadowing statement, a 1935 *Philadelphia Tribune* article titled "Slum Analysis," asserted: "The slums of Philadelphia are no accident. They are planned slums . . . the unregulated tenement manipulators in their mad scramble for profits use the Negro as a pawn and use the middle class white families as suckers, making them pay at both ends."[19] The quotation charged the city with employing structural violence in the name of profit. It reveals that the slums were not the creation of stereotypically lazy, criminal, and unworthy black people, but rather of those who would capitalize monetarily on poor conditions.

Five years after the end of World War II, Mantua changed. The assimilated ethnic white people who had arrived to Mantua earlier in the century began moving out of the neighborhood while black people steadily took up residence. This phenomenon is not unlike what occurred in city neighborhoods across the North and the West. This period saw a spike in "white flight," as white men who had served in the war used their G.I. Bill benefits to acquire low-interest loans to purchase homes in suburban neighborhoods like Levittown near New York City and Chester near Philadelphia, where restrictive covenants illegally or legally prevented black people from buying houses. This essentially left city neighborhoods like Mantua to black people, which were commonly referred to by monikers like "Black Bottom." By 1950, in the Twenty-Fourth Ward (where Mantua was situated), black residents became the majority.

Mainstream purveyors of history have for decades infused the "culture of poverty" concept into the narrative of black neighborhoods. The concept indicates that when black people move to an area, the neighborhood naturally becomes "bad" because of the degenerate nature of black people. It presents black residents as somehow atypical of the mainstream working class and devoid of positive values and pride. In the 1950s, there was no culture of poverty. As historian Matt Delmont noted, "the 'block bottom' was a vibrant neighborhood of businesses and row homes, 15 to 20 percent of which were owned by black families."[20]

Of course, the culture of poverty concept does not take into account several key factors that include the role of the government and racism. While the federal government provided subsidies to those who moved to the suburbs, local municipalities cut civil services in black neighborhoods. This combined with the fact that the housing infrastructures were deteriorating gave the appearance that black people created the ghetto themselves. Even if housing infrastructure was not deteriorating, homes that exist in predominantly black neighborhoods are monetarily worth less according to appraisals. Delmont explained the role white homeowner associations played in the eventual drop in home values in West Philadelphia. Those associations practiced "defensive localism," which allowed white residents to perpetuate stereotypes regarding black residents and their perceived pathological ways.[21]

The culture of poverty concept that these homeowners associations attached to black neighbors points to the violence that occurs in the black neighborhoods as proof of flawed collective character. It omits the fact that city authorities and law enforcement took part in, and sometimes benefited from, the vice that was allowed to fester in black neighborhoods. By now, it is clear that white criminals and governmental agencies infused drugs and alcohol into black neighborhoods and thus ramped up the violence that occurred surrounding the debilitating and addicting substances. Further, many of the jobs that black people followed to these cities during the Great Migrations of World Wars I and II moved to the Sun Belt, where manufacturers took advantage of subsidies and lower tax rates. Rather than looking to the government that created the bleak circumstances, the culture of poverty theory assigns low moral standards to black residents of city neighborhoods. In light of the theory, poor did not mean lacking money but rather lacking the American values of hard work and individual advancement. The simplified concept does not acknowledge the pride that black residents took in their neighborhoods.

"The atmosphere and recipe for growing up to be a strong, idealistic, friendly, peaceful person was down 'da bottom,'" declared lifetime Mantua resident Ardie Stuart Brown. A third-generation college student, she rejected the term "impoverished" as it was used to describe the character of people from her area. Although she qualified that she could not account for everyone in the neighborhood, she was clear about the pride she had in being a resident: "I wasn't from up the way; I'm from the Black Bottom, and I had some of the most fantastic neighbors," she exclaimed.[22] Brown went on to become director of the Spring School of the Arts.

Herman Wrice was another representative of the Mantua community. Like so many other black Philadelphians, Wrice, who was born in 1937, participated in the second Great Migration. He and his mother moved from West Virginia to the Philadelphia area in hopes of more economic opportunity. They lived briefly in Chester but quickly moved to Mantua. Similar to many youth in his neighborhood, Wrice participated in high school sports but also found his way to trouble. He was reportedly a member of a street gang called the Flames.[23] In 1957, a local Catholic priest and neighborhood mentor confronted Wrice about using his leadership and influence in a different way. He allowed Wrice to coordinate activities in a church gymnasium, where youth played basketball and where dances were sometimes held. Several young people who could not afford the cover charge ($0.25) to enter a dance one night, made the fatal choice to take the money. Unfortunately, they robbed a University of Pennsylvania Korean exchange student. In the process of taking his money, they beat him to death. This crime had two effects. The first was the reaction of Penn officials to make the area around campus safer. Improving safety involved increased security and expansion; both initiatives chafed nearby neighbors. The second was more personal. Wrice, who had been in charge of accepting the admissions fees, felt partially guilty for the act of violence. At that point, he decided to find a better way for youth that did not involve robbing or killing.

Wrice and many of his neighbors faced issues of unemployment, the dearth of quality housing, segregated education, and the vastness poverty. To relieve problems of housing, the city provided a public housing complex called Mantua Hall in 1959. When it opened the next year, at eighteen stories it became the tallest structure in West Philadelphia. Thousands of black and several white tenants took up residency in the structure. In 1960, Wrice moved into the newly built complex, where he took a job as a cook. After work, he spent time coaching youth and leading a Cub Scout troop. Even with his housing situation secure, Wrice still had to confront trouble in his neighborhood. A few years after moving into Mantua Hall, Wrice's wife, Jean, was at a store when gang members fired a shotgun blast. Deeply concerned about his own family and the future of his neighborhood, Wrice called a meeting of gang leaders to discuss better options for youth. As a result of the meeting, Wrice and family friend Andrew Jenkins started the Young Great Society. The Young Greats, as they were called, vowed to take responsibility for their own lives and to make life better for neighborhood children.[24] Wrice, Jenkins, and representatives of the Young Greats participated in negotiations with Penn years later.

Regarding Mantua Hall, there was excitement about the prospect of new housing at first, but as civil service waned and public policy constricted the liberty of public housing residents, some of the tenants became embittered. By 1968, nearly every resident in the complex was black. The government, with the help of racism, had effectively cornered black residents. While the government authorized the construction of new housing units in white areas of the city, black West Philadelphians had far fewer options. As a result, West Philadelphia became home to the second largest black population in the city.[25]

As industry began to move from the city to the suburbs and to the Sunbelt, life in Mantua and much of West Philadelphia became more of a struggle for its residents. Black workers were the last hired and first fired, leaving them to work in low-wage jobs, if any at all. Discrimination or stringent apprentice requirements often prevented black West Philadelphians from joining the craft unions. As a result, day work presented the best option for many of the black men who had moved from South for opportunity.[26] Leaders such as the Rev. Leon Sullivan, who had been organizing on behalf of workers since the 1950s, pointed out that if black workers had had better access to the trades, they might have benefited from the urban renewal effort that eventually led to the loss of their homes. Sullivan established the Opportunities Industrialization Center in Philadelphia to help unskilled workers gain access to decent paying jobs. The fact that there were so many unemployed or underemployed people so close to the school was problematic for the Ivy university that sought to improve its status as a serious research and world-class institution.

Urban Ivy leaders were familiar with Penn's predicament as well as that of other elite universities in cities. In 1957, several presidents and chancellors met to discuss the need to deal with issues of the cities they occupied that affected life for students and university officials. Issues that concerned the presidents and chancellors included the increase in joblessness, crime, and overcrowding in the areas around their campuses. These university leaders had always pushed to shield their students from the troubling issues that occurred off campus. As most of the students before the period had come from wealthy families, remaining secluded from the masses was typical. When the second Great Migration occurred in the mid-twentieth century, however, seclusion was no longer an option for the elite, white campuses.

At the 1957 meeting, Penn President Gaylord Harnwell met with Lawrence Kimpton, president of the University of Chicago, Grayson Kirk, president of Columbia, Nathan Pusey of Harvard, A. Whitney Griswold of Yale, and Julius Stratton, chancellor of Massachusetts Institute of Technology to discuss how their universities could "ameliorate their respective neighborhoods," Rodin explained.[27] That meeting is crucial evidence of the awareness of university officials of their stature as elite institutions and their status as urban universities. The leaders agreed that their universities' participation in urban renewal was prudent for the time.[28] This essentially meant that Penn's and Columbia's leadership chose to attach themselves to slum clearance and neighborhood disruption without really consulting the people who lived in the neighborhood but were not affiliated with the universities.

Penn's endeavors to expand via urban renewal worked smoothly in part because of its vast network of power brokers. A trustee of the university, Edward Hopkinson Jr., was the chair of the Philadelphia City Planning Commission until 1955 when another Penn trustee (former dean of the School of Architecture Holmes Perkins) took over the role.[29] Then, yet another trustee, Gustave Amsterdam, who dealt in real estate development, chaired the city's Redevelopment Authority, which also aided the implementation of the university's plans to increase its holdings. In short, Penn's network of influence was wide enough to accommodate whatever decisions university officials made. This situation proved convenient when opportunities arose for property and land acquisition. Manifestly, the neighborhood of Mantua and Black Bottom died and "University City" was born.

Penn's influence was strong, as officials at the institution were able to redesign transportation routes in the city. In their book, *Becoming Penn*, University of Pennsylvania scholars John Puckett and Mark Lloyd described the work that university president Harold Stassen and alumni like Hopkinson did in the 1950s to get the trolley lines moved underground to become a subway. Puckett and Lloyd cited the account of the president when he stated that the university "mobilized the alumni to come to the City Council in great numbers" to convince the council and other citizens that "this was a *real* need and had *real* support."[30] Penn benefited from the fact that Hopkinson was also chairman of the executive committee of the Philadelphia Transportation Company. Moving the train system below ground lessened the public congestion and traffic on campus and greatly worked in favor of Penn establishing a contained campus. The university also benefited from the city's decision to create a nearby turnpike and build a freeway that allowed further dissection of the neighborhood. Monetary offers to homeowners from Penn and the city helped to thin the neighborhood as well. Remaining residents understandably grew fearful of the direction Penn and the city moved. With the West Philadelphia neighborhoods logged as part of the "University City Urban Renewal Area," Penn, along with institutions like Drexel, the Philadelphia College of Pharmacy and Science, Presbyterian

Hospital, and the Philadelphia College of Osteopathy formed the West Philadelphia Corporation (WPC).[31]

The WPC represented the interests of the nonprofit private institutions and worked in conjunction with the Philadelphia Industrial Development Corporation (PIDC), which the city's Chamber of Commerce and city government operated jointly.[32] The PIDC funded a land bank and purchased abandoned commercial and private properties to improve and sell to speculating industrial leaders. Eventually, the PIDC also offered low-interest loans to companies. Although other institutions participated, Penn acted as the primary stakeholder for the group. Thus began Penn's most extensive expansion program until that point. In this case, private institutional and governmental agency cooperation allowed for an Ivy League school to take over city blocks (165 acres) and homes. President Harnwell, whom many observers have characterized as a caring leader concerned with the goodwill of the community, presented a physical development plan to the trustees with a completion date of 1975.

Students at urban universities often receive solemn admonishments about going astray of campus into the "iconic ghetto" that former University of Pennsylvania sociologist Elijah Anderson described.[33] The threat of the mostly black and brown spaces looms in the mind of those who only have tangential interactions with the ghetto. In practice that meant students at Columbia University in New York City were warned not to enter Morningside Park in Harlem and to be sure to take the Broadway exit and not Amsterdam Avenue at the 116th Street stop if they were to stay safe. In the case of Penn, the campus map that students received came with a bold black line of demarcation indicating the area beyond Fortieth Street that meant danger and also happened to be where predominantly black people lived. According to a story captured by scholar Harvey Etienne, when Penn students did venture to an Acme grocery store on the edge of the black neighborhood in the 1950s and 1960s, they referred to it as the "Black Me" store. Using language similar to that describing Columbia, Etienne explained that "the years between 1930 and 1990 represented the time when the university attempted to fortify itself against the effects of deindustrialization and the movement of many poor and working-class families into West Philadelphia communities. The integration and subsequent racial tipping of several of those communities into predominantly African American neighborhoods furthered the university's resolve to redevelop its environs."[34]

The federal government assisted Penn's expansion effort with the American Housing Act of 1949 and the amended legislation of 1959. That legislation came to life, in part, because of the efforts of Penn's business vice president John Moore, who along with representatives of the University of Chicago and New York University crafted the proposal for expansion of institutions of higher education. The part that Moore worked on, Section 112, amended the act to make it possible for universities and hospitals to be considered as part of a municipality's redevelopment plan. The act passed in 1959 after representatives like Moore testified to the Senate Committee on Banking and Currency. This worked in favor of private institutions and the cities. "No institution," however, "achieved a greater expansion of its campus core or made more use of urban renewal tools than Penn" in the postwar period, asserted Puckett and Lloyd.[35]

Members of the black community understood the ramifications of urban renewal. Philadelphia's black newspaper, the *Philadelphia Tribune*, featured a story titled "Urban Renewal Means Negro Removal, Says Community Planning Official"[36] in which Doris Hamilton, a member of the Mantua Community Planners, Inc. (MCP), said plainly, "We knew we did not want urban renewal in our neighborhood." The MCP started as a way to soften the blows of urban renewal and to benefit the most vulnerable in the neighborhoods. Joan Countryman, a city planner, was a member of the committee. Prior to joining the committee, she had participated with the Northern Student Movement, which had helped residents of low-income areas in northern cities fight for tenant rights.[37]

In the MCP, Countryman, Hamilton, and other members sought to prevent institutions like Penn from using urban renewal to tear down buildings in neighborhoods. To accomplish that, MCP garnered funds to renovate the buildings and retain the character of the neighborhoods.[38] The plan was to work with private developers to purchase homes that MCP employees and community members could renovate together. Then, once fixed and safely habitable, the homes would be sold to the residents at a significantly discounted price.[39] The president of MCP, Andrew Jenkins, explained that revitalizing the neighborhood required the intentional cooperation of those living in Mantua. In that way, MCP efforts at renewal allowed community members to have a say in their residential destinies. To be sure of the needs of the people from the neighborhood, MCP conducted a survey to find out how many of the 25,000 residents made use of government assistance, how many renters versus owners lived there, and how many bars/clubs existed.[40] The survey was meant to help with zoning, which MCP claimed was a problem.

The reality for so many of Mantua and West Philadelphia residents was that, at their expense, universities like Penn expanded their campuses to make room for the growth that occurred with the arrival of veterans taking advantage of the G.I. Bill and baby boomers benefiting from their parents' economic advantages. All the while, cities like Philadelphia were clearing up what they deemed "blighted" areas. In West Philadelphia, that meant the extirpation of the Mantua neighborhood and the cultivation of University City and the science research center.

To counter the ill effects that urban renewal was having on residential housing in Mantua, MCP created "grief centers." Open twenty-four hours a day, the three offices that MCP staffed catered to residents who had problems with their landlords or who had been evicted. The MCP staffers would investigate complaints and seek to advocate on behalf of the residents in hopes of positive resolutions.

The University City Science Center was set to cost $100 million in a neighborhood consisting of some twenty blocks. The homeowners and renters who received compensation to move found that they had to pay higher rents and mortgages in the new neighborhoods but received fewer amenities. Residents in some of the condemned properties received a meager $50 to $150 for moving expenses.[41] The science center was supposed to bring jobs, but the mostly black neighbors did not benefit largely from construction employment in a significant way, partly because of previous practices of segregation.[42] To improve Penn, residents faced the loss of their homes or increased cost of living, and still their job prospects did not improve.

In addition to Penn, black people in the city had other problems. Black Philadelphia had been quite active in the push against institutional racism. Often the narrative of the Philadelphia freedom movement is male-centric with the focus on leaders such as Cecil B. Moore. As was the case with the black liberation movement in general, however, black women in Philadelphia were in the vanguard of campaigns on the ground. Sadie Alexander, the first black woman to receive a PhD in economics in the United States and the first black woman to earn a JD from Penn, had been active as part of the Fellowship Commission, which pushed desperately for the Fair Employment Practices Commission to become a permanent body in the city.[43] That effort created job opportunities for black people within municipality offices. Historian Lisa Levenstein, in her study of black women in poverty, highlighted low-income mother-activists who participated in and led the charge to desegregate and equalize education for their children. Their activism mirrored that which scholar Rhonda Williams described in Baltimore, Maryland. Activism in both cities further illustrated the need to situate northern struggles in the civil rights narrative.

At the primary, secondary, and tertiary level, education presented a battlefront for black Philadelphians. In postwar Philadelphia, black schoolchildren were "plagued by a pernicious combination of mismanagement and deliberate racial segregation and academic tracking," Levenstein explained.[44] Black parents in Philadelphia experienced educational racism in the same way parents in southern towns and cities did. Levenstein pointed out that "by confining African American students to segregated underfunded, overcrowded, and understaffed schools, the system as a whole impeded teachers' efforts and made it difficult for most black students to succeed."[45] Black female activists like Gladys Thomas, who was the director of the NAACP's educational committee, took up the charge to equalize and desegregate education. She is still an active community leader for the NAACP and faith initiatives.

By the mid-1960s, segregation in Philadelphia was glaring, with black students making up more than 96 percent of the student body at high schools like West Philadelphia, Franklin, and William Penn. Historian Matt Delmont highlighted the discriminatory nature of education in his work on Philadelphia youth culture. He clearly demonstrated how, even when school district officials outwardly issued statements regarding the move toward integration, the Philadelphia schools in the 1960s became more segregated. By linking education to zoning and housing, and by pointing to market choices, school board officials could claim innocence regarding racial segregation and the inequitable distribution of resources.[46] Those officials were not innocent and neither was the segregation that incurred.

Black people challenged segregation in education in a number of ways. On the airwaves, Georgie Woods, a disc jockey for the WDAS AM radio station in Philadelphia, used music and his voice to discuss the problems of racism that black Philadelphians met.[47] Educational Equity League leader Floyd Logan initiated a protracted campaign that studied the disparate educational opportunities of black and white students and created a proposal to address the discrimination. Logan worked for more than three decades, from the 1940s to the 1970s, to ensure progress. Where Logan's approach involved the tireless tasks of research and the appeal of moral suasion, Cecil B. Moore, the former Mumford Point Marine and head of the Philadelphia NAACP, took a different tack. From 1963 to 1967, Moore led a campaign to desegregate Girard College, a school started for fatherless white boys. Rather than waiting for a court to rule that the private school must be opened to black youth, Moore led a legendary direct action campaign.[48] Black residents from every walk of life marched to protest the recalcitrant segregation. One marcher was Florence Early, an early childhood educator and mother of future Penn alumnus Gerald Early. The marchers called their campaign to desegregate Girard "going to the wall," in reference to the wall surrounding the school.[49] It took a multiple front attack strategy to penetrate the wall of segregation that surrounded the school. Black Philadelphians like Moore, Logan, and Early were bringing the fight against institutional racism to the perpetrators; in this case, black parents and supporters chose Girard as their target. They eventually won the battle, and Girard desegregated.

Given the often inadequate and largely segregated schooling afforded to black children throughout the nation, the poor quality yet expensive housing available in black neighborhoods, the inability of black workers to navigate the unions, and the abusive policing of black bodies, many were not surprised to witness the urban rebellion that took place in Philadelphia in 1964. The rebellion in Philadelphia was just one to occur during the long, hot summer of that year. Others occurred in Harlem, Rochester, Patterson, and Chicago, spaces where large black populations existed. As the Kerner Commission report indicated, these uprisings were the result of a particular interaction usually between black citizens and law enforcement; however, the fuel for these rebellions had been building for at least a half century before exploding in 1964.[50]

In late August, when reform politics involving voting campaigns and working within the existing political systems did not yield the results the masses of black Philadelphians desired, the most disenfranchised and disaffected took to the streets to lodge their displeasure. They indicted President Johnson's Great Society platform as generally inadequate while noting the inability of city and federal government programs like urban renewal and model cities to meet the needs of the people. Despite the efforts of those like Moore, who had aggressively fought institutional racism in Philadelphia, anger and hopelessness spurned residents to lash out via forms of property destruction and looting.[51] The exclusive whiteness of institutions like Penn became a problem for some activists.

Walter Palmer, an activist from Philadelphia, challenged Penn's whiteness. Also a resident of the Black Bottom, Palmer had a long and interesting relationship with Penn. The university marked the place where he was first arrested at the age of twelve for stealing from a residence hall.[52] Fortunately, that was not his last interaction with the university. Palmer and his family, in 1955, started the Black Peoples' University, which acted as a community education resource. A Penn professor who noticed Palmer's work in the neighborhood, asked Palmer to lecture in 1962, which further bolstered his relationship with Penn. A lifelong activist, Palmer answered the call of his community again when in 1964 Penn and its partner institutions announced plans for the University City Science Center. When asked why he joined the struggle against institutional expansion, Palmer responded that he and his friends were going to lose their homes.

Like Ardie Stuart Brown, Palmer indicated that the Black Bottom did not suffer from a culture of poverty, and that many of the families were working- or middle-class homeowners. Penn alumnus and Philadelphia resident during the period Gerald Early remembered West Philadelphia in much the same way. He recalled that West Philadelphia and neighborhoods like Mantua were places where the aspiring black middle class moved.[53] For Palmer the activist, that made Penn's aggressive acts of expansion that much more egregious. Palmer correctly noted that to receive urban renewal subsidies and matching funds, a developer had to prove that the area suffered from blight. He claimed to observe Penn representatives purchasing rental properties and allowing them to decay so that the university could eventually declare the area blighted. Philadelphia residents like Palmer, Brown, or Early would not have considered the neighborhoods in Mantua and the Black Bottom blighted, but the university and government agencies eventually did.

Although a large number of black residents lived near Penn, very few lived and studied on campus.[54] There was no institution in the Ivy League that could lay claim to being an educational oasis for black students at any point in their histories. Some schools did better than others to accommodate meager black admissions, but each institution had been racially and economically exclusive from their origins. Penn, like most of the other Ivies, had black professional school and even undergraduate alumni in the late nineteenth and early twentieth centuries. Scholar Wayne Glasker noted that these students experienced discrimination and outright segregation within Penn itself. He mentioned the cafeteria as a space that was reserved for white students only. Of course, some of the early black Penn students were welcomed as long as they provided a function on an athletic team.

Black men had participated as athletes at Penn since the 1920s. In the postwar period, a basketball player named John Edgar Wideman came to Penn on scholarship. Originally from the Homewood neighborhood of Pittsburgh, Wideman arrived at Penn in 1959. He remembered being one of potentially ten black students in the entire class. Knowing that education and basketball was his opportunity to overcome the oppression of the ghetto, he took a shot on the Ivy League school across the mountains.[55] What he found was the "intensity of whiteness" that one black Penn alumnus described.[56]

One of the few black students on the entire campus, Wideman walked the fine line of establishing a bond with the other black students who did not always share experiences outside of their skin color or with white students who understood black people in the abstract. Wideman recalled a story of a white student in the dormitory berating him about the fact that Wideman did not know the bluesman Big Bill Boonzy. In addition to his higher socioeconomic status, the white student lorded his knowledge of one obscure part of the black experience over the Pittsburgh native, who had no choice but to live the black experience daily. With one small instance of cultural appropriation and condescension, Wideman was made to feel the full thrust of his otherness. Years later, he wrote: "I don't believe that pompous ass could have known, because I didn't know at the moment, how much he was hurting me." He wondered to himself: "why did that smartass white son of a bitch have so much power over me? Why could he confuse me, turn me inside out, make me doubt myself."[57] Considering the small number of black students at Penn, he was not alone in that feeling. Without the comfort or reassurance of an organization like the Students' Afro-American Society (SAAS), which students founded in 1967, the handful of black students in the early 1960s had to survive on what Wideman called "the island of University."[58]

Wideman and the few other black students at Penn had to adopt strategies to survive culturally and emotionally. "To maintain any semblance of dignity and confidence" at the university, Wideman said: "I had to learn to construct a shell around myself." He admitted that he "adopted the strategy of slaves, the oppressed, and the powerless." Of the benefits of Black Studies, Wideman later wrote, "Knowledge of my racial past, of the worldwide struggle of people of color against the domination of Europeans would have been invaluable. . . . History could have taught me I was not alone, my situation was not unique."[59]

During the mid-1960s, officials at Penn had a change of perspective regarding admissions. With the black freedom movement thronging in Philadelphia and throughout the nation, Penn officials could not ignore its stark whiteness in a black neighborhood, especially after the 1964 rebellion in North Philadelphia. To increase the black presence on campus, the institution took several different approaches. One such approach involved an exchange program with historically black Morgan State College in Baltimore. There were similar exchange programs throughout the Ivy League. Princeton exchanged with Lincoln University in Pennsylvania, Brown with Tougaloo College, and Dartmouth with Talledega College. Regarding Penn's exchange with Morgan State, faculty and students had the opportunity to spend time at each other's institutions. That method may have boosted numbers for a short period, but the few Penn students who were traditionally enrolled looked forward to a more sustainable increase.

Culturally, as was the case elsewhere, black students at Penn had to adjust to life in a predominantly white institution. Self-confidence and a sense of belonging were issues that directly affected the students. The social environment was relatively familiar to a large portion of the white student population who had attended racially exclusive and socially elite high schools. That was not the case for the vast majority of black students. As a black alumnus from Dartmouth explained: "so many of us came to school not believing we were smart, but I always knew I could compete."[60] There is no way to quantify the Ivy alumnus's assertion, but he pointed out some of the trials that the few black students who attended Ivy schools faced. The lack of confidence affected those students during and after graduation, but at least the black students understood that if they could do well at an Ivy institution like Penn, they could potentially succeed in other areas of life. To boost confidence and a sense of belonging, the students created their own network in the SAAS.[61] That network, like so many others, became more politicized in the late 1960s.

By 1967, Penn officials had teased out the idea of intentionally diversifying the student body. Glasker discusses some of the intricacies of navigating the move toward higher black admissions. A committee of faculty and staff members (all white) met as part of the Committee on Undergraduate Admissions. Subsequently, race became an explicit part of the list of subjective factors. It is important to note that race had, of course, always been an implicit part of the subjective factors that admissions counselors considered when inviting students to attend Penn. Being white had almost always been a bonus regarding admissions. The committee now suggested 90 percent of admissions remain based on test scores and grades, while 10 percent be reserved for special admissions. The special admissions category broke down into 5 percent for athletes, 2 percent for children of Penn affiliates (trustees, faculty, administrators, and staff) and special interest (Pennsylvania politicians) admits, and 3 percent for those from lower socioeconomic backgrounds (most likely black). In the 1967–1968 school year, seventy-one students were admitted under the Penn affiliate/special admit category. The same year Penn invited eighty-five black students to attend. The next year, 125 black students were admitted.[62] The number of black Penn matriculants more than doubled between 1968 and 1969 (from 62 to 150). Certainly, the committee report and work of the faculty contributed greatly to the increase, but the activism of black people on and off campus also played a significant part.

The mood at Penn regarding the role of students in decision making was changing. As scholar Wayne Glasker stated, "Penn was no stranger to protests and sit-ins."[63] In opposition to the war, students (mostly white) pressured their university to break ties with the U.S. Air Force and to disallow the Dow chemical company to recruit on campus. In the 1950s and 1960s, Penn researchers assisted the air force with two projects, "Spice Rack" and "Summit."[64] According to Glasker, after students protested the projects, university officials looked to transfer the contracts to the independent University City Science Center. The students set their sights on a new target. As the nation escalated the number of troops in Vietnam, Penn students in April 1967 held a demonstration at College Hall. The 1967 action lasted more than two days. Months later, students again protested in a different building to prevent CIA and Dow recruiters from working on campus.

Across the nation, black students were rebelling on campuses. Black Studies became a major issue, but so too was student power. Not far from Penn, at historically black Cheyney State College, students demanded control over the student newspaper and transparency regarding the college's budget. Students also protested at Temple University when a white fraternity put on a minstrel show.[65] The Temple students pointed out the need to refine the culture of their university with a Black Studies curriculum, which would teach all students just how inappropriate blackface shows were. At both Temple and Cheyney, the Black Student League acted to empower their fellow students and to advance black goals.

In Philadelphia, there was most certainly a culture of activism in place when, arguably, the most tragic event of the year—Martin Luther King Jr.'s assassination—occurred. King came to the Philadelphia area in 1948 to study at Crozer Theological Seminary. During his time in school, King worked in the black community, and people in the area embraced him even before his national fame. News of his death had a personal effect on many in the city.[66] Black students at Penn, as their peers had done at all the Ivies, loudly mourned the death of King. As occurred at the other institutions, black students at Penn called for a boycott of classes on April 5. City officials, fearing a black rebellion like others that had been reported since news of King's assassination, ordered that groups larger than fifteen could not assemble in public areas. In the face of the order, members of the SAAS met on campus, then marched off campus in the middle of the street for several blocks before heading back to campus. The demonstrators did not face legal repercussions for their action.

In another act of resistance that responded to King's death, SAAS led an effort to get signatures for a petition that would support open housing.[67] The issue of housing was one that King had raised not long before his death. Housing was also an issue of importance in West Philadelphia. The protestations of student groups SAAS and SDS, as well as that of the Community Involvement Council, indicated the coalition that was building against institutional expansion. After getting 2,148 signatures, SAAS delivered the petition to the House of Representatives. They were taking to heart the message that King advisor Bayard Rustin shared in an opinion editorial after his friend's death: "Tears Are Cheap; Action, Alas, So Dear."[68] Rustin said that to effectively repent for the sin of King's murder, the nation and its citizens had to begin by first "acknowledging one's guilt and expressing one's sorrow," then by "dedicating and committing one's self to better conduct in the future." Penn students knew that it was not enough to just feel bad about the acts of individual and institutional racism, but that they should strike out at racism with whatever weapons were available. Back on campus, SAAS called for "Black Week" to educate their peers and to honor fallen black heroes such as King, Medgar Evers, and Malcolm X.

The students exhibited a new black consciousness because of their exposure to the movement in Philadelphia and elsewhere. Sometimes representatives of the movement came to campus to share news. In 1967 and 1968, influential and charismatic leaders like Dick Gregory, Floyd McKissick, and Muhammad Ali came to speak with the Penn student body and to meet privately with members of the SAAS.[69] The leaders urged the students to use their power to help the larger movement.

Taking up that charge, SAAS members exercised their Black Student Power in late April 1968, when they blocked entrances and exits to a bank that a white Penn alumnus owned. The students demonstrated because the financial institution did not employ a single black person. Although located in an almost entirely black neighborhood, the bank took black people's money but refused to hire them. When the owner attempted to explain that he had not personally witnessed any racial discrimination in hiring practices, the SAAS pointed to the experiments that it had conducted with the help of white allies. The group had two black people unsuccessfully try to fill advertised positions at the bank. When the SAAS's white ally applied, he miraculously received a job offer. After learning this, the owner indicated that two black people would be hired immediately. That story was a perfect illustration of Black Student Power—black students using their status and influence as students and representatives of the black intelligentsia to effect change on behalf of the larger struggle for freedom.

The Penn student activists joined young people and other activists in Philadelphia and elsewhere who favored disruption. On the streets of Philadelphia, Walter Palmer participated in demonstrations. Collaborating with activist mothers, he led a secondary school walkout for more resources that involved more than 50,000 students from across the city in November 1967. Less than a year later, he helped host the second national Black Power Conference in Philadelphia. The gathering welcomed more than 4,000 black freedom fighters from cultural nationalists like Maulana Karenga of the U.S. organization to more moderate negotiators like Whitney Young of the National Urban League to revolutionaries like Max Stanford of the Revolutionary Action Movement. Neighborhood control was a topic of discussion and was relevant in the city where powerful white institutions commandeered acres of land and living spaces with the help of public policies.[70]

Karenga also attended the conference on Black Studies that the Black Student Alliance at Yale hosted. His comments there provided some insight into how Black Power advocates viewed white institutional expansion. In thinking of the black neighborhoods as part of an oppressed colony, he said that black people should "try desperately to keep the outside world from imposing its authority" on the community.[71] America's "values are communicated best through its university system." Expansion and the usurpation of land in the neighborhoods communicated a message to black people. Providing advice to universities like Penn and Columbia, he said: "the first thing I would propose for a university is nonintervention . . . that is not taking over things in the black community, tearing down buildings and putting up your [the university's] things." He continued: "Stop imposing yourself through projects that only benefit you and the white community, or the business community."[72]

Based on its history, student body, faculty, and administration, the expansion of the campus further into West Philadelphia would mostly benefit the insular white community on campus and those ostensibly white-owned construction companies that would receive contracts to build the edifices.

By the time Karenga made those comments in the fall of 1968, Penn President Harnwell and many Penn affiliates had admitted the need to improve the relationship between the university and the community. That included students and faculty members providing "service" in the nearby neighborhoods. To that notion, one Black Power advocate scoffed. Gerald McWhorter (now Abdul Alkalimat), who held a master's degree from the University of Chicago, also attended the Black Studies conference, where he stated: "the university . . . must conceive of itself as a *servant* (original emphasis) of the community. This servant relationship to the community must be defined cooperatively, for only in that way can the university maintain a balance between relating to what is and relating to what ought to be,"[73] an admonition that certainly applied to Penn.

While black activists tried to concentrate power in Philadelphia and other urban centers, white politicians sought to exert power at the national level. Candidates such as Eugene McCarthy, George McGovern, and Robert Kennedy fought to be the Democratic Party's presidential candidate. They mostly agreed that the nation had to end the war in Vietnam with or without a victory. Johnson, who faced severe criticism because of his administration's decisions regarding the conflict in Vietnam, chose to not seek reelection. Matters came to a head in the summer of 1968 when the Democratic National Convention in Chicago drew thousands of protesters and demonstrators who wanted to shine a light on the key issues of the period: the war, institutional racism, and youth empowerment. Political life, for the Democrats, became even more complicated when the seemingly most popular primary candidate, Robert Kennedy, lost his life to an assassin in California. As the Democratic Party fell into disarray, the Republican Party had a clear candidate in Richard Nixon, who claimed to speak for the silent majority in his calls for law and order. Nixon, unlike the many young people who believed American troops did not belong in Southeast Asia, believed that victory was possible. His desire to continue the efforts in Vietnam, as well as his criticism of liberalism and outright disgust with radical activism, found support in the majority of U.S. voters who elected him as president.

During the 1940s and 1950s black citizens had had to endure organized white resistance to merely move in to West Philadelphia neighborhoods and attain an education. By the late 1960s, however, black residents attempted to organize to resist the encroaching will of educational institutions even more powerful than the homeowners associations that attempted to keep black residents out of the neighborhood. Universities like Penn and Drexel and other proponents of the science center comprised a nearly unstoppable foe for black people who wanted to keep their neighborhood intact. After struggling to get in, there must have been great disappointment at the prospect of having to leave. Many in West Philadelphia and the city in general believed they had no choice but to protest and agitate on behalf of their homes and lives. National politics and policies had not done enough to improve their quality of life. That meant they had to agitate in the arenas of education, jobs, and housing. If politicians could not (or would not) take up their issues, then local community members had to highlight matters of importance and advocate on behalf of those issues themselves.

Considering the expansion of institutions into West Philadelphia, some residents believed the neighborhoods were under attack. To make room for University City high school, the city used eminent domain to acquire land in Mantua between Thirty-Sixth and Thirty-Eighth and Market Streets. For neighborhood people whose children attended West Philadelphia High School, a new high school was not necessarily negative. The issue was that people had to lose homes for the children (most likely white) of those who would work at the science center to attend school. In perhaps a prescient move, officials placed the education of some students over the housing needs for black residents.[74]

Penn, the city, and federal offices colluded further when Philadelphia became a "model city." The model cities program was part of President Johnson's War on Poverty, and was meant to incorporate community leaders in the decision making related to development and aid funding that came from the federal government. Although Philadelphia participated in the model cities program, the experience was not always positive or empowering for the citizens in the poor communities of color. As participants in the Area-Wide Council—a community group that involved a large contingent of black and Puerto Rican members—citizens faced the partisan nature of federal and municipal politics. At the same time that militant black factions were demanding their rights in cities like Chicago, Los Angeles, Newark, and Detroit, in Philadelphia black freedom fighters engaged in school demonstrations. The Great Society that Johnson envisioned did not manifest itself in the model cities program in Philadelphia. The citizen-participants met with disillusionment when Republican candidate Richard Nixon won the presidency and took office. Philadelphians who had been hopeful about the model cities program were also disappointed in their Democratic mayor, James Tate. The mayor, some claimed, was fearful of the potential power that community members could have if they united to improve their spaces with government funds.[75]

In late 1967, the state of Pennsylvania greatly assisted Penn's expansion plans when the commonwealth passed a bill creating the Pennsylvania Higher Education Facilities Authority. The new agency sought to "to provide educational facilities at nonprofit institutions of higher education in the Commonwealth of Pennsylvania; to provide short-term loans for working capital; and [to create] the Pennsylvania Higher Educational Facilities Authority as a body corporate and politic with power to acquire, construct, improve, equip, furnish, operate, lease, and dispose of projects and provide short-term loans."[76] When Penn acquired the blocks adjacent to that of the new high school, people in Mantua clearly saw the pattern and began mobilizing against the elite institution. The land acquisitions for the science center, high school, and university perfectly illustrated Mollenkopf's concept of the pro-growth coalition that favored large business, government (at all levels), and developers over small businesses and private owners. That coalition was responsible for the engineering of modern cities. Unfortunately for some, the government-assisted growth of University City and Penn meant the waning and death of Mantua—unless someone checked the expanding institutions.

That someone was the Rev. Edward Sims, who, in fall 1968, stood up to the Ivy League university to protect a small experimental school. The community activist's stand was significant on several counts. The first is that he sought to defend the experimental school that he and others of the Volunteer Community Resource Center believed was necessary, especially in light of the deep segregation prevalent in the Philadelphia school districts. Second, Sims and his organization were aware that they faced an American institution that produced the most powerful brokers in society and had the political and financial support of the government; yet, he and the VCRC still acted. Third, in its effort to provide educational opportunity to its students, the grand majority of whom were white, Penn was destroying black younger students' educational chances with its expansionist efforts. Sims, in the spirit of the black freedom movement, publicly declared his opposition to the powerful white institution's plans.[77] The struggle over the Walnut Center that housed the experimental school became a symbol of both black resistance and Penn's power. The battle was not new, but the forces of history converged upon the Ivy university. As scholar Wayne Glasker astutely noted about the Penn controversy: "geography is destiny."[78]

In terms of the university's geography, several factors collided. There was urban renewal, a need for science-based research at the government level, and a growing push toward law and order. In the poverty stricken areas around Penn, property values were dropping and there were people committing crimes of opportunity. The Mantua-West Philadelphia community faced many problems in the late 1960s. In addition to crime and expansion, residents suffered at the hands of slumlords who refused to sustain livable conditions for their residents.[79] Owners of rental properties rarely were fined for code violations, but rent prices continued to increase. Some slumlords in the Penn area admitted to holding out in speculation that the university would eventually purchase their residential buildings.[80] Those owners who took advantage of renters in West Philadelphia knew that they would not face many (if any) reprisals from the city and essentially acted with impunity.

There were other problems pestering Mantua residents, including a large population of rats. In addition to the sheer annoyance that rodents presented, the presence of rats created a public health issue because of the diseases they spread. Citing a lack of funds, the Mantua Community Vector Control Unit sought grants to treat the problem.[81] To some residents, it must have seemed like an invasion at every level. If they could not repel the rodents from their homes, then there was little chance of fighting back a powerful Ivy League university.

In the midst of some depressing conditions, there were positive aspects of life for residents. The Walnut Street Center represented a bright spot. It was founded in 1966 to operate as an experimental school for neighborhood children. The university took over the lease of the community center in 1967. At that point, the children of university officials and faculty used the community center with the mostly black children from Powelton and Mantua, making the experimental school one of the few integrated spaces for education in the city. In 1968–1969, when the university announced its intention to convert the center to student living space as part of a "super block" renovation, many in the community were dismayed. The designs for the super block outlined campus growth but meant the displacement of nearly 2,700 residents. Along with their homes, the residents worried that the 133 students who used the Walnut Street Center would not be able to find another site because the rents had risen as a result of the new construction and expansion undertaken by institutions like Penn and Drexel.[82] Part of the student and community activism against expansion included the effort to ensure the sustainability of the Walnut Street Center.

When the university's planner later determined that the Walnut Street Center would not provide enough space for student housing, plans were made to raze the community center and instead create 600-space parking garage.[83] The *Daily Pennsylvanian* brought up a problem of privilege by highlighting the pernicious nature of parking in Philadelphia and especially around Penn. For those who could afford a car, not finding a space was highly annoying. The paper emphasized the increased efforts of traffic police to tow cars illegally parked in the area surrounding Penn.[84] Students often parked illegally, which led to one more fee for students who were caught. As David Cohen, an undergraduate student at the time jokingly remembered, "the real controversy was over parking!"[85] Philadelphians of all types battled for space at every level.

In the same issue of the school paper that described the community protest against the plans to remove the Walnut Street Center, an article pointed out that a Penn nursing student, who was presumably white, became a victim of an attack by a "black about 25 years old" in the Forty-Fourth Street building where she lived.[86] According to the *Philadelphia Tribune*, Mantua experienced the highest rates of crime in the city.

Philadelphia unquestionably had an intense gang problem, and Mantua became an area for turf battles.[87] The presence of undereducated, underemployed, and neglected young people spelled trouble in the city and Penn. Issues of crime also led to the dedication of a new community center that could have complemented the mini-school. The impetus for the new community center was the murder of Mantua teenager Stanley Workman, to whom the new center was dedicated. Workman was shot to death in West Philadelphia. Both young people and adults from neighborhood could enjoy the space, but tutors were available to the youth after school. Mantua Community Planners, Inc., sponsored the new Stanley Workman Community Center.[88] The safety and use of space in the area was of utmost importance to the university and the community.

The university's plans to demolish the Walnut Street Center provoked some community members to protest. The Rev. Edward Sims led the charge. He made it known that there would be "a strong negative reaction" to the university's intention to remove the experimental school. Making it plain, the Rev. Sims stated that removing the Walnut Street Center "is not going to help [the University's] failing image one iota." Sims noted sadly that "I don't see anybody winning on this issue." Further, he lamented, "the community will lose."[89]

The issues and conflicts of the neighborhood pressed against Penn officials who were searching for ways to compete against the university's Ivy peers. Although Penn's image in the neighboring poor black community was at stake, so too was the university's status in the predominantly white and rich Ivy League. Prospective students and parents compared and contrasted the resources of the various institutions. If there was overcrowding in the residence halls, safety issues, and a lack of parking on campus, then Penn could potentially fall behind its Ivy peers in the eyes of prospective students. Indeed, part of the impetus for the expansion was to create a space that was similar to Harvard Square, with commercial amenities and a closed campus feel.[90] When it came to prioritizing the image of the university to disparate audiences, Penn officials made the crucial choice of ranking Penn's image in the Ivy League above that of improving its image in the eyes of black West Philadelphia neighbors.

That is why community residents felt inclined to protest; they had suffered regularly and paid highly for their substandard homes, but the idea of having to leave was too much. The same sentiment floated for resources, such as the mini-school, that were available to their children. White and black students from Penn sympathized with the causes of the nearby community. An American Council of Education report on the 1968–1969 student demonstrations at Penn explained: "Two issues dominated the student-led confrontation." The first "centered around classified, defense-related research. The second stemmed from the University's relationship to its neighboring community. The two issues were interrelated." In a succinct observation, the report noted that "the two basic issues of the February 1969 sit-in intersected at the point of the University 'presence' in the University City Science Center."[91]

Even though Sims declared that the community would "mobilize" to keep the mini-school and homes, he was not always able to count on the help of all of his white allies. John Seley, a leader of Penn's student-led mostly white Community Involvement Council (CIC), explained that struggling via protests on campus was futile because the university's intention to remove the community center was part of the state's development plan. "What they're going to have to do is fight the whole state. . . . Direct confrontation will not work," Seley predicted.[92] He suggested that the community should take the fight to the courts. Seley's statement called into question the stability of the alliance between black community members and white allies. This was a challenge for the white and black activists in the larger New Left coalition. Some proponents of Black Power questioned the loyalty and dependability of white radical activists when it came to following the lead of black people. This scenario played out in organizations like Student Nonviolent Coordinating Committee (SNCC) and the Congress of Racial Equality (CORE), but also at the local level.

There was also the potential for university reprisals if students chose to demonstrate. The president of Cheyney State expelled nine students who had participated in a campus protest the previous fall. Some of those Cheyney State students eventually faced indictment in Delaware County.[93] Penn students, black and white, knew that the same fate could befall them if they violated campus regulations regarding protest. Incidentally, losing student status would expose the young people to the draft in the midst of the Vietnam conflict.

With the threat of expulsion ever-present, CIC members learned, just as some members of SNCC and CORE had earlier, that as white people they could be more effective sharing the message of black freedom with their white peers. Part of the CIC's new approach was to put on what it called "Liberation Week." The idea was to provide the mostly white Penn students with a "relevant educational experience," according to member Ira Harkavy.[94] Some of the relevant education offered during the week included lectures from Rev. James Woodruff, an Episcopalian priest who served as chaplain at several historically black colleges in Nashville and was an advocate of black liberation theology. In 1967, Rev. Woodruff came to Philadelphia to work on community outreach on behalf of the church. The CIC also invited SNCC regional director John Wilson, who worked throughout the South and in Chicago. The lectures, in combination with films, exposed the nearly all white student body to aspects of the movement. Indeed, the black freedom struggle was quickly overrunning the borders of campus.

In addition to issues surrounding Penn's expansion, members of the Students' Afro-American Society (SAAS) pushed the issue of Black Studies. Peer institutions like Yale, Harvard, Brown, Cornell, and Princeton had already committed to establishing programs. In Philadelphia, leaders like Walt Palmer offered courses in black history and culture in community centers and on college campuses. He participated in a campaign to create a Philadelphia institution that dedicated itself to the black experience in America. In January 1969, according to the student newspaper, a committee of Penn administrators and faculty members was preparing to launch a program the next year. A committee member indicated that the group had been consulting with black students informally about the major.[95] In that way, black students sought to advance black goals on and off campus.

In February, SAAS held "Black Week," which had been conceived of after the murder of Dr. King. The group believed that it was the responsibility of the university to provide information on the black experience, especially in lieu of the fact that there was not definitive Black Studies program. By the time of Penn's Black Week (February 16–22), members of Harvard's Association of African and Afro-American Students were finalizing the curriculum plan for a Black Studies program.[96] Penn's SAAS was only consulting informally with faculty members regarding Black Studies at that point, so Black Week was meant to provide information to the campus until there was a more substantive plan implemented. This coincidentally occurred during the week that the protests against the science center and expansion on campus began. The black student group had chosen the dates to honor the memory of Malcolm X, who had been killed four years earlier on February 21.

On February 17, the day before the sit-in, Black Power advocate and poet/playwright Amiri Baraka (formerly Leroi Jones) put on two of his plays at Penn. Although the SAAS did not sponsor the event, the members benefited from the artist's visit. In the hours before the performance, Baraka directed comments to SAAS members, black youth from the community, and others in attendance. "The black man must control his own space," Baraka declared to the crowd of 2,000.[97] While he spoke in generalities, the leader of the Black Arts Movement might have been speaking to the controversy of space in Mantua and West Philadelphia that confronted black residents. Baraka continued: "The problem for white America is that they must learn they cannot control our lives." He may have been hopeful in his assessment of white people, as Penn's ability to purchase land and buildings in the surrounding neighborhoods actually meant the white American institution could, in fact, determine the life choices of black people. To counter this kind of intrusion into black lives, Baraka pointed to the need for Black Power and Black Nationalism. After his lecture to the general audience, the speaker met in a closed meeting with SAAS members.

The day that Baraka was on campus, the student newspaper ran an article titled "Disruption Marks Nation's Campuses," which detailed student struggles for Black Studies and black-controlled spaces at institutions like San Francisco State College, Duke University, and the University of Wisconsin.[98] Of particular note to readers was the description of the bomb that had exploded at San Francisco State and injured a campus security guard. The situation at those other campuses must have piqued the interest of Penn officials.

Another source for information on campus rebellion was radical historian Howard Zinn's book *Disobedience and Democracy: Nine Fallacies on Law and Order*, which was released that winter. Zinn had long been a supporter of student activism, particularly that of the SNCC.[99] In observing campus protests in the late 1960s, Zinn claimed that in order to keep peace many educational institutions sacrificed expression and the right to dissent. Incidentally, President Harnwell did not receive a review of the book until after the demonstrations at Penn had ended.[100] The February 17 issue of the *Daily Pennsylvanian* also described the student campaign against the antiballistic missiles system that researchers were set to study at the science center.

Like Penn officials, the staff of the student newspaper worried about the potential of violence during the demonstration at the science center construction site that the SDS had planned for February 18. In a piece titled "Caution, Not Violence," the staff encouraged the SDS and community activists to avoid violence. If the protest turned violent, the paper argued, the message of the university's complicity with war research and institutional bullying would be lost. Resisting arrest might incite violence. Interestingly, the writers indicated that they had faith that the nearly all white members of Penn's SDS chapter would remain peaceful, but were concerned that the black people coming from the neighborhoods would not. "We think the blacks from the community might be more likely to resist arrest, since they are faced with a gut issue of losing their homes" and resistance seemed a justifiable response.[101]

The assumption that the mostly white members of SDS could restrain themselves while black residents could not reflected some of the prevalent stereotypes of the period. To be certain, black Philadelphians rebelled violently in 1964, as did black citizens of nearby New Jersey in 1967. They reacted to what they perceived as police brutality, but that did not necessarily mean that black people in West Philadelphia would do so in 1969. During the same period, white activists, including those affiliated with the SDS, had participated in violent rebellions. So, the extra concern for black violence may have been stilted. Then, given the record of the Civil Rights Movement, perhaps white violence should have been assumed. Along those lines, the poor relationship between Philadelphia police and black citizens was cause for worry. Ultimately, the staff believed that "violence can only harden SDS members and West Philadelphia residents, thus leading to more violence."[102]

Episodes of violence and disruption racked the nation and the world in 1969. In Los Angeles members of the Black Panther Party, John

Huggins and Alprentice "Bunchy" Carter, got into a shoot-out with members of Maulana Karenga's US organization on the UCLA campus.[103] And in February 1969, the Nixon administration ratcheted up the bombing efforts in Vietnam in an effort to achieve "peace with honor." Violence loomed.

In the third week of February, the Rev. Sims accepted an invitation to a rally planned by Penn's SDS chapter. The students pushed against expansion as a result of the construction of the science center and against secret war research at the university. Much in the same way as Columbia's SDS chapter had at the gym site the year before, Penn's SDS orchestrated a demonstration at the science center construction site on February 18. Nearly 250 Philadelphia-area students representing higher education institutions that were part of the science center consortium gathered to watch a performance by Guerrilla Theatre.[104]

An American Council on Education report suggested that perhaps the SDS was acting in retribution for a lack of satisfaction with President Harnwell's tepid response to the group's demands of a month earlier to prohibit controversial research at the science center. Irrespective of motive, in conjunction with students from Drexel, Bryn Mawr, Temple, and Villanova, the SDS staged a demonstration on the morning of February 18. Like demonstrators in other cities, the SDS used protest theater to illustrate their point and performed a play at College Hall. The play depicted the displacement of West Philadelphia residents. The actors used props to show a dog in a house being thrown out onto the street while a "mad scientist" took the dog's place.

Rather than leave the building after the performance, the growing group of demonstrators made the decision to stage a sit-in to more effectively dramatize their protest. In much the same way that leadership at times waivered during the Columbia crisis, SDS members had not set a course of action after the performance. Eventually the students formed a steering committee to organize next steps that included food, bedding, and entertainment as the demonstrators intended to remain in the building. The demonstrators also elected not to close off the building. The Penn demonstrators made sure not to obstruct entrances and exits and allowed employees to move about freely.

The students' actions reflected the agreement of the Mundheim Committee, which had created a set of guidelines that would allow

Figure 6.1. University of Pennsylvania President Gaylord Harnwell addresses the press during the College Hall sit-in of 1969. Courtesy of University of Pennsylvania Archives and Records Center.

demonstrations as long as they did not impede working operations.[105] Written in 1967 by a committee of administrators, faculty, and students led by Penn law professor Robert Mundheim, the guidelines stated that "in keeping with the nature of the University[,] a spirit of reason should prevail in any demonstrations and counter-demonstrations which may take place on campus." Moreover, "demonstrators and others must refrain from physical violence, from damage to property, from prevention of entry to or exit from buildings, and from interference with the normal conduct of University business."[106] However, in February 1969, the protesters did not impart any physical violence, damage property, or prevent entrance and egress from buildings, but they did interfere with the normal operation of university business because the typical business of Penn involved the forced displacement of West Philadelphia residents.

The demonstrators developed three demands. The first was to return the land that the university acquired for the science center to the community via Renewal Housing, Inc., a nonprofit community advocacy entity that focused on rehabilitating homes and neighborhoods using local labor. The goal of the organization was to keep neighborhoods intact. The second demand was that the university establish a fund for low-income housing in the areas where residents had lost homes under the auspices of Penn's expansion. The third was to prohibit classified military research at the new science center.

One-time SDS member Ira Harkavy led the CIC into the demonstration. The mostly white student group, whose sole intention was to interact with the surrounding neighborhoods, charged the university with encroachment. Before the sit-in, members of the council had put together a tutoring project for black students from a nearby alternative school.[107] From their experiences with various community members, CIC members like Harkavy learned the significance of the science center not just in terms of defense research but in the loss of homes that university expansion threatened. Harkavy had grown up in New York City with a "civil rights orientation," as his father and uncle had marched with Dr. King. While an underclassman at Penn, Harkavy established a relationship with community leaders like the Rev. Sims, Herman Wrice, and Walter Palmer.[108] They made an indelible impression on the white student, who took his neighbors' struggle to heart. "We are a rich institution living next to a poor black community and the only way we see blacks is through a car window," he stated in January 1969.[109] Harkavy remembers walking through the nearby neighborhoods where he became familiar with the issues affecting the people and recalls that he may have gained credibility with the neighbors when they saw he had an issue of the black-owned and operated *Philadelphia Tribune* in his back pocket.[110]

Upon hearing news of the sit-in, administrators mobilized immediately to deal with the students. John Russell, the vice provost for student affairs, acted as a key negotiator. The next day (February 19), the group of protesters agreed on the following demands: that all the land acquired for the University City Science Center would be turned over to a black staffed community organization, Renewal Housing, Inc.; that the university and the West Philadelphia Corporation would provide funding for new housing; and that the University City Science Center would not be allowed to conduct research that could be used for war purposes.

One report explained that "some 800 members of faculty and academic staff attended [an] unprecedented all-University faculty meeting" to discuss the sit-in and demands of the students.[111] The president, in the historic meeting with the faculty and faculty senate advisory committee, suggested that a junta of all interested parties be called and also that the university pledge an immediate $25,000 toward the provision of housing. In a unique move, members of the faculty senate advisory committee agreed to donate 1 percent of one year's salary toward the effort.[112] Many faculty members cared deeply about the issues of poverty and housing in the city, but the steps that the senate advisory committee took displayed its membership's commitment.

Members of the black student organization had scheduled a meeting with the trustees of the university on February 19 to discuss their own grievances before the hearing of the SDS-planned demonstration. Some of those grievances included increased black admissions, which had been on the rise but was still not satisfactory, and the introduction of a Black Studies program. In unity with the SDS and the community protesters, however, the SAAS allowed the demonstrators to take their scheduled time with the trustees to negotiate.

Early on, some of the community organizations opposing the science center were not part of the negotiations. Renewal Housing, Inc., participated, but that was only one representative. Other community representatives actually missed a meeting held with the trustees. University documents characterized the missed appointment as a lack of organization, but there is an alternative interpretation. There were power dynamics at play during the period. The trustees were extremely influential men in industry and other fields. When they called meetings, typically people moved quickly to accommodate. By not attending a meeting with the trustees, community members altered the momentum of power by forcing the trustees to wait. If the trustees moved forward without serious consultation with the community, then the university opened itself to even more criticism of institutional bullying. In that particular moment, because of the university's history, the community representatives had the power. Rarely did the balance of power favor working class and poor black people. Taking advantage of the moment, by February 20 representatives of twenty different organizations such as Sims's VCRC, Herman Wrice's Young Great Society, Walter Palmer's Black People's Unity Movement and the Black United Front, and Andrew Jenkins of the Mantua Planners Committee, Inc., came to express the unity of West Philadelphia black residents in their stance against institutional expansion. Their presence and discourse led the students and others to refocus attention on the needs of the community.

Upon meeting directly with the trustees, the students, community members, and faculty negotiated agreements. On February 29, a university press release announced news of a quadripartite commission. The new commission was established "to coordinate community and university development and as a mechanism for securing community consent to development plans."[113] The news release quoted from a document the trustees had penned several days earlier that explained the commission would consist of five community members, five Penn students, five Penn faculty members (four of whom had to reside in West Philadelphia), and five trustees or representatives of trustees.[114] In spite of the fact that Penn had commandeered most of the territory it outlined in the 1948 master plan, the community and students could count the creation of the commission as a victory, as Penn could no longer afford to push into the neighborhoods in a typical paternalistic manner. After realizing the error of their unchecked growth policy, the trustees took a different tack: "in keeping with the principle of accountability and responsibility of the University to the surrounding community the members of the Board of Trustees individually and collectively agree to concert their efforts through the corporations, businesses, institutions, and agencies to which they have access" to develop the community in collaboration with the neighborhoods.[115]

The quadripartite commission would have the power to "review and approve all existing plans involving future land acquisition and/or development of currently owned land contiguous to existing residential neighborhoods," according to the university press release. Fundraising would also be a charge of the committee, as it proposed $10 million for the creation of new housing when residential properties had to be demolished. Other money would be set aside for the function of the quadripartite committee. The issue of funds was significant. According to a letter to the president from a trustee, the plan was to acquire $2.5 million from commercial financial institutions in the city and FHA-guaranteed financing from mutual savings banks. The bulk of the funding, according to the letter, was to come from "the Federal Government and it will be our intention to work closely with the Mayor's office and his housing associates and with officials in HUD [Housing and Urban Development] in Washington."[116]

By depending so heavily on money from the government, residents not associated with the university still lost money. Ostensibly those Americans who resided in West Philadelphia paid taxes, and if that were the case then the university would be borrowing money from the government that took money from the residents to give back to the residents in the way of housing. All the while, Penn still benefited from government money to build exclusive housing for its students and affiliates. Although not practical, the entire interchange of funds for development could have been avoided if Penn chose not to expand so aggressively. As it were, the university came out ahead again.

Other than with the politicians and municipal officials, Penn had not, until that point, invited the opportunity to work closely with the black community in West Philadelphia. The quadripartite commission proposal reflected the members' awareness of urban universities like Penn taking advantage of neighborhoods that had little chance of resisting an institution's will to expand. The document claimed in a hopeful tone that "this proposal creates an unprecedented opportunity for an urban university to pioneer in the establishment of an acceptable pattern of institutional involvement in the problems of its neighbors in the community."[117]

The quadripartite commission came together rather quickly after a relatively peaceful but disruptive five-day demonstration on campus that involved community members and students. Those in positions of power at Penn did not have to use much if any imagination to understand the potential for heightened drama if the university did not bend in its position on expansion. In a letter to President Harnwell on February 24, 1969, the chairman of the board of trustees, William Day, wrote: "There are obviously many things we have learned from this experience, not the least of which is a dislike for having to conduct serious discussions knowing that the confrontation that we see on other campuses [like Columbia's] could envelope the University, most especially because of the presence and possible undue influence of non-University persons whose prime motivations may be those of disruption."[118] To be sure, the penchant for disruption of some "non-University persons" had actually motivated the trustees to take the unprecedented steps of incorporating a community perspective into the business of expansion.

Fearing that violence and chaos could visit Penn's campus, concerned university affiliates signed a petition indicating their support for a group calling itself the Committee to Prevent Another Columbia.[119] Nearly 250 people signed the document, but they could not slow the momentum of the campus protesters. The work that the university officials did was to prevent what happened at institutions like Columbia. There was, in essence, a "Columbia Effect," that led the trustees and other university officials to consider negotiating before more serious disruption occurred. Penn Professor Robert Rutman had been proud of the reaction of the university to the demonstrations, noting that "the entire demonstration was conducted without a trace of violence." More explicitly, Rutman stated: "At the start, the situation had all the ingredients of a second Columbia (meaning the student rebellion of April 1968), and everyone from the trustees to the students was aware of this."[120] According to a report by the American Council of Education, university officials were quite careful about choosing which student representatives with whom to negotiate. When the labor committee and more radical elements of the SDS threatened to sink negotiations, university officials were anxious to reach out to moderate elements. This became even more acute when the black community members arrived. Philadelphia teetered on the verge of violence after Dr. King's assassination and Penn affiliates, by way of proximity, could observe rebels who had reached frustration with their inability access opportunity and be heard. This proximity and the real or imagined threat of black violence motivated the Penn officials' sense of urgency.

In addition to the Committee to Prevent Another Columbia, the demonstrating students also met the indignation of a local Veterans of Foreign Wars (VFW) and American Legion post. Retired Col. Robert McClain had been a motor machinist mate, second class, in the U.S. Navy during World War II and was a mail carrier in 1969. He believed that the SDS participated in the demonstrations to plant seeds of anarchy and advance communism. The retired colonel explained that FBI director J. Edgar Hoover made it clear that "SDS flies two flags, the black flag of anarchy and the red flag of communism," and neither was tolerable in America.[121] Replying to a WCAU-TV editorial that assessed the number of participants in the protest at 1 percent of the student population, McClain declared that those who were protesting (whom he referred to as anarchists) should have been heavily censured: "The VFW cannot accept anarchy on the campuses of our universities, colleges, and high schools" for any reason. The news network suggested that the demonstrations successfully drew attention to the callousness with which the university treated its neighbors.

McClain claimed that the protesters' primary goal was to remove the Naval Reserve Officers' Training Corps from campus and that the students just tagged on the issue of housing. Further, the colonel suggested, the SDS took up the community's complaints when faced with the majority opposition of Penn students to SDS tactics. It was true that the SDS wanted the Reserved Officers' Training Corps (ROTC) removed from campus. Perhaps to McClain, the SDS's opposition to the ROTC and behavior was unpatriotic. As a veteran and member of the white working class, his opposition to the demonstrations was not surprising.[122] With respect to the community concerns, whether the SDS coalesced with black community members by way of pressure from other students was of little consequence. What mattered was that the coalition was in a place of power to discuss community issues.

The Penn chairman of the board of trustees, William Day, bolstered the quadripartite commission's suggestions. He explained that rather than a capitulation to students, the negotiated settlement of the commission was "a carefully worked out agreement" between all the parties.[123] That meant little to McClain, who stated: "If it took a sit-in to call the attention of the Trustees and we excuse anarchy because of it, then we must charge the Trustees with neglect of their duties." The VFW representative decried the "defiance of authority" that the protesters showed.[124] This was not an insignificant point because it spoke to the generational differences of culture. Many from McClain's generation celebrated respect for authority and remaining within the lines of order. The same was true for many from the student demonstrators' generation, but the culture had changed for some to allow questioning of authority. In Mc-Clain's opinion, the public had no obligation to fund institutions that allowed students to demonstrate on campus. To be sure, Penn is a privately funded institution. After the 1965 Higher Education Act, universities (private and public) received and dispensed federal funding that students received in the way of loans and grants. Otherwise, universities like Penn did not deal in public monies.

The fact that Penn made use of some state-appropriated money spurned state legislators to threaten the university if it did not rein in its dissidents. "If there are disorders, then throw them [the disorderly students] out of school or in jail," said Democratic State Representative Martin Mullins. "The people in the Commonwealth [Pennsylvania] are not going to keep tolerating this kind of foolishness on campuses."[125] Joining Mullins in lambasting college officials for their inability to maintain discipline on their campuses, Democratic State Representative Eugene Gelfand admonished: "If there's any more of this [disorders on campuses], it's going to affect the budgets. . . . The boys [in the legislature] are not happy about this."[126] Of course the budget of Penn was not in peril, but the sentiment of the political officials at the time was clear.

No matter when the students added the community's concerns about losing homes to their platform, some residents had unconditional support for them. "Those kids are terrific," stated Marvin Judson, a welder from the neighborhood. Regarding the McClain and the VFW, Judson issued sharp criticism: "Did you ever hear the American Legion come out and condemn racism and poverty? . . . Who gives a damn what those dopey veterans' groups think anyway? . . . All they know how to do is dress up in those dumb getups on July 4."[127]

Individual residents advocated the students' actions as well. Jessie Baker, a nurse's aide, believed that the Penn students did a good thing by demonstrating. "Yes, the students were right," she said.[128] She then explained a problem that black Americans had faced in their struggle for freedom throughout the nation. "It's about time somebody listened. We've been saying this for years, but nobody ever took any notice of us," Baker clarified. Her remarks reflected the sentiments of black people in Mississippi who experienced the terroristic acts of white racists for more than a century. When, in the summer of 1964, those black southerners found that the FBI arrived in Philadelphia, Mississippi, to investigate the murders of two courageous white activists (and one brave black Mississippi activist), some wondered if black life was as valuable as white because the FBI had not been outwardly present to investigate the previous murders of black citizens. Years later, in Philadelphia, Pennsylvania, Baker noted that black people had been voicing concerns about expansion and that perhaps those concerns were not worth addressing until white people (students) drew attention to the matter.

Other residents applauded the efforts of the students, but were wary about the commitment of the young activists. "I can't help being suspicious because, most of these kids were white," admitted housewife Rosa Lee Tindell.[129] She suggested that the students' actions may have been youthful hijinks or a "school-boy prank." Because people in the community had grown accustomed to the broken promises of policies and institutions that claimed to act on behalf of the most vulnerable, Tindell could not let herself believe that Penn would actually follow through with the inexpensive housing for displaced community members the university promised in the negotiations. Incredulously, she asked a *Philadelphia Tribune* journalist: "you don't think Penn is really going to give us that low-cost housing like they said they were, do you?"

An ostensibly young resident, Cynthia Lewis, supported the students' efforts, but wanted to see the methods of Black Power employed. "I'm hip. The white students should do their thing among their own people . . . while we ge[t] our ourselves (black people) together right here," the high school student opined.[130] Black Power advocates insisted that white people take the struggle for black freedom back to their communities, where they could most effectively communicate with white people. Black people, claimed Black Power leaders, needed to be in the vanguard on issues that affected the community or the community became subject to the decision-making power of outsiders. In this instance, mostly white students were definitely taking up the issue of black freedom with white administrators and trustees.

One area resident could appreciate what the students did but wished they had been more militant in their approach. Rachael Walker, a waitress, said: "My only complaint is that they were all so prim and proper."[131] In the city, demonstrations sometimes took on a disruptive or destructive tone. Philadelphia activist Walt Palmer remembered running a line of barbed wire across a street to prevent traffic from disrupting a protest.

Students like Ira Harkavy, who was an associate of Palmer's, believed that more militant acts than the sit-in would have "detracted from the issue of expansion." Walker predicted that perhaps because the action was so moderate "nothing will come of it."[132] She suggested that "if they would've put those big shots up against the wall, they would've gotten somewhere." Her call for militancy mirrored that of the Black Panthers and Black Power advocates like poet Amiri Baraka, who metaphorically employed the phrase: "Up against the wall, motherfucker, this is a stick up!"[133]

While supportive of the student agitators, there was a theme among residents of not expecting great progress with the university. Like many poor black people in the nation, some of the residents were disillusioned and did not have faith in white-controlled systems and structures. "What difference does it make," Percy Henderson asked.[134] Facing the insurmountable odds of poverty nearly paralyzed some people's ability to hope. Exasperated with poor circumstances, Henderson said: "We all know our housing has been bad, and it's going to stay bad." Succinctly summing up the position in which black residents found themselves in relation to Penn's expansion, Marvin Alsion, a mechanic's helper, conceded: "These houses might not be palaces, I'll admit," but "they're a lot better than being out in the street."[135] Their homes were in need of repair, sometimes infested with rodents, and even burglarized at times, but the meager structures in the way of Penn's planned construction meant the world to the inhabitants. Those shabby places represented the only piece of control over life that some residents had. The idea that a university, representing other powerful institutions, wanted to provide services to people whom black residents would likely never know, and that this university could move people out of their homes reminded the black residents just how powerless they actually were.

The sit-in and ensuing negotiations caught the attention of some of the most influential people in Philadelphia. A Penn faculty member claimed that the protest and settlement was "the greatest victory in the history of the American university."[136] Another Penn professor was also pleased with the outcome: "Thus, there comes about out of this sit-in, significant potentialities for interrelating the university and the community."[137] In a comment to the *New York Times*, William L. Day, chair of Penn's board of trustees, pointed up the fact that Penn students, faculty, and staff had been serving the surrounding community. The efforts, although valiant, were apparently not enough to keep community members from voicing their concerns about the university. They, along with their student allies, "focused people's minds on the need to do more in this area," Day said.[138]

In contrast to Columbia University trustees' reaction to the campus crisis the year before, Penn trustees seemed to be more open to engaging in the issues that the students raised. Day claimed that the demonstrations and the agreements that resulted from it "offered a great opportunity for all of us."[139] Student Robert Fried bolstered that point: "It's true that the university has been committed to social change. But the question that we want to address . . . is social change for whom, social change for what? Social change has not taken into consideration the people we are trying to help."[140]

For the administration and trustees directly involved in bringing the demonstrations to an end, the Penn demonstrations were undoubtedly trying and exhausting. To those who only had the opportunity to observe the development of the demonstrations through the media or by word of mouth, the protests may have been blown out of proportion. To contextualize the demonstrations and quell the anxieties of university supporters, Harnwell sent a letter to Penn alumni and donors.[141] Looking to distance the occurrences at Penn from those on other campuses, he wrote: "it was a continuous dialogue between sincerely concerned groups, and in its broader aspects was a most significant educational experience for all participants."

Although Harnwell did not explicitly acknowledge it, he and other university officials could only take advantage of those educational experiences because community members and students brought their protests onto campus. Until then, many at the university seemed satisfied to let the experience be that of primarily community members. Harnwell made it clear that although it was "characterized in the press as a 'sit-in,' in which emphasis on the negative aspects of occurrences on campuses today," the demonstrations brought to the fore "able leadership" while avoiding "hazardous extremes."[142] He claimed the events "achieved a constructive consensus." To clarify what actually occurred, the president attempted to summarize how he perceived the events unfolding. In doing so, he emphasized that "the demonstration was legal and civilized" and that the university rules and regulation were "scrupulously respected." The crowd of several hundred did not block passages or prevent "academic or administrative activity," the president reported.

By pointing out that the protesters' actions were in line with the policy, the president highlighted the effectiveness of the administration in decision making. Also, by downplaying the magnitude of the demonstrations in challenging the university, the president eased the anxieties of would-be donors. In spite of a peaceful protest in College Hall, the students and community members achieved progress in their goal of checking university expansion. University officials like Harnwell knew what protesting groups were capable of, and they did well to engage the demonstrators to reach an agreement before Penn's campus resembled Columbia's the previous year. The letter indicated that the welfare of the surrounding community was a personal concern for many of the administrators, faculty, and students. One could argue, however, that these demonstrations had to occur before the coalition could voice what the president referred to as their "convictions" about the neighborhoods.[143]

The intended audience for Harnwell's letter was a group of people that provided a great deal of support and funding for the university, and the intention was to mollify any fears they might have had about the protests. The language, however, is notable. Harnwell celebrated the legality and civilized behavior of the protesters. The destruction of homes and displacement of Mantua residents was both legal and civilized according to first-world standards, but the result was injurious to people who were largely powerless. The legal and civilized actions that demonstrators took did not physically harm or displace anyone or anyone's property. For the people in the community, in terms of space, the legal and civilized actions of the university had often proven to be detrimental.

Harnwell also accentuated the idea that no one went to hazardous extremes, but he did not define what that meant. Perhaps for him, the destruction of school property and the threats of violence he observed at other institutions constituted a hazardous extreme. But what, might community members have considered to be "hazardous extremes" in Penn's approach to university expansion? Many argued that purchasing "super blocks" and extirpating entire neighborhoods was extremely hazardous to those living around Penn. They asked just how much space a university needed and to what ends would the university go to get the territory. Harnwell began the last paragraph of the letter by stating: "We [university officials] share the widespread indignation over the wave of disruption that has swept so many other campuses," which presumably was meant to have a reassuring effect on the readers.[144]

Those observing from outside the United States lent an interesting perspective. An article in the U.K. newspaper the *Guardian* inferred that Penn's administration had planned and coordinated the sit-in. "The students were intelligent enough to plan the sit-in with all the protesting bodies and with officials of the university itself," journalist Alistair Cooke reported.[145] The reporter considered the sit-in and negotiations "unique in the recent history of student uprisings" because it lacked the disruption that other campus rebellions featured. Cooke noted that the issue of the science center and expansion was as controversial to Penn students and West Philadelphia activists as the gymnasium in Morningside Park was to Columbia students and Harlem activists the year before. The difference, according to the *Guardian*, was the measured approach of the Penn students who with cooperation from the administration overrode the more radical elements of the New Left to actually negotiate demands. "It (the demonstration) was, in a sense, the first university sit-in not controlled by any of the innumerable bodies of the New Left, by anarchists, by random rowdies, or by professional student agitators who flit from State to State and campus to campus to provide what they call 'guerilla leadership.'" That assertion was, of course, untrue, but there was a less dramatic tone associated with the Penn protest.

When trying to measure the negative effect of the sit-in on monetary gifts and donations, Penn director of development E. Craig Sweeten claimed that the damage was minimal at best. In a letter responding to a survey regarding alumni reaction, he indicated that by late March 1969, many alumni had contacted the university with negative reactions but a goodly number had reacted positively as well. He wrote that although some alumni expressed their desire to withhold monetary gifts, he could only identify one alumnus who specifically indicated that he was canceling his bequest of $100,000.[146] Sweeten also replied that another alumnus who had never given more the $100 gave $5,000 to the university along with a note congratulating the president on the way he handled the situation.

Looking back a year later, a report by the American Council on Education suggested that there were "five factors chiefly responsible for the relative stability" of the campus during the demonstrations. Those factors contributed to what the report considered to be a "positive conclusion."[147] The first factor was the ability of Penn officials to deal with the moderate rather than radical elements of the protesting group. Dissension among the demonstrators regarding strategies and goals, the report indicated, may have allowed the university officials to shape the direction of negotiations. A second reason was that the university and students had agreed upon demonstration guidelines for voicing their concerns as a group or crowd. The fact that there was a certain amount of trust that had been established between officials like vice provost for student affairs John Russell and the demonstrating students marked a third factor. In addition to the trust of administrators like Russell, the trustees put forth an effort to listen to students' concerns on the ground. Russell, for instance, communicated constantly with the city police to ensure that law enforcement did not aggravate the situation by storming campus. Then, of course, several faculty members played key roles as liaisons to the administration and students.

A fourth reason for stability, according to the report, was that university officials readily agreed to refrain from conducting any "military-related" research in the science center. Then, regarding housing, the report claims that the university "maintained a flexible posture" and made headway with demonstrators by submitting the proposal for the quadripartite commission and funds for low-income housing. Finally, the report contended that a fifth factor for a constructive conclusion to the sit-in was the absence of any major media presence. Penn officials had chosen not to give many if any interviews and the students only gave a few. This may have curtailed some of the posturing that often occurred with oppositional groups within the media. Overall, the report by the American Council on Education celebrated the role of Penn officials and not necessarily the students and community members who brought the issue to the consciousness of the officials. Perhaps the tone resulted from the author's connection the university itself. American Council on Education executive secretary and author of the report Richard A. Humphrey wrote a kindly letter to President Harnwell in 1970, stating: "this alum should warmly acknowledge the impressive job you have done for all of us. . . . We are all in your debt."[148]

Changes at Penn occurred following the demonstrations. An immediate result was the university's agreement to host a conference on student power. On March 27–30, a month after the College Hall takeover, the conference at Penn featured student activists and leaders from as far away as South Africa and France as well as student leaders closer to home. Domestic dissidents included Thomas Hayden from the SDS and James Turner, an activist with the Afro-American Society at Northwestern and founding director of Cornell's Africana Studies and Research Center. The goal of the conference was "to assess the nature and direction of student unrest throughout the world," said an article in the student paper.[149]

The sit-ins were, as scholar Wayne Glasker put it, an "accelerator" regarding other aspects of life at Penn. Just weeks after the demonstration, the university put together a committee on Afro-American Studies. As did some black students at Cornell, members of Penn's SAAS wanted an autonomous School of Black Studies that offered a separate curriculum at the undergraduate and graduate levels. Not surprisingly, university officials demurred on the idea of a separate school for Black Studies but did eventually approve a program in Afro-American Studies. To run the program, the university hired Penn and Oxford alumnus John Edgar Wideman. A luminary in the field of literature, Wideman took his post in spring 1972. Yale and Princeton alumnus Robert Engs came to teach black history. Engs had been a counselor for the Princeton Cooperative Schools Program. Federal Judge A. Leon Higginbotham taught courses on race and the law. In 1974, Houston Baker succeeded Wideman as director of the program. Baker came from Yale and the University of Virginia, where he was a professor in the Department of English.[150] It took struggle at Penn to make gains for black people on and off campus.

Life also changed for Harnwell. In spite of the kind words from alumni like Humphrey, Harnwell made the decision to resign in 1969. By 1970, he had joined the ranks of the majority of Ivy presidents who chose (and would choose) not to continue as leaders of their institutions. Students made it known that they wanted to be a part of the decision making and were part of the search committee for the new president.[151]

In recent years, Penn has gained a reputation for its university-community relations. With the arrival of the Barbara and Edward Netter Center for Community Partnerships, the university has in some ways become a national model for other urban colleges. The Ivy school in West Philadelphia has not always enjoyed such a positive reputation with the nearby neighborhoods, but the perception of the university has improved over the past five decades. As Penn grew in the 1990s and early 2000s, its leadership learned from the bullish expansion program it had adhered to in the postwar era. Even with the more community-inclusive approach to growth that Penn took, some still recognize the results of Penn's presence as threatening to the welfare of low-income neighbors who could not afford to enroll in the university or to even shop at the retail stores that catered to the primarily white middle- and upper-class students. It is clear that the adjacent blocks and neighborhoods are still under-resourced and suffer from neglect, but Penn thrives.

Looking back, Penn celebrates its progress. The university benefited from its engagement with the neighboring black community. Netter Center director Ira Harkavy, who as a student protested against Penn's expansion in the 1960s, indicated that in order to compete with Harvard, Penn had to be the best in an area in which Harvard could not compete.[152] Harvard, which is separated from Boston by the Charles River and enclosed in Cambridge because of its own expansion into working-class white neighborhoods, was not adjacent to a black urban area. Based on Penn's close proximity to a black ghetto, the choice of revitalization gave the Philadelphia Ivy a competitive advantage in at least one way. Another way involved the University City Science Center. In 1986, Penn president and historian Sheldon Hackney modestly considered the science center as one of three best known examples of the cooperation between student preparation, technological research and development, and vocational skills training.[153] The West Philadelphia Corporation became the West Philadelphia Partnership, restructuring "to include equal numbers of directors from neighborhood organizations, individuals, and the institutions involved in the affairs of the West Philadelphia community," Hackney said.[154] Additionally, Penn established the Office of Community-Oriented Policy Studies to innovate theories and practices that encouraged cooperation between the university and surrounding neighborhoods. Hackney knowingly admitted that "this new awareness results from the [university's] experience of the sixties." The lesson was that cooperation between an Ivy League institution and its neighbors involved the "experts" of the university both teaching and learning within the parameters of mutual respect. Only then could the university and community share.

Political scientist Elizabeth Strom aptly surmised that universities in urban areas not only have social and economic concerns to confront, but they also face the necessity of establishing and cultivating political strategies to lubricate the universities' development plans. Penn's political strategies in the twentieth century grew from the urban renewal movement. Strom noted that "over 45 percent of Penn's total square footage . . . was added" in the 1950s–1970s.[155] When the federal government plan (Section 112 of the American Housing Act of 1949) stipulated that municipalities could use university investment and expansion as part of the city's larger plan and that the federal government would match funding, a natural relationship formed between institutions like Penn and Columbia and their respective cities. These elite schools, encouraged by government entities, acted aggressively in their pursuit of growth and caused residential opposition that led to student engagement in community matters in a battle over who was worthy of place and space.

7

Blue Bulldogs and Black Panthers

Yale, New Haven, and Black Imaginings

At Yale I came to realize that my presence violated one of
the deepest taboos in American Life—the racial boundary
hedged around the life of the mind.
—Phillip M. Richards, 2006

New Haven, Connecticut, home of Yale University, garnered national
attention in 1970 for two reasons. That year, the city hosted the murder
trials of Bobby Seale and Ericka Huggins, members of the Black Panther
Party for Self Defense, as well as twelve others.[1] The well-covered courtroom drama reached households across the nation as Black Nationalism
itself seemed to be on trial. Images of Bobby Seale with tape over his
mouth symbolized, to many, the inability of black America to effectively
tell its side of the national narrative. To those who were not sympathetic
to the Panthers, the tape worked to impede, what non-sympathizers
considered, divisive rhetoric.[2]

Also in 1970, Yale became ground zero for opponents of U.S. intervention in the Vietnam War during the May Day protest. Hundreds of
students from across the country descended upon the campus to protest
the nation's escalation in the war effort and to demand that Yale extri-
cate itself from making any contributions to the controversial conflict in
Southeast Asia. Rebellion and resistance with regard to race, racism, and
war were prevalent on and off campus. The Panthers, whose style and
affect was catching, could be clearly identified as representatives of Black
Power in their apparel, stances, rhetoric and actions.

This chapter argues that for as important as the militancy of the Panthers was to the movement, so too was the methodical campaign that
black students waged for the first recognized Black Studies program in
the Ivy League. Those students contributed as much to Black Power as

the firearm-wielding, Mao Tse-tung quoting Black Panthers. Similarly, the challenge to the traditional curriculum of Yale matched the spirit of the push against the war that mostly white students made on the campus. The rise of Black Studies in the Ivy League played a significant role in the ascendance of youth and counterculture, as well as youth empowerment.

The efforts of black student activists were paying dividends as the Ivy League steadily increased its population of African American learners. According to an article in *Yale Alumni Magazine*, the eight Ivy League institutions and their "Sister Schools" (Mount Holyoke College, Vassar College, Wellesley College, Smith College, Radcliffe College, Bryn Mawr College, and Barnard College) doubled their black student acceptance rates between the 1967–1968 and 1968–1969 school years.[3] The article indicated that institutional officials realized that perhaps they had not been as committed to equalizing educational opportunity in the past as they should have been. Members of black student organizations on Ivy campuses helped administrators to recognize the potential for the good institutions could do if they opened their doors to previously nontraditional students.

Admission was only the first step in creating better life chances for black students. Once on campus, many black students needed to feel a sense of belonging. The article insightfully pointed out that even though university officials urged a good number of the black students in the late 1960s to apply and the university recruited them, the students often felt as though they unfairly bore the burden of their adjustment. The isolation that black students felt on Ivy campuses was psychologically damaging. From dating to the curriculum, these new students confronted the fact that they were what modern social scientists call the "other." Of course, the phenomenon was not new for black students at predominantly white institutions (PWIs), but that did not remove the anxiety that came with being the other in their scholastic and living environments.

In an effort to feel more at home, black students pushed to create a sense of belonging by demanding, requesting, and negotiating spaces that allowed them to be and learn about themselves. As the article aptly put it, "Colleges and universities have been among the first institutions in the society to feel the full effect of the new concern among Negroes with black pride and black self-determination."[4] Educational centers like Yale and its peers were almost perfect for the campaign for Black Student Power. Indeed, university campuses were main venues for a rising black consciousness. Black students, particularly in the late 1960s and early 1970s, wanted education on their own terms, which included not sacrificing their black identity.

A Dartmouth trustee noted that "tradition alone is a vacuum," and the *Yale Alumni Magazine* article affirmed that statement, noting that "traditional ways of doing things are . . . being given a second look—although at times such reexamination has needed the impetus of student protest before reluctant faculty and administration members were willing" to address the changes students suggested.[5] Yale did not face the type of major turmoil that Columbia, Cornell, and Harvard did in part because of the line of communication that the members of the Black Student Alliance of Yale (BSAY) and the Kingman Brewster–led administration.[6] Similar to the observations concerning the Student Afro-American Society (SAS) at Columbia, those who witnessed the activism of BSAY saw how effective the student group's efforts were. "Its ability to get things done ha[d] far outreached that of any other student organizations."[7]

The BSAY started unofficially as the Yale Discussion Group on Negro Affairs in 1964 with the fourteen black freshmen admits to the class of 1968. In the winter of 1964, black Yale students invited their peers from other Ivy and northeastern schools to campus for a dance mixer. This dance was significant because it represented a way for black students to openly socialize on campus when they were often shunned from doing so in other areas of campus life, and it began a yearly event that some students within the black Ivy League community called "Spook Weekend." Spook, of course, did not refer to members of the CIA (many of whom came from Yale), but rather to black people. As was the case with other words that white people used derogatorily against black people, members of the black community co-opted the word and used it for their own purposes. Thus, Spook Weekend (like the Penn Relays) became a phrase synonymous with black camaraderie and enjoyment. Before there were substantial numbers of black students at each of the Ivy institutions, the few would take the weekend to meet and discuss life in isolation while enjoying the company of similarly situated souls.[8]

Figure 7.1. Yale University student and progenitor of the first recognized Black Studies unit in the Ivy League, Armstead Robinson. Courtesy of Yale University Library, Manuscript and Archives.

The weekend hosted by Yale black students gave birth to the BSAY and eventually the black culture center (Afro-America). As Armstead Robinson, who arrived at Yale in the fall of 1964, remembered, the BSAY formed because "we (black students) felt a need to assert our sense of positive self-identification."[9] He emphasized that they "tried to create a normal social situation for themselves." That sense of normalcy seemed to be elusive in the traditionally white and privileged spaces of Ivy campuses. Concerning living arrangements, before the formation of the group black students had to live with white roommates. It was likely part of the university's plan to integrate the students into "Yale" life, but for some students it had the opposite effect. Some of the black students felt as though their rights to choose roommates had been abrogated, an issue that became one of the early points of protest for black students.

Between 1965 and 1968, Yale black students strengthened their community ties. Members of the BSAY participated in black history events in the local elementary and secondary schools. Other members tutored the younger students in hopes of illustrating the benefits of education. The black freedom movement's achievements in accommodations and voting for black people provided the background as students at Yale tried to show that they were relevant to the off-campus community as well. By the fall of 1968, black people and the BSAY, which listed 100 members, had gained strength.

A *Yale Alumni Magazine* article posed vital questions to readers: "How do you maintain a black identity in a white environment? How do you take advantage of what college can offer without being swallowed up by the white brand of cultural particularism?"[10] Four black Yale students (members of BSAY) their experience at one of the most admired higher education institutions in the world. The four students were Armstead Robinson (class of 1968); Raymond Nunn (class of 1969); Glenn E. deChabert (1970); and Larry Thompson (1972). Robinson, the oldest, explained that to be black and at Yale was a "fundamental contradiction."[11] He noted that "Yale . . . is the epitome of whiteness." Raymond Nunn echoed that sentiment, claiming that "Yale is the epitome of white, Anglo-Saxon, high Protestantism," and asserted that there was no possible way for a black student to have "total positive identification with Yale."[12] Nunn opined that he could never fully be a "Yale Man." He understood what being a Yale man had meant historically and he observed the status of Yale alumni in society; those images were not to what he aspired. He could not see himself occupying the same place in society because the position of powerful white men seemed to be instrumental to the powerlessness of so many in the black community.

Nunn's words smacked of the double consciousness about which Harvard alumnus W.E.B. Du Bois wrote in *The Souls of Black Folk*. The erudite work discussed the near impossibility of being both American and African when black people in the United States could not fully be either in the early twentieth century. In the same way that Du Bois found himself "at Harvard but not of Harvard" in the late nineteenth century,

254 BLUE BULLDOGS AND BLACK PANTHERS

Nunn was at Yale but certainly not *of* Yale in the 1960s. The sense of not quite belonging was not just in the mind of black students; some Yale officials made them feel that way. As Donald Ogilvie remembered about his first year at the university, campus police constantly made black students show their identification while on campus.[13] Those officers, who, according to Ogilvie, were not asking to see the identification of white students, could not conceive of the black students as Yale men.

Being at Yale (and in the Ivy League in general) evoked strange feelings for some black students. For Robinson, it was somewhat difficult to be recruited to the elite school and, as he put it, "coddled" by the white power structure while trying to maintain his black consciousness. Growing up in legally or de facto segregated environments handicapped some black students from the outset, observed the BSAY's first president Glenn deChabert. Upon arriving at Yale, the black student, according to deChabert, had to defend the importance and even equality of his blackness in a white bastion. Robinson asked rhetorically why a black student should come to Yale if there was the potential to feel isolated and discriminated against. Interestingly, he invoked his southern background as part of the reason for choosing to attend Yale. As a child of the South, he detested the overt racism that he faced in Virginia, where white residents (even by the time Robinson had left for college) participated in massive resistance to the 1954 Brown v. Board of Education decision. He optimistically believed that perhaps such intense racism would not exist in New Haven, Connecticut—a Union state that had been part of the Underground Railroad. To his disappointment, he encountered what he perceived as racism in spite of Yale's northern roots. As college attendance has not ever been mandatory, Robinson had the opportunity and choice to drop out or to attend another university. Dropping out, of course, would have flown in the face of the long-held black tradition of striving for education at all costs. Attending another university was also not an easily accessible option because Yale made the cost of attending much lower than the cost would have been at other institutions. That, too, was a part of the privilege associated with Ivy institutions. Each of the Ivies could afford to offer financial aid packages that covered the educational and living expenses of the new recruits.[14]

Robinson felt obligated to make the university more hospitable to black students who followed him. In 1964, when he arrived, Yale enrolled its largest class of black learners—14 of 1,050. As Brown University alumnus Barry Beckham had noted, a black student like him or Robinson could have been satisfied in believing (erroneously) he was just one of the very few black men in the nation who was intelligent enough to attend Yale. In Robinson's words, fourteen black students in his class "just wouldn't make it."[15] Employing a phrase popular in the black community at the time, Robinson did not mean that black students could not achieve; rather, he meant that only fourteen black students in a class of 1,050 was not satisfactory. That inspired him and his peers to do something about the small number of black students.

Like the black male students at Cornell in 1906 who came together to form a study group and then the fraternity Alpha Phi Alpha, the few black students in Yale's class of 1968 "found each other" for the sake of encouragement and support.[16] Thompson stated it explicitly: "Blacks have a habit of either dropping out or doing badly academically at this place unless they can get together with other blacks."[17] Albeit blunt, Thompson's point is bolstered by scholarship regarding black student retention.[18] Forty-five years later an African American student at Brown made the very same point: "when looking for a support system, if you constantly need to explain why you're feeling a certain way, that's exhausting." The student expressed that there is a "certain empowerment in knowing that there is a community that totally understands what you're going through."[19]

In the discussion of black student acclimation to college life, race is a primary but not the only factor. Robinson, deChabert, Thompson, and Nunn were either in or just past their teenage years. Life for most teenage men is difficult enough without having to focus on their race daily. The student, deChabert, put it aptly when he explained that most of black men who arrive on campus were alone for the first time in their lives. Furthermore, they were attempting to "develop a sense of self or self-consciousness."[20] That process, deChabert pointed out, was constantly disrupted by white students asking questions about what they called the "black problem." Although black students wanted others to understand them and the problems of their community, it became onerous and time-consuming to explain all things black to students, staff, and faculty members who had been exposed to few outside of their own white race.

Then, of course, there is the anxiety to achieve that comes along with being one of the first or few of one's race to attend an elite institution. Just as baseball legend Jackie Robinson felt immense pressure to succeed on behalf of his race, so too did black students. The students and the hall of fame ball player knew from experience that their failures would likely be judged in terms of their race and not individual shortcomings.[21] At the same time, however, if they succeeded, white observers often claimed that black students achieved in spite of their race or because they were exceptional. To be sure, any student who could afford to pay or had scored highly enough to attend an Ivy League school was exceptional in many ways, but the feeling of being separated from the race was troublesome. The inability to fit in created a certain kind of anxiety.

In part, the anxiety resulted from white peers' and officials' misunderstanding the intentions of black students in attending Yale and other Ivy institutions. Thompson suggested that once at Yale, many of the students, faculty, and administration treated him as though he was trying to escape his blackness and landed at the university. "From the time I walked in the doors, I began to notice that implicit in the minds of white students (and also some of the administration and faculty) was the assumption that by coming Yale I wanted 'in,' and that I meant to sever my ties with the black community," Nunn revealed.[22] Yale wanted him to assimilate to whiteness, he asserted. That, of course, had been the case with ethnic Europeans and Jews throughout the history of the Ivies, but the case was different as it concerned black Americans. For black American culture was very much American, but many of those at Yale did not perceive black culture and history in that way. Assessing the curriculum, Nunn claimed that "the education is geared to make him [the black student] as white as possible." In describing the interaction between white Yale affiliates and himself, Nunn explained that it was difficult for them to fathom that he would not aspire to be like them and eventually live in an environment steeped in white culture.

Attending an Ivy institution certainly invoked anxiety for black students and even caused them to question their presence. Like Beckham at Brown, Armstead Robinson wondered if Yale admitted him to merely enhance the lives of the white students. If that were the case, then Robinson believed it to be an act of paternalism. In his view, by inviting black students to attend at that moment in history, white university officials were acting as if they had done a favor for black students and the black community in general, while doing so actually helped white students to gain more experiences that allowed them to achieve in society. Without a confident self-identity, black students often suffered academically and, worse, psychologically. Robinson suggested that white students and alumni view Yale as "the epitome of all that is beauty and truth and light in America"; however, as a black student he viewed "Yale as having a rather limited function" in that it could "provide certain intellectual training and tools" that he could use to reform or dismantle the structures that Yale and the other Ivy institutions had supported for generations.[23]

Critics wondered whether black students, who sought higher numbers of black admits, faculty, administrators, and cultural spaces, were attempting to make Yale black. Robinson responded: "I don't think we're asking Yale to become black. . . . We accept that Yale is going to be white[,] but being here can have a certain functional utility" for blackness if the institution were to mobilize the appropriate resources.[24] For black students, that meant the creation of an Afro-American Studies program and space for black culture. Nunn saw himself as a "spy" at Yale, learning the white power structure. Perhaps his self-assessment was dramatic, but many young black people viewed attending white institutions similarly. As Nunn explained, "I'm beginning to know Yale, its functions, its operations within larger society." Nunn's explanation meshed well with the mission of Black Power that Stokely Carmichael outlined in his book *Black Power*. Carmichael's work discussed the function of white institutions in the movement for black freedom. According to the Black Power imperative, those from the black community were meant to use the resources of white institutions to improve black life.

Recent scholarship has characterized black students like those agitating at Yale as revolutionaries or participants in a metaphorical revolution on college campuses.[25] The movement to enhance the curriculum may have seemed revolutionary, and some students viewed it that way. Yale student Donald Ogilvie referred to his role in improving life for his peers as "a warrior. . . . I had to go out and kill the lion."[26] But in contrast to the young people who were uprooting colonialism abroad in the 1960s, domestic black students on college campuses were quite militant at times but mostly reformist in nature. "I don't see myself, quite frankly, as leading a revolution," stated Nunn. He did, however, see himself as potentially relevant "to whoever is going to try to revolutionize this country and make it a decent place for black people."[27] In sympathy with that statement, Dartmouth College alumnus and former Afro-American Society president Wallace Ford II remembered that he was not a militant, but rather he was dogmatic about creating opportunities for black people in the elite white space where he found himself.[28] Rather than revolutionaries, black student agitators at Yale viewed themselves as equals when addressing the representatives of the administration. In some ways, enforcing the equality of humanness among black and white people was revolutionary; however, students like deChabert took a much more simplistic view of their interactions. "We have not had to go the faculty or administration meeting and fall on our knees to ask for anything," he explained. Instead, "we have always confronted them . . . as . . . equal by virtue of the fact that we had done our homework."[29] Perhaps more than revolution, the Yale black students who advocated an Afro-American Studies program, a space for black culture, and higher numbers of black Yale affiliates sought the *evolution* of their American institution. In the Ivy League, most of the black students who participated in demonstrations and actions to advance opportunity on campus made it clear they did not, ultimately, want to hurt their institutions but rather to enrich the American establishments in the new age of black freedom.

The methods that black student activists employed at Yale and elsewhere in the Ivy League were under scrutiny as well. The president and future presidents of the United States campaigned against the demonstrations and protests that members of black organizations made on college campuses. The actions of Ivy League black students were that much more visible because of the place that those institutions held in the American mind and because of the educational centers' locations. In addition, the image of the black students looking and acting differently than their mostly white peers captured the imaginations of those who did not attend Ivy institutions. Many white and black people outside of those universities could not understand why some black students in these elite spaces were not complacent and satisfied with the fact that they were part of the best that America had to offer. Some militants, who were attempting to bring democracy to the streets (as the refrain went), wondered why black students were not doing more for the outside community. Black students at Yale believed that by organizing, learning the system, and bringing their talent back to their community they were a critical part of the struggle. To help in that effort, a Black Studies unit could have been quite useful, contended the students.

When members of the BSAY proposed the Afro-American Studies program, one administrator viewed the suggestion as significant on two accounts. Provost Charles Taylor Jr. believed that in one way, Black Studies was important because it allowed black students to recover the history and culture that the traditional curriculum of Yale had long ignored and outright neglected. The second reason he believed the proposal was effective concerned the idea that the "deficiency [of courses pertaining to black culture and life] ill serves Yale's white students, and the society in which they will play significant roles, by failing to offer them the opportunity to understand what it is to be a black American."[30]

Taylor's statement is revealing on several levels. The first is the clear awareness that Yale men were unreservedly supposed to "play significant roles" in American society. Second, he situated Black Studies as something that would ultimately benefit white students and white America. In recent decades, scholars like Derrick Bell and Kimberlé Crenshaw have advanced what they have termed critical race and interest convergence theories, which describe the willingness of white society and institutions to address the needs of black Americans as long as the actions benefits the majority race more.[31] Decisions could not be made just for the benefit of black citizens, even if they were righteous, contended critical race theorists.

According to Bell and others, white society and institutions were unwilling to make concessions for the sake of righteousness alone but rather for the sake of advancing white America. They pointed to the 1863 Emancipation Proclamation, the 1954 Brown v. Board decision, and even the 1964 Civil Rights Act as points that had been celebrated for the justice delivered to black people, when in fact white people benefited the most. Lincoln's Emancipation Proclamation did not free many if any black people but it did make it possible for black men to enlist in the military, allowing for a Union (federal) victory. When delivering its ruling on the Brown v. Board decision, the U.S. Supreme Court referred to the Cold War and America's image as a free democracy as a rationale for the decision. Critical race theorists also assert that the Civil Rights Act of 1964 passed because it made commerce with white business owners possible and, therefore, added to the wealth of those who had for so long tolerated segregation.[32] In the case of Black Studies at Yale, the idea was acceptable to at least one administrator because it would enhance the skill set of the white students, who, in his mind, were going on to lead the world anyway. These white young men were the sons of the men who were currently making decisions on behalf of the nation regarding world policy.

The creation of the Afro-American Study Group that Yale professor of political science Robert Dahl chaired was the administration's and faculty's attempt to rectify what Armstead Robinson called the "criminally insensitive" manner in which the university had interacted with black people in the past.[33] Students are necessarily transitory with regard to their collegiate careers and most complete their degrees within four years. During this era, even those who became campus demonstrators and activists usually graduated "on time." Students who observed peers staying beyond four years sometimes referred to them as "super seniors." Although the term could have been used as one of derision, it was generally used in fun. Risking derision for not graduating on time, Robinson and his classmate Donald Ogilvie made the crucial decision to remain an extra semester so that they could help the university plan a campus conference on the importance of a curriculum that included black history and culture. That conference, which hosted 150 students and scholars from around the nation, became the immediate precursor to the Black Studies program at Yale.[34]

In addition to students and scholars of the black experience, the 1968 conference featured national figures such as Yale alumnus McGeorge Bundy, who headed the philanthropic Ford Foundation. Bundy had also served as national security advisor to U.S. presidents John F. Kennedy and Lyndon B. Johnson as national security advisor and as a dean at Harvard University. Bundy had experience with the tenuous relationship of Ivy institutions to black America. He oversaw the $10 million grant that Columbia University received to improve its relations with the surrounding black communities of Harlem and Morningside Heights.[35] Invited by black students, Bundy found himself at the Yale conference articulating reasons for the implementation of a black-centered curriculum. Recently, the presence of Bundy and the role of the Ford Foundation in the making of Black Studies has become a point of controversy. At least one scholar links the arrival of Black Studies primarily to funding from philanthropic organizations (like the Ford Foundation) and not necessarily to the activism and agitation of black students who pushed vigorously for Black Studies.[36] However, the most accepted narrative in scholarly circles maintains that the demonstrations and negotiations of student activists provided the main impetus for change, and funding provided a supplemental push for the new field of study's arrival on hundreds of campuses during the late 1960s and early 1970s.

At the end of the Yale conference, the Afro-American Studies advisory committee had made the decision to create a proposal for a Black Studies major at Yale. Incidentally, Robinson, who took up the title of "super senior" because of his intricate role in planning the conference and then planning for the new major, eventually graduated under the tutelage of eminent historian C. Vann Woodward. He went on to receive a PhD in American history with an emphasis on the Civil War and founded the Carter G. Woodson Institute for Afro-American and African Studies at the University of Virginia. Yale and the University of Virginia were only two of the many educational institutions that Robinson consulted with to create Black Studies programs. He was a conduit of Black Power in white institutions.

Convincing Yale to add a Black Studies program required countless meetings in various departments across the university. The significance of students meeting with faculty members and decision makers to help them understand the viability and importance of adding the black experience to the curriculum cannot be minimized. Few college students ever commented on the general curriculum and still fewer thought to alter it. Robinson, the BSAY, and other black students who made this push at Yale (and at San Francisco State University and elsewhere) were particularly bold in their demands. For at least one student, the issue at hand could be summed up in one word: "truth." Donald Ogilvie, thirty-three years later, revealed that "we were frustrated with the lack of truth in the college curriculum."[37] Until then, Western civilization was Yale's untested truth.

To shore up the gaps of truth in the curriculum, members of the BSAY proposed Black Studies at Yale. In May 1969 Robinson declared: "Afro-American Studies was simply a rebellion against implicit racist assumptions that Yale courses had."[38] He exclaimed, "this nonsense can't be, and we demanded that either Yale reform itself . . . or else not have any blacks at all." Astute in his analyses of the critiques of Black Studies as being anti-intellectual, Robinson shot back: "the definition of intellectualism up to this point has been racist." He pointed to the fact that the role of black people had been neglected (often intentionally so), which as a practice is the opposite of intellectualism. By pushing for access to more knowledge, Robinson and other black students helped fulfill Yale's role as a purveyor of intellectualism. As one faculty member remembered three decades later, the beauty of the push for Black Studies was the fact that Yale's "African-American students undertook a tremendous task of educating the administration, the faculty and the other students."[39] The new unit met with approval, the professor believed, because "in an age of unruly protests, they used polite diplomacy, reason and research." At a time when administrators wondered nervously if Columbia-scale demonstrations could happen at Yale, it seemed the unruliness elsewhere helped to clarify the importance of Afro-American Studies.

The perceived lack of available material to analyze in such a program presented another point of argument for the mostly white faculty opponents of Black Studies. SNCC member and founding chairman of University of Massachusetts at Amherst's Black Studies department Michael Thelwell spoke directly to the inadequacy of that argument. "The rhetoric . . . barely conceals a most vulgar political and professional self-interest" in maintaining what had worked for white faculty throughout the ages.[40] Further, it may have revealed "an overt old-fashioned paternalism." Those faculty members upheld the fallacy that there was not sufficient material to support Black Studies as a significant field of interest in the academy. If that were factual, reasoned Thelwell, "it would constitute the strongest possible confirmation of the covert racism and cultural chauvinism which informs the intellectual and scholarly establishment." This line of thinking resulted in what Thelwell called "intellectual colonialism."[41] In couching the argument of insufficient material in such a term, Thelwell invoked images of the European and American colonial insistence on the infusion of Western culture in place of the cultural and historical connections known to natives of the occupied territories. Placing Black Studies into the curriculum would be sensible because the material, which was handily available, covered Americans who had been in the country well before it achieved nationhood. Just as colonialism was under attack worldwide, Thelwell supported the idea of removing vestiges of intellectual colonialism in higher education. The fight against neo-colonialism became a plank of SNCC campaign in the mid-1960s and was apparent in Thelwell's contestation of arguments opposing this new field of study in the latter part of the decade. He, too, was a purveyor of Black Power.

Opponents argued that the subjects housed within Black Studies could be covered in the traditional disciplines. Thelwell checked that argument by showing that those departments had had plenty of time before discussions of a Black Studies curriculum to prepare courses on the black experience, but they had not done so. Another black scholar, Jesse McDade (who later headed Brown University's Afro-American Studies program), made the same point regarding the representation of the black experience in courses until that point. "Whites have had hundreds of years to slowly incorporate Black Studies into relevant subject matter, and they have not done so. We [proponents of Black Studies] feel that it is safe to assume they never will, and probably would do a poor job if they did."[42] In the chance that the black experience received attention in the traditional courses, McDade observed that the discussion usually focused on slavery and its role in building Western civilization. That, he exclaimed, was only a part of the narrative of black life. Frankly, said McDade, "at this point in history, when Blacks can see what Whites have done to them, said about them, and written about them, they [black people] would be very foolish to let White people continue to 'leave Black people out of courses.'"

Similarly, where Black Studies promised the employment of black faculty to teach these classes in the new unit, traditional departments had not exerted sufficient effort to hire black scholars until that point. The conspicuously low numbers of black scholars on faculty at PWIs and especially in the Ivy League certified Thelwell's contention. He questioned whether white faculty members were any more prepared (and committed) to recruit black faculty members than they were the years before Black Studies arrived. Certainly, the desire to do so at the exclusion of the new unit was suspicious. The dearth of courses regarding the black experience was noticeable. In the semester after Yale black students led the effort for a Black Studies program, Professor Sydney Mintz, who was on the Afro-American studies committee, remarked on the interesting curricular phenomenon in spring 1969. "It's just that something's in the air. . . . The faculty and the administration have been persuaded that something they should have given attention to really deserves it now." [43] The "something" in the air was pressure from students around the nation—and at Yale in particular—to refresh the traditional curriculum. The fact that the rush was on to create "black courses" in light of the protests and demonstrations added further evidence to Thelwell's claim about the faculty not pressing to teach about or analyze the experience of black people. In that way, it was the mostly white faculty not the students who were reactionary. The push for Black Studies was part of other student demands about ending the war in Vietnam and opening up the university to coeducation.

Thelwell, although a supporter of Black Studies, cautioned against recruiting black faculty members from historically black colleges and universities (HBCUs) for the interdisciplinary units.[44] Doing this would make a Black Studies program guilty of disadvantaging black institutions in a way similar to PWIs. Scholar-activist Vincent Harding, who helped to found the Institute of the Black World, supported the effort to create Black Studies but also worried about a brain drain from black institutions.[45] Instead, Thelwell suggested, Black Studies units should look to work with HBCUs toward cooperation and mutual uplift.

Thelwell cut off another point against the rise of Black Studies. White faculty members in universities, he claimed, naturally opposed the creation of the new unit because Black Studies would draw resources and students from the traditional disciplines in the humanities and social sciences. Armstead Robinson's advisor for his undergraduate major in history, C. Vann Woodward, was one faculty member who was not in favor of Black Studies as a standalone unit. In a pamphlet entitled *Black Studies: Myths and Realities* (1969), the Sterling Professor of History conceded that "American history, the white man's version, could profit from an infusion of 'soul' " because of the neglectful lack of attention given the subject until then.[46]

Although Woodward could admit that the work of white historians had been insufficient, he was not willing to wholeheartedly support the rising call for black self-determination on campus. By stating that some "soul" should be infused in the traditional "white man's version" of history, Woodward was still asking that the subject be taught on the terms established by white scholars. About the prospect of a separate Black Studies curriculum, he said: "Either black history is an essential part of American history and must be included by all American historians, or it is unessential and can be segregated and left to black historians."[47] The statement assumed that black history and culture could not be an essential part of the traditional American narrative and still leave room for black historians to address the subject. "Negro history" he suggested, "is too important to be entirely [left] to Negro historians." What was remarkable about that particular statement was the fact that no one considered "white" history in the same way. Thus far, it had been perfectly acceptable for the overwhelming majority of white American scholars to write the history of the nation without worrying (aloud anyway) that white history may be too important to leave to white historians. Woodward, who researched the black experience in the Jim Crow South, may have believed that with employment of Black Studies, scholars like him would become obsolete or unnecessary. If that were the case, then Thelwell's point about the academic self-interest of white faculty members and scholars was that much more salient. Whatever the case, leaving the interpretation of history and culture to just one race—white or black—would, Thelwell claimed, "result in a fantastically abstract history."[48] One can only gather that until the 1960s, the soulless American historical narrative that students from kindergarten to graduate school imbibed was what Woodward feared a separate black curriculum to be—"fantastically abstract history."

In addition to the argument about competition for resources and students, some white faculty members questioned the objectivity that black scholars could have in researching and presenting material on the black cultural and historical experience. Thelwell dismissed this outright, as all of the humanities and social sciences would be undermined if such a measurement were applied to what was traditionally European- and American-based material. Another point that opponents made was that unqualified (by traditional university standards) Black Studies instructors would indoctrinate rather than educate students. Thelwell highlighted the irony of such concern for black students that existed in the new age of enlightenment. For all the years that black students could not attend (or minimally so) because of quotas and outright racial animus, some of these faculty members were not as worried about the needs of black students as they were when Black Studies threatened to arrive in the late 1960s. If the opponents of the new unit were realistic with themselves, asserted Thelwell, they would acknowledge that the "intellectual establishment . . . has always been the willing servant of wealth and power [and] in service to established power, which has, in this country, always been antithetical to the interests of black people."[49] The material and ideas that students and educators of Black Studies covered would necessarily challenge the established power structure.

Although few could deny the fact that the material providing the basis for Afro-American studies was conspicuously new to the traditional curriculum of Yale, there were those who questioned the methodology and pedagogy that educators would use to disseminate the information. Some questioned the potential rigor of Black Studies courses. Yale alumnus John Silber, who received a PhD in 1956, commented on the value of Black Studies. As president of Boston University in 1971, he called Black and Ethnic Studies a fad. "These demands for shallow and intellectually empty ethnic [and black] studies will disappear; or, universities will disappear," he predicted.[50] Yale black student deChabert put those concerns to rest: "Black people aren't asking for courses where they can go into the class and as a result of their environmental experiences be able to pull an honors or a high pass without any work. . . . They're asking for courses that could lead to something better in terms of their own thought."[51] Black students felt the need to justify the existence of courses covering the black experience and to show that they would not benefit specifically from their own environmental experiences. White students had for centuries, though, benefited from just that—their own environmental experiences provided an advantage to them without the traditional courses and educators being questioned about rigor or objectivity. That was the privilege of whiteness that prevailed in most institutions of higher education. When confronted with a change to the traditional curriculum, issues of depth and quality concerning the subject matter came to the fore of many white (and some black) critics' minds. In a direct challenge to the curriculum that existed before the arrival of Afro-American Studies and to traditional notions of rigor, Robinson cogently argued that "I hope that the Afro-American Studies program can begin a movement away from defining rigor in terms of how many pages long your paper is as opposed to the quality of thought contained in the paper."[52]

In terms of research, Yale black students analyzed the role of Black Studies as a new field of inquiry. According to Raymond Nunn, before the advent of Black Studies white male scholars or authors who made the slightest effort to "research" black experiences would be considered "experts" in mainstream (meaning white) scholarly circles.[53] The movement for Black Studies called on scholars of all races, for the first time, to meticulously focus on the history and culture of black people from the black perspective: "What we're calling for now is for people to do some really intensive reflection about what black America is, what our role in America has been, what we've done. . . . That's rigor," Nunn exclaimed. He put on notice all those scholars and writers who had, as one white official at Columbia University stated, "cut across the negro."[54] In this new era, Nunn warned, they would be "severely questioned."[55]

Perhaps the most popular term used by black student activists in the late 1960s and early 1970s was "relevance." For the new generation of black students, the utility of traditional Ivy curriculum was a point of contention. At institutions like Yale, no black students could deny the extensiveness of European and early white American culture in the curriculum. For white students, that meant that the curriculum reflected the work and contributions of their ancestors. As one student indicated, a white student could very well trace his lineage back to the figures that the professor discussed in a literature, history, or art course. That made the curriculum relevant to that white student and others like him. Black students, on the other hand, would find much less to relate to, and thus the course would be much less relevant.

With that in mind, the students were questioning the utility of education and how receiving an education could benefit the black community in general. Robinson aptly summarized the rising sentiment of black collegiates: "The relevance question . . . has to do with how well the educational process communicates ideas that have vitality and meaning for people's lives." This rebellion against the idea that there is only (to use a phrase made common in a subsequent era) the "Eurocentric" point of view, or that the Eurocentric point of view is the only acceptable position, provided the base off which campus radicals leapt, claimed Robinson.[56] Scholars such as Harold Cruse, who had visited Yale in 1968, cogently argued that the traditional concepts of culture in the university and elsewhere were inadequate. Such a stilted view of culture and history is detrimental, claimed Cruse and young Robinson. Discussing the need for education to be relevant, Robinson worried that "Ivory-towerism deprives the educational process of its most vital function: to prepare students for the society in which they must live."[57] In that way, according to Robinson and Cruse, the curriculum without Black Studies was not only anti-intellectual but also irrelevant.

To drive home the point that that the traditional curriculum was anti-intellectual in nature, Robinson recalled a personal experience of taking an American history course at Yale. "We saw blacks three times: the first time we saw them as happy slaves; next we saw them after the Civil War when they were wandering around confused and dazed, not knowing what to do; then, we didn't see them until the sixties, when they started raising hell."[58] The frustration that Robinson encapsulated in his brief summation represented what many African Americans had recognized in some form or another for decades. University of Pennsylvania alumnus Gerald Early confirmed the bleak portrayals of black citizens in his own education. Even though he grew up in a northern city with a historic black population, he rarely if ever learned anything (other than slavery) about black people when in school.[59] Black Studies, then, helped to solve the problem of anti-intellectualism that plagued the Ivy League and traditional curricula around the nation. Further, as BSAY member Craig Foster (class of 1970) stated, the students won the right to Black Studies because "we knew that our best weapon was our intellect. We made a strong rational argument that stood on its merits."[60]

After discussions with faculty members, the students and faculty group decided it was best to not make Black Studies a standalone major but rather one that could be shaped around existing majors. Taking this approach, the proposal for Black Studies met with little resistance, which was not the case at other institutions. At Columbia, a year later, students took over a building for a Black Studies Institute while campus demonstrations arose at Cornell and Harvard. On December 12, the Yale University News Bureau issued a press release, which stated that "for the first time, a new curriculum at Yale has been developed, not by the faculty alone but jointly with students. . . . Although many colleges, including Yale, have been offering individual courses in Afro-American Studies, the new Yale program is the first of a major university that makes this subject a field of study leading to a B.A. degree."[61] Those at the Ivy League institution in New Haven could once again boast that Yale was on the cutting edge of educational advancement. The press release (perhaps intentionally) did not take into account the fact that it took a coalition of working class students of color to create a program of Black Studies at San Francisco State University and that program inspired the one that sprouted at the elite Yale. The narrative of history has been kind to those with the most, and classism infected the way that the privileged power elite perceived themselves. Issues of class conflict aside, as a result of the unanimous vote of the Yale faculty Course of Study Committee, the proposal for Black Studies became a guideline for the new program.[62] Recognizing its privileged place in higher education, committee chair Robert Dahl proudly stated that Yale could have a "great influence" on other universities and colleges that were considering Black Studies programs.[63] It was an added bonus, he admitted, when he "realized we were rather ahead of other schools."

Back at Yale, the original Afro-American Studies advisory committee consisted of Robinson, sociology professor James A. Mau, history and American studies professor William S. McFeely, psychology professor Leonard W. Doob, psychiatry professor James P. Comer, English instructor Houston A. Baker, assistant dean of undergraduate affairs Paul B. Jones, and political science professor Robert Dahl. Roy S. Bryce-Laporte, professor of sociology, acted as the new director after the university brought him to Yale from his position at an institution in Europe. Most of the committee members were white, but they knew the potential value of Black Studies. The committee stated that "the experience of black people in the world is not merely a suitable object for serious academic study and teaching but one too relevant, vital, important, and rich in content to ignore."[64] Committee member Robert Dahl bolstered that point when he took note of the lack of knowledge concerning black history and culture. "It is hard to say which is more appalling . . . the ignorance of whites about black people or the ignorance of Afro-Americans about their own experience," he pondered. An expert on Caribbean culture, white anthropology professor Sidney Mintz, who received his PhD from Columbia, acted as the head of the faculty committee charged with overseeing the new program. Once Robinson and Ogilvie graduated, history major Dwight Raiford and American studies major Charles Finch served on the committee.

To be sure, there were scholars, like Mintz, who engaged black people in their research and teaching at Yale. C. Vann Woodward, author of the popular work *The Strange Career of Jim Crow*, researched topics that involved the black experience in the post-Reconstruction South. Although Woodward fashioned himself as a friend of the black community, he did not believe in the effectiveness of the Afro-American studies program, as he feared it might lead to racial isolation at the university. Woodward, who in 1965 proudly marched with Dr. King in Selma, was not willing to wholeheartedly support a program of Black Studies, which would have ostensibly hired black scholars for the faculty. It is questionable how many black faculty members Woodward assisted his department of history in hiring before the advent of Afro-American Studies. In 1969, the year after the program was approved, there was not one U.S.-born black person working as a tenure track professor in Yale's history department. In all of Yale, there was one black professor working in the department of English (Michael Cooke, born in Jamaica) and a professor of psychiatry in the Yale Child Study Center (James Comer, born in Indiana). Both had attended Yale.[65] John Blassingame, who received his PhD from Yale, became the first U.S.-born black member of the history department's faculty in 1971. Prior to the arrival of Blassingame, perhaps either Woodward's efforts in the campaign to integrate his department were lacking or it had not been a pressing issue to his history colleagues. In either case, Afro-American Studies sought to and eventually succeeded in employing black scholars in the humanities and social sciences much earlier than many other departments and units. Incidentally, Woodward later opposed affirmative action, another program instituted to present employment opportunities to those who had been previously shut out because of their race.

In "The Integrationist Ethic as a Basis for Scholarly Endeavors," Harold Cruse commented on the reaction to student activism surrounding demands for Black Studies. "In response to pressure for Black Studies," Cruse noted, "whites often attempt to speed to piecemeal integrative processes in favor of black integrationists," and in opposition to black separatists. He observed: "Another response to the demands of Black Studies involves questioning the validity of separatist doctrines." The proposal that black people would conceive of, create, and operate a unit focused on the study of African descended people in a white space was controversial. Black Studies, according to Cruse, was part of the black cultural nationalism movement, and he suggested that the traditional methods of educating had resulted in the cultural "retardation of the black bourgeoisie" and "intellectual class." To catch up, the young members of the black bourgeoisie pushed for an immediate remedy of the curriculum and not a "slow reformist" approach, Cruse explained. "They do not desire slow change; they demand rapid change" in the way they learned. Cruse interpreted the youth as saying: "We are going to study black history with an eye toward it being socially functional. We are going to have Black Studies with the understanding that this is a new social method of dealing with the infirmities of our society." Universities like Yale were part of what Cruse called the "cultural apparatus." As such, Cruse asserted, Black Studies had to "initiate a critical examination of, and critical approach into, the manifestations of . . . the cultural apparatus."[66]

There at the birth of the Afro-American Studies program, Bryce-Laporte represented an important and interesting choice for founding director. He had advocated for the program from the beginning: "Black Studies is the way by which respect is to be given to blacks and knowledge about blacks."[67] The leaders of three Black Studies programs at Ivy institutions in the late 1960s and early 1970s came from Latin America or the Caribbean: Bryce-Laporte at Yale, Ewart Guinier at Harvard, and Erroll G. Hill at Dartmouth. Thelwell, who ran the University of Massachusetts Afro-American Studies Department was also West Indian. This represented an interesting dynamic that quietly stirred conversations amongst U.S.-born black scholars. Although West Indian scholars and those from other parts of the African diaspora were clearly aware of the effects of racism, and colonialism in particular, their experience differed from that of black scholars who were born and reared in the United States. Having a nation in which black people held influential governmental posts and where black people made decisions on behalf of the country differentiated those West Indians from U.S.-born black people, who had in general been shut out from decision making on a large scale. Still, the spirit of Pan-Africanism drew together black people irrespective of their nations of origins. The same spirit that inspired

U.S.-born black people to support Garvey and Stokely Carmichael encouraged the support of foreign-born Black Studies chairs.

Bryce-Laporte, regardless of his country of origin, meant a great deal to Yale and especially to his students. Donald Ogilvie, one of the students who helped bring Black Studies into existence, remembered the professor as being "not all academician and not all activist."[68] That was an important combination for the early leaders of Black Studies programs. The experience of another of Bryce-Laporte's students provides an example of the benefits of having a Black Studies department and of black freedom in general. Henry Louis Gates Jr., who went on to become director of the Hutchins Center for African and African American Research at Harvard, expressed his gratitude for Bryce-Laporte's role in changing the trajectory of his life in his freshman year (1969). "A different model was available to me" he said, explaining that Bryce-Laporte inspired him to follow in his mentor's footsteps.[69] The possibilities and life chances of black students increased when they saw the variety and viability of options created in the academy.

The difference between Yale and some of the other institutions that established Black Studies programs early on was the sheer access to resources available to the Ivy League university. The university hired Charles Davis to take over the Afro-American studies program from Bryce-Laporte. Yale also acquired the assistance of literary icon Arna Bontemps, of Harlem Renaissance fame, to oversee the extensive collection of the famed author James Weldon Johnson, which was housed in the Beinecke Rare Book and Manuscript Library. In a similar manner during the period, Dartmouth College hired the accomplished jazz musician Don Cherry and Columbia University gave a post to social scientist Charles V. Hamilton, who co-wrote the very influential *Black Power* with activist Stokely Carmichael. Some of those who observed the employment of these figures in predominantly white elite schools worried about the future of historically black colleges and universities that might not be able to compete with the resources that elite private white institutions could offer. One document describing Afro-American Studies at Yale pointed out that in addition to those materials in the Beinecke Library, Yale had documents and papers germane to Black Studies in the Divinity School and Peabody Museum Anthropology Library. Those resources did not take into account others available in the city of New

Haven, the state of Connecticut, and in nearby New York City, which would all be quite attractive to scholars.[70] Taking note of the resources at Yale, nine fellows of the Danforth Foundation came to the New Haven campus to study in the 1969–1970 school year.

Another issue with the Black Studies program concerned the inter-disciplinary nature of the major and the potentiality of graduate study in the new field. Until the mid-twentieth century, university and college curricula had functioned largely on a core set of traditional disciplines in the humanities, social sciences, and applied sciences. Black Studies presented a challenge because it relied upon a combination of mostly the humanities and social sciences. This presented a problem for some, but for others, like Armstead Robinson, the interdisciplinarity of the program called for a larger university investment. If different depart-ments and units were a part of the curriculum and shared faculty, then the Afro-American Studies program would be securely implanted in the university. As Robinson indicated, to remove the Afro-American Stud-ies program in the future would require Yale "to literally tear away at the university structure."[71] There were no graduate programs in the new field and so, according to traditional standards, that meant there were no "experts" in the specific discipline of Black Studies.

In the same way that black students at Columbia and Penn coalesced with black community members off campus, so too did Yale students. In New Haven, members of the BSAY joined the Black Coalition, which consisted of community organizations and action groups. As was the case with Columbia University and Morningside Heights, Yale fostered a town-gown relationship with New Haven. The students on campus, because of their blackness, viewed themselves as surrogates of the off-campus black community. Historically there had been some apprehension on the part of community members when it came to relationships with university on any level but even with black students. To repair the relationship, black students arranged a situation with the university that allowed them to get paid through federal work study to tutor local black youth. Undoubt-edly, the students were doing positive work as both representatives of the university and of the black community; however, for some, tutoring was only a conduit to a sense of engagement the university students did not feel on campus. One BSAY member stated that tutoring "let's you escape the isolation of Yale while clearly doing something worthwhile."[72]

Yale's provost, Charles Taylor applauded the BSAY in the same way that Brown University's president Raymond Heffner and Dartmouth College's president John Dickey credited the black student groups on their campuses. Taylor asserted, "I think the BSAY, by virtue of what it has accomplished, has made two points worthy of national notice: first, that a rigorous program of intellectual substance can be developed on student initiative and receive fully faculty support, even in the atmosphere of racial self-consciousness; and second, that this happened at Yale much faster and more effectively because the students' approach to the problem, while urgent, was itself rational and critical. Such a demonstration could go far to restore faith in rational argument as an appropriate means of persuasion on national campuses."[73] Taylor's statement about the approach that Yale black students took is worthy of some analysis. The activism of students on college campuses elsewhere and that of demonstrators (not students) in urban areas also made Afro-American Studies possible. Taylor was not alone in his desire for rational discourse. Some, like famed psychologist Kenneth Clark (alumnus of Columbia University), believed that much of the action that demonstrators took for Black Studies was irrational. After students demonstrated on the campus of Antioch College, where Clark was a trustee, he stated that higher education institutions were in trouble: "to succumb to any form of dogmatism, to institutionalize the irrational is to fail in fulfilling this important obligation . . . [of] the custodians of the rational and intellectual approach to the study and eventual solution of difficult and complex human problems."[74] In protest, he resigned his post as trustee of Antioch.

Yale black students and white officials could meet on relatively peaceful terms because all of the parties were aware of the actions of young people and activists elsewhere. This was also the case at Dartmouth, where the students had unusual access to administrators and, most notably, the trustees. The provost at Yale indicated that reason and rational argument had been abandoned on many campuses and that the work of black students at Yale provided a successful example of a demonstration that worked. Although Provost Taylor was correct about the critical role that black Yale students played in negotiating with school officials, his intimation (similar to Clark's) that many of the campus rebellions had been irrational revealed his own bias as part of an older generation. Outside the walls of academe, older (born before World War II) white people in power domestically and abroad could not understand why black and other oppressed groups rebelled loudly and sometimes violently. This must have had to do with the privilege of those who had participated in the system that led to the oppression of black and brown people. In that system, there was room for oppressors to discuss issues rationally amongst themselves without ever having to seriously consider the ideas and desires of the oppressed.

When oppressed groups finally rebelled in ways outside of the strictures that oppressive groups had set for themselves, the oppressed groups appeared irrational to the oppressors. Moderate and sometimes liberal reaction to the black freedom movement (and strains of it, like Black Studies) of the 1960s displayed this best. Many allies claimed to sympathize with the demands and requests of black people as long as those black people used the courts (such as in Clark's Brown v. Board case), but those allies just could not go along with the tactics of rebelling black people who disrupted the system. The moderates, liberals, and even conservatives on issues of racial justice likely did not take into account the very methodical and rational struggle for freedom that had been in place since slavery reigned in the United States. Black people had written letters, requested audience with leaders, made valiant attempts at the moral suasion of those who opposed black rights. Even when these oppressed citizens finally succeeded in the courts or in legislation, there were still those white power stalwarts who refused to enforce the decisions and laws.

Black freedom fighters, out of exasperation with the slowness of progress, finally acted against the system with boycotts, sit-ins, takeovers, and even threats of violence; to some white and black investors in the system the actions of the protesters seemed irrational. In taking another vantage point, to some freedom fighters irrationality meant employing the same failing tactics while hoping for different outcomes. The students, who took over buildings and shut down campuses, believed they acted rationally and made reasonable demands. Some, of course, were more reasonable by traditional standards than others, but the black campus movement was not the result of students going insane or losing their minds; in fact, many scholars cogently argued the contrary. The students had become conscious of themselves as black people and as privileged representatives of the race, which led them toward militant action in some cases but not necessarily toward irrationality. It could also be argued that Yale officials, by endorsing Afro-American studies, finally acted reasonably toward black people, and by accommodating the requests and demands of their black students actually provided a model for campuses across the nation.

It was not just the older generation and conservatives who questioned the tactics of black campus activists. White student radicals did as well. Just four years earlier (1964), white students had been part of the contingent from Yale that went to Mississippi to register voters and challenge black oppression. An issue that rankled concerned white students in 1968 was the black agitators' need for separatism at times. As white college students also believed in racial equity and sacrificed their student status with demonstrations, some wondered why they could not always join like-minded black activists. Black student activists took the questions that white campus demonstrators asked about integrated efforts into account, but there were times when black students needed to act on their own behalf. Robinson addressed those concerns: "Some SDS types are upset because we don't want to cooperate and share our movement, telling them all that's going on."[75]

At Yale, Robinson challenged the SDS decision to not help or support black demands unless BSAY leadership shared their plans with the radical mostly white new left organization. He characterized such conditional support as racist, indicating that it was the "sweet racist line . . . to assume that they [white radicals] can be in on the planning of a black thing."[76] Black youth pushed against the notion that black people needed white assistance to achieve goals. BSAY members worried that the SDS was attempting to use black people "as a catalyst for their revolution," as Nunn put it. At Princeton, Columbia, and Cornell black student groups faced similar relational dynamics with the local SDS chapters.

Back at Yale, members of the BSAY were not ready to involve white radicals in the design phases of their campaigns. "We have no workable framework for white radicals at this time and in the foreseeable future, deChabert noted.[77] Testing the limits of the desires of white allies to be useful to the black freedom movement, he suggested that "if these people are sincere in their fights against oppression and what-not," they will be available to black activists whenever the black community should have the need for them. The issues that black student demonstrators raised were too important to allow anyone other than conscious members of the black community to interfere, they argued. Robinson exclaimed: "I'll be damned if I'm going to let them take things that are important to me and use them for themselves."

If relevance was a key term for Black Power advocates and other participants in the freedom movement, then so too was "self-determination." For the purpose of Plack Power, self-determination meant allowing black people to make decisions about and choose the direction of their movement. The call for self-determination stemmed from the historical phenomenon of some traditional civil rights groups and organizations that consisted of mostly black members seemingly yielding to the influence of the white members and financial supporters. Kendi (formerly Rogers) does well to point this out for HBCUs in *The Black Campus Movement*, but in advocacy organizations like the SCLC, NAACP, and Urban League there was a similar dynamic because of the close relationship that its leadership had to powerful white figures. Black Power advocates criticized those groups because the ties of the more traditional organizations stymied their abilities to make what Black Power activists considered to be the purest decisions on behalf of the community. In the 1950s, the NAACP backed away from its pursuit of the United Nations' charges against the United States for its ill treatment of black citizens, and Whitney Young (on behalf of the National Urban League) refused to damage relationships with corporate America and the government in the 1960s.[78] Black Power leaders like Carmichael, Newton, Ericka Huggins, and Rap Brown experimented with the idea of not catering to the desires or influence of members of the white establishment or even white radicals. Of course, their organizations still accepted money from white donors, but the Black Power leaders made it clear that they should be left to design and implement freedom strategies themselves. The work of the younger black leaders greatly inspired the attitudes and direction of the campus campaigns at Yale and in the Ivy League in the late 1960s.

Building Black Studies was not a burden that all black students were willing to bear. The narrative of the historical past that scholars craft often leads those in the present to believe that virtually everyone in the race sympathized with or even participated with the campaigns of the black freedom movement. This was not the case, but the attention that scholars pay to those agents of change can, at times, give the impression of total engagement. At Yale, some black students merely watched the campaign for the Afro-American Studies program unfurl, while others eschewed the issue altogether. Still other students remained intently focused on their studies in an effort to achieve the primary goal of most students at the university: graduation. A sophomore at the time, Kurt Schmoke, who went on to become the mayor of Baltimore, was not part of the effort to bring Black Studies to Yale in 1969. The former mayor and Yale Corporation (board of trustees) member recalled decades later that "I was among those underclassmen who were not immediately convinced of the need to create a separate program for what was often referred to as 'black studies.'"[79]

The task of those who sought to install the new unit was no different than that of black leaders who had attempted to "sell the Negro to himself."[80] In addition to the public outside of campus and Yale officials on campus, Black Studies advocates had to sell the idea to their black classmates and peers. Schmoke, who spoke at an Afro-American Studies memorial in 2002, admitted that he "came to appreciate why it was essential for a great university to have a quality program of African American studies." He noted that "the establishment of this department has enriched the quality of the academic life of this University." Inserting some levity regarding his earlier position on Black Studies, he conceded, "Fortunately . . . BSAY leaders paid no attention to me on this issue."[81] Indeed, it was lucky for Robinson, Ogilvie, and the rest of their comrades that they did not relent to the opposition or the lack of support they received from some of their peers. Schmoke, like so many others who chose not to participate in aspects of the black freedom movement, could only view the results admiringly while acknowledging the work of those who made sacrifices.

Just as not every black student supported Black Studies, not all black scholars in the academy endorsed the idea of a black-controlled and exclusively black-led unit within the hallowed halls of academe. Thomas Sowell, an alumnus of two Ivies, Harvard and Columbia, and a professor at Cornell, believed theoretically in Black Studies but opposed the programs he observed in 1969. He made the point that, based on the available research and scholastic resources, Black Studies could work at a minimal number of institutions, but at that point it was not feasible for programs to be effective at a higher number of universities. In his estimation, asking students to take degrees in the programs available amounted "to a fraud and a criminal waste of time for students whose intellectual skills will be desperately needed by the black community."[82]

Sowell abhorred the thought that the student advocates for Black Studies placed so much weight on relevance. He understood their protests to mean calls for more discussion about black life, which Sowell thought was unnecessary. The black community, he asserted, had an acute need for experts in law, medicine, and business. For him, the strong emphasis on humanities and the softer sciences would not be as beneficial to the immediate needs of the ghetto. Although Sowell has been controversial in some progressive scholarly circles, he, as one of few black men who had attended an Ivy League university in the 1950s and taught at one in the 1960s, provided a unique perspective on the pressures that some black college students faced. Those pressures, he said, included "guilt at his advantages over family and friends in the ghetto, frustration and ambivalence in dealing with white people and institutions, and a brutal academic competition with students who have been given much better preparation for it."[83] Then, of course, these young people were still coming of age, which was difficult enough in itself.

Harvard's first black full professor and one of the university's first African American administrators Martin Kilson agreed with Sowell. The desire of black campus militants to contribute to the community was misguided, said Kilson. In their rush for their units to be relevant to the masses of black people, he predicted, Black Studies advocates would eschew academic work in favor of social services and outreach. By his measure, the students could not very well cover the humanities and social sciences while also acting as practitioners in the community. To be sure, the phenomenon of studying and practicing happened in many disciplines (i.e., medicine, education, law, etc.) throughout the university, but for some reason it unsettled Kilson. He believed that if the idea was to make relevant contributions, then such a concept would best serve the community college where perhaps Black Studies programs could focus on the development of nurses and technicians. According to Kilson, it would not, however, work best in a university setting, where professors were ostensibly supposed to be training future academicians and policy makers. In the end, Kilson added, the push for Black Studies was really an attempt for black students to "demonstrate they have some worth."[84] For Kilson, the concept that the black students had worth was foregone, and that rendered the student-designed versions of Black Studies programs unnecessary and potentially irrelevant. The Harvard alumnus was not alone in his critique of the Black Studies units that students proposed. Integrationist leaders like Roy Wilkins and Bayard Rustin as well as literary figures like George Schuyler staunchly opposed even the creation of Black Studies—let alone its place in the university.

Regarding the guilt of advantages, Sowell explained that the militancy of black students on campus allowed them to, in one way, reach back to those in the ghetto not privileged enough to attend elite schools. By protesting and demonstrating, they could be useful to the movement in the era of relevance, claimed Sowell. He maintained that the manifestation of the need to bond with those less fortunate (militant demonstrations), created a situation in which higher education institutions foolishly satiated student demands out of fear that their schools might end up like the buildings that burned in the ghettoes during the long, hot summers. With that in mind, Sowell predicted that Black Studies could serve, abandon, or "exploit the suffering of black people."[85] Black Studies, and the centers built around the discipline, however, could also potentially ease those feelings of anxiety that Sowell admitted he and other black students had.

Fellow Harvard alumnus Kilson criticized the approach that student activists, like those in BSAY and the African and Afro-American Society (Afro) of Harvard, took toward establishing Black Studies. He viewed their impassioned campaign as antithetical to the "self-detached" scholarship of intellectuals such as Carter G. Woodson, Rayford Logan, and W.E.B. Du Bois. Rather than objective research and scholarly activity, Kilson believed that Black Studies advocates favored the "politicization of the organization and teaching of Afro-American Studies in colleges and universities."[86] Further, he noted, the progenitors of the systematic study of black culture, unlike the Black Studies advocates of the late 1960s, "were sensitive and modest human beings, not given to arrogant behavior or vengeful activity."[87] In that comment, Kilson addressed the behavior of those who demonstrated for the new unit. The Harvard professor did not expound on what he meant by arrogant behavior or vengeful activity, but his statement clearly indicated that he did not view the majority of demonstrators for Black Studies as productive to life on a university or college campus.

Born in 1931 and reared in an era that featured black American leaders who advocated powerfully for the racial integration of white institutions, Kilson did not believe that a program of study built exclusively for and by black people could stand within American society. "Negroes can master the best skills, tools, and habits in the humanities and social sciences only through unfettered interaction with white colleagues."[88] Furthermore, denying white participation in a Black Studies unit would amount to "black racist rot" in his estimation. Kilson, who would have otherwise been admired in black America, represented an older generation to the younger black generation that had been exposed to the ideas and philosophies of Black Power.[89] Although Kilson and others of his generation faced down racial discrimination in their own way, the newer generation looked to their own race for expertise in the study of black life, history, and culture. The idea that black people needed white people to succeed chafed members of the younger generation of students.

The conflicting stances of Kilson, Sowell, and Black Studies advocates mirrored the stances of civil rights leaders like Roy Wilkins and younger Black Power leaders like Carmichael and Cleveland Sellers in SNCC.[90] Earlier in the century, a similar debate about approaches to freedom existed between Marcus Garvey and Du Bois. Where Garvey had looked to take advantage of the Jim Crow desires of white America by creating a black economy and culture, Du Bois sought to open up all areas of white society to benefit black citizens. In the 1960s, Malcolm X and the Nation of Islam picked up where Garvey left off while King and Wilkins carried on the approach of Du Bois. More than any other, Malcolm X had a tremendous influence on militant black youth.[91] Kilson identified the ambitions of Malcolm X and the new Black Power activists as racist. He believed the same about most Black Studies units, pointing out that while Black Studies arose as a result of white racism the programs and departments were to be housed in white institutions.

Kilson, like Sowell, also addressed the issue of class in the rise of Black Studies. Kilson claimed that the various campaigns for Black Studies had been commandeered by the style and affectations of "lower-class" black youth; that middle-class black students had initiated the movement but later adapted the language and tactics of the urban ghettoes.[92] This scenario called for black students who attended Ivy League schools to perform their street blackness so as to remain credible to those outside the university. The reliance of black students on the lower socioeconomic class for style and methodology dismayed Kilson. He asserted, not incorrectly, that black students coming from a working and poverty class in 1967–1969 took over the Black Studies movement and brought with them Black Nationalist ideologies and a disdain for white traditionalism. He also stated that the members of the new cohort of black students were not used to the rigor that was typical of elite universities like Harvard and Yale. As a result, the new leadership cared more for cultural aggrandizement than rigor of scholarship. Rather than compete head-to-head with their white peers in the academic setting, the new black students focused on their militant posture to veil their insecurities, Kilson suggested. Speaking to the same sense of guilt that Sowell described, Kilson opined that middle-class black students tried to outdo their working and poverty class peers in terms of militancy out of a sense of obligation to the race and guilt regarding their own success.[93] He called the scenario "pathetic" and felt that most of the proposals for Black Studies were "academically shortsighted and deficient, anti-intellectual, politically bizarre, and—not the least—catharsis-prone."[94]

The Harvard professor's remarks reflected the respectability politics featured in the Civil Rights Movement. That aspect of the modern Civil Rights Movement contrasted with the lower socio-class's expectations. Elements of the black working and middle class, many of whom were male and veterans of World War II or the Korean War, reacted during the Civil Rights Movement out of a need to protect their investments. For instance, many owned homes and cars and believed strongly that America could be a place of advancement with the appropriate amount of determination and work. The underclass in the most poverty-stricken rural and urban areas, however, lacked much if any faith that the system could work for them.[95]

When the Civil Rights Movement made legislative and court gains like the 1954 Brown v. Board case, the 1964 Rights Act, the 1965 Voting Rights Act, and the 1968 Fair Housing Act, middle-class black people typically benefited. To achieve those goals, activists relied upon marches and boycotts in combination with the work of attorneys and black leaders such as Thurgood Marshall, Martin Luther King Jr., and Roy Wilkins. Although some members of the black community took advantage of those gains, those who could not afford to shop, had lost all faith in elected officials, and certainly had no money to purchase a home were left behind. Their approach to freedom was markedly and necessarily different than that of those black members of the middle and upper classes. When members of the underclass reacted to their exasperating circumstances by burning, looting, and violence, their actions unsettled those in the middle and upper classes who quickly denounced the "riot-ing" as irrational and unproductive to the causes of the race.

Civil rights leaders and appointed government officials voiced their opposition to Black Studies as well. Wilkins saw the students' efforts for autonomous Black Studies programs as a reflection of their hurt pride. Furthermore, he posited their campaigns were a "retreat from the tough and trying battle of a minority for dignity and equality."[96] As a front, the students called the black critics of Black Studies "Uncle Toms" and white detractors racist to mask the illogicality of the proposal for black-controlled units. Wilkins referred to Black Studies as "Jim Crow studies." He reminded students that if the institutions make use of tax money, creating all-black centers or institutes would be illegal according to the 1964 Civil Rights Act. Harvard alumnus Andrew Brimmer, ap-pointed to the board of governors of the Federal Reserve, had a similar but more nuanced take on Black Studies. He said that the black centers that were housing the new discipline on campuses throughout the na-tion were actually "a series of sheltered workshops in which black stu-dents languish during a considerable part of their college careers and then leave the campus ill-equipped to perform in a world which is plac-ing an increasingly heavy premium on technical skills and a vigorous intellect."[97] Black Studies, then, acted to "cripple young people—rather than strengthen their ability to compete in an economy of expanding opportunities," he emphasized. Brimmer knew from experience that the students needed to broaden their horizons at every chance.

Norman Hill, who at the time was the associate director of the A. Philip Randolph Institute, rightly indicated that the future of the Civil Rights Movement was at stake with the rise of Black Studies. Literally, those who took up Black Studies became the caretakers of the move-ment's memories with their teaching and research. Hill, who was also black, soberly commented on the miniscule number of black PhD recipients in the fields that would comprise Black Studies, and pointed to the fact that there simply were not enough to be placed at all the institutions where students demanded programs. The statistics, he said, made the students demands "unrealistic."[98] He also pointed to the inferior education they would receive if they did not have instructors trained at the highest level. What Hill essentially addressed was the institutional racism that made the pursuit of Black Studies difficult.

Had universities and colleges not abdicated their duties to investigate the experiences of nonwhite ethnic and racial groups, there probably would not have been a call for Black Studies in the first place. Also, had PWIs not denied entrance to black students as part of their institutional allegiance to Jim Crow, then black students would not have been saddled with the sense of otherness that overwhelmed them when they arrived at historically white colleges. Black students sought to fix the problems that institutional racism caused, but they met challenges from the likes of Hill. He believed that the so-called white allies that went along with Black Studies proposals often wanted to live out their fantasies of a black revolution and identify with the oppressed, when in fact those white allies would always have an advantage over their black counterparts. Many militants made similar assertions. With those concerns in mind, Hill stated emphatically that he was "wholeheartedly in support of black studies," but that the units had to be built on solid ground in order to be useful to the race.[99]

Nathan Hare was a stalwart of the Black Studies movement in the late 1960s. The director of the nation's first Black Studies department at San Francisco State College, he emphatically declared that "Afro-Americans must first blackwash then revamp the existing educational system and revolutionize America."[100] Hare chided peers like Kilson in the professoriate, saying that "to remain impartial in the educational arena is to allow the current partiality to whiteness to fester." Furthermore, "black education must be based on both ideological and pedagogical blackness." The need for Black Studies, according to Hare, was urgent, and until Black Studies was implemented at all levels of education, the system would suffer.

Black Studies might have a place in the university, conceded Kilson, but not in the way that black militant students conceived. In his version, "a Black Studies program must ward against producing a jack-of-all-disciplines but a master of none."[101] To avoid that, students should be encouraged to emphasize or "master" one discipline while being exposed to the others. Operating under the assumption that undergraduate education at a university is essentially preparation for future academic training, the professional trades (such as law or business), or government, Kilson indicated that having exposure to interdisciplinary studies was good, but selection committees of graduate schools and employers preferred mastery of a discipline. Yale's program of study did ensure that students took up a major in a single discipline to go along with the concentration in Afro-American Studies, and the same protocol was in place at Harvard.

Although Kilson was a well-esteemed scholar, his position concerning Black Studies met formidable opposition. While Kilson focused on the myth of Black Studies, Thelwell charged the Harvard scholar to pay attention to the myth of access that existed in a white-dominated socioeconomic power structure. Thelwell indicted Kilson and others of a brazen class contempt in their immediate ridicule of Black Studies proposals. Bitingly, Thelwell's critique continued to include what he viewed as the abiding belief of opponents of Black Studies in "a thoroughly uncritical acceptance of the methods, goals, and educational practices of white America save for its traditional exclusion of black people."[102]

Ivy institutions attempted to acquire the best talent for their fledgling Black Studies programs. Social scientist Charles V. Hamilton left Roosevelt University in Chicago to work for Columbia University in the City of New York. Roosevelt, in contrast to Columbia, had a larger population of black students and a relatively short institutional history. In spite of that, before Hamilton left for Columbia, Roosevelt featured one of the most dynamic and well-known political scientists of the era. Hamilton's book, *Black Power*, provided a guide for many of the actions that youth took to achieve Black Power. During the latter part of 1968 and the early part of 1969, black students at Columbia, riding the momentum of their victorious campaign against the construction of a gymnasium in a nearby Harlem park, demonstrated loudly for a Black Studies institute. The students, as members of Columbia's Students' Afro-American Society, were aware of the BSAY victory for Afro-American Studies at Yale, and they wanted their own. With the resources available to the second-largest landholding institution in New York City, the Ivy League school brought Hamilton to Columbia to accommodate the demands of the SAS and its white supporters.

In an article written for the *New York Post*, journalist Fern Marja Eckman interviewed Hamilton about his early impressions of the movement for Black Studies, the campaign for the institute at Columbia, and his thoughts toward the future of the discipline.[103] The interview, conducted in Hamilton's office on 114th street where students and community protesters had demonstrated just months earlier, revealed interesting aspects about the fledgling discipline. He remembered that when he came to Columbia, "my image at one point—because of my association with Stokely and so forth—was revolutionary." That, of course, was off-putting to some who irrationally feared the destruction that Black Power promised to wreak on established white institutions.

Many white (and some black) faculty members wondered whether qualified scholars or popular activists would be used to lead the new Black Studies programs. In some cases, black scholars did not have similar pedigrees as traditional white faculty. For instance, the erudite Harold Cruse could not boast a college degree, but his analysis of racial dynamics in the United States and abroad in his classic tome *The Crisis of the Negro Intellectual* (1967) was (and is) unassailable. As a result, he was invited to teach in the Black Studies program and eventually earned tenure at the University of Michigan. One could cogently argue that a scholar who could achieve tenure at one of the nation's finest research institutions was, ultimately, "qualified." Certainly, a lack of qualifications was not the case for University of Chicago alumnus Charles Hamilton, who, like most Black Studies instructors, took very seriously his charge to expose young minds to the daunting issues that faced black America in a systematic scholastic way. In the interview with Hamilton, Eckman raised the issue of student power and how it should be handled in the classroom. Hamilton, the consummate teacher, explained that as the professor he retained control of nearly all aspects of the course curriculum and facilitated and guided the discussions, but most of all he required the students to put their challenges on paper and test them against the evidence of research.

At Columbia, a key element of the SAS's protest for a Black Studies institute, was that students (ostensibly members of the SAS) should have the power to hire and tenure faculty. This demand was quite popular with young people, but was not supported by those who had made their careers in higher education institutions as faculty members. Hamilton believed strongly that students should be consulted regarding the employment of instructors for an institute, but he pulled up short on the option of students making personnel decisions. He advocated "a strong element of consultation, yes," he told Eckman, "but I'm not prepared at this juncture to give students the authority for hiring and firing personnel, promotions, tenure."[104] When confronted with the question of whether he would give more power to the requests and demands of black students than to other students at the university, Hamilton replied: "No, no."

Hamilton also responded to Harvard professor Martin Kilson's criticism of Black Studies becoming an ideological venue to preach the goodness of black people. Although the two scholars were on opposite ends of the spectrum with regard to their opinions of Black Power and its place in American society, Hamilton agreed that Black Studies was no place for "proselytizing" and that "where that happens, I will condemn it."[105] He said: "I'm not arguing here for objectivity because I don't believe in a value-free social science," echoing the stance that Thelwell had taken. "We have enough to do by examining all aspects on an academic level without getting into the ideological," Hamilton explained. In assessing Kilson's position on Black Studies, Hamilton believed that the Harvard administrator's anxieties got the best of him. In fear of the potential for black cultural "chestbeating," Hamilton claimed that Kilson "tunes out the whole [Black Studies] thing because of that," and "I think that is wrong." Hamilton declared that "there is a whole area of approach to this subject matter which maintains the field called [Black Studies]."[106]

Hamilton, like Thelwell and others, aggressively allayed apprehensiveness about Black Studies regarding standards. "The black struggle is not going to be advanced until and unless we develop a very, very, clear high caliber of expertise," he exclaimed as he pushed against the notion of black (and other students) sliding in Black Studies courses. Continuing, he noted that "the black community, which I'm intensely interested in, needs high caliber economists, high caliber lawyers." Where Kilson may have made assumptions about what would happen in Black Studies units, Hamilton was deeply invested in the outcomes of the students' efforts while matriculating through the course of study. If the leaders of the new field allowed students to not achieve excellence and then go on to receive a degree, the future of the black community would be endangered. In such a scenario, Hamilton shuddered at the thought that students "would go into the Harlem community with insufficient tools . . . [and] I'm just not going to do that." Deeply sensitive to the needs of black America, Hamilton was adamant about giving the black community the best: "Dammit, that's the way I feel about it," he affirmed.[107] Hamilton claimed that by focusing on the material and the interpretations and analysis given to the material, black and white learners would meet on a level plane. Although the viewpoints of the students would be colored by race and socioeconomic status, there would be value in studying the differences that arise.

Although Hamilton had no outright reservations about a separate unit for the study of the black experience, he was not pleased with the vast majority of Black Studies units that sprung up, in his view, as a political response to pressure that black students placed on mostly white institutions. He claimed to have surveyed more than eighty programs and believed that nearly all of them were, in his words, "worthless." Realizing that their institutions had done a poor job of covering the experience of black people domestically and internationally, many officials at higher education institutions throughout the United States tried to hastily patch the gaps with makeshift "Black Studies" units, according to Hamilton. That, he opined, did a disservice to the students and the institutions. If officials at these colleges and universities were forthright they would "admit to the students that [the institutions] can't get the talent, that [they] can't get the materials." Doing so would allow the students the option of assessing their role at the institutions and to leave if they deemed that necessary. As for why he and Columbia moved slower than other Ivy institutions, Hamilton clarified that he was "girding up for what is called the protracted struggle."[108]

Black Studies courses were available at Columbia, but there was no program or institute. Unlike Yale, Harvard, Princeton, Dartmouth, Cornell, Brown, and Penn, which had established programs in the 1960s and early 1970s, Columbia did not have a program of Black Studies until the 1980s. The lack of an established program did not seem to bother

Hamilton because his desire was for a sustainable, substantive unit. Perhaps, his "take our time" approach placed his university at a disadvantage with its peers in terms of what it had to offer potential students and faculty members. Hamilton valued careful progress, but it is possible that by not exploiting the momentum of the era, students missed out on an important opportunity to participate in the advancement of freedom by way of study.

Just as black students were aware of what the traditional Yale student was expected to do in society and the world, BSAY student Raymond Nunn understood his role for black students elsewhere. He revealed that "I saw the [Black Studies] major as something that had national importance."[109] Regarding Black Studies, he explained that "in working for the Afro-American studies major here we were very aware that if we could get something done here, we would help create the momentum to get things done other places." That for him and the other BSAY members meant that they bequeathed something to future generations of students and, hopefully, to larger society. Other institutions benefited from the work that the BSAY did, which became clearer as Black Studies programs, departments, and centers developed throughout across the country. Nunn's sentiment regarding the usefulness of the Yale campaign for Afro-American Studies fell in line with the intentions of so many generations of black leaders. Providing opportunity and life chances for black people in the future was the nature and underlying impetus of the black freedom movement.

With respect to the gains of Black Power and the larger struggle, Black Studies has been one of the most enduring legacies. Robinson reinforced Nunn's point: "The view that we had while working on the program was that here was a chance to strike a blow, to begin to reform American education so it corresponds to reality."[110] "I hope," Robinson declared, "it has as much influence as it can have." Evidence of the Yale campaign's effectiveness existed in the fact that Harvard, or as Robinson put, "our sister school to the north," modeled its Black Studies program after Yale's. At Yale in 1969, at least one black student appreciated the direction that his university took regarding the curriculum and resources arranged for the students. He noted that "Yale has made a solid beginning toward responding positively to the needs of black students. More is needed, and I hope it will come."[111]

Figure 7.2. A Black Panther Party member addresses a crowd at Yale University in May 1970. Courtesy of Yale University Archives.

In reflecting on the importance of Black Studies, Nunn took note of what could be possible at HBCUs. "A principal concern of mine was that we get some conservative black administrators on black college campuses to realize that they had the real potential to do something even greater than we could ever hope to get accomplished at Yale."[112] Although most HBCUs had black student bodies and administrations, they did not have institutional programs of Black Studies. At Howard, in 1968, black students protested for Black Studies and more importantly for a "Black University." Those students pushed their administrators to believe that if it were important to create the systematic study of people of African descent, then such an endeavor should take place at a black institution. The students sought to move the administrators beyond Negro advancement to Black Power. The creation of Black Studies units at HBCUs signaled self-determination to the new generation of black activists.

Black students at Yale and other Ivies recognized that if they were to be valued as Americans they would have to make a lasting impression on the nation's narrative. The notion of doing for black people, most of whom they would likely never meet, ran "through the minds of students on this particular campus and on campuses throughout the nation," explained deChabert. Although Ivy Leaguers realized that they were part of the elite and lived an exclusive life with their white peers, they also knew that they could never wholly be a part of that life. They realized that no matter how much opportunity they enjoyed as students, they were linked to the fortune of the rest of black America. Nunn, who was a part of a predominately white senior society at Yale, summarized it beautifully, "I wear three-piece suits because I like them . . . and at the same time I'm always cognizant of the fact that my destiny is inextricably bound up with the destiny of all black people."[113] The sense that the students' destinies were tied to that of black America created a network of brotherhood that fueled racial advancement on and off campus. It was almost like a "black man's burden" that students like Nunn happily shouldered.

Black people off campus in New Haven were attempting to chart a destiny for themselves. A local group, the Black Coalition, organized after

Figure 7.3. Black Panther Party member Steve Long at Yale University in May 1970. He, along with other Panthers, were in New Haven to observe the murder trial of Bobby Seale and to participate in the May Day antiwar demonstrations on campus. Courtesy of Yale University Library Manuscript and Archives.

residents rebelled violently in 1967 to police repression and poverty conditions.[114] The Black Coalition, consisting of neighborhood associations and advocacy groups, pushed the university to be more accessible to its neighbors. The national Black Panther Party for Self Defense had established a chapter in New Haven that experienced internal strife. As early as March 1969, Erica Huggins and other Panthers came to campus to share ideas about the establishment of free medical clinics in black communities, similar to the one the party had set up in Los Angeles.[115] The meeting ended when the group of one hundred students and activists left because of a bomb threat. There was no bomb, but the Panthers, by attempting to organize on campus, became a threat to the status quo. Although the black student population increased by 1969, most of the black people affiliated with Yale had historically worked in service capacities.[116] They came from the sizable black population (more than 27 percent) in New Haven that provided the impetus for the Panthers to mobilize. As had been the case in the cities where most of the urban Ivies existed, urban renewal unsettled black communities. Yale, like Penn, Columbia, and Harvard, took advantage of the governmental push, buying up large tracts of blighted neighborhoods and displacing residents. For that and other reasons, many of the black residents' attitudes toward Yale did not point to affection.

In the fall of 1969, the Panthers convened with students on campus to discuss the legal struggles that the party underwent nationally. By then, the New Haven chapter of the Panthers had organized a rally for the members who had been jailed in connection to the murder of Alex Rackley, an alleged government informer who infiltrated the chapter. Nearly 5,000 residents, students, and activists came together to protest what they called the mistreatment of the women who had been arrested. Several were either pregnant or had children but were not receiving proper prenatal health care within the local jail facility. In December, acting on behalf the mostly white campus chapter of the SDS, students went from classroom to classroom seeking financial and moral support for the imprisoned Panthers. As a result of the action, five students were suspended. Later in the spring, at the same time that white groups were offering their support of the Panthers, the university also heard from William Kunstler, the white attorney representing the party, who spoke on campus regarding the court proceedings.[117]

Figure 7.4. New Haven Youth on campus at Yale University during May Day and Black Panther trial demonstrations of 1970. Courtesy of Yale University Archives.

As Kunstler defended the Panthers, President Nixon extended U.S. attacks into Cambodia and Laos, instigating militant antiwar protests throughout the nation. Students were in the vanguard of the demonstrations. Indeed, 1970 was shaping up to be tumultuous for the country and Yale. Even Ivy status could not prevent the colonial institution from the rebellion of youth, black, white, and other.

In May 1970, university students and antiwar activists and supporters of the Panthers held an action on campus that drew the attention of the nation. Phillip M. Richards, a black alumnus who arrived in 1967, remembered the buzz on campus and in society the week of the trial. "It was a week in which apocalyptic rumors of the imminent physical destruction of spread throughout the academic communities of the East," he wrote nearly four decades later.[118] The heightened anxiety may have been a result, in part, of the very high usage of drugs like marijuana and acid that he also remembers being popular among students on campus. Richards was not altogether comfortable with the approach that the activists took to their issues and tried to avoid their demonstrations. What occurred that year was overwhelming for many students.

The Yale administration, under the leadership of Kingman Brewster, was preparing for student action weeks before the May Day demonstrations. Brewster had appointed Henry "Sam" Chauncey as an assistant whose sole purpose was to prevent the "death and destruction" of the university, Chauncey said.[119] He and others studied the administrative responses to student demonstrations at universities in the Ivy League and discovered that "throwing police at students" had not been a successful strategy. It caused more turmoil and even worked to radicalize more students. Chauncey learned this from Harvard University School of Law professor Archibald Cox, who by 1970 had great experience with negotiating student unrest on Ivy campuses. Cox investigated the famous Columbia 1968 uprisings and helped navigate the 1969 strike on Harvard's campus. In both cases, the administration called police onto campus, which reinvigorated activism. The potential for a flare up on the pristine elite campus that involved the Black Panthers, whom J. Edgar Hoover had characterized as the greatest threat to American security, was imminent and officials feared that violence would befall the university.

To avoid the tumult that its peer institutions faced, Yale administrators employed several methods. One included allowing the activists to gather unmolested by campus and city police. On a different score, administrators like Chauncey ensured that the most radical activist element was removed entirely from the demonstrations. He remembered that, perhaps illegally, he arranged for the bus bringing members of the Weathermen to New Haven to meet with severe mechanical problems.[120] The Weathermen had been known to use violence in their demonstrations. Chauncey believed he was saving the institution with the act of sabotage.

Brewster launched another offensive to diffuse the demonstrators: charm. Unlike Ivy presidents Grayson Kirk and Nathaniel Pusey, Brewster had an affable relationship with many students and was unafraid to interact with them. Despite his avowed liberalism, his goals were the same as his administrative peers—to keep radicalism from taking a stronghold on campus—but his disarming style differentiated him from other presidents. He sympathized with the students, even going so far as to admit that he was "skeptical of the ability of black revolutionaries to achieve a fair trial anywhere in the United States," including New

Haven.[121] That quotation ran on the front page of the *New York Times*. Observing the reaction of the nation, and especially that of authorities, to the Civil Rights Movement and Black Power Movement influenced Brewster's opinion of the prospects of achieving fairness in the court system for black people.

Because of the tension of the moment, the president declared that it would be difficult to uphold traditional academic standards and suspended normal grading procedures. He called on students, as well as faculty and staff, to prepare for the nearly 15,000 activists who were expected to arrive between May 1 and 3. Brewster was doing as much as he could to accommodate the students and demonstrators in order to avoid violence, including providing food and first aid to the visitors. As the trial began, interest heightened among the supporters of the Black Power advocates in the courtroom. On campus, there was disruption to daily operations, but there was little to no violence.

Black Power, Black Studies, and the Black Panthers came to Yale's campus in 1968–1970. The students who advocated for Black Studies on campus did not draw as much attention as the Black Panthers in New Haven did, but they were very much part of the same liberation movement. The Afro-American Studies program at Yale and Black Studies units at institutions throughout the nation filled in the gaps of truth. Furthermore, according to black Yale student Kurt Schmoke, who achieved fame in 1970 when he called upon Yale administrators for guidance in the midst of racial tension, "It [Afro-American Studies] has improved the Yale of today and will make this great University greater in the future."[122] Schmoke made that statement decades later, but at the time of the unit's conception he did not support Afro-American Studies. Those who did bring Black Studies to life, as well as those who exposed the mostly upper-class white students, alumni, and officials of Yale to the black experience on and off campus, took ownership of the Ivy League.

8

Black Studies the Hard Way

Fair Harvard Makes Curricular Changes

So fell the walls of academic exclusion which had previously
surrounded the ivory tower.
—The First Thirty Years of the Afro-American Studies
Department, 1999

"No baby was ever born under more adverse circumstances," observed
Harvard University administrator Henry Rosovsky thirty years after
the founding of the Afro-American Studies Department.[1] His statement could have applied to many of the Black Studies units that started
during the period. Just as Yale had to work out the details of a viable program to intellectually explore the black experience, so too did the other
universities and colleges in the Ivy League. After Yale initiated the
process for its Afro-American Studies program, Cornell and Harvard
found themselves in a race to establish their own Black Studies units.
Between 1968 and 1970, students, in different ways, pressured the Ivy
League to include black people in their curricula and lives on campus.
Yale's alumni magazine boasted that the New Haven Ivy would have the
first Afro-American Studies unit at a major university.[2] Of course, San
Francisco State College established the first Black Studies unit in 1968
after students and faculty had been teaching courses and conceiving
of a program in the preceding years. Still, the colleges and universities
of the Ivy League had to live up their missions of being in the vanguard of knowledge production and analysis. Students at Harvard and
Cornell took that challenge to heart.

This chapter and chapter 9 will delve into the arrival of Black Studies units to Harvard and Cornell. The birth of Afro-American Studies
at those two Ivies was not easy. In 1969, Black Studies came the hard
way, as it maneuvered around tradition and navigated bureaucracy. This

chapter will highlight the actors who used research, negotiations, and a strike to bring black culture to the nation's first and most popular university, Harvard.

As was the case with campaigns on the other Ivy campuses, the students fed off of each other's energy to advance their own goals. The uprising at Columbia over institutional ties to the war and expansion helped the causes at Harvard and Cornell. The push for Black Studies at Yale did as well. Harvard student Ernest Wilson III recollected that on a broader scale, activists like Malcolm X (who visited Harvard three times before his death), H. Rap Brown, and Stokely Carmichael affected them greatly, but the interaction they had with their "counterparts at Yale, Stanford, Howard, Princeton, Columbia and other institutions" meant just as much.[3] On campus Wilson and his peers benefited from the coaching of graduate students like Arnold Rampersad and Nell Irvin Painter (who went on to become world renowned scholars). The *Harvard Journal of Negro Affairs*, first published in 1964, allowed students some access to insights regarding black issues as well as opportunities to write and edit. By the next year, Harvard enrolled its largest class of black students up until that point; it included fifty black men. Life was slowly evolving for black students and faculty on campus, but it was still not quite welcoming at the elite institution in Cambridge.

Ernest Wilson III was one of the fifty new black students in 1966. His exposure in life was atypical of most American children because of his family's activism and success. He had come from a well-established family in Washington, D.C., where his father was an administrator at Howard University. Wilson was the descendant of three generations of college graduates, with one maternal relative being among the first to graduate from Howard Institute. Other family members attended and graduated from Harvard University as early as 1910 and 1942. As a child of the black elite, Wilson participated in black social organizations such as Jack and Jill, which provided him with a network of similarly situated young black people. When he was a teenager, Wilson worked as a page for the U.S. Supreme Court and was a stand-out student at Capitol Hill High School in Washington, D.C., where his best friends were the children of world leaders from nations such Niger and Saudi Arabia. With his father working as a dean of international students on Howard's campus, Wilson had the opportunity at a very young age to interact with black American leaders and figures from the continent of Africa and the diaspora. Wilson's family also hosted scholarly giants like Alain Locke and Sterling Brown.

Wilson's family was socioeconomically successful and politically active. His aunt was an original signatory to the document titled "We Charge Genocide," which was crafted by black communist leader William Patterson for submission to the United Nations in 1951 in an effort to indict the United States for its inhumane treatment of black people. Wilson's family's background and politics regarding race relations helped to shape his worldview before he ever decided to apply to Harvard. He came to the university quite aware of its prestige and its ability to unlock the doors of access in the world; he was also conscious of the struggle for black freedom that existed in the nation and world. Wilson was undoubtedly attracted to Harvard's acclaim, but he was not at all intimidated by the pedigree of his fellow white classmates, as he recognized his place in what Du Bois and others termed the Talented Tenth.[4]

Wilson's background was similar to that of Robert L. Hall, who had arrived a year earlier than Wilson. Originally from Tallahassee, Florida, Hall grew up on the campus of Florida A&M much the same way that Wilson grew up on the campus of Howard. Hall's father, Robert Harry Hall, worked as an accountant and his mother, Mary Susan Washington Hall, as a secretary at Florida A&M. A self-described "campus brat," Hall learned early on of the value of a college education. With Florida A&M being one of the most popular universities open to black students in the South, he had the opportunity to interact with the nation's leading black figures. His parents had both graduated from historically black Hampton University. Both Wilson and Hall soaked in the bourgeoning Civil Rights Movement in their respective cities. In Hall's Tallahassee, his family participated in a bus boycott that took cues from that which Martin Luther King Jr. led in Montgomery, Alabama. The two black Harvard men had parents connected to what Hall called the "black matrix." Their parents sought to uplift the race in organizations like the Carter G. Woodson Club, Omega Psi Phi Fraternity, Inc., and Delta Sigma Theta Sorority, Inc. Wilson and Hall both attended secondary school with mostly white students.

Hall had been recruited to St. Paul's School in Concord, New Hampshire, with the assistance of a black Episcopalian priest from Tallahassee who pressured Episcopal schools throughout the country to recruit and admit black students. At St. Paul's School, Hall became the second black student to attend the northern preparatory academy. Incidentally, he was a schoolmate of eventual Yale alumnus, Democratic U.S. senator, and presidential candidate John Kerry. Hall, because he graduated from St. Paul's, was a beneficiary of Harvard's prep school rating system, which moved prep school graduates farther along in the application process. According to Hall, 25 percent of his class at St. Paul's ended up enrolling at Harvard. Aside from being racial standouts in high school, Both Hall and Wilson distinguished themselves as popular and involved students. Both were athletes and participated in debate and other activities. Also, both had international experiences, with Hall studying abroad in France and Wilson's father heading the international program at Howard. After his travels, Hall came to Harvard in 1965 as one of forty black men; Wilson came as one of fifty black men in 1966. For both of them and their families, college life was not at all foreign.[5] Neither young man was actively recruited to Harvard, but rather they applied on their own volition. Even so, as Wilson stated, "Harvard was not a big deal." In their privileged lives before Harvard, they learned early to compete against their white peers, not fear them.

Hall and Wilson may not have represented the typical black student at Harvard, but they were not at all unique. Black figures such as famed Brooklyn Dodgers catcher Roy Campanella sent his son, Roy Campanella Jr. to Harvard and leftist attorney Conrad Lynn, who defended in court the likes of black self-defense advocate and ex-patriot Robert F. Williams, enrolled his daughter, Suzanne Lynn, in Radcliffe in the mid-1960s.

Life for the black students at Harvard and similar institutions was uneasy. As was the case with some black students at other institutions (then and now), there was a creeping sense that they perhaps did not belong in the white Anglo Saxon Protestant enclave. Although the number of black undergraduates increased, there was a large contingent of the white student demographic that constantly remained the same. Even as the black student percentage at Harvard rose, by the late 1960s it still had not eclipsed the percentage of alumni sons—the grand majority of whom were white.[6] Observing the growing black numbers, bold and discourteous white students wondered aloud if their fellow black students were admitted under special circumstances and not because of their talent. Some of the black students could have responded that they (white students) were admitted under the special circumstance of being a preferred prep school student or the son of an alumnus. When asking the question, however, what the white students really wanted to know was whether they had been admitted because they were black.[7]

On a different note, some black students felt as though they were not doing everything they could do for black people because they were at the Ivy League school. "Many of us were beginning to feel slightly guilty for being at Harvard while Mississippi was . . . Mississippi," wrote Ernest Wilson years later.[8] The feeling was similar to what today is referred to as "survivor's guilt." The Harvard black learners were unlike most of their peers in the nation—black or otherwise. They were quite conspicuous on campus but they also stood out in many of their communities. Henry Rosovsky claimed that the guilt spurred a sense of obligation to ensure that the education that they received was of "relevance" to the lives of the black masses. That echoed Cornell President James Perkins's point about the utility of the curriculum. Based on the rhetoric of the movements of the time, if those few black students were the chosen ones of their communities, then it was imperative that they gain knowledge and skills to empower the same neighborhoods while at the top university. Many Americans had for centuries used education as a wedge between those who could afford it and those who could not. The feeling of duty to the black community off campus, whether positive or not, created an additional burden for students.

The race consciousness that they were acquiring made it unlikely that they could focus solely on their studies without fear of disappointing the race or community if they did not succeed. The students, no matter what their socioeconomic background, were undergoing personal transformations. Ernest Wilson III called the state of transition "questing" in hopes of understanding what it meant to be black on a white campus.[9] He, along with his racial peers, wrestled with the alienation that young people his age experienced but also with the idea of fitting into the movement. The black students were experiencing, what Princeton-trained psychologist William Cross termed, "the Negro to Black conversion" in the midst of the movement for black consciousness.[10] On campus, that may

Figure 8.1. Barnard College students Ntzoke Shange (left) and Thulani Davis holding signs and marching with Princeton University student Rod Hamilton (behind Shange and Davis) and Harvard University student Ernest Wilson III (to right of Davis) in a 1967 United Nations antiwar demonstration in New York City. Courtesy of Thulani Davis.

have involved black students joining the Harvard and Radcliffe Association of African and Afro-American Student known as Afro. As part of Afro, one could serve on various committees, including the Negro Studies Committee, which focused on exposing the students to the art and literary works of black creators.

Hall recalled being on Afro's Negro Studies Committee and meeting the editor of *Liberator* magazine, Daniel Watts. Founded in 1960, by 1964 the *Liberator* was a periodical that billed itself as "the voice of the Afro-American protest movement in America and the liberation movement of Africa."[11] Based in New York, Daniel Watts and the *Liberator* had amassed a following of militant black activists and nationalists in the late 1960s. Hall's interaction with Watts when the editor visited Harvard in 1965 for a lecture was life-altering. Along with meeting Watts, reading the *Autobiography of Malcolm X* captured Hall's imagination and helped him to see the possibilities of blackness and understand the demands

302 | BLACK STUDIES THE HARD WAY

of movement making. After those experiences, Hall intensified his activities. He even taught black history courses at Norfolk Prison Colony,
where Malcolm X was once an inmate.[12]

Hall was not alone in his conversion. For Wilson, it was Stokely Carmichael's book, *Black Power: The Politics of Liberation*, that helped shape
his consciousness. Another student, Dru King, who was the son of a
medical doctor, had joined forces with the Student Nonviolent Coordinating Committee (SNCC) in the Boston neighborhood of Roxbury.
Students like Leslie "Skip" Griffin involved himself in the work of some
of the black churches in Roxbury as well. In 1967 students like King, Griffin, Wilson, and Hall, as well as black students from Dartmouth, Boston
University, Northeastern University, and Wellesley College joined SNCC
activists in the area to organize a symposium called "Black Power and
the Talented Tenth." The symposium called together the privileged black
campus learners from the Northeast and people from the local community who struggled against institutional racism.[13] Students came from
institutions like Columbia University and Barnard College to learn from
the seasoned SNCC activists and their peers.[14] Living in an area next to
an urban center allowed Harvard and Radcliffe black students to make
these kinds of alliances and host these types of events; whereas doing so
was much less practicable for students at Cornell.

Black students could not afford to only focus on issues that affected
them or the black community if they were to sustain themselves at the
elite institution. They set about piercing the culture of Harvard by working in areas where black students had traditionally not been present.
One wrote for the school newspaper; another for the humor publication
the *Harvard Lampoon*. Others sang in the Harvard Glee Club and joined
houses that had not previously welcomed black members. Pioneering
black students attempted to embed themselves in traditional Harvard
cocurricular activities as well.

In the United States, the movement for black freedom was changing
to address the needs of black people in economically depressed urban
areas and in spaces where institutional racism reigned. In the spring
of 1967, Harvard black student Charles J. Hamilton Jr. (no relation to
Charles V. Hamilton of *Black Power* fame), wrote about the conference
and the SNCC's turn toward northern slums in the school's newspaper,
The Harvard Crimson. Leaders like James Forman, who was featured at

the Black Power and the Talented Tenth conference, simultaneously appealed to and taunted black students at Harvard. "I'm fighting for your mind, Baby, just like Whitey," Forman told an audience of black students, insinuating that black student had removed themselves mentally from the black community.[15] He warned that as privileged black students they had the power to liberate or oppress the black masses, "Your very presence in this American educational institution is, by example, oppressing your black brothers and sisters."

Sensitive to the jab, Hamilton, the student, questioned Forman and SNCC's understanding of the commitment of black intellectuals to the movement. The conscious black student at Harvard is "proudly intellectual and even prouder of having reached Harvard," Hamilton wrote. Ernest Wilson III described regular discussions that lasted to the early morning hours about how they, as Harvard men, could use their privilege to help the masses. He took seriously his place in the Talented Tenth. Thulani Davis, a student from Barnard College in New York City who attended the conference, found Forman's comments laughably condescending.[16] Davis, who grew up on Hampton University's campus in Virginia the daughter of an administrator and teacher, was intimately familiar with the desegregation movements of the South. Skip Griffin's family actually won a lawsuit against the State of Virginia for its accommodation of the massive resistance movement to impede the desegregation of public schools.[17] So some Ivy League students could not only recognize the movement, they had lived it.

Davis believed that Forman and some of the SNCC activists misjudged their audience by claiming the students were not interested in the movement. For years, students like her had been organizing in various capacities on behalf of the Civil Rights Movement. Additionally, in the early 1960s, there had a been a successful group called the Northern Student Movement operating in areas like Boston, New Haven, and New York. Black students like Bill Strickland and white ally students like Peter Countryman worked from their campuses to contribute to SNCC's efforts. What Hamilton and Davis teased out is that which Ernest Wilson III described as being "on the sharp edge of the knife." Simply put, he explained the false dichotomous choices that were being thrust upon them. "We feared that we would either be sellouts to the white man or Black Panther communists without having any options in between. In retrospect, it was irrational, but it was a very real feeling of ambiguity and pain," he remembered.

Although students were incapable of devoting all their time to the movement, they sought to innovate and create in ways that even SNCC could not recognize. Hamilton asserted that the students, who faced marginalization in the white environs of Harvard and from the hardcore activists in the movement, "will not be intimidated for [their] hard work or antagonized for their efforts to 'make it'" at an Ivy League university.[18] With the black students' privilege came pressure from a number of different angles. In the face of the pressure, Harvard and Radcliffe black students excelled on campus and worked with members of the black community in Roxbury to advance freedom causes through their tutorials of children and organization of black businesses. Hamilton critiqued SNCC for deriding the work of students while uplifting the "kind of street-oriented, ultrahip, political lingo that makes all SNCC statements sound distressingly similar." The point was, according to Hamilton, SNCC and the movement needed students from Ivy League and elite universities to represent the black intelligentsia and to infiltrate the same institutions at which SNCC demanded change.

In the 1968 edition of the *Harvard Journal of Negro Affairs*, Robert L. Hall attempted to merge the interests of SNCC and Harvard's black student group Afro with his account of "SNCC's Appeal to Northern Students." Writing the article while working on the assembly line in the Chrysler plant in Newark, Delaware, he focused on the need for students to take action and to think of themselves as part of the black collective. Hall also refused to be portrayed as a "sellout" because he attended and excelled at Harvard. Northern black students at universities and colleges like Harvard had to balance their activism on and off campus, claimed Hall.[19] The off-campus activism included organizing, tutoring, and protesting the war. The on-campus activism pointed toward Black Studies.

Much the same way that Columbia, Penn, Brown, and Yale students understood they had the support of the neighboring black community, Harvard students enjoyed the support of black activists and community members who were involved in the movements for black freedom and against the Vietnam conflict. The turmoil surrounding the war in Vietnam has often been depicted as the domain of white radical activists in the New Left; however, the most current studies have revealed that black students and agitators demonstrated against the war with similar verve. Opposition to the conflict in Southeast Asia was a plank of SNCC's anti-imperialism platform. Students also took to heart the words of Martin Luther King Jr., who came out publicly against the war in his sermon at Riverside Baptist Church in 1967. At historically black Southern University in Louisiana, students took over buildings on campus to end mandatory ROTC training during the war. In New York City, black Columbia students participated in the national antiwar demonstration in 1967. Similarly, black students at Harvard moved to check the university's ties to war research. Robert L. Hall at Harvard was one of the students who raised his voice against the war. On the steps of Widener Library, Hall decried the nation's involvement in the conflict and explained how the war was draining the black community of necessary resources at a most inopportune time.[20] In the midst of pushing against the U.S. war effort, the students recognized there was work to do on behalf of black people back on campus. In March 1968, King came to Harvard's campus to discuss his views against U.S. intervention into Southeast Asia. Less than a month later, King died at the hands of a white gunman. The beloved leader's death sharpened many students' attention to the issues that he had highlighted in life. Hall recalled later that "King's assassination was definitely a galvanic event . . . if not THE galvanic event that crystallized and gave force to the nascent Black Studies movement at Harvard."[21]

At the same time that black students at Harvard chose which part, if any, they would play in the black liberation movement, white student members of the SDS were tactically poking at the university. As one of the largest chapters of the SDS in the nation, Harvard's group had been active on two fronts. The first was the school's relationship to the war effort; the second was expansion. Harvard officials, in the 1940s, had already created policies that prohibited professors from doing government-funded classified research on campus transparency was required in regard to all government-contracted studies. Unlike at Columbia, the SDS did not discover private links to the Institute for Defense Analyses. There was, however, controversy at Harvard and Columbia over the institutions allowing Dow Chemical Company to recruit on campus. Seeking the brightest employees, recruiters for companies naturally gravitated to college campuses and especially elite universities. Perhaps at another moment in time the presence of Dow's recruiters would not have been cause for controversy, but with scenes of the Vietnam War shown nightly on television, young people and Americans in general could see the effects napalm had on the earth and on human flesh. And Dow Chemical had helped to develop it.[22]

Mostly white followers of the SDS mobilized to prevent Dow's recruitment of students. In its information campaign, the SDS asked students and university officials to see recruitment to its logical end. Their view was that if Harvard officials allowed a chemical company known for providing the tools of mass and heinous destruction in Vietnam to recruit on campus, then Harvard tacitly supported U.S. involvement in the conflict. The SDS questioned the practical use of the liberal education they received, asking if should it be applied for life or death. The SDS also pointed out that even when working with a private company like Dow, indirectly the university was partnering with the government to assist in the war effort. The issue was important to many of the 1,000 Harvard students who had attended the 1967 march on the Pentagon to end the Vietnam conflict.[23]

With that in their minds on October 25, 1967, SDS members, along with hundreds of followers and sympathizers, staged a sit-in during a Dow recruiter's presentation on campus. They refused to allow the recruiter to leave until he pledged not to return. In spite of threats from a dean promising disciplinary action, the 300 students refused to end their demonstration. Hearing that the university had contacted the police to remove demonstrators, SDS leadership had to decide on a course of action. It chose prudence over escalated confrontation. The all-day sit-in ended the same evening, but not before students, including some who had not even participated in the protest, handed their identification cards to the dean to signify their solidarity with the demonstrators.[24]

Even though the faculty voted to punish the leaders and participants in the protest, the students of Harvard won a larger victory. As a result of the SDS's effort, the faculty decided to add a student representative body to advise the faculty on campus matters. In an extremely hierarchal decision-making structure, it was a progressive step. Additionally, the SDS observed that students could be inspired to action and it learned how the university would react to a mass demonstration.

"A Justified Demonstration" read the headlines of *The Harvard Crimson* (student newspaper) the next day. In support of the action, the paper asserted that dissent on the controversial issue of Vietnam (and the weapons used in the conflict) was necessary and not one that could be addressed solely by traditional political mechanisms. *The Harvard Crimson* went a step further in declaring that the administration should not punish students for making a stand on behalf of morality. Although the university should not prevent private companies from coming to campus to recruit, stated the paper, the university should inform such companies of the welcome they might receive from students. That would determine whether the companies actually wanted to continue recruitment.[25] Dow recruiters came once more, several months later. Instead of students protesting the Dow recruiter, they shifted their attention to the university administration and held a demonstration in University Hall. The president, Nathaniel Pusey, was displeased with the form of the activists' protest, decrying the "wastage of time."[26] The demonstrators, he said, "play at being revolutionaries." Whether it was for a revolutionary purpose was debatable, but the students of Harvard were mobilizing in ways that administrators could not fathom. However it was characterized, according to Pusey, "it was quite clear that . . . [it] was a direct assault upon the authority of the University and upon rational processes and accepted procedures."[27] Pusey's assessment was correct.

The world-famous demonstrations at Columbia University and at the Chicago Democratic National Convention of 1968 shocked administrators across the nation and at the same time energized the morale of student organizers. The authors of the book *The Harvard Strike* were reporters for the student radio station WHRB-FM in 1968–1969. After observing the buildup of events at Harvard, they pointed out that "the events at Columbia also affected Harvard's radicals. The success of the demonstrations put pressure on the leaders of the Harvard chapter [of SDS] to organize a similar uprising." After a week-long demonstration, the administration of Columbia called in a thousand New York police officers to remove the student demonstrators who had taken over five buildings. Sometimes brutally, the officers arrested more than 700 people and much of the scene appeared in photographs and film footage in the media. The violence provoked a six-week strike at Columbia. As a result of the demonstrations and negotiations, university officials agreed to cut ties with the Institute for Defense Analyses (IDA) and denounce U.S. participation in the war; end the construction of the gymnasium in Morningside Park and reconsider expansion into the surrounding neighborhoods; and establish a student senate that allowed students a voice in university governance. Too, The president of Columbia University resigned.

The conflict between liberalism and radicalism came to a head at the Democratic National Convention in October 1968. Harvard students were not instrumental in the major disruption that the Yippies and other radicals led in Chicago. Many students throughout the nation, however, supported the nomination of Robert Kennedy before he was assassinated. They then looked to Eugene McCarthy, who publicly opposed the war. When the Democrats chose to nominate Vice President Hubert H. Humphrey, who continued to support President Lyndon B. Johnson's war agenda, disillusionment with the political system overcame many students. For students, some of the most disturbing images involved the police use of violence to detain demonstrators. Young people everywhere were outwardly upset with the authority figures who were supposed to be representing their ideals. The educational and governance systems at institutions like Harvard became the prey and young disillusioned activists became the hunters.

The most visible representation of the military on campus was the ROTC program, which blended education and war preparedness. Although not a requirement, students could take ROTC courses for credit toward graduation. Also, the ROTC instructors were classified as professors but were paid and evaluated by the U.S. Department of Defense. The officers that the ROTC developed joined the military to train enlistees and recruits to function in war. As the students put it, ROTC was "crucial to the war effort" in that it supplied, by their accounting, "85% of the Army's junior officers." Those officers did not make policy, they implemented it.[28] "Since SDS sides with the people oppressed by US imperialism, it opposes agents of that oppression—like ROTC," said an SDS statement. In the face of the thousands dying in the conflict, students believed that the university had to distance itself from all aspects of war making. University officials and faculty did not necessarily disagree, but the trustees refused to approve the removal of the program because a controversial war was occurring. Mistakenly, the administration and caretakers of the university underestimated the will of young people.

As the ROTC controversy simmered, the campaign to check Harvard's physical expansion into Cambridge and Roxbury gained steam. Housing and education have always been points of controversy for poor and black people in America. The situation was no different in Cambridge and Roxbury. Harvard residential, educational, and medical buildings were taking up a lot of space in the area. By the 1960s, Harvard and Massachusetts Institute of Technology owned more than 10 percent of Cambridge's land, but neither university, because of their tax-exempt status, paid municipal taxes. Harvard contributed $100,000 yearly, but private owners paid at a higher rate.[29] Over the course of a decade (1960–1970), the university accumulated more than 1,000 dwellings only to raze them in order to construct newer housing for students. Then, Harvard needed more space to expand the John F. Kennedy School of Government in honor of the slain alumnus and U.S. president. The most acclaimed and influential policy analysts came to work in the Harvard school. The university also intended to build its Affiliated Hospitals Center in Roxbury, a working-class enclave of Boston with a very high black population. The center would combine the services of several area hospitals and clinics, while rerouting the training of medical students to one facility.

In a scenario typical of other universities' expansion into residential areas, tenants who lived in university-owned homes faced relocation with very few resources or options for equivalent affordable housing.[30] Between 1960 and 1969, the rent in Cambridge for a two-bedroom unit doubled. According to an SDS document, the Cambridge Rent Control Referendum Campaign found that Harvard-owned apartments featured some of the highest rents with the poorest upkeep of all Cambridge rental units.[31] At the same time, the demographics of the city shifted as the population declined. Few could deny that a hospital center was important to train future physicians, but equally, a similar few could deny the justness of affordable housing in Cambridge and Roxbury.

The optics of Ivy League institutions that physically expanded into black and economically downtrodden neighborhoods were jarring. In this case, the richest university in the world (Harvard had an endowment of well over $1 billion) was moving poor people out to prepare the world for nearly all-white, soon-to-be rich professionals. Concerned undergraduate and medical students alike attempted to alter the course of the university's expansion by working with a faction of the SDS called the Worker Student Alliance to organize demonstrations and tenant groups. They appealed to the university to either stop expanding or to at least provide comparable lower-income alternatives to tenants who faced eviction. The expansion resisters charged the Ivy institution with attempting to engineer an "Imperial City" that catered to only wealthy and middle-class white residents.[32] It just so happened that wealthy and middle-class white people comprised the grand majority of the faculty and student bodies of Harvard.

The institution, in doing what most institutions do when controversy arises, created a committee to study the impact of expansion. The committee that faculty member James Q. Wilson headed reported that, indeed, if housing business continued as it had, Cambridge would become a homogeneous white, middle- to upper-class city.[33] In order to retain a socioeconomically and racially diverse Cambridge, Harvard had to be intentional, the report indicated. Perhaps that meant facilitating the availability of low-income housing in the areas. For university officials and caretakers, however, ceasing expansion was not a viable option. As was the case with Columbia and Penn in 1968, conflict over housing and expansion ensued at Harvard in spring 1969.

The three major issues that grabbed the attention of students were ROTC, expansion, and Black Studies. The black Harvard and Radcliffe students were more determined than ever to achieve their goal of bringing Black Studies to the hallowed halls of the institution. The group of students who launched the campaign formed what they called the Ad Hoc Committee of Black Studies. Although the black student group Afro already existed, this particular collection of students focused entirely on the establishment of Black Studies. It is notable that one of the co-chairs of the committee was Octavia Hudson, an honor student at Radcliffe. As was the case at Pembroke and Barnard College, black women were leading the charge on issues affecting black students. Ernest Wilson III and Hudson were joined by Lani Guinier (daughter of political and labor leader Ewart Guinier), Robert Hall, Robert Listenbee, Fran Farmer, Charles J. Hamilton, Herbert Nickens, and later Constance Hilliard. Together they approached university officials about the importance of featuring the black experience in the curriculum. According to Hall, they collected more than 1,100 signatures of Harvard students in support of having a Black Studies unit. They delivered the petition to the administration in University Hall.[34] Wilson recalled the sophistication of the young people looking to modify the university. "In retrospect," he said, "it is rather remarkable that a dozen or so undergraduates in their late teens or early twenties negotiated" so well with faculty members and university officials.[35] "We managed those tough times with some sophistication and savvy," Wilson reminisced. He thought that regarding Afro-American Studies "we didn't always get it right," but "we got it together."[36] Such a statement reflected the sentiment of the movement for black freedom. Furthermore, Wilson and his peers represented the ideas of Black Power in a mature manner.

The students' use of Black Power as inspiration for their campaign did not sit well with all their advisors. As far back as 1967, Martin Kilson perceived Black Power to be "crude in conception, crass in inspiration, rugged and opportunistic in mode, and devoid of aesthetic."[37] Kilson represented the older guard of black intellectuals and leaders who believed that progress could only be achieved through the traditional political system. He referred to the militant nationalist movement as "black radical infantilism" because of leaders' call for separate black entities, and he believed the philosophies of Black Power grew out of a "deep-seated racist . . . outlook."

Kilson was a junior professor at the time, and was still one of the only black professionals on campus. Like other black people in similar circumstances, Kilson felt pressured to respond to all things black, and he did not disappoint in his responses. In taking the position that he did, Kilson let his colleagues and institution know that he was not a threat to the university and did not support the militant Black Power Movement. He was not opposed to the idea of Black Studies, but he did not want it to become a substitute for political advancement in the larger system. In spite of being a "stone contrarian," as one student characterized him, Kilson was for black students at Harvard what Carl Fields was for black students at Princeton.[38] Kilson and black Assistant Dean Archie Epps III were like lifelines to students. As one of the only black professors in Harvard College, Kilson generously opened his home to students. He allowed them to share their feelings openly, sympathized with their plight, and helped them clarify their goals. This he did out of his sense of obligation to the race not because it would further his career. He did not always agree with the students and their causes, but according to multiple sources, Kilson was "absolutely instrumental in the intellectual development" of the students who knew him in the period.[39] Kilson accomplished all this while establishing himself as a stalwart scholar of African and Afro-American politics.

As part of the Ad Hoc Committee of Black Studies, the students put together binders filled with the dossiers of the most renowned scholars of black history, literature, and culture. Their purpose was to provide the university with as many possible candidates for hire as possible. In a move that is atypical for students, they organized subcommittees to reach out to black scholars at predominantly white and historically black colleges and universities to recruit. They surveyed "who's doing what at Howard and who's doing what at Yale," according to Wilson, who did not want to leave room for doubt when it came time for the university to move toward Afro-American studies. The students strategically anticipated the criticism about the quality of candidates, so they moved to check the argument by doing research early.[40]

In January 1969, the faculty committee charged with designing the program at Harvard made several suggestions.[41] One that became controversial was that Afro-American Studies be offered in conjunction with another major. Another issue was whether the unit would be a program or a department that tenured its own faculty. The proposal was unique among the other Ivy proposals because of its early emphasis on the graduate training. Whereas Yale's and Cornell's proposals concentrated on undergraduate learning, Henry Rosovsky, the chair of the Afro-American Studies committee at Harvard, focused on providing opportunities for black graduate students so that the university could help shape the field's professoriate.[42] Born to a Jewish family in Germany, economic historian Professor Rosovsky was keenly aware of the need to create access for those different than what was perceived as the norm. That is why he supported the committee's suggestion of Harvard "setting aside" fifteen to twenty "five-year fellowships for black students with the potential to become scholars of the first rank" in various fields throughout the university.[43]

Afro-American Studies, if established, was to serve a number of different purposes. Dissatisfaction with the college experience was relatively common among students, but there was something "special" about the lives that black students lived on campus, claimed Rosovsky. "The black student experience is not simply a mode of the general student experience" it has a "unique character of its own" a committee report read.[44] Black students confronted something beyond the angst that all young people have. Because of a dearth of black coverage in the course offerings, few black students, and hardly any black professors on campus, observers could note the lack of value placed on blackness in the culture of the nation and university. The students were left to defend their blackness. Making Afro-American Studies available to themselves and the students who followed them "would help the black student to justify his separation from the larger black community" and show that the separation was not "permanent," Rosovsky believed. As Howard University and University of Chicago alumnus E. Franklin Frazier noted, the members of the black middle class suffered from a lack of security in both the world they wanted to occupy and the one in which they resided. Afro-American Studies would provide answers for their intellectual curiosity while also showing the outside world that they had not forgotten their blackness.

For many black people who have entered historically white spaces, the burden of belonging and feeling welcome has been on the black visitors. Wilson admitted that, at times, they felt like "refugees from another place and another culture."[45] In that way, black students had to work hard to educate white people without unsettling their white hosts to the point that they might deny further access. With that in mind, black students in the late 1960s took the lead in making themselves feel more comfortable on campus irrespective of the behavior of their hosts. Afro-American Studies was an avenue toward that comfort. Black students wanted an experience that affirmed them not just as students but as humans. They asserted that far too few white people had ample practice in viewing black people as human equals. That was evidenced, according to students, in the hiring practices of Harvard. From contracting to faculty appointments, black workers were scant. As did the students at Penn and Columbia, Harvard black students also claimed that the university discriminated against black residents by charging too much for rent and using a process that "squeezes poor people out," according to a report[46] Students claimed that if it was not outright racism, then the university was certainly guilty of indifference to racism in its business and academic policies.

Another important issue was determining who would implement Afro-American studies. The students on each of the Ivy campuses made it clear that black people should spearhead the effort and operate the units. They were sure that if they were not experts in any other subject, black people were fluent in blackness and therefore capable of administering the field. Black students from the earlier periods who desired to study black people and culture often had to chart their own courses. Such was the case with Harvard alumni like Du Bois, Carter G. Woodson, and William Leo Hansberry. To remedy the situation, the report suggested that the university "secure the appointment of at least 10 tenure, term, and visiting faculty members by 1969."[47] It also called for student representatives of Afro to sit on the personnel committees.

The committee did not overlook the need for cocurricular educational opportunities. It pinpointed the need for black advisors and tutors as well as a geographic space that allowed black students to feel normal. "The lack of older blacks available as advisers" was a problem for particularly first-year students, the report found. In terms of African American student success, the sort of informal and formal counsel that upperclassmen passed on to younger students provided the assurance that was necessary for success. It also helped the older students feel as though they belonged and were useful at their university. All could agree that the university would benefit from having black people present at the undergraduate, graduate, faculty, staff, and administrative levels.

Part of the problem, the committee admitted, was getting black students to Harvard. The stigma of elitism and exclusiveness associated with the nation's first university dissuaded some from applying. One of the main deterrents, however, was the fact that Harvard rarely recruited any students black or otherwise. Because of its reputation, the university was always in the position to turn qualified students away. The report wisely noted that "this will not work with black students." The competition for achieving black students meant that Harvard needed to get beyond its general modus operandi to use more progressive recruiting techniques. Those new techniques, in addition to functioning Afro-American Studies department, were necessary steps toward attracting black students.

The committee also took into account potential charges for "reverse discrimination." Rosovsky, himself an immigrant, knew that at least in the Department of Economics, the brightest foreign students were sought out and enrolled into the university. The immigrating students, although bright, had some difficulties with the language and culture of the United States and the university. To bridge this gap, the university helped refine their language abilities so that they could better deal with the content of the major course of study. The committee claimed that it hoped to approach black students using the same method. As the committee put it, "If it is possible to discriminate in favor of foreigners, it should be at least as justifiable to do so on behalf of one's own fellow citizens." Those fellow citizens just so happened to be black.

By spring 1969, Harvard was making progress with regard to an Afro-American Studies department. The black students who demanded the unit, however, were not always pleased with the rate of progress or the ideas that the Standing Committee on Afro-American Studies had. One concern was whether the program of study would be available to the class of 1972; another was the number of courses necessary to complete the major.[48] The committee, in April 1969, admitted that it would be difficult to solidify everything for the major by the fall of that year. The university's faculty governing body that approved new units had not done so, and the students were anxious. On a different note, the students observed that the way that the committee had outlined the major, it would require them to take on the burden of extra courses so that they could "double major."

The original outline called for the Afro-American Studies major to be combined with a traditional major, which would add some legitimacy to the new field. That would, hopefully, assist the students in their quests for graduate or professional school, which was the path of many Harvard undergraduates. The committee members believed that allowing the students to concentrate in Afro-American Studies while taking up another major kept them from being marginalized with a major in such a new field of study. The black students advocating the Afro-American Studies major believed otherwise. "We reject this notion," the students declared.[49] They believed that if Black Studies was important enough to be an academic unit, then it should have been important enough to be a stand-alone major requiring the same number of credits as traditional majors.

The students also pointed out that the committee and the faculty governing body wanted to plan out all facets of course offerings, but that doing so wrested some decision-making power from the new director or chair of the department and further institutionalized racism. They based their reasoning on the fact that the faculty governing body was almost all white and most members had no dealings with subject matter covering the black experience. The students envisioned the incoming chair as a black person whose academic focus was on issues directly concerning black people. The new (ostensibly black) leader would be coming into a situation where mostly white people would have determined the direction of the program despite having little to know expertise in the subject. The new chair should have the discretion to determine the nuances for the multidisciplinary major, the students stated. Even the Standing Committee on African American Studies could not foresee all of the needs the new unit would have.[50]

On April 21, 1969, a day before the faculty was to meet and discuss the creation of the unit, the members of the student group Afro made an appeal. Decrying the fact that some of the changes in the proposal that the Standing Committee on Afro-American Studies made several weeks earlier had not been revealed to the wider audience of potential majors, the student group called the move a "flagrant disregard for black student opinion."[51] It wanted to help shape the direction of the unit. In an effort to amend the proposal submitted by the committee, Afro publicly proposed that students would hold a "set number" of seats as part of the decision-making board for the unit. The desire to have some control over the unit's direction was reflective of the kind of rebellion against what black people believed was institutional racism. Self-determination at every level was a baseline premise of Black Power. At Harvard, that campaign resulted in three black students from Afro having seats on a committee that would vote to (or not to) tenure faculty members.

The prospect of black students having so much decision-making control, not surprisingly, unsettled many faculty members. Some pointed out that in matters of rank and tenure, only senior professors had a vote. If the undergraduate students were allowed to sit on a committee that determined a faculty member's tenure and rank status, then those students would be able to do what even junior faculty members and graduate students could not. Educationally, such a concept was highly abnormal. It was too much for even Afro-American Studies advocate Rosovsky, who likened the potential move to an "academic Munich," referring to the city where British Prime Minister Neville Chamberlain signed an agreement that effectively signified the appeasement of Hitler's Nazi regime.[52] This statement took on even more import when considering Rososvky's biography. His family had fled Germany during the Holocaust and he was on faculty at Berkeley during the free speech movement that many students held up as a model of campus activism. Those experiences made him sensitive to the demonstrations of Harvard students.

Between January, when the Rosovsky report was submitted, and April 22, when Afro demanded an amendment to the committee's proposal, the campus environment became stormy. The SDS had several successful disruptive actions, and the radical leadership come together to plan its major spring offensive. The April planning meeting yielded a proposal for a major militant action. That proposal manifested in the SDS's occupation of University Hall on April 9, 1969. The group issued a set of demands to the president calling for the removal of the ROTC program and scholarships associated with it. The scholarship money saved from ROTC should be reinvested into scholarships for all students. The SDS also wanted students whose scholarships had been revoked or reduced because of their participation in previous demonstrations to be fully reinstated. The radicals demanded the lowering of rent in university-owned units in Cambridge and Roxbury to 1968 levels; cessation to the razing of homes in Roxbury for the hospital facilities center; and cessation to the razing of homes for the Kennedy School. Just as demonstrators at Columbia University a year before had renamed Hamilton Hall as Malcolm X University, student activists at Harvard renamed University Hall as Che Guevara Hall.

As they liberated the new Guevara Hall, SDS leadership went to work determining next steps and securing the building. The administrators were ushered out while onlookers and followers were welcomed inside. The only press representatives allowed were members of the student newspaper and radio show staff members. Forty years after the strike, a participant, graduate Jon Wiener, wrote in *The Nation* magazine about demonstrators discovering files in the president's office that linked the university to CIA operations and war research. In an underground radical newspaper called the *Old Mole*, Wiener published the findings in an article entitled "Reading the Mail of the Ruling Class."[53] Wiener's find was similar to those of radical students like Bob Feldman, who had uncovered Columbia University's relationship to IDA in 1968. Perhaps not all the materials that students found at Harvard were private, but they were certainly not intended for public dissemination.

That students had read through sensitive files was of great concern to administrators, some of whom believed that was reason enough to end the protest immediately. The first black administrator at Harvard, Archie Epps III, who reportedly got off a few good punches at demonstrators when they removed him from the building, commented that when the students began distributing information from the files about "the personal affairs of faculty members" it was time for the occupiers to leave.[54] The administration could not allow students to "rifle and duplicate the Faculty personnel files and financial records," said the president.[55] He explained that the administration had to do something "if the freedom of the University was not to be surrendered."

As the students at Harvard pilfered documents and occupied the building, the faculty and administration met to figure out an end to the demonstration. The president, Pusey, was taken aback by the audacity of the students' action. He was in no mood to negotiate. Pusey, whom one student representative on the disciplinary committee remembered fifteen years after the takeovers, "was too aloof, he didn't understand the urgency of the situation."[56] The president understood the action to be rebellious and disrespectful to the traditions of Harvard. Members of the faculty, many of whom were distressed by the occupation, attempted to calm the situation by discussing the demands and attempting negotiations with the students. They understood what a demonstration such as this could do to a university after observing the Columbia crisis, where the faculty had split along ideological lines and many members lost faith in the administration. Some observers of the Harvard crisis explained it best: "Everyone had heard about the experiences at Berkeley and Columbia where the faculty's fragmentation had left deep scars."[57] Harvard's faculty was determined to at least try to work together to bring a resolution to the protests.

Unlike Columbia's president Grayson Kirk, who called the police to remove demonstrators after a week, Pusey made the decision to call in the police to remove the several hundred occupiers at Harvard after two days of negotiations. He believed it better to take quick action to remove the students, but the result was not all positive for him. Police presence, as observers of the Columbia mass arrest pointed out, adds a special dimension to demonstrations. The 400 police officers who arrived on Harvard's campus did not take care to peacefully arrest the protesters. Blood was spilled as the officers bludgeoned students with their clubs and violently removed agitators who did not make the process easy for the authorities. As onlookers observed and members of the media reported, police arrested almost 200 activists.

Most Harvard students were not present for the arrests nor was the majority necessarily favorable of the occupation. However, the presence of police and violence helped to influence the sympathy of students and faculty members regarding the issues that the SDS raised. When the SDS proposed a strike, they had the support of a large contingent of the student body. White students like the moderate leader of the Young Democrats (and as of 2016 the U.S. Senate Minority Leader) Charles "Chuck" Schumer detested the thought of a violent reaction of police and worked to create an enduring student voice in decision making.[58] Design and Architecture graduate students Melvin Hacker and Doug Engel, in sympathy with the demonstrations, created the iconic red fist design that became emblematic of the strike at Harvard and youth rebellion around the world.[59] The demonstrations garnered support.

"As students of Harvard, and as Black students in a white environment, we join with all other members of the Harvard community in deploring and condemning acts of brutality perpetrated by the Administration against students in the University Hall demonstration," declared an Afro position paper.[60] Afro intentionally indicated that it was the administration and not police that committed the acts of brutality. This took the attention away from the police officers, who regularly used force to handle citizens, and placed it on the administrators who made the decision to employ the police. In that way, the nearly all-white police force became a tool for the white power structure at Harvard and around the world.

The position paper read: "The events at Harvard the past week are indicative of a rising national ambience of traditional American militarism and racism."[61] The paper linked the student action and the university's response of calling the police to the arrival of "troops" in the ghetto of Chicago after "three hours of minor disturbances" and the ineffectiveness of the Paris Peace Talks to conclude the Vietnam War. Considering the administration's unresponsiveness to issues and quick decision to call the "local storm troopers," the Afro Paper claimed that "Harvard's winter pledges to Afro and SDS came to spring putrescence with the resort to violence and denial of Black Studies." Afro-American Studies had not actually been denied yet, but it had been tabled as a topic of faculty discussion. For the interested students, that was tantamount to denial.

The position paper also noted what it viewed as institutional spin. "The Administration has skillfully projected the image of giving in to the dissenters' demands, while in reality making no substantive changes," the position paper read, focusing especially on "the history of Black student efforts to effect significant academic and social changes" as an example. Unfortunately for Afro, by the time of the SDS demonstration, the program of Afro-American Studies had morphed into something unrecognizable. "The Afro-American Studies Program, as now conceived by the university, even if it were to be temporary, is ... far from what Black students [originally] envisioned such a program to be," the paper observed. In effect, with the current iteration of the unit, there may as well "be no program on Afro-American Studies at all."[62] For Afro, a program that did not intimately involve student participation regarding the programs planning and governance was one not worthy of authorization.

Although members of Afro had been working on the Standing Committee on Afro-American Studies all along, when SDS led the strike against Harvard, the militant wing of Afro took advantage of the momentum of student power to make the unit better reflect its original proposal. The newer version stipulated black student participation at every level of the unit's operation, from hiring to promotion to the creation of the curriculum. This worked well for both Afro and the SDS. The wider white following of the SDS benefited Afro because the mostly white activists and followers brought Afro's issue to places it may not have gone if Afro-American Studies remained only a black issue. Further, it added wider resonance to Afro's call for the unit. The SDS gained a certain amount of credibility at the height of Black Power by aligning itself with black activists and taking on a distinctly black issue as part of its protest platform. During the planning for the spring offensive, Afro-American

Studies was not part of the SDS's discussions. Adding an element of explicit blackness to a campus demonstration also promised to ignite deep concern in faculty and administrators, as evidenced by the reaction to black student activism at Columbia University and elsewhere.

It was a whirlwind time on campus. The entire faculty was set to meet to discuss the issues that the SDS had raised and to address the revised proposal of Afro. Most of the faculty members, claimed several professors in a document, deplored "the entry of police into any university" but they also deplored the "forcible occupation of University Hall." They could tell by surrounding events at other institutions that Harvard could very well meet with disaster if university representatives did not take students' concerns seriously and confront them squarely.

On April 22, the faculty of Harvard met and voted in the majority to approve the amended Afro-American Studies proposal. Concern about the potential for violence and destruction loomed over the campus. The faculty members were worried about students potentially harming rare paintings in the Fogg Museum in much the same way that Columbia president Grayson Kirk worried over the Rembrandt painting in his office when students occupied the university's administration building a year earlier. Then, news of Cornell's black students' demonstration at the university library in Ithaca, New York, frightened the book loving faculty at Harvard. Faculty members took turns standing twenty-four-hour guard at the library to ensure demonstrators did not destroy any of the precious paintings and first edition books. In those high-anxiety days, everything must have seemed unsafe for all involved.

Rosovsky, who had led a committee to explore Afro-American Studies and submitted a report on what the committee believed it should look like, wondered whether the decision they (faculty members) were making with regard to Afro-American Studies was being made under the pressure of threat or of their own volition. He remembered that at the all-faculty meeting, a black representative of Afro suggested to the professors that "not to pass this resolution [which included the new stipulations] is a serious mistake . . . it would be a mistake from which this University might not be able to recover."[63] The Afro representative also reminded the faculty that black student activists had chosen not to demonstrate in any dramatic way sooner, hinting that there was a possibility of disruption in the future. The faculty did not have to look any farther than Columbia and Penn the year before or Cornell at that very moment, which was experiencing a serious disturbance at the same time as Harvard, to see the potential for black Ivy League student activism to flare up. Indeed, in 1969 hundreds of colleges and universities in nearly every state confronted what scholar Ibram Kendi called the "apex" of black student activism.[64] No institution was safe from demonstrating students, not even the most prestigious. Rosovsky concluded that the decision to approve the Afro-American Studies proposal, with the amendments that the black student group made, could not be "interpreted as anything else but action in the face of threats."[65]

There was some dissension in the faculty vote. Rosovsky recalled that junior faculty tended to vote affirmatively for the proposal while those who voted in the opposition were largely senior professors. The junior professors were closer in age to the protesting students and saw undergraduate students more frequently than their senior colleagues. They typically had been at the university a shorter period than the associate and full professors. That meant, Rosovsky hypothesized, the juniors were not quite as entrenched in Harvard culture and tradition as the older faculty members. In fact, Rosovsky observed some rebellion from the junior faculty, who intentionally sought to check the vote of their elder colleagues. The sentiment, according to Rosovsky, was "if the old bastards oppose the black demands, we [junior faculty members] might as well back them [the black demands]."[66] The faculty was torn as some remained sympathetic with the cause but opposed the method of the students. Still, others saw the opportunity to progress with Afro-American Studies, in spite of its atypical arrival. Perhaps, Rosovsky opined, it was "liberal guilt" that motivated some to vote how they did. Either way, the faculty voted to approve.

Although there was some difference in opinion among the faculty, some members wanted to set the record straight. They claimed that during this vote and previous votes regarding the demonstrations of April, the faculty remained relatively unified. Well aware that the eyes of the world were upon them, the faculty members pointed out that the events at Harvard were unlike what occurred at Cornell. A key difference, they said, was that black students at Harvard did not use "guns, violence, or threats" and that the proposal was not a "summary demand," but rather a revision of previous work.[67] For their part, the faculty believed that "the new program for our black students may well become a model of relevance both to scholarship in a new field and to the peaceful evolution of democratic institutions in the United States."

Looking back on the drama that surrounded the founding of Afro-American Studies, Rosovsky believed both the university and students made some missteps in their approach to the new unit. Concerning the university, the professor-turned-administrator cited a "crisis of authority" in handling the needs of black students, who needed more than admission to be healthy and effective students at Harvard.[68] Rosovsky criticized the "rather traditional" approach of the university in establishing committees, which tend to slow down processes. By his observation, this left black students feeling "patronized or rejected." He spoke of the "implicit quota" system that the university had for students from what he called underdeveloped countries. The institution was attempting to cover its social obligations by admitting such students. He stated plainly that "if we had social obligations to foreigners, clearly we had at least equally urgent obligations toward American Negroes—sometimes described as foreigners in our midst."[69] Ernest Wilson III bolstered that sentiment when he commented on feeling like a refugee at his own school.

Rosovsky soundly defeated numerous arguments against the establishment of Afro-American Studies. When he heard the contention that creating the unit was more a political response than an intellectual one, Rosovsky pointed out that in the postwar era Harvard created units for Russian and Chinese Studies that did not exist before. He insightfully noted that it was not the great curiosity in Tolstoy and the Ming Dynasty that motivated the faculty to quickly create programs. It was, instead, the fact that the Russia and the Soviet Union gained political power in Central and Eastern Europe while simultaneously acquiring nuclear power. That China became home to a communist revolution drew the immediate attention of the United States and American universities. With that in mind, Rosovsky suggested that "national needs" made certain areas of study more pertinent for the time. If there was some political impetus for doing so, then, he said, "I would conclude that more political activity of this type would be highly desirable."[70] In essence, the professor illustrated that education could be relevant to the needs of society, which was a key concern for young black people.

After the controversy of the vote, Rosovsky worried that what precipitated the vote may have caused irreparable damage to Afro-American Studies such that it would be hindered in the future. He believed the demonstrations and the pressure that students placed on the faculty to vote affirmatively for the new unit diminished all that was good about Harvard. Understanding that protest was part of the zeitgeist, he blamed the white faculty for capitulating to the threat of more demonstrations. Rosovsky feared that the seemingly quick decision to approve set a dangerous precedent regarding university operations. The students argued that there was nothing quick about the decision to approve Afro-American Studies; that the reason they activated was to move along a painfully slow process so that Harvard, after 333 years of existence, could systematically study the plight of African descended people. At the time, Rosovsky's fear was legitimate in the sense that life was changing quickly at Harvard and all throughout the nation and world. Black people, with a heightened consciousness and militancy, abhorred the gradualism that liberal and conservative white people had imposed on black progress for centuries. Black Power was as much a challenge to white racism as it was to gradualism. "That it happened at a place as sound as Harvard may well signal that a deep-going malaise is spreading into the value system on which the modern university is based," said one faculty member.[71] Although many had come from privileged backgrounds and had experiences that set them apart from the masses, the students pushing for Afro-American Studies were still black, and they were part of the social movements that even exclusive Harvard could not deny. Indeed, claimed another professor, "Harvard is living through revolutionary times," and while many acts seem irrational, there was a great "productive energy" released that allowed for university officials to reflectively consider the course of humanity.[72] That was the plan of the student agitators.

In the fall of 1969, the Standing Committee on Afro-American Studies issued a new report that discussed the progress and hindrances the new unit was experiencing as it prepared for its premiere in the fall of 1970. Some news was quite encouraging. Nearly seventy students in the class of 1972 chose to concentrate in Afro-American Studies, which already had seventeen courses slated for the fall and spring terms of 1970. To chair the department, Harvard identified someone who attended the university as an undergraduate and had intimate ties to the institution.

The faculty chose Ewart Guinier, who had been a visiting professor at Harvard, to lead Afro-American Studies. His daughter, Lani, was one of the students who led the push for the unit. Without much fanfare, the faculty recommended he be offered full professorship and tenure. That act alone illustrated the institution's ability to act quickly with regard to hiring black faculty when it was expedient. Few if any other black professors had been promoted to full professorship at the university. The agitation led to advancements for not only their lives but those of faculty members as well. Where there was an argument that few "qualified" scholars were available for hire at Harvard and similar schools before the advent of demonstrations, afterward the universities' powers of selection must have improved immensely. The committee boasted that Guinier was coming to Harvard with a "rich background in community and academic experience," which included work with unions, politics, and association with Columbia University's Urban Center.[73] Born the son of Jamaican parents in Panama, Guinier had, at one point, run for Manhattan Borough president. He held a master's degree from Columbia University's Teachers College and a PhD from New York University. Incidentally, he had been available to work in the professoriate before April 1969.

Regarding the progress of Afro-American Studies, the struggle did not end with its approval. A report assessing the unit's evolution in the three years after its approval noted: "Within the department student contributions have been invaluable." To "separate the work" that students have done for the department from that of faculty members would have been "sheer sophistry," according to the report. Two thousand students took Afro-American Studies courses during the short period, pointing out the relevance and popularity of the subject. The department featured esteemed full-time faculty members but also invited visiting instructors such as Hoyt Fuller, who established the *Black World* journal (formerly *The Negro Digest*); Rhody McCoy who famously negotiated for community control of schools in the Ocean Hill-Brownsville section of New York City; eminent Marxist historian Herbert Aptheker; acclaimed author C.L.R. James; and even activists such as Stokely Carmichael and Ivanhoe Donaldson. Not without needs, the new department struggled to acquire lines for tenured professors from the university. In higher education, a unit thrives on its tenured professors who do much of the important committee work and establish the scholarly reputation of the unit. Tenured professors also receive more competitive salaries and benefits, which can make a unit that much more attractive. The report called Harvard "'soft' on honoring it commitments" to adequately fund and staff the unit.[74] In spite of the struggle, by 1972, of the fourteen students who majored in Afro-American Studies, ten graduated with honors and eleven went on to postgraduate education.[75] The benefit of fifty years reveals that not only did Afro-American Studies survive it all, but the unit thrived and became a model, attracting top scholars and students from around the world.

As devoted as the members of Afro were to Afro-American Studies, black students took on other issues as well. In the winter of 1969, a new group was formed that incorporated all the different black student groups and their off-campus allies. The Organization of Black Unity (OBU) concentrated on black employment at Harvard. The group pointed to the very small percentage of black workers that the university hired. Considering the institutional push to expand, the university could at least focus on employing some of the people from the areas into which it planned to grow, stated OBU. In November, the black group brought the issue to Professor Archibald Cox of the Harvard Law School.[76] Cox, who focused on arbitration and labor law, was an advisor in the Kennedy administration. Additionally, Cox headed the commission that investigated the 1968 Columbia crisis. Later, he became famous for the confrontation he had with President Richard M. Nixon during the Watergate scandal that led to Nixon terminating him as special prosecutor. Before that crisis, he honed his arbitrary and investigatory skills at Harvard in winter 1969.

"Checking out the blatantly racist employment practices of Harvard University, and finding the same insidious patterns of discrimination on all its campus constructions sites" led the Harvard-Radcliffe Association of African and Afro-American Students (AAAAS) and OBU to issue demands that would constitute a "*meaningful* and *effective* program of affirmative action," according to an AAAAS-OBU document.[77] The student group demanded a minimum "20% of the skilled, semi-skilled, and general work force on all construction projects be composed of black and Third World Worker." It also requested a training program; consultation with the Contractors Association of Boston, the Urban League, and the United Community Construction Workers regarding all new construction projects; that the university hire a compliance officer to ensure that black workers were treated fairly and that the compliance officer would be chosen by the United Community Construction Workers and AAAAS; that a black man should be hired as a crew chief; and finally that no "minority workers" would see reprisals as a result of the demands. AAAAS and OBU also demanded that the classifications of current black workers be changed from the titles of "helper" and "painter's assistant" to titles that would draw higher wages. The group gave the university until December 2 at 9:00 A.M. to satisfy the demands.

In response, Cox and other university representatives never denied that Harvard had a problem with hiring black workers. In correspondence with Leslie "Skip" Griffin, president of Afro, one administrator proposed working groups to explore ways to improve hiring in the three planned major construction sites (School of Design, Kennedy School, and Affiliated Hospitals Center). The administrator admitted needing assistance in finding "appropriate minority contractors" to help with consultation and contracting.[78] OBU sent a response to the administrator indicating that a committee should be formed, "headed by an appointee of O.B.U. from each school within the university, plus one member of O.B.U.'s labor committee, and Mr. Archibald Cox, Administrative Vice-President [L. Gard] Wiggins, and two faculty members or administrators." The committee would have veto power regarding any matters concerning workers of color. Again, black students, using Black Power as a model, fought to control the issues most affecting the lives of black people.

On November 30, administrators sent a short letter explaining that the university was amenable to a joint committee, and that "Harvard's policy and practices in respect to minority group employment can be strengthened and improved" with OBU's help. Cox followed up with a document outlining the university responses, as well as "concrete action taken in response to OBU's demands," and a list of all the construction properties on which the institution was currently working or had planned.[79] By December 2, no official agreement had been met, but Harvard was on notice that their hiring practices reflected institutional racism.

In a "Statement by Harvard University Regarding Discussions with the Organization of Black Unity," administrators regretted "our inability to reach an understanding today with O.B.U." The statement read: "Harvard University is most anxious to join with the Organization of Black Unity . . . in affirmative action to increase the employment of black and other minority workers." A major issue of contention was the demand that 20 percent of the workers be black or "minority."[80] Harvard representatives indicated that reaching such a high percentage was nearly impossible considering the low percentage of black people in the Boston metropolitan area, the low number of black skilled union workers, and the relatively low percentage of black general workers. Further, increasing the number of hires, changing the titles of workers, and increasing wages may have put the projects beyond their budget allocations.[81] Finally, some believed that it was indeed racist to guarantee 20 percent employment to any race of workers let alone black workers. As it was, white construction employees never before had to worry about guarantees for employment; construction work had been normalized as white.

On December 11, one hundred activists following the lead of the OBU escalated the protest by staging demonstrations at Gund Hall, which was under construction and was the university's esteemed faculty dining house. In a press release, the OBU explained that it intentionally stopped construction at Gund and sent the construction workers home "with the support from the greater Boston Black community" to point out that only 5 percent of those working at the site were black "despite the availability of qualified people in the Black community who need jobs." The press release indicated that the OBU did "not act frivolously or irresponsibly in renewing its protest activities" and that in addition to the general support of the "Roxbury-Boston-Cambridge community," OBU also had the backing of the National Offices of the Urban League and Southern Christian Leadership Conference, which had "pledged full support."[82] In a follow-up press release, the OBU announced its takeover of the Faculty Dining Club, "a place where Harvard Faculty members relax in leisure and comfort and dine in elegance ignoring the fact that black people are suffering at the hands of Harvard's Racist Policies perpetuating the oppression of black people." The demonstrators said they chose to "inconvenience" the faculty until the university found a way to address and actualize each of OBU's demands. To get them to leave, Cox instructed the university attorneys to file a Middlesex County court injunction and restraining orders against the demonstrators.[83] The members of the OBU and AAAAS argued that black people had been "restrained" from work at Harvard for too long.

Members of the newly formed Association of Black Faculty Members, Fellows and Administrators of Harvard University differentiated themselves from their white peers to immediately stand with the OBU. The group of black Harvard professionals made a public statement in an "appeal with the University that no reprisals be taken against students who participate in appropriate student demonstrations in an effort to correct existing inequities in employment opportunities which fall under the purview of the University."[84] They found the demonstrations to be appropriate and necessary to improve the institution with regard to employment. Conceiving of the demonstration in terms of morality, the black professionals explained that reprimanding the students for their demonstrations at Gund Hall and the Faculty Dining Club would only punish "those who seek to right the wrong" of Harvard, and reprisals against the students would permit "those who exercise the wrong . . . to escape with immunity." In their view, those who exercised wrong were the university's decision makers who had consistently overlooked black workers in the past. On a practical note, the black professional group believed that castigating the students would, no doubt, lead to more escalation that may bring "additional forces" to campus. Those additional forces, hinted the statement, did not include students but rather local community members who had no jobs to lose and ill feelings toward the institution. The urban setting of the university could potentially work against the institution if matters intensified, according to the group.

One of the black faculty members to sign the statement was law professor Derrick Bell. Bell had worked in the Department of Justice and with the NAACP. In coordination with the likes of Thurgood Marshall and Constance Baker Motley, he helped win James Meredith's admission to the University of Mississippi. Meredith later attended and graduated Columbia University Law School. Bell arrived on campus because of the earlier protests of AAAAS and black law students. When the controversy over hiring arose, he accepted an appointment on the committee that was formed to reevaluate the titles and pay of black workers on university sites. Rather than focus solely on his own work and research, Bell and his fellow black Harvard professionals moved beyond their scholarly duties to bolster the efforts of students protesting for freedom. Likely, most professors did not feel obligated to wade into matters concerning the employment of wage workers, but black professors and administrators did. They, too, risked their status and respect among colleagues.

The campaign to increase the number of black workers at Harvard and to bring Afro-American Studies to campus realized Black Power's goals of pride, unification, and economic advancement. Students allied themselves with the black working class. They received the support of the black administrators and professionals at Harvard. The cross-class coalition illustrated the potential for black progress on multiple levels. The campaign also showed the ability of the Harvard learners to employ their Black Student Power by using their privileged status. In focusing on contractors, painters' assistants, and wage workers, the members of AAAAS and the OBU had nothing to gain, as most of them would go on to successful salaried careers. The spirit of collective identity and advancement inspired them to create better life chances for others. Moreover, students joining with black professionals and the black working class demonstrated one of the few effective ways of attacking what they viewed as an institution entrenched in racism. Through their dogged efforts to change the nation's oldest university, students attempted to make Harvard their own.

9

Africana Ambitions

The Defense of Blackness at Cornell University

Why then did black students have to virtually fight a war just
to get a few courses about ourselves?
—Thomas Jones, 1994

Scholars have done well to cover the April 1969 demonstrations at
Cornell University that led black students to arm themselves, but the
activities of black students before that moment were perhaps even more
militant and informative about the tribulations faced by administrators
and the university. This chapter will discuss the reactionary Willard
Straight Hall takeover, but it will focus more on the methodical arrival
of Afro-American Studies at Cornell.

As Harvard affiliates dealt with the turmoil of activism that led to
Black Studies, Cornell University confronted its own crises. Protests, fist
fights, burning crosses, water hoses, and white nationalism all seemed
to be images that belonged in the South, but the Ivy League institution
in upstate New York experienced that and more in the late 1960s. On
the way to Black Studies at Cornell, drama descended upon the beautiful campus in the Finger Lakes Region. Upon arriving, the Black Studies unit at Cornell provided a new model of autonomy in its reporting
structure.

By 1969, black students were not new to Cornell and neither was
protest. As Thomas H. Jones, a leader of Cornell's Afro-American Society (AAS) in the late 1960s, explained, "anger and anguish" fueled the
demonstrations that made the prestigious institution famous.[1] So too,
though, did fear and frustration. Cornell gained notoriety when images
of students carrying firearms and donning bandoliers flashed around
the world in April 1969. Many on and off campus were awed at the state
of student activism and the boldness of black students in reacting to

their circumstances. The students were also unsettled that they had to go to such extremes. "The confrontation at Cornell was born in the efforts of African-American students such as myself to learn something about what had happened to us as a people," said Jones. "We wanted to know . . . how we had come to be such a powerless and disrespected people"; Cornell and other Ivy League institutions, Jones contended, were not providing the answer to that question. So black students activated to gain the respect and power they believed they deserved. To achieve Black Power they used Black Student Power.

At Cornell and elsewhere in 1968–1969 black students pushed the limits of acceptable dissent. They wanted, as Jones put it, to "draw the line" with regard to what they viewed as racism. After watching their peers on urban streets in conflict with police or abroad fighting the Viet Cong or on campus demonstrating, the activist black students at Cornell believed that they were part of the generation that had to overcome tradition and decorum to usher in change. To do so, they understood they had to confront fear and potentially death. It seemed like a very high price to pay to have a Black Studies program. Jones compared the words of university founder Ezra Cornell with the reality for black students in 1969: "I would found an institution where any person can find instruction in any study." That may have been the founder's desire, but black students understood the statement to mean every subject as long as it was not centered on the black experience. Jones asked logically: if the founder wanted students to have access to any subject, "why then did black students have to virtually fight a war just to get a few courses about ourselves? Why did we have to struggle to obtain culturally-supportive living accommodations for those of us who preferred them?" Perhaps the answer was that tradition and decorum reigned, and white men largely determined both. Black Cornellians would see about that.

Much had changed in the world since the days when Jerome "Brud" Holland played football and the university would not let black women stay on campus. In 1963, Cornell authorized its Committee on Special Education Projects (COSEP) to make arrangements to better accommodate black life on campus. Those accommodations included admission, housing, and retention resources. It was one of the earliest of the programs directed toward black recruitment at Ivy League universities. James A. Perkins, the new president of Cornell, commissioned COSEP during his first year in the position. His establishment of COSEP did not surprise his contemporaries because of Perkins's service to the United Negro College Fund (UNCF) and the Ford Foundation. Perkins took over as chair of the UNCF, which was founded by Cornell alumnus Frederick Douglass Patterson, in 1966.[2]

In contrast to Grayson Kirk of Columbia and Nathan Pusey of Harvard, Perkins had liberal leanings, but he came from a similar privileged background. Perkins was reared as a Quaker and graduated from Swarthmore College, where he pledged Delta Upsilon Fraternity, Inc. He earned his doctorate in political science from Princeton. Like Dartmouth president John Dickey, who served on U.S. President Truman's Civil Rights Committee, Perkins intimately understood the value of education for black people through his service and work. Before the Willard Straight Hall takeover, a Harvard student who was active in demonstrations for Afro-American Studies remembered: "Perkins was considered to be a good liberal who had something to teach the Rosovsky Committee and the Ad Hoc Committee of Black Students about how to handle race relations."[3] Perkins's liberalism was renowned.

Just as the Foundation Years and A Better Chance programs assisted black students from "disadvantaged" backgrounds to attend Dartmouth, Cornell's COSEP sought black learners with high potential for success in college from urban areas and public schools. The students who arrived at Cornell, according to Perkins, were "a new kind of black young person" for the institution.[4] The new students were, he said, "often the product of a childhood in a Northern ghetto or a Southern rural community that cannot be comprehended by" those who were "adult, white, secure, and successful in America." Just after a major demonstration at Cornell in 1969, the president astutely observed of COSEP students, "by now it must be clear to everyone, he [the student taking advantage of COSEP] is not an average, middle-class American who happens to be black." During the period, that proved true time and again with the students at Cornell and elsewhere in the Ivy League.

At the moment that the COSEP initiative began, America's urban centers confronted poverty, overcrowding, crime, and drugs. Many black urban residents faced unemployment and underemployment, poor relationships with law enforcement, unequal access to quality public education, and a general lack of resources. The young people who took advantage of COSEP observed closely when altercations surrounding brutal police interactions with residents flared into physical rebellion during the Long Hot Summers of 1964–1968. In upstate New York in 1964, black residents reacted violently in Rochester (not far from Ithaca) when police arrested a black youth at a party and the community rebelled.[5] That summer, a similar episode took place in Harlem while women in Philadelphia and Jersey City had confrontations with police that sparked upheaval and the destruction of property. Many of these young learners, who came from cities where rebellions had occurred, were attracted to Malcolm X's message of racial pride, unity, separatism, and self-defense. Some arrived on campus with a more militant attitude about black freedom than of their predecessors. Of course, earlier black students shared the spirit of advancement on campus, but the students who arrived in the mid-1960s differed in their methodological approach in ways that the Cornell administration had not before witnessed.[6]

Although their enrollment at Cornell meant new opportunities for some of the students who were not part of the tradition pool of Ivy matriculants, their arrival did not always invoke celebration. For instance, one of the few black professors at Cornell in the mid-1960s, Harvard alumnus Thomas Sowell, referred to them as "hoodlums" and considered their work less than standard. Scholar Donald Downs, who wrote extensively about the black student experience in the late 1960s, explained that COSEP's successes in attracting and accommodating some black students were met with "overt racism, institutional racism, and cultural confrontations," not to mention "a lack of mutual understanding" between white and black Cornellians.[7] The rural setting of Ithaca was idyllic, but it was not what many of the black students knew. In addition, there were the typical slights from white students and problems with access to an adequate social life for black students. In the 1960s, black students wanting to pledge a traditionally white fraternity or sorority often faced outright rejection. Integration was an honorable goal, but it did not seem to be working for black or white people on campus.

The COSEP students needed a lifeline and they found it in graduate student and assistant dean Gloria Joseph. She was for black Cornellians what Martin Kilson and Archie Epps were for black Harvardians, what Carl Fields was for black Princetonians, and what Elliott Skinner was for black Columbians. She knew exactly what the new students felt. "Our parents had hopes and dreams for us . . . but no money."[8] She made Cornell more tolerable and even fun for students. They described her as a savior and her resourcefulness provided them with a support system. She kept their confidence and provided solace during the stressful times that urban students endured so far away from the city. Joseph also helped them to navigate acts of covert and overt racism.

The ineffectiveness of the racial integration efforts at Cornell led black students to believe they had to establish their own accommodations separate from those offered to all students. Malcolm X's views bolstered the ideas of the students. When black students could not pledge and live at white fraternity or sorority houses, they instead established parallel living quarters. That same scenario caused early black Cornellians to form Alpha Phi Alpha Fraternity, Inc., in 1906. Sixty years later, the rejection from white culture and the self-determination of black students inspired the young learners to establish the Elmwood House for black men.[9] As was the case during the desegregation era at Cornell (1900–1945), black women were still having issues with their white housemates. Some white women had problems with the afros that black women wore but others had problems with the smell of the relaxer that some black women used. Other white women took offense to the outward and unapologetic blackness that black women displayed in the dorms from their decorations to their loud soul music. The conflicts gave birth to the Wari Cooperative House for black women in 1967. After decades of ill treatment, black women took it upon themselves to, with the assistance of COSEP, live with each other to avoid unnecessary confrontations. Fourteen young women took advantage of the opportunity to enjoy cooperative black living.

The idea of separatism worked well for some black students, but the idea chafed a number of university officials. The officials believed that for as much as black students stood to gain from Cornell, white people at Cornell stood to gain as much from the presence of black people. That would have worked best if the students could successfully integrate. Unfortunately, history and human nature pressed against the interracial notion. After years of trying to make themselves feel welcome, some black students in the mid-1960s relented to some white students' desires to keep their social circles white. Taking to heart the separatism that Black

Power advocates espoused in 1965–1967, black students saw clear logic in creating separate living quarters. When black students took up residence in the Elmwood and Wari houses, white administrators regretted that students would not have more opportunity to interact. Better preparation for the arrival and residence of black students would have prevented the perceived need for separate circumstances.

Just as the founders of Alpha Phi Alpha organized a fraternity to support themselves and to represent the interest of black students, students in 1966 founded Cornell's Afro-American Society (AAS). Its establishment was typical of similar organizations throughout the Ivy League. Initially it focused on black presence and networking, but with the entrance of higher numbers of politicized and radically oriented students, AAS evolved. Students used AAS and similar organizations for different reasons. Some wanted simply to associate with other black students while others believed AAS could lead the charge to reform the campus culture and policies. Still other students saw AAS as a vessel that could bring them to Vincent Harding's river of the black liberation struggle. Although there were multiple ideologies that existed in the minds of AAS members, the militant black activist contingent came to fore in the late 1960s.

The students of the AAS, like their peers at Harvard, also met with activists from the Student Nonviolent Coordinating Committee (SNCC) to discuss their role in the movement. They had the opportunity to meet with Cleveland Sellers and Michael Thelwell, who had been very influential in the SNCC's organizing efforts in the South. They were present for Stokely Carmichael's call for Black Power and the transition that the organization made to the northern struggle against institutional racism. In Boston, when SNCC activists participated in the Black Power and Talented Tenth conference, James Forman aggressively critiqued black students, claiming that they were not prepared for struggle because of their attachment to the white establishment. That sentiment rankled some black Ivy League students, who pointed out that attaining an education at an elite institution was not a detriment to the movement but an asset that could be used to advance the cause. At Cornell, Sellers and Thelwell also challenged the credentials of the black students, who suggested they were becoming militant but only to militantly integrate white society. If they were to be useful to the community, they would need to take up Black Power, which at some point would require racial separatism and unreserved allegiance to the uneducated and undereducated black community. Otherwise, according to the SNCC leaders, they were mere objects of the bourgeoisie. Where Harvard students chafed at such charges, many in the leadership of Cornell's AAS gravitated toward the position of Sellers and Thelwell. Here, again, the outside influence of SNCC helped to determine the direction of life on campus for black students in the Ivy League.[10]

Complications came along with more militant leadership of the AAS and the arrival of Black Power on campus. The new black consciousness challenged standing relationships between black and white students. At Harvard, Ernest Wilson III remembered there was a time when it was impolitic to be seen in public with white people even if they were friends or allies. The militants, he remembered, either shamed or shunned those black students. As a member of the black elite class, this tore at his conscience.[11] Students made analogous statements at Cornell during the period. To be black, in the minds of some, meant to be black exclusively. Interracial dating and even socializing threatened, according to that line of thinking, one's legitimacy as black. Middle-class black students who grew up in desegregated and integrated environments sometimes clashed with the students coming from nearly all-black economically impoverished neighborhoods over how to proceed at Cornell.[12] In the way of youth, some students pressured others to choose sides racially, ideologically, and methodologically. A more radical faction of AAS formed, calling itself the Black Liberation Front.

In March 1968, members of the AAS met with faculty members to discuss the creation of courses in Black Studies. They decided on at least two courses that needed to be taught and that the right faculty members needed to be the instructors. This became clear when controversy erupted over the statements of a visiting white economics professor. That month, black students enrolled in McPhelin's Economics 103 course took offense to the instructor's characterization of black youth from urban areas as pathological and perverted, while acknowledging the effects of poverty.[13] Throughout the course, McPhelin, a priest who had taught in the Philippines, described the durable groups of people who had confronted poverty, become stronger from the experience, and advanced. In his discussion about the American ghetto and slums, he talked of

children learning to survive as if they were in the jungle and impoverished youths' innate or learned predilection toward crime. He attempted
to compare and contrast groups around the world that reacted to poverty in different periods, illustrating that some American groups did not
have the will or wherewithal to climb out of their poor circumstances.
McPhelin never specifically mentioned black people.[14]

Black students, who came from some of the slums and ghettoes to
which McPhelin referred, recognized the tone and direction of the comments as covertly racist, implying that certain racial and ethnic groups
in America and elsewhere could actually thrive because of poverty while
other groups—like black people—could not get past it. Under the leadership of John Garner, a leader of the AAS, several black students in the
course complained to the Department of Economics chair, which led
to an investigation at the departmental and university level. Some in-
vestigators and observers supported the professor's right to assess and
characterize the topic as he saw fit; after all, he was supposed to be the
expert. Others, however, believed that his line of thought and presentation contributed to the narrative of black and poor people being unworthy, lazy, shiftless, and criminalistic by nature.[15]

To be sure, McPhelin's comments were in line with the way that many
white people stereotyped black communities during the period. Students during commission hearings referred to the popular 1965 Daniel
Moynihan Report, which, in an effort to explain that antiblack racism
was a cause of poverty for large segments of the black community, characterized the black family as broken and even deleterious to progress.[16]
At Cornell, white students created a petition to support McPhelin,
while some black students searched for a way to better educate their
peers.

Black students, for as long as they had attended predominantly white
institutions (and even some historically black ones), endured comments
from professors that belittled, infantilized, and blamed black people for
their circumstances in the United States. The new times and audience
challenged McPhelin, who had taught the course the same way previously.
The times ushered in a militant pride for black people, who resisted all
forms of colonization, including educational colonization. The young
learners at Cornell saw themselves as the black intelligentsia and responsible for checking racism in education. They brought the situation

to a head on April 4, which happened to be the day that James Earl Ray shot and killed Dr. King in Memphis. Before getting news of the assassination, the students went to the Department of Economics and held a sit-in, denouncing McPhelin and the way that the university responded. They wanted black-centered courses to prevent the sort of deficit model that professors like McPhelin used to characterize those in poverty (particularly black people), and they wanted McPhelin relieved of his duties.[17]

The problems surrounding McPhelin's lectures were exacerbated when news of King's death arrived. People throughout the nation and in Ithaca grieved the loss of King, whose consistent leadership and focus on respectable rebellion challenged white America to live up to the nation's promises. By 1968, many young black people maintained a deep respect for King but did not take up his abiding allegiance to nonviolence as a way of life. Many from the younger generation began to view King and his lieutenants as part of the old guard of civil rights activists who had almost become impediments in the era of Black Power. At Cornell in particular, messages of integration and the beloved community did not particularly resonate when students faced with white fraternities and residents who mistreated them because of their race. Still, King's death was a realization to even moderate, middle-class black students that they were threats in the eyes of some Americans. In an environment where black learners made up only 250 in a student body of thousands, many black students believed they had to react to defend themselves.

Their reactions were rational. Black students reported hearing cap guns go off in dormitories when some white students found out about the assassination. Black graduate student Cleveland Donald remembered black and white students engaging in fisticuffs, with shots being fired. Some black students reported receiving death threats. Being in rural Ithaca did not comfort some of the urban black students, who felt removed from safety. Naturally, they banned together and set about arming themselves. Many of the narratives of black reactions to King's death have often been spun in such a way that black people angrily destroyed property and called for violence. There has been little room to reveal the sheer fear that many black people felt at the thought of the most respectable, nonviolent representative of the race being targeted. By allowing room for fear in the narrative, black people once again become human.

Fearful black college students reacted as many Americans would if they felt threatened.

From April 4 to 6, properties blazed on and off campus. In Ithaca someone threw a rock through the window of a newspaper office. Other businesses in town burned as well, including a bar and a bookstore. Back on campus, the chapel went up in flames.[18] Just as black women learned that racism was expensive at Cornell in the early part of the twentieth century, white university caretakers learned the same lesson in the late 1960s. Racism had a cost not only in terms of money for repairs but also with regard to the disrespect of that which white institutions held sacred. Typically, in moments of racial tension, black houses of worship burned, but the tables were turned on Cornell's campus in the wake of King's death.

Burning, grieving, and destruction all occurred at the same time black students were trying to move the university toward a more inclusive curriculum. With the image of King fresh in their minds, fifty black students met with faculty members to solidify plans for new courses covering the black experience. The black students emphatically demanded that these courses be exclusive to them even if white professors taught the classes. The faculty members and concerned black students agreed that the courses should indeed be taught and that it would have been best to offer the courses through the Center for Research in Education as an "experiment." Among those in agreement were black undergraduate and graduate students and white professors. The group assigned a committee to take the idea to the university body that decided on coursework.[19]

Realizing that the courses, as they were conceived, would likely come under the auspices of the College of Arts and Sciences, which would also need to approve the classes, the students and faculty reconsidered to whom the courses should be offered. The racial exclusivity of the courses became an issue, and to avoid anticipated conflict, the committee that proposed the courses decided it was best to make admission to the courses by way of instructor permission only. That allowed the professor the latitude to determine those who had backgrounds that would be best conducive to a successful class. It worked. The classes were approved and were to be offered that fall, on one condition: the department chair and professor teaching the course had to ensure that white students would not be rejected from the course because of their race. On that issue, the college committee stood firm.[20] Those approving committee members, with their unshakeable commitment to racial fairness (to white students), would have been very useful when black women could not stay in the Sage College dormitory in the early twentieth century or later when black students could not pledge white fraternities.

When the two classes were filled, there was a minor controversy. In the economics course, there were twelve black students and one white student. The problem was that the professor had initially accepted fifteen black students and four white students, which upset the black students who had protested for the class to be exclusively black. To accommodate, some of the white students dropped the course but so too did some black students, who were protesting the fact that one white student was remaining. To onlookers, it must have seemed irrational of the black students to cause a stir about the racial composition of the class, but that sort of logic had been used for years in the Ivy League. Additionally, the black students knew that the discussion that black people have regarding issues affecting the race can be skewed by either white gaze or the insertion of opinions from those outside the community. In the end, the economics and the literature courses, both taught by white professors, continued without further interruption.

By the time the courses started, several students and faculty on campus had been exploring the prospect of a Black Studies program. To get a sense of the type of unit they wanted to start, in July students visited other universities that were already in the process of establishing Black Studies programs. They went to Harvard, Boston University, Northeastern University, the University of Chicago, Northwestern University, Lincoln University in Pennsylvania, and Howard University. Cornell students protested, demonstrated, and negotiated for the program. It is extraordinary that students, undergraduate and graduate, took it upon themselves to research other academic units—over their summer break no less.[21] In October, the university issued a press release announcing an advisory committee, which consisted of undergraduate and graduate members, men and women, all in AAS. The press release indicated that the committee would submit a finalized proposal for a Black Studies unit.[22] It included students Paul Du Bois, Gayla Cook, Betran Cooper, Sandra Hearn, Dalton Jones, Tom Jones, Fenton Sands, and Janet

Williams as well as administrators Stuart Brown Jr., Faye Edwards, and David Knapp. Also included were professors Chandler Morse, Dan McCall, Benjamin Nichols, and William Whyte.

Equally important as the type of program was the information sharing that occurred among students from all of the universities. The campus campaigns at the various institutions influenced each other. For instance, when Cornell students attended the "Toward a Black University" conference at Howard University in November, their conception of what they wanted in a Black Studies unit evolved greatly. The Cornell students discovered they wanted a standalone black institute, perhaps even an all-black college.[23] Cornell students also met fate in graduate student James Turner. In May 1968, at Northwestern, Turner was in the vanguard of a rebellion that brought Black Studies into existence, an experience served him and Cornell University well.[24] The activist students at each of the institutions laid the groundwork for an entire academic discipline.

In addition to thinking about how the unit would be structured, the students commandeered space as well. In December, six black students took over a campus house, proclaiming it the home of the "Afro-American Institute." In doing so, the students told the white people in the building that they had to leave because the house was for institute members only. The white professor and employees left. Under the leadership of black student John Garner, the demonstrators were pushing for their black college.

The campaign of the militant wing of the AAS emanated heat during the cold Ithaca winter. The next demonstration led to disciplinary trouble for AAS members. Carrying toy guns, several black students enter Day Hall, where President Perkins's was located, to re-emphasize the demand for a black college. During the course of their demonstration, the students tipped over a vending machine, damaging it. For the students, the autonomous college was nonnegotiable. In the eyes of the administrators, the students were plainly destructive, even if they raised valid points about restructuring the university. As a result, the university pressed charges against the students who had damaged the property.[25]

More AAS demonstrations took place in mid-December. One included students marking the hallway outside of Perkins's office as a "seminar" to illustrate the need for space. When the president sent out a cart of drinks and snacks, the students tipped that over too. Another demonstration involved taking down thousands of books from shelves in a library to show they had no "relevance." They wanted a better catalogue of books regarding black life and culture. Additionally, students demanded a black psychiatrist or psychologist for the counseling center, highlighting the point that black students experienced a form of stress that could perhaps be best understood by someone who may have experienced similar stressors because of race. Then, protesting students disrupted a basketball game to state their demands. This all occurred as students throughout the university prepared for finals.[26] The black demonstrators believed that if racism had to disrupt their lives, then it should disrupt everyone else's life as well. They wanted a new black college that featured black faculty, staff, administrators, and of course students so that the work they did would be available to the black community. The AAS wanted all of this at its elite white institution; it wanted to blacken the ivy.

In justification of the black college, the AAS sent a letter to Perkins: "The Black brother realizes that he must continue his education at white institutions in order to gain technical skills unavailable elsewhere which he can apply to Black situations."[27] What the brother found at Cornell was not useful to him or his community. "Therefore . . . he is demanding that the predominantly white institution develop a program which fits his needs." AAS members believed that they had multiple responsibilities. They were responsible for acquiring skills, for bringing those skills back to the community, and for improving their university. "We do not believe that the institutions [of higher education] can stand still and survive, nor will we allow them to do so." The AAS did not support the status quo and felt "morally committed to acquire an education by whatever means, which will be relevant to the community from which we have come." So, they protested.

On the issue of autonomy and black control, the students were adamant. Likening racism to a disease, they reasoned that liberal-minded white people had finally become aware (with the assistance of black people) that racism had sickened them. AAS members did not believe that the same white people who had just learned of the disease could "diagnose and cure" themselves. That, they claimed is what the administration proposed to do by allowing white officials to participate in defining, designing, and implementing Black Studies. If that were to occur, the AAS contended, the unit would be based in the same racism that had afflicted white people up until this point. That was why it was essential that black people design a program for black students, who could then help the larger black community. Ostensibly, students could look to black professors for guidance, but that was not the case at Cornell because "at Cornell University they are too few" or had no desire to start a Black Studies unit. The AAS demanded that black students take the lead in defining, designing, and implementing the program. What, then, would be the role of white professionals and students? The AAS responded that "we do not require that white [students] benefit although they might. . . . Our aim is the creation of a Black College . . . within a white university which will deal with the problem of Black America."[28] There would be some white students who, conceivably, "might be able to empathize with the Afro-American experience to an extent that would permit them to participate validly in some course, at least conditionally," explained a document that discussed the goals of the unit.[29]

The president responded in favor of most of the demands regarding a Black Studies unit, space, and a black psychiatrist, but he could not agree to an all-black college because that would be a matter for the faculty.[30] To implement their vision of Black Studies, AAS members also made their choice of a director for the new institute. They selected recent Northwestern graduate and activist James Turner, whom some had met previously. On January 11, they communicated their desire for Turner to the president, and by January 20 Turner was interviewing on campus. After some consultation, the students and the candidate determined that it was best to have a center and that a college might not have been practicable. The center could oversee a major in Afro-American Studies and feature its own faculty (not joint-appointed with another unit) while reporting directly to the provost of the university. The president had proposed a budget of $175,000 for the 1969–1970 school year. By the end of the month, the university sent a letter to James Turner expressing its unofficial approval of a center for Black Studies, a major and minor in Black Studies, and instructions regarding the creation of a graduate minor and major.[31] Black students, in negotiation with the mostly white administration, were building an institution one step at a time.

Just months earlier, black students had been protesting the presence of an instructor they thought was racist, but now black students reveled in the options they had for courses and instruction. Because of the planning that started as far back as December, some of the most influential members of the black activist and arts communities offered courses for the spring term.[32] Like the Harvard activists, they not only wanted intellectuals but those who had acted on behalf of the community. With that in mind, the students did not need the instructors to have doctorates. Renowned poet Don Lee (later Haki Madhubuti) taught a freshman seminar while SNCC activists Cleveland Sellers Jr. and Michael Thelwell offered classes on black ideologies and literature. Madhubuti founded the Third World Press, which published the works of Sonia Sanchez, Gwendolyn Brooks, Margaret Walker, and Amiri Baraka. Thelwell became the founding chair of the Afro-American Studies Department at the University of Massachusetts. And Sellers, who had been present when Black Power was introduced in Greenwood, Mississippi, and when police killed black student activists near the campus of South Carolina State College, went on to earn a master's degree from Harvard and eventually become president of Voorhees College. Each instructor shared their life experiences and work with Cornell students.

While enjoying those courses and instructors in the spring of 1969, AAS members continued to revise the proposal for what they were calling the Center for Afro-American Studies. By the time the students and James Turner (who was still not an official employee of the university) finished negotiating with the administration, the budget for the oncoming year had been increased to $215,000. On April 10, the Cornell Board of Trustees manifested the vision of audacious students by approving the degree-granting center. The next month, James Turner officially accepted the position of director with the power to hire faculty members (upon approval of a university oversight committee).

Between the board's approval of the center in early April and Turner's acceptance of the directorship in May, Cornell experienced one of the most tumultuous moments of its history. On April 18, at nearly 2:00 A.M., black women awoke to the sound of a rock breaking glass in the Wari House. Outside, they found a cross burning on the porch. The year before black students had reported that their lives had been threatened after the assassination of Dr. King, but they had witnessed nothing so blatantly threatening and racist as a burning cross on the porch of their residence. The Ku Klux Klan historically used the burning cross as a threat to black people and a symbol of white Christian supremacy. That one burned so far North and on a college campus surprised some people, but it frightened and infuriated black students, who grew up hearing stories about the Klan and racial violence. Years later, a black student characterized the act as a "threat on the lives of a group of African Americans living together, studying and attempting to find their place in the world at Cornell."[33] The world at Cornell, at that moment, was perilous. Granted some of the women in the Wari House had, with their demonstrations, been threatening tradition but not death. Whoever burned the cross on the porch implicitly or explicitly threatened black life. The victims of the hate crime reacted quickly.

The cross burned the same night that the university student conduct board decided the disciplinary fate of the black students who had participated in the December 1968 demonstrations. After hours, the deliberating board determined that three students were culpable for the destruction of the vending machine and should be punished for their actions. Reprimand involved notifying the students' parents and the placement of a letter detailing the offenses in each student's permanent record.[34] Effectively, that meant that none of the black students were to be expelled or suspended, which was acceptable to some students but not all, particularly those who believed that black students were let off too easily. It was also unacceptable to some black students who believed that the December demonstrators should not have been punished at all. As students considered the implications of the disciplinary board's decision, the fire truck sirens rang out on campus. The firefighters arrived to answer the call at the Wari House, and to false calls elsewhere on campus. Then, more than one hundred black students, leaving a party, mobilized to Willard Straight Hall. Scholar Donald Downs claimed that the AAS had already devised a protest action in case the decision did not go in the black students' favor. He indicated that the Straight Hall takeover was not a reaction to the cross burning, but rather part of a larger campaign of disruption that the AAS had been planning and waging all school year.[35]

At Straight, the AAS demonstrators took the keys from the custodians and relieved them of their duties in a manner similar to that of Association of Black Collegians members who took over the New South building on Princeton's campus the previous month. Then, the Cornell agitators woke the residential staff and parents who had been staying in the student union. Over the airwaves, AAS members announced the takeover on the student radio station, exclaiming that black people were in rebellion. One of the leaders of the takeover, Edward Whitfield, remembered that the group had not planned to stay in the building for more than a few hours and that the intention was simply to disrupt. Just as white radical allies did at Princeton during the New South takeover, members of the SDS interposed themselves between counterprotesters, authorities, and administrators by surrounding the building in support of the black demonstrators. Cleveland Donald, who was inside, remembered that initially "we [black students] were not armed when we entered the building," but there was an intense attitude of "urgency."[36] Downs, in deviation from that narrative, pointed out there were some demonstrators who originally had small makeshift weapons inside but no firearms. Whitfield, who grew up in Little Rock, Arkansas, during the Central High School crisis in 1957, soberly recognized the significance of angry white mobs forming to check black agitators. Protection quickly became a priority.

After finding out about the cross-burning, the Straight occupiers were undeniably and understandably defensive. They recognized how high the stakes were as they barricaded themselves in the building. Some began cooking while others studied. It was, after all, nearing final exams. Making an interesting point about the narrative associated with black protesters in the Ivy League during the period, one Cornell student remarked: "I think there's a mythology out there that suggests that all of these movements—be it at Cornell, Columbia, or anyplace—represented kind of a group of black thugs or something from the ghetto." They may have been from urban centers and they may have maintained a militant attitude about racial advancement and opportunity, but the young people were intelligent and wanted to achieve. The student believed that some viewed the activists as "people who couldn't read, write, compute—people who . . . just came up and raised a lot of hell and took stuff over and then left."[37] The student knew they were more than that but worried that others did not.

The action was perfectly timed to coincide with the annual parents' weekend when those who typically financed the education of the mostly white students came to see how their children lived and how their tuition payments were used. It was also a time that the institution put on its best face to reassure the parents that in loco parentis remained intact. Only certain parents could afford the time and money it took to visit their children in Ithaca. Many of the parents, university officials, and students could not have predicted the turmoil that ensued the night of April 18 and the early morning of April 19. Inside Straight, the black protesters pounded on doors and yelled to awaken the sleeping parents in an effort to get them out of the building. The sound and sight of the all-black contingent frightened some parents as they hurried out of Straight. They certainly had not made tuition payments to receive such treatment.

Similarly, the parents of black students had not allowed their children to attend the Ivy League university in Ithaca with any inclination that a cross might be burned on their doorstep. The parents of black students hoped that their children did not have to be called racial epithets, threatened, and denied opportunities because they were black. Equally, though, most black parents did not send their young persons to Cornell to become race rebels but rather to make life better for themselves and their families. The news that their children took over a campus building was not always welcome. Students, adhering to the protocol that nearly all student protesters followed when taking over buildings, called their parents from Straight. Some of the students remembered their parents being upset and telling them to leave.

At that point, those students faced a lonely, life-altering decision. They could defy the wishes of their parents, the administration, and fellow students by staying in the building to demand that the reprimand of the three black students for the December demonstrations be nullified, that there be a full investigation of the cross burning, and that secure housing be made available to black students. Or they could leave the building, knowing that they had successfully disrupted life at Cornell while drawing attention to their concerns. The choices were very difficult and personal. Either way, they had already committed acts that would be embedded in their conscience forever.

Many parents on and off campus were unhappy but so too were white student counterprotesters. During the actions of black student groups at each of the Ivies, counterprotesters attempted to neutralize and mitigate the effects of the demonstrations. At Cornell, Delta Upsilon fraternity men were in the vanguard of the opposition during the morning of April 19. Delta Upsilon Fraternity, Inc. was, incidentally, the fraternity that President Perkins had pledged while an undergraduate. White athletes comprised much of its membership and they believed that they were perhaps the last line of defense for the university's honor, as the administration seemed to capitulate to the whims of black students too often. Acting on behalf of what they viewed as righteousness, the fraternity members entered Straight to confront the occupiers. Their counteraction escalated the demonstration to the point of violence. Fisticuffs ensued, and the AAS men and women forced the Delta Upsilon vigilantes out of the building. The action of the fraternity, more than any strategy meeting, helped AAS leadership decide that the occupiers would not just stay in the building, but they would take up firearms to defend themselves.

Tom Jones mentioned anger and anguish as motivators for black student activists' protests during the period, but there was another element that was equally motivating: fear. Knowing that someone burned a cross on the porch of the Wari House, knowing that the white fraternity members just physically attacked them, knowing that some AAS members had received death threats months earlier, and knowing about the rumors circling that there were armed white men off campus ready to come to Cornell to eradicate the black problem made the decision to arm themselves prudent.[38] Although the decision was logical, it was also frightening for some of the occupiers who were forced to come to grips with the magnitude of what was occurring. If the Delta Upsilon men or other counterprotesters returned, the college experience of the demonstrating black students would become one that potentially teetered between life and death. Although the Straight occupiers, now armed, may have been perceived as the most threatening group at the moment, they were certainly not the most dangerous. There were thousands of white students on campus, many of whom owned firearms. Between the awareness of those numbers and that of the weapons available to those outside the building, a heightened paranoia arrested some of the demonstrators.

There was another issue at play: black masculinity and manhood. The arrival of Black Nationalism, according to graduate student Cleveland Donald, shaped black male Cornellians' sense of manhood to include protection of the black community and particularly black women. He surmised that before Black Power fully took hold on campus, black men dated and maintained frivolous relationships with white women not for potential marriage purposes but to fulfill mutual sexual desires. Black Nationalism and its emphasis on racial unity and manhood, explained Donald, required that black men relate to black female students differently. That included black men ceasing sexual relations with white women while glorifying and protecting the idea of black womanhood. At the same time, claimed Donald, black women, who had been neglected and rejected before, were expected to devote themselves to black men for the sake of the community and movement. In effect, this could occur while black men took leadership positions for themselves in organizations like the AAS, enforcing what scholar Stephanie Dunn referred to as a "dangerous primitive black male image."[39] Black manhood, then, became an outward push for power and control that was on display in a starkly white space. With the advent of Black Nationalism, criticizing black people in the presence of white people became taboo. That allowed the black students to appear unified when, in fact, there was likely tension that existed between various factions, including men and women.[40]

The men and women of the AAS made decisions on behalf of the group, but there was present, during the Straight Hall takeover, the sensitivity associated with centuries of black emasculation. Burning crosses on the lawns of black homes without retribution from black men embodied that emasculation. Years of black men choosing the survival of themselves and their families over counterattacking white supremacists even at the risk of death had psychological and historical consequences. From the Deacons for Self Defense to SNCC to the Black Panthers, one of the goals was for black men to be able to act assertively in defense of their families and communities—especially black women.[41] Many black men wanted to defend themselves and black womanhood in the way that white men had claimed to do for centuries. At the thought that black men might have harmed a white woman, white men mobilized to lethally punish the perpetrator and to make it known to larger society that such behavior was unacceptable.

White institutions and individuals had historically taken advantage of and abused black women. In surviving those atrocities, black women and men called on the newer generation to "draw the line" to which Jones referred—to do what their ancestors could not do in the face of crippling oppression. Some suggested that the urban rebellions and the Black Power Movement of the period influenced AAS members to arm themselves. Black power critic Martin Kilson wrote in 1968 that "Negro or Black manhood is being affirmed by a riotous attack on white dominated society" and that "for the Black Power advocates . . . riots have first a romantic and psycho-cultural relevance."[42] The men of the AAS believed they were Black Power advocates and felt it was their duty to take up arms to defend black womanhood from white terror. "Historically the white boy has made the black woman a target of racism and inhumanity," wrote one of the occupiers later, "no longer will we allow our women to be harmed in any fashion by this white boy."[43] In addition to protecting the notion of black womanhood, they were protecting their friends. Whether arming themselves was a romantic notion was of little consequence in the moment.

The idea that women could not defend themselves was based, in part, in hegemonic masculinity, but the actions of those who shouldered firearms took the threats, cross burning, and fraternity invasion as a challenge to black womanhood, black manhood, and black life. Months and years earlier, like so many black organizations, there was tension surrounding the all-male leadership of the AAS and female participation. That tension was surely not resolved by the time of the takeover. In the morning hours of April 19, Andre McLaughlin, a black female student, recalled wondering how the situation had devolved so quickly as to necessitate firearms and declarations of the men's willingness to die to protect women. Could the decision to bear arms have been the result of misguided notions of manhood? Was it the result of romanticized notions of Black Power? Or, was it the need to feel secure and basic self-defense? Regardless of the justification, the AAS reacted resoundingly and officials believed the demonstrators were ready to die if necessary.

The invasion of the Delta Upsilon members and the AAS occupiers arming themselves in Straight spelled disaster for Cornell's administration. Perkins was loath to call the local police onto campus because he and others recognized what philosopher Charles Frankel explained a year after demonstrations involving the police at Columbia, Cornell, Harvard and elsewhere: "on lookers bring certain conditioned reflexes to the spectacle" the Columbia professor wrote. For students, whether they sympathize with the demands of demonstrators or are mostly apathetic, turning the police on protesters will cause merely sympathetic and apathetic onlookers to become supporters of their fellow students who have faced the perceived violent wrath of the outside police force, he noted. In the eyes of observers, "young people spill their own blood in the struggle[, but the] old call in the cops to do their dirty work," wrote Frankel.[44] The contrast was stark to young people.

In addition to the optics, there was the very practical matter of numbers. In a speech that he gave after the demonstration, Perkins revealed that there was a total thirty-nine police on the Ithaca force and there were well over a hundred students in Straight. Considering that Harvard, days earlier, had called 400 Boston and Cambridge officers to remove 200 protesters, Perkins believed that a contingent from the Ithaca force that may have been able to show up would have been instantly overwhelmed, further antagonizing the situation. Had the police been overrun, then the next option for the president was to call in the National Guard, which was the worst-case scenario for any university president or state governor.

Police violence had the potential to tear a university apart, and Perkins knew it. Not calling the police to extract the occupiers, however, also galled those who believed in law and order, academic freedom, and respect for the university in general. Perkins, an avowed liberal, was in a most unenviable position between black militants and the protection of a white institution. On April 20, with violence, in one form or another, looming over Cornell, President Perkins acceded to the AAS's demands that the demonstrating students (from December or April) would not be punished by the university, there would be an investigation of the cross burning, and the university would establish secure housing units for black students. This decision made the president popular with no one, especially the faculty as well as many alumni, donors, and parents. The decision did, however prevent further violence. With that in mind, he watched black students like Eric Evans, Edward Whitfield, and others vacate Straight Hall with rifles pointed upward and cartridges reportedly empty (a picture later showed a round in the breech of Eric Evan's rifle). The men of AAS surrounded the women as they walked out because some AAS members believed they may yet be ambushed by white vigilantes. Photographers from multiple news organizations snapped the infamous photos of the scene. Perkins had to answer to many constituencies.[45]

The president stated sadly: "The fact that our efforts for black students should have grown from the good will of my administration and should have erupted into such violent feeling, has been a source of more sorrow and distress to me than I can possibly say."[46] The statement featured a hint of paternalism and bewilderment. Like Jones, Perkins mentioned anguish: "Cornell's anguish of the past week has unquestionably drawn the attention of the nation because here we have reflected the anguish of the nation." It was time, believed some AAS members, that white institutional America experienced the anguish with which much of black America constantly dealt.

"I would like to speak about two matters regarding events at Cornell that have occupied the attention of the nation," began Perkins in a public statement.[47] Guns and the background of the building seizure were the matters he addressed. With regard to the firearms that AAS students bore, the president said that "in the interest of avoiding what seemed at the time to be much too great a risk of bloodshed," he decided to concede to the demands of the students. The idea, however, that large amounts of students were "armed to the teeth" and no one defended the institution was fallacious. He correctly noted that relatively few students had firearms but optically the image of students exiting Straight with bandoliers draped around them and rifles pointed upward may have given a different impression. That the students were black with afros surely added to the spectacle as well.

Perkins also discussed the experience of black students. He said: "I have no reason to doubt that our black students have been subjected to threats, insults, and intimidation here at Cornell that no white person would tolerate if he were in their place." After conceding that, the president suggested that while most of the black students at Cornell were sincere in creating racial reconciliation, "a small group of black students" has worked to resist "and on occasion undermine" the university's efforts to help. With the state of things then, he wondered if COSEP would

Figure 9.1. Members of the Afro-American Society and other black students exiting Willard Straight Hall after taking over the student union building in a demonstration for Black Studies, safety for black on-campus residences, and cultural space, among other issues. Courtesy of Carl A. Kroch Library, Cornell University.

survive the intimidation that has come from the "black side as well as the white."

Reassuring the public that Cornell was safe, Perkins explained that within a week of the demonstration, "new and thorough regulations are already in force" that prohibited firearms on campus. The president declared that all firearms were banned on April 23, and on the morning of April 25 university officials collected firearm, rifles, and shotguns and issued receipts to students who could not get them back until they returned home.[48] Before the Straight Hall takeover there were no pat rules about having firearms. Ithaca was rural; students as well as townspeople hunted and carried weapons regularly. In the United States, however, there is a phenomenon that involves white America recognizing the flaws in processes and operations only when black people participate. For instance, the state of California, under Governor Ronald Reagan, was up until 1967 an open carry state. That was until members of the Black Panther Party for Self Defense conducted armed patrols of their neighborhoods, ensuring that the police acted within the law when contacting citizens. Conservatives, moderates, and liberals alike proposed and voted for the Mulford bill, which tightened firearm laws. Governor Ronald Reagan (who toted pistols regularly during his movie career) signed the Mulford Act into law.

At Cornell, the same principle applied. Firearm ownership on campus was not an issue of great concern until unhappy black students, many from urban areas, reacted to a perceived threat by bearing weapons. Only then did the university discover that having weapons in a space where alcohol and drugs were prevalent and where emotionally charged young adults dwelled was potentially dangerous. This was not lost on the Cornell Community of Anthropologists, which presented a signed petition that decried the "deep-seated hypocrisy in the minds of white Americans."[49] Its petition read: "Blacks who have demanded human respect for themselves have been murdered by white members of a white system." Human respect meant the right to live without death threats and crosses burning at one's residence. The reaction of the Cornell community regarding firearms was conveniently hasty, the petition noted: "The majority of the Cornell Community condemned the presence of guns in the Black students' hands without an adequate consideration of the context of the events and situations on campus and on national . . . levels." That the university moved to check firearm presence on campus after black students armed themselves was, according to the statement, "a discredit to the Cornell community." Despite the criticism, the president, administration, and most of the faculty believed banning firearms on campus was essential if they were ever to regain a semblance of peace on campus.

The banning of weapons on campus was an important step, conceded some faculty members, but it was not impressive in lieu of the real threat the university faced. There were professors who claimed that Tom Jones and the AAS had threatened them personally. The president's statement about banning firearms on campus was not completely reassuring to them. As one professor conjectured, "The guns are several blocks away instead of inside this room."⁵⁰ Some contended that as menacing as firearms were, it was the threat to academic freedom that most challenged the university. Professors like famed white historian Walter LaFeber decided to resign because the administration and faculty voted to reverse the reprimand of the student demonstrators from December and not to punish the protesters of April. There was a minority of faculty members who threatened to leave the university because of decisions made by Perkins and other administrators. If the AAS intended to "destroy this university, I say let [them] try it," exclaimed another professor.⁵¹ He believed that the university could "survive the expulsion or departure of no matter what number of students and the destruction of buildings," as long as it adhered to the principle of academic freedom. The AAS's push to design exclusively black courses and to determine whether disciplinary decisions were valid opposed the professor's view of academic freedom.

A majority of faculty members voted to nullify the reprimand, but not all did so with their dignity intact. Of his affirmative vote, one professor said at an all-faculty meeting in Barton Hall: "I will vote for nullification from fear. . . . I will lose some self-respect doing so; I want you [the thousands of students who were present] to know I terribly resent this."⁵² The professor was not alone. The faculty, too, was in a precarious situation. They needed the freedom to teach and operate without fear of coercion from either the administration or students, but they also needed the confidence of their students to be effective.

Their frustration was largely with the Perkins administration. A faculty member made it clear that he represented a group that wanted to move forward in peace with the students. "In fear for your safety, we put aside our principles" he said.⁵³ Another capped those sentiments: "We hear you, we care, we are trying to understand you and want together with you to do something. . . . We want to be your friends."⁵⁴ Incidentally, LaFeber did not resign, but black economics Professor Thomas

Sowell did. Not all students wanted the faculty to approve nullification. Some wore on their bodies signs that read: "Agreements Made Under Duress Are Not Binding."[55]

President Perkins understood that the future of the university was uncertain. Desperate to pull the faculty and administration back together, the beleaguered university president said, "I hope that we may be able to expunge to the fullest extent possible the seizure of Willard Straight Hall from the records of this University and the incidents connected therewith."[56] That was impossible. Someone started a campaign to unseat Perkins. Believing the university could not continue with him at the helm, a leaflet appeared featuring a drawing of an ostensibly white woman dressed in flowing robe with long straight hair and her breast exposed seated in a rocking chair, smiling. On the lap of the woman, who was apparently supposed to represent the university, was a darkened unclothed infant with curly hair and a rifle in his hand smiling at the milk that flowed from the woman's breast. A text box above the infant read: "Hail, Oh Hail, CORNELL." Emboldened in block letters at the top of the sheet was the phrase: PERKINS MUST GO."[57] The "artwork" infantilized black activists at Cornell and depicted them as violent; yet the image implied that they were dependent on the teat of the university. That characterized the way that some viewed the relationship of black students to the school. Cornell affiliates were split in their reactions to the demonstrations. The only consolation for Perkins was that the campus was, as one public affairs administrator pithily put it, "without coffins."[58]

This was the atmosphere James Turner entered when he officially accepted his position in late May. He could not solve all of Cornell's problems concerning race, but he could create a Black Studies center that was, as he put it, "a prototype of faculty-student relations."[59] In his vision the new Africana Studies and Research Center would be "a community of scholars: teachers and students." Africana, a term that Turner coined, referred to the three major geographical and cultural contexts of the black experience: Africa, the African Diaspora (primarily the Caribbean), and America. In that way, students began their scholarly inquiries based in philosophies of the "African Continuum and African Constitution," he said.[60] Turner's conception of the center called for mostly small courses for students and an intensive focus on research. In his plan there were five elements that were essential for the center's success: an awareness that "Black Studies is a field still being born"; that initiative of defining and establishing the field "must be ours"—meaning that of black people; the collaboration of scholars and students around the nation; "a unified, rather than a conventionally understood academic-discipline-bound, approach"; and an understanding that the establishment of the field would take years and not weeks or months.

Turner indicated that the courses and research would center on areas that had been neglected with regard to the black historical and contemporary experience. In emphasizing that the unit's focus would be on Africa, the Caribbean, and the United States, the center was different from many other Black Studies units that focused primarily on the black experience in the United States. Turner suggested comparative studies of black slavery and urban life as well as exploration of a black aesthetic and arts. To engage studies in these and other fields, the center needed a state of the art library with ample archival material that could be made available to academic and nonacademic audiences. Not wanting to recreate that which had already been proven to work, he also pointed to the need to review the efforts of others at different universities throughout the nation who were building Black Studies units.

For theoretical grounding, Turner and the Cornell students looked toward the Institute of the Black World that was developing in Atlanta.[61] Thought leaders such as Vincent Harding, Gerald McWhorter, and William Strickland counseled Turner on the need for praxis. The new center leader understood that learning for learning's sake had its place, but the goal was to "identify the enemy within the black community, within our own people, within ourselves," which was what Harding taught.[62] Black activists and thought leaders throughout the nation were constructing models for the field. Cornell and Turner were part of that community.

The role that students played in shaping the curriculum and recruiting faculty and staff for the Africana Studies and Research Center (ASRC) was notable, but more remarkable was its autonomy within the university, which Turner commented on: "The Africana Center is organizationally different from other university units called 'centers.' It is not . . . composed of a loose confederation of faculty who hold appointments in other departments."[63] Most of those units in the Ivy League were programs, which operated with joint-appointed faculty members or departments that featured several full-time but mostly joint-appointed faculty members. This would not work well for the ASRC, Turner said. "As a general principle," he noted, "joint faculty appointments are avoided because they would compromise the Center's distinction, and the integrity of its purpose." Although he was new to the academy, Turner sagely surmised that "a centralized faculty can better provide a cogent and integrated curriculum." As many Black Studies units found out, many unforeseen problems arose when sharing faculty.[64] By having its own faculty, the center avoided unnecessary turmoil.

Turner was able to acquire some of the most acclaimed black intellectuals in the nation to act as instructors and professors, including John Henrik Clarke, who personally mentored Malcolm X and Kwame Nkrumah. Like some of the other members of the faculty, Clarke was not formally trained in the academy but learned the role of African people by studying the available documents in the Schomburg Center for Black History and Culture and elsewhere. He provided the Cornell students with an important perspective as someone who worked in public history.[65]

Finally, the ASRC director reported not to the College of Arts and Sciences but rather to the provost's office, which was unique among the dozens of units that arose during the period. Considering the ability of black students, staff, and community members to determine the direction of the new ASRC, the unit was, as scholar Donald Downs aptly characterized it, "the most militant in the country."[66] The students made sure of it. Turner, writing for *Ebony* magazine in August 1969, explained that relying on the same models of education that had intellectually colonized young people before would only lead to more oppression in the future.[67] To undo the effects of mental colonization, the students and black people in general needed a model of self-determination and definition, which was what the center intended to provide.

The ASRC did well to prepare students for life after Cornell. One of the main questions about Black Studies was what could majoring in the interdisciplinary field ever do for students. Apparently, it could greatly enhance the life chances of the majoring students, most of whom were black, and it could positively affect the lives of black people not enrolled in Ivy institutions. An article reported that by 1973, four years after the establishment of the ASRC, of the Straight Hall demonstrators one had completed his PhD and four others were enrolled in doctoral pro-grams; six participants matriculated into either law or medical school; one wrote a book for children while also writing a play that showed on Broadway; another earned a master's degree at Harvard; and one went to work for the government of Tanzania.[68] By most standards, that was a good record for students majoring in any academic field but especially one the students helped to design.

Cornell, in the Ivy League, had the opportunity once again to be a leader in higher education, but, like Harvard, had to do it the hard way. There were ideological battles in which Harvardians and Cornellians of all political orientations engaged. Those skirmishes did not just play out on campus but in the national media. The elite universities, protective of their traditions and culture, were unprepared for the newest genera-tion of black learners who did not seek to blend into what had already been established in terms of race relations. Black Nationalism and Black Power challenged the students to live out the freedom movement, which had changed in tenor and methodology, on campus. In responding to the challenge, activist black students at Cornell found university offi-cials still trying to catch up to the integration imperative. In embracing racial separatism and demanding the right to control aspects of the cur-riculum and university governance, the black Ivy agitators confounded liberal white officials in their efforts to remake Cornell.

Conclusion

Welcome to the Class

"The disorders on these campuses are reflections in part of the disorders in the larger society—disorders in our social arrangements, and disorders in the way we think about these arrangements," wrote Columbia University philosophy professor and former U.S. Assistant Secretary of State Charles Frankel in 1968.[1] The Vietnam conflict and unchecked militarization, along with racism and poverty, represented the disorders to which the philosopher referred. To him, the Ivy League universities were a laboratory for the concentrated problems of the nation. In his book, *Education and the Barricades*, Frankel asked if students had a right to demand power. Some black Ivy Leaguers, with their actions, answered in the affirmative—that they had the right to create better life chances for those in their communities; that they had a right to the power that came along with learning about their history and culture; and that they had the right to use the elite white institutions to acquire human rights and build Black Power.

Life was unpredictable on Ivy League campuses in the postwar era. The population of higher education institutions expanded as youth culture arose. The values of the nation were changing and the struggle for what was and what would be bubbled over onto campus. War invaded so many aspects of life that it was difficult for students to determine where the interests of the government ended and where the missions of their universities began. Race and all the tension it evokes picked away at the relative calm of Ivy institutions. There was also the fact that the majority of people on college campuses were attempting to discover their identities while battling hormones and studying for exams. Cornell's president James Perkins candidly admitted: "Maintaining peace and stability on a university campus in the late 1960s is an entirely new ball game."[2] It certainly was.

Racism, of course, existed in the Ivy League in the postwar era. In most cases, however, it was not racial animus that threatened black students but rather racial neglect. The Ancient Eight were constructed and maintained for the advancement of a certain demographic: well-to-do white men. Institutions such as those in the Ivy League reflected the values and mores of the nation. The group that had the most access to the Ancient Eight focused, often narrowly, on their families' wealth and their own opportunities to succeed. In creating their networks of success, many of the young white men from socioeconomically comfortable families did not think about black people other than when they needed service. So, even when white alumni and affiliates of the schools were open to black students and employees coming to campus, there was no infrastructure and support system in place to ensure a healthy transition for the new demographic.

The transition of some of these black newcomers, whether or not they had previously been in predominantly white educational environments, was a source of friction on each of the Ivy campuses. They clearly brought with them more than their clothes; black students packed the hopes and ambitions of their communities as well as the attitudes and spirit of the movements that arose in their neighborhoods. Friction sometimes yielded fire when no one in authority knew how to relate to or empathize with black students. The white authority figures never had to practice relating to black people and sympathizing with their plights before the substantial arrival of the new students.

In addition to surviving and studying, black Ivy students used every method available to them to improve themselves and their institutions. Sometimes that included organizing, employing militant rhetoric, cajoling administrators, coalescing with other groups, boycotting classes, taking over buildings, and even striking until their demands were met. Seasoned student activists wrote that "the purpose of a strike is not to demonstrate that students can fight with police and soldiers on the streets. It is to promote and achieve change."[3] Thankfully, black students did not always have to implement strikes to alter policies that they believed prohibited their advancement. When they found it necessary, however, black students risked a great deal to prove their points.

Negotiating between traditional Ivy League culture and that of black students in the postwar era was an education unto itself. In acquiring that education, various groups learned different lessons. Institutional officials learned, sometimes the hard way, that opening the doors to black people was not enough. Having a racially diverse campus; a curriculum that showed an awareness of the black experience; and cocurricular experiences and spaces required the commitment, intentionality, analysis, assessment, and resources of the institutions themselves. It also required patience, of which black students in the latter part of the postwar era seemed to be short. Along those lines, officials learned that their liberalism would not save them from the wrath of young black people who did not feel grateful for their opportunities to be with rich white people. Those students learned that voicing their concerns rather than suffering often led to accommodations. Survival and assimilation could not satisfy their desires to feel as though they were truly a part of the Ivy League. Students also learned that no matter what their struggles were, to some in the outside activist community Ivy League black students could never be truly devoted to the cause. In that vein, the student agitators understood that, concerning their role on campus, they were fighting against the stereotypes of some white people and also against those of black people who could not quite imagine their lives.

Many of the black students during the postwar period disrupted the consciousness of decision makers and their fellow students in white institutions. In unsettling the status quo at the staid institutions, black students, arguably more than any others, promoted and achieved change at schools that predated the nation. Between 1945 and 1975, they were never more than 13 percent of the student population at any of the Ancient Eight, even those urban Ivies that resided in black and brown neighborhoods. All of those black students, in some manner, resisted the racial discrimination that had existed in the Ivy League for centuries. The percentage of black students who participated in demonstrations and spoke out against what they viewed as institutional racism was, of course, smaller. Although their numbers were small, they took up causes that were bigger than their individual selves.

Contemporary scholars have the luxury of knowing whether the students' bids for black advancement were successful. When, in the postwar era, students moved from survival to establishing their identities and accommodating spaces on campus, they did not know what the results of their campaigns would be. Personally, there was little to gain for student activists who rebelled against their universities. For their efforts they were not guaranteed more money in scholarships or positioning themselves to attain better marks in their classes. In fact, they risked all of their standing and potentially their lives if they lost their student exemption status during the war. Unselfishly, the student demonstrators often activated for students they would not meet and for those who would not ever experience the life of an elite student. That fact fits into the faith that students had in collective progress and humanity.

Collective progress and humanity were themes in the new field that the students inspired. Black Studies intended to serve multiple purposes, and it succeeded. One such purpose was to intellectually stimulate learners, another was to give students on campus a sense of belonging, and finally another was to give back to the off campus black community. This was especially important at predominantly white institutions (PWIs), which had greatly changed in terms of demographics over the decade of the 1960s. At the beginning of the decade only 200,000 black students attended PWIs. By 1970, 500,000 black students (6 percent of the black collegiate population) were enrolled at PWIs.[4] These newcomers to PWIs benefited from the thorough educational, political, and psychological work that their predecessors had done to create a curriculum and space on campus that allowed the students to feel not only respected but uplifted. Additionally, Black Studies inspired nonblack students and scholars to create other fields of study, such as Chicano and Latino Studies, Women's and Gender Studies, Native American Studies, and Jewish Studies. Using Black Studies as an interdisciplinary model, the new fields claimed their space in the academy.

The work that black Ivy students did to create and participate in the field of Black Studies was critical in reshaping conceptions about the culture and life of black people inside and outside of the academy. "Black Studies programs remain one of the enduring and outstanding legacies of the Black Power Movement," wrote scholar Peniel Joseph.[5] In these programs, the long stream of black radical consciousness that was present in early scholars such as Harvard alumni W.E.B. Du Bois, Carter G. Woodson, and William Leo Hansberry and others affected the scholastic journey of thousands of students. The Black Studies programs, departments, centers, and institutes at Ivy institutions are now points of pride and their faculties are world-renowned. The institutions and the faculty owe a debt of thanks to disruptive black students. Considering the auspicious arrival of the units in some of the Ivy institutions, the fact that the units remain and thrive is reason for celebration.[6]

Beyond Black Studies, students created opportunities for others. Stepping outside the bounds of traditional student life, they boldly challenged hiring practices at their institutions. In doing so, jobs opened for black faculty members, administrators, contractors, construction workers, and staff in all capacities. Additionally, those students helped to get better conditions for workers. Learning from and seeing black people in positions of authority, however, did not just benefit black students. Many more nonblack Ivy students and officials grew scholastically, socially, and personally by knowing the black employees. That phenomenon seemed to manifest one-time Harvard Law School Professor Derrick Bell's interest-convergence theory, which indicated that white America would make concessions to black people with respect to racial progress as long as those concessions held equal if not more benefits for white people.[7] The presence of the Civil Rights Movement and Black Power Movement on Ivy League campuses was mutually beneficial to white and black affiliates.

The changes that those agitators advocated endure. The unlikely changes in space and culture enhanced the Ancient Eight. These alterations to the look and culture of America's finest educational centers resulted partly because of the will of good-hearted white administrators who sympathized with the Civil Rights Movement but mostly because black agents pushed these schools toward progress. Twenty years after becoming the first black administrator at Princeton University, and one of the first in the Ivy League, Carl Fields commented on the need to create an accurate narrative of history when he noted emphatically the need to "recognize the role that blacks have played and still play in this very racist but congenial institution."[8] He was referring specifically to Princeton, which by 2002 could count almost 2,400 black alumni, but the sentiment extended to all American institutions that benefited from black people acting on behalf of justice to improve life for others. "To give white university authorities the credit for the initial discovery of black talent" in terms of black admissions, curricular changes, and space additions, "would be wrong," according to Fields. It largely took the efforts of black agents to enhance the experience of black people on these elite campuses.

Scholar Randall M. Jelks sagely reminded academic peers that there is a tendency in renderings of African American history to "valorize 'resistance,' but more often than not people 'endure.'"[9] As the cases of black students in the Ivy League teach, resistance and endurance are frequently the same. Even as some had to leave, many of the early desegregators remained enrolled and dignified under unimaginable strain. They finished their degrees and continued their work of modeling consistent progress. While enrolled as students, however, few black pioneers acted in the way that some contemporary observers of history would consider resistance or rebellion. The small number of black students helped each other maintain their respectability on campus to later take their fight for racial equality and advancement to larger society. They eventually exhibited leadership for the next generations of black students who entered the Ivy League in the postwar era. The students in the 1960s took advantage of the black freedom movement that the early black Ivy Leaguers and others helped to create. Not able to withstand society's broken promises of integration and fairness any longer, black students in the Ancient Eight allowed everyone associated with their institutions to share in their discomfort. Not all of the students participated willingly in the campus campaigns of disruption, but each student of color (whether they identified as black or Negro) contributed to the recalibration of life in the Ivy League by enduring. Their presence was a teacher and the later demands of black students became the assignments for white institutional America.

According to a 2014 *Journal of Blacks in Higher Education* survey of admissions at the nation's highest ranked research universities, black students (which included U.S. born and foreign-born people of African descent) made up 10.4 percent of the enrolled freshman class: Princeton enrolled 8.1; Harvard enrolled 10.7; Penn enrolled 9.7; Brown enrolled 9.1; Dartmouth enrolled 8.4; and Cornell enrolled 8.1. Leading the Ivy League, Columbia University enrolled the most, with black students making up 14.1 percent of the 2,291 students accepted.[10] Although current students and activists make convincing arguments about the need for more racial diversity, those numbers would have been unthinkable before the work of black students and officials in the postwar era.

Michelle Obama (nee Robinson), who in 1985 submitted her undergraduate thesis on black Princeton alumni in relation to the black community, would have been happy to note that the black Ivy alumni of the postwar era continued to create access and opportunity for black people. After graduating with a degree in sociology, the future first lady attained a law degree from Harvard. With her education, she, like so many other alumni, used her skills for the good of the community as an attorney. The subjects of her study blazed the trail for her and her husband to follow. The black students, staff, and administrators in the Ivy League during the postwar era were manifestations of the hopes and dreams of generations of American citizens who had resisted oppression by fighting for education. In much of American society it would have been enough for the few that enrolled in the elite institutions to achieve academically and to provide a good life for their families. They, however, came from a different tradition that called on them to take from the past and give to the future. The black learners did not ask to be racial pioneers and freedom fighters; they responded to their circumstances. In doing so, they inserted blackness into the culture of eight of the nation's oldest and most valued institutions. For a brief period, those students blackened ivy.

Many of the students who attended and graduated Ivy institutions in the postwar era have succeeded in terms of society and their careers. Following the lead of black pioneers like Du Bois, Raymond Pace, and Sadie Alexander, the postwar generation continued to lobby on behalf of black freedom in their professional lives.

Those affiliated with Princeton became educators (like Bob Engs and Gerald Horne), as well as physicians and attorneys. Would-be Princeton attendee Bruce Wright, who had been accepted to the university and then denied upon arrival, became an attorney. Just as he tested segregation at Princeton, he challenged the inequity of the judicial system from the bench in the New York City Criminal Court. Confronting what today is referred to as the prison industrial complex, he worked to lower bails. He eventually became an associate justice on the New York State Supreme Court. He could look to his own experiences for motivation to advance the freedom rights of others. In 2001, Princeton undergraduate students learned of the university's mistreatment of Wright and made him an honorary member of their class. John L. Howard (class of 1947), the first black student to receive an undergraduate degree from Princeton, went to Cornell University Medical School and received his MD degree. Robert Rivers (Princeton class of 1953) followed the path of Howard into health care. Rivers, after graduating Harvard University Medical School, became a vascular surgeon and dean of minority affairs at the University of Rochester. He also became a trustee of Princeton University in 1969. As a testament of his devotion to the university, Rivers sent three of his children to Princeton. Shearwood McClelland Jr. (class of 1969) graduated Princeton and became an orthopedic surgeon. In an effort to provide quality health care to black people, he still works at Harlem Hospital in New York City. His son, Shearwood McClelland III completed an MD degree at Columbia University School of Medicine. Ralph Austin (class of 1973) became a practicing physician in Georgia.

Black Princeton alumni are well represented in law and other fields. Charles Shorter, who graduated in 1963, attained a graduate degree from Columbia before taking up a career as a real estate advisor and adjunct professor at the Columbia University Graduate School of Architecture Planning and Preservation. Brent Henry, class of 1969, earned a JD and a master's degree from Yale University. He is currently general counsel for Partners Healthcare in Boston. Vera Marcus (class of 1973) practices law in Benicia, California, and Carolyn Upshaw, who earned a law degree as well as an MBA, practices law in Michigan.

Brown University's black alumni achieved just as highly in the professions. Barry Beckham (class of 1966) became a novelist and eventually wrote *The Black Student's Guide to Colleges* (1982) before establishing his own publishing group. Phil Lord (class of 1970) became an attorney and activist for tenant rights and community development in Philadelphia. Spencer Crew (class of 1973) chose a career in public history after earning a PhD. He was the director of the National Underground Railroad Museum in Cincinnati and the Smithsonian Institution's National Museum of American History in Washington, D.C. Sandra Prioleau Crew, who graduated Pembroke College in 1971, married Crew in 1972. Their two children graduated from Brown. Also in the class of 1971 was Sheryl Brissett Chapman (née Grooms) who eventually earned a doctorate in education from Harvard University and is executive director of the National Center for Children and Families in Bethesda, Maryland.

Black graduates of Dartmouth continued to ascend in their professional lives while still focusing on issues of inclusion. Forester "Woody" Lee (class of 1968) earned an MD degree from Yale University, where he is currently the associate dean of multicultural affairs. Bill McCurine (class of 1969) became a magistrate judge in southern California after earning a master's degree from Oxford University and a law degree from Harvard. Wallace Ford II (class of 1970) received a JD from Harvard University Law School and practiced in New York, where he served in the David Dinkins administration. He also wrote a novel and is an instructor and chair of the public administration department at Medgar Evers College in New York. Former Conservative Vice Lord members Allan "Tiny" Evans and Henry Jordan both graduated in 1971. Jordan earned a law degree and returned to Chicago, as did Evans. Evans eventually earned a master's, counseled gang members, and worked for the Chicago Public School District. Conservative Vice Lord founder Edward "Pepilow" Perry attended Dartmouth but did not graduate and met an untimely death in 1980.

Columbia black graduates from the postwar period also continued to advance the cause of freedom. Hilton Clark stopped attending the university in 1964 to join the Mississippi movement with CORE and SNCC. He later became a New York City councilman. SAS member William "Bill" Sales (PhD class of 1968) continued to organize in New York until eventually joining the professoriate at Seton Hall University. He wrote a book about Malcolm X's Organization of Afro-American Unity. Barnard graduate Thulani Davis (class of 1970) remains prolific in the arts. She became a nationally renowned journalist, screenwriter, documentarian, songwriter, poet, and professor; Davis is currently on faculty in the Department of African American Studies at the University of Wisconsin–Madison. White SDS leader Mark Rudd left Columbia before graduating. He co-founded the Weather Underground and remained on the run until surfacing in the 1980s. Rudd published his memoirs in 2009.

Those who struggled for racial advancement at the University of Pennsylvania maintain the spirit of struggle. John Edgar Wideman (class of 1962) won a Rhodes Scholarship to Oxford University. Upon returning in 1966, he began teaching in the English Department at Penn where he helped found the Black Studies unit. White student Ira Harkavy (class of 1970) earned a PhD in history from Penn and eventually took a post with the university as director and associate vice president of the university's Netter Center for Community Partnerships. John Seley, another white student who protested Penn's expansion in the postwar period, earned a PhD from Penn and is currently a professor in the City University of New York Graduate Center. Gerald Early (class of 1975) was inspired by his interactions with Wideman to take up English and Afro-American Studies. Early received a PhD from Cornell where he worked at the Africana Center for Research and Study with James Turner, and eventually joined the professoriate in the Department of Black Studies at Washington University in St. Louis. He is currently the chair of the Department of African and African American Studies and is the Merle Kling Professor of Modern Letters. The Rev. Edward Sims, a black West Philadelphia community member who opposed Penn, continued to struggle for black rights and authored the book, *Black Family Rituals: Rites of Passage for the African American Family* (2008). Herman Wrice, also a representative of the black community in Philadelphia, died in 2000. In the years after his demonstrations against Penn, he started the Mantua Against Drugs organization and worked to rid neighborhoods of crack cocaine. Walter Palmer, after protesting Penn, eventually earned a JD. While continuing his community activism, he later became a lecturer at Penn in the School of Social Policy and Practice and the Department of Urban Studies. The University City Science Center thrives and the neighborhood immediately surrounding Penn has changed decidedly in terms of race. Mantua is a memory, but University City lives.

Thanks to black students, Yale University currently has an excellent Department of African American Studies. Most who shaped the unit have met with success and some have suffered untimely deaths. After graduating, Donald Ogilvie (class of 1968) carried on his relationship with the New Haven black community when he took a job with Yale as director of the office for community affairs. He eventually acquired a degree from Yale's School of Management and became a consultant for many high-end clients. Keeping with his commitment to creating access, he also worked with the U.S. Agency for International Development in Somalia. He died in 2003. Armstead Robinson (class of 1969) completed a PhD and joined the professoriate at the University of Virginia. There, he founded the Carter G. Woodson Institute for Afro-American and African Studies and continued to help found Black Studies programs at educational institutions across the nation while contributing scholarship to the literature. Robinson died in 1995. Raymond Nunn (class of 1969) attended Harvard Law and maintains a successful career in entertainment. He worked for ABC News as a bureau chief in Beirut in the 1980s and eventually became director of new program development for the Oprah Winfrey show and Harpo Productions.

Other Black Yalies associated with Afro-American Studies continued their education and service as well. Unfortunately, like Robinson, Glenn E. deChabert (class of 1970) died young. Before passing, he earned a law degree from the University of Pennsylvania in 1979. Larry Thompson (class of 1972) eventually attained a law degree and became chairman of the Securities Clearing Group. He is currently general counsel and vice chairman for Depository Trust and Clearing House Corporation. In the realm of politics, Yale alumnus Kurt Schmoke, who chose not to support the creation of an Afro-American Studies unit, excelled. Schmoke enjoyed a Rhodes scholarship to Oxford, earned a JD from Harvard Law, entered politics, and become Baltimore's first black mayor. Another prominent student to be associated with the department at Yale is Henry Louis Gates Jr. (class of 1972), who earned a PhD from the University of Cambridge. By 1975 Gates was secretary of the African American Studies Department at Yale and eventually rose to associate professor in the unit before leaving to teach at Cornell and later Harvard. He is currently director of Harvard's Hutchins Center for African and African American Research. An annual lecture at Yale was established and named for Gates in 2012.

Students from Harvard took their place in the leadership class as well. After earning his PhD in English in 1973, Arnold Rampersad became a renowned biographer. He authored many books and won the MacArthur Genius Grant. He is currently the Sara Hart Kimball Professor in the Humanities at Stanford University. Nell Irvin Painter gained much acclaim as a scholar after achieving her doctorate in history in 1974. She is the Edwards Professor (emerita) of American History at Princeton University. Robert L. Hall (class of 1969) acquired a doctorate and entered the academy by joining the professoriate. His work was published widely and he is currently professor (emeritus) in the Department of African-American Studies at Northeastern University. Years after becoming a professor himself, Hall encountered a faculty member who was at Harvard at the time of the building takeovers of 1969. The Harvard professor, perhaps jokingly, stated that he was glad Hall was currently not armed, revealing a fear he had during the demonstrations. Ernest Wilson III (class of 1970), like Hall, also earned a PhD. Wilson worked for the White House National Security Council and served as chairman of the board of the Corporation for Public Broadcasting. Currently, he is dean of the Annenberg School for Communication and Journalism at the University of Southern California.

Not surprisingly, women who graduated from Radcliffe College also excelled. Suzanne Lynn (class of 1971) followed in her father's footsteps. She graduated Columbia University Law School and worked in the New York attorney general's office. She investigated the headline-snatching 1988 Tawana Brawley rape case. Her Radcliffe classmate, Lani Guinier (daughter of Ewart Guinier), also went into law after earning a JD at Yale Law School. She garnered fame when President Bill Clinton, whom she had known in law school, attempted to nominate her as assistant attorney general of the United States. Facing pressure from conservative members of Congress, he withdrew the nomination. She led an exemplary law career in practice and scholarship, becoming the first black woman to be tenured professor at Harvard Law School. Guinier is currently the Bennett Boskey Professor of Law at Harvard.

Leslie "Skip" Griffin, after achieving a BA degree, attained a master's in education from Harvard. He became the director of the African-American Institute and associate dean of student affairs at Northeastern University. He also was the director of community affairs and public relations at the Boston Globe. Two years after Griffin graduated, Cornel West arrived at Harvard for his undergraduate work. He finished in 1974 and pursued a PhD at Princeton. West became perhaps one of the best known black alumni of Harvard in the modern era. Like Gates, he took advantage of the field of Black Studies in becoming a professor in Yale's program of African American Studies and directing the program at Princeton. He became arguably the nation's most well-known scholar, winning an American Book Award and appearing frequently in the media. He maintained an activist agenda for social justice throughout his career. After retiring from Princeton and Union Theological Seminary, West is currently Professor of the Practice of Public Philosophy at Harvard University Divinity School with a joint appointment in the Department of African and African-American Studies.

Many of the black students and staff who engaged in activism at Cornell continued to push for justice and had lucrative careers. Thomas Jones eventually apologized for the role he played in intimidating officials at Cornell in 1969. Jones earned an MBA and had a successful career with TIAA CREF, working his way to president before moving to Citigroup Inc. Global Investment Management where he was chairman and CEO. In addition to serving on the boards of the Federal Reserve Bank of New York, Freddie Mac, and Pepsi Bottling Co., he sat on Cornell University's board of trustees. Edward Whitfield remains an activist willing to agitate in the realm of education and democracy. After leaving Ithaca in 1970, he taught in the Malcolm X Liberation University that opened in Greensboro, North Carolina. He has worked for the Beloved Community Center (named after the King's Beloved Community) and later co-founded the Fund for Democratic Communities. He currently serves on the advisory board of the Dream Defenders, the antiracist, antipatriarchy, and antiwar collective that formed after the shooting death of Trayvon Martin in Sanford, Florida.

The black alumni of these prestigious institutions have directly or indirectly created access for people from their communities. Not all graduates and attendees have maintained the posture they took at the height of the Civil Rights Movement and Black Power Movement, but their entrance into American institutions after their time in the Ivy League helped to make opportunity for others.

After the police-involved deaths of unarmed and legally armed black citizens in 2013–2016, black student activism on Ivy campuses reignited. Criticizing the dearth of black students and faculty members as well as what they considered privilege of the white students and professionals, black students organized to demonstrate their displeasure. At Yale, they rallied around a black service worker who lost his job as a custodian in John C. Calhoun Hall after he broke a stained glass window that featured an image of an enslaved person laboring. The students also protested when a "master" of a campus residential area suggested that students should not be upset when their white peers dressed as people of color for

Halloween. Black Yale students with their allies issued a set of demands that called for an increase in black faculty and administrators, more directed mental health resources for black students, requirements for all Yale students to take courses in Ethnic Studies (including African American Studies), a budget increase of $2 million for each culture center, a cessation of the term "master" in the housing system, and the removal of prominent slaveholder John C. Calhoun's name from a campus building.

Others recently activated in the Ivy League as well. Princeton students formed the Black Justice League. In a similar fashion to the Yale students, the organization demanded that Princeton publicly acknowledge Woodrow Wilson as a racist and remove his name for the School of Public and International Affairs; allow black students to name an affinity space on campus; require Princeton students to take courses on the black experience; and require faculty and staff to undergo cultural competency training. Black students at Harvard launched a Twitter campaign called "#itooamharvard," which sought to bring awareness to the issues that they regularly confronted on campus. Using video and photos they poignantly illustrated what it meant to be a black Harvardian.

Black students in the Ivy League have always been marginalized to some degree. From the 1800s to the present, they have been something of a spectacle even as they gained greater access to the eight elite institutions. Because of their race, they stood apart from their school peers, and because of their opportunity to enroll, they were unique among their racial peers. Life on campus was complex for these students. From Martin Delaney to Cornel West to the Obama family, students of every generation challenged their institutions to be more accommodating and accessible to black students. In doing so, they improved and enriched the American leadership class by adding talent to the homogenous pool of traditional leaders. In their own ways, students in the decades after World War II highlighted the issue of race in the most elite and white environments. Taking advantage of their student status, they upended the ivory tower to determine whose Ivy League would stand.

ACKNOWLEDGMENTS

I am thankful to MY students, including Jonathan "Hightop" Pulphus (thanks for the scholarly assistance), Alisha "Niecy" Sonnier, Christopher "Frat" Walter, Trevor "Old School" Woolfolk, Josh "Lil Big Bro" Jones, Marissa "Pricey" Price, Kyle "Comic Book" Lawrence, Shadé "Slim" Phoenix, Jason "Curly Fro" Ebinger, Sarah "Nashty" Nash, Noelle "Favorite" Janak, Gold "Standard" Gladney, Michelle "Ella" Fitzgerald, Isaac "Mr. Miracle" Singleton, Amber "Ms. Advocacy" Overton, Chris "All Heart" Bell, William "Fifty" Smith, Jonathan "Mr. President" Long, Etefia "Analyst" Umana, Jr. (thanks for the research assistance), Christopher "Karl" Winston, Ian "Holy" McPherson, Divine "the Senator" Shelton, PJ "Car Troubles" Sims, Deionna "I'll Fix It" Ferguson, and the other student activists who were brave enough to press for justice in the streets and on campus; I learned so much from you and your peers. Know that I have written this book for you and your followers. I am also hoping to set a good example for the graduate students with whom I have worked: Dorian "Prof." Brown, Chris "Jarhead" Ketcherside, Bryan "Tats" Winston, Cherrell "Grad Getter" Johnson, Latrina "Oh Lord" Parker, Dazialee "Teach" Goodwin, T. K. "iThink" Smith, and Mike "Big Lil Bro" Jones.

I must give thanks to those who shared their time and resources to make this book possible. Clara "Close-the-Deal" Platter, acquisition editor at New York University Press, took a chance on me and this book, and I am proud to know her. Amy "Amazing" Klopfenstein, Maura "Move-it-Along" Neville, and Molly "Hawkeye" Morrison were clutch players as well. I thank also Phil Leventhal, who helped me to shape ideas early on, and Paul Cronin for assistance with the image. Thanks also to Eddie Goldman and Bob Feldman. So many colleagues and friends read parts of the manuscript and made helpful comments. They include Howard Rambsy II (you remember when we chased down the car thieves?), Ibram Kendi, Joy Ann Williamson-Lott, Gregory S. Parks,

Stephen Berry, V. P. Franklin, Abdul Alkalimat, Derrick White, Sonya Ramsey, Prudence Cumberbatch, Zebulon Miletsky, Kelton Edmonds, and Brett Wilkinson. Oh, and Terence Farmer deserves a special shout for the magic he made for the family during hard times. Thanks to the Camp Sarah Lawrence Crew: Komozi Woodard, Jeanne Theoharis, Lynnell Thomas, Ayesha Hardison, Shannon King, Hasan Jeffries, Natanya Duncan, Peter Levy, Kristopher Burrell, Laura Hill, Mary Barr, Crystal Moton, Say Burgin, Aliyah Dunn-Salahuddin, Tahir Butt, Verdis Robinson, Balthazar Becker, John S. Portlock, and Ujju Aggarwal. At Saint Louis University, my first thank you goes to the superstar library staff, and especially Martha Allen, T. K. Smith, and the entire interlibrary loan squad. Then, of course, I had wonderful colleagues who asked all the right questions and read materials: Lorri "The Jeweler" Glover, George "Sage" Ndege, Eddie "Consistency" Clark, Dan "So St. Louis" Schlafly, and the late Norm White. Thanks also to my former SLU colleagues Wendy "Pinky Up" Blocker and LaTanya "Queen Mother" Buck (hilarious times we had; you are the certified best)! My mentors in the academy and life, Robert E. Weems Jr., Carol E. Anderson, Travis Threats, Gerald Early, Robert Harris Jr., Genna Rae "God Mother" McNeil, Antonio Tillis, Charles Jones, Akinyele Umoja, Jeffrey O. G. Ogbar, Dr. Donald Suggs, Shirley and Harry Portwood, Earleen Patterson, and the dearly departed Felix Armfield and Rudolph G. Wilson fortified and sustained me as I researched and wrote.

To the young professionals and citizens with whom I worked during the Ferguson uprising, I say thank you for helping me understand the moment and what it means to be ten toes down. I send a special thanks to Brittney Packnett, Charli Cooksey (sorry again for that night), Tishaura Jones, Justin Hansford, Kira Van Niel (duck!), Michael Butler, Dwaun Warmack, Kayla Reed, Johnetta Elzie, Marva Robinson, Rasheen Aldridge, Jonathan Fenderson, Jamala Rogers, Etefia Umana Sr., Malik Ahmed, the Rev. Rodney Francis, Leah Gunning-Francis, the Rev. Traci Blacmon, Amy Hunter, Chris King, Reena Carol, Kira Hudson Banks, Ashley Gray, Aleidra Allen, and the many others I saw in the street. I am glad I had the chance to be with real life freedom fighters.

I am extremely appreciative for the generosity of those who allowed me to interview them. Sam Anderson, Spencer Crew, Thulani Davis, Gerald Early, Wallace Ford II, Robert L. Hall (you deserve a special shout out for the extra assistance you rendered), Gerald Horne (you are a role model and Brother), Ira Harkavy, Woody Lee, Phil Lord, Walter Palmer, and Ernest Wilson III, I hope I conveyed the spirit of your message and work with this book.

I deeply appreciate the institutional support I have received. Saint Louis University was very generous in providing research stipends to complete the project. I had some of the most supportive colleagues in the Lou! Along those lines, I am so thankful for the advocacy and kindness I have received from my new colleagues at Loyola Marymount University. Dean Robbin Crabtree, your encouragement sustains me; thank you for believing in me. To Profs. Marne Campbell, Adilifu Nama, Jennifer Williams, Diane White-Clayton, Barbara Lang, and Darnise Martin, and senior administrative assistant Elizabeth Faulkner, I say: Onward, AFAM!

Finally, I must acknowledge my family of blood and bond. My brothers (Van and Adrian) and my sister (Alanna) have been supportive in their own ways even while they have faced tragedy. Their children and grandchildren have proven to be good people, if not *active* (what used to be called bad-booty). We do not speak frequently, but I appreciate you all. My father, Alphonso, is everything I have ever wanted to be. His care for God, family, and community is inspirational and aspirational for me. We lost my mother, Annie Lee, when I was writing this book. She taught me to fight when I was young and reminded me how to fight as she struggled with cancer. There was no quit in her as she battled to her last breath. I am so glad she chose me to rear. I must thank her for sending us Simone Andora "Peanut" Bradley. That girlchild is just as pretty and rebellious as her heavenly grandmother ever was—they have the same spirit. Simone, thanks for looking like your Grandma and Mama and for letting me know who I am supposed to be. To my A-1 Day-1, Traice "T. Webb" Bradley, what a gift I found in you. You are perfect in every capacity (except laundry). You are the only one who can put up with my kind of crazy; thanks for you.

This book is dedicated to Annie Lee Bradley and all the rebellious youth with justice on their minds.

NOTES

FOREWORD

1 See, for example, Lana Stein, *Holding Bureaucrats Accountable: Politicians and Professionals in St. Louis* (Tuscaloosa: University of Alabama Press, 1991), 72–75; John Wright, *Discovering African American St. Louis: A Guide to Historic Sites* (St. Louis: Missouri Historical Society Press, 2002); and "Integration Threatens to Close St. Louis Hospital," *Jet*, October 26, 1961, 51.

2 Bill Bradley, *Life on the Run* (New York: Vintage Books, 1995).

3 See, for example, Gerald Horne, *Black and Red: W.E.B. Du Bois and the Afro-American Response to the Cold War, 1944–1963* (Albany: State University of New York Press, 1986).

4 Horne is completing an exploration of jazz music in a forthcoming book.

5 See Gerald Horne, *The Deepest South: The U.S., Brazil and the African Slave Trade* (New York: New York University Press, 2007); Gerald Horne, *Black and Brown: African Americans and the Mexican Revolution* (New York: New York University Press, 2005); Gerald Horne, *Race to Revolution: The U.S. and Cuba During Slavery and Jim Crow* (New York: Monthly Review Press, 2014); Gerald Horne, *Confronting Black Jacobins: The U.S., the Haitian Revolution and the Origins of the Dominican Republic* (New York: Monthly Review Press, 2015).

6 Subsequently, I mentored his son, Taj Robeson Frazier, a graduate of Penn, then grad school at Berkeley (where I attended law school) and now a professor at the University of Southern California. I counseled him, read multiple drafts, then "blurbed" his book on African Americans and China before it was published by Duke University Press to sustained applause from critics. See Taj Robeson Frazier, *The East Is Black: Cold War China in the Black Radical Imagination* (Durham, NC: Duke University Press, 2015).

7 See, for example, Clark Terry, *Clark: The Autobiography of Clark Terry* (Berkeley: University of California Press, 2011), 75, 77–81, 83–94, passim.

8 At the California carceral facility, one of my students was Donald De Freeze, who was involved in the abduction of heiress Patty Hearst, then involved with another Princeton classmate, Steve Weed; I lent this inmate, then known as Cinque, homage to a famous slave rebel of the nineteenth century, a copy of Friedrich Engels's *The Origins of the Family, Private Property and the State*, which I assume will never be returned since he perished in an infamous shootout with the Los Angeles police in 1974. See Steven Weed, *My Search for Patty Hearst* (New York: Crown, 1976).

9 Gerald Horne, *From the Barrel of a Gun: The United States and the War Against Zimbabwe, 1965–1980* (Chapel Hill: University of North Carolina Press, 2001). I am presently working on a book on the United States and South Africa—a venture that took me to Cape Town and Fort Hare University in December 2016.

10 Gerald Horne, *Paul Robeson: The Artist as Revolutionary* (London: Pluto, 2016). Additionally, when researching my Robeson biography in his papers at Howard, I incidentally encountered a letter written by Williams to Robeson making the request.

PREFACE

1 Original emphasis. Memorial Service for Carl A. Fields, October 1998, box 15, Carl A. Fields Papers, Princeton University Archives.

2 Carol Kammen, *Part and Apart: The Black Experience at Cornell, 1865–1945* (Ithaca: Cornell University Library, 2009).

3 Vera Marcus, interviewed by Brenda Tindal, tape recording, April 2012, Seely G. Mudd Manuscript Library, Princeton University Archives.

INTRODUCTION

1 The institutions that comprise the Ivy League or Ancient Eight are Harvard, Yale, Princeton, Penn, Columbia, Brown, Dartmouth, and Cornell. In the twentieth century, sports journalist began referring to the institutions as the Ivy League as the schools fiercely battled each other in athletics on campuses where the colonial edifices were decorated with ivy. For the sake of consistency in the book, the eight institutions will be referred to as members of the Ivy League even when describing the long period before the term arose.

2 "Confirmation of Barack Obama's Cabinet," https://en.wikipedia.org, accessed December 15, 2017; "Barack Obama Cabinet Members," http://cabinet-members .insidegov.com, accessed December 15, 2017.

3 Michelle L. Robinson, "Princeton-Educated Blacks and the Black Community" (undergraduate thesis, Princeton University, 1985), 1, www.politico.com, accessed November 6, 2016.

4 Angie Drobnic Holan, "Digging Up Dirt on Michelle Obama," www.politifact .com, accessed November 6, 2016; Charles C. Johnson, "A Detailed Look at Obama's Radical College Past . . . And We're Not Talking about Barack," www .theblaze.com, accessed November 6, 2016; Kathleen Henehan, "Hannity Repeatedly Distorts Passage in Michelle Obama's Senior Thesis to Suggest Alumni Views on Race are Her Own," www.mediamatters.org, accessed November 6, 2016.

5 Americanrevolution02, *Breaking News: Breitbart's Incriminating Unedited Video (Obama Is a RACIST by His Own Admission)*, YouTube video, March 1, 2012, www.youtube.com, accessed November 6, 2016.

6 For a complete discussion of Ivy League institutions and the making of the United States as a nation, see Craig Wilder, *Ebony and Ivy: Race, Slavery, and the Troubled History of America's Universities* (New York: Bloomsbury Press, 2013).

7 E. S. Hubbell, "Letter to the Editor," *Princeton Alumni Weekly*, April 22, 1969, 5.
8 Jerome Karabel, *The Chosen: The Hidden History of Admission and Exclusion at Harvard, Yale, and Princeton* (Boston: Houghton Mifflin, 2005), 2–9.
9 James A. Perkins, interview by Keith R. Johnson, audio cassette, 1994, archive 47-8-2795, Rare and Manuscript Collections, Carl A. Kroch Library, Cornell University.
10 For information on the free speech movement, please see, Robert Cohen, *Freedom's Orator: Mario Savio and the Radical Legacy of the 1960s* (New York: Oxford University Press, 2009).
11 Marcia Synnott, ed., *The Half-Opened Door: Discrimination in Admissions at Harvard, Yale, and Princeton, 1900–1977* (Westport, CT: Greenwood Press, 1979); Geoffrey Kabaservice, *The Guardians: Kingman Brewster, His Circle, and the Liberal Establishment* (New York: Henry Holt, 2004), 49 and 66; Karabel, *Chosen*; Wilder, *Ebony and Ivy*; Wayne Glasker, *Black Students in the Ivory Tower: African American Student Activism at the University of Pennsylvania, 1967–1990* (Amherst: University of Massachusetts Press, 2002); Stefan Bradley, "The Southern-Most Ivy: Princeton University from Jim Crow Admissions to Anti-Apartheid Protests, 1794-1969," *American Studies* 51, no. 3/4 (2010): 109–130.
12 Hasan Jeffries, *Bloody Lowndes: Civil Rights and Black Power in Alabama's Black Belt* (New York: New York University Press, 2009); Kevin Mumford, *Newark: A History of Race, Rights, and Riots in America* (New York: New York University Press, 2008); Thomas Sugrue, *The Origins of Urban Crisis: Race and Inequality in Postwar Detroit* (Princeton: Princeton University Press, 1996).
13 Abbott Lawrence Lowell to Roscoe Conkling Bruce (senior), December 14, 1922, and January 6, 1923; Bruce to Lowell, January 4, 1923; and clippings from the *Boston Transcript*, January 11, 1923, and *New York World*, January 12, 1923, "Negroes" folder 42, Abbott Lawrence Lowell Papers, Nathan Marsh Pusey Library, Harvard University; Synnott, *Half-Opened Door*, 247n.
14 Synnott, *Half-Opened Door*, 49.
15 Carl Fields, "One University's Response to Today's Negro Student," *University: A Princeton Quarterly*, no. 36 (Spring 1968): 14.
16 Synnott, *Half-Opened Door*, 200.
17 "Financial Aid Practices in Ivy Group Colleges: Subcommittee Report to Ivy Presidents," Black Students file, Brown University Archives.
18 Ernest Wilson, III, interview by author, October 28, 2016, digital recording. Hereafter, Wilson interview.
19 Thomas W. Jones, "Reflections on the Sixties and Nineties," speech delivered at Cornell University, April 19, 1994, Cornell University Archives.
20 Wilson interview.
21 Javier C. Hernandez, "A High Achiever Poised to Scale New Heights," *New York Times*, November 30, 2008, A23.
22 "Afro-American Studies," press release, January 22, 1969, HUF124.2, Harvard University Archives.

23   James Turner, "An Approach to Black Studies: Concept and Plan of the Africana
     Studies and Research Center at Cornell University," 14/17/1821, folder 4, box 1,
     Rare and Manuscript Collections, Carl A. Kroch Library, Cornell University.

24   James Turner, "Student Perspective: Black Students and Their Changing Perspec-
     tive," *Ebony*, August 1969, 137.

25   The literature surrounding black student activism on white campuses has grown
     immensely in the last decades. See William Exum, *Paradoxes of Protest: Black
     Student Activism at a White University* (Philadelphia: Temple University Press,
     1985), 36–45; Richard McCormick, *The Black Student Protest Movement at
     Rutgers* (New Brunswick, NJ: Rutgers University Press, 1990); Donald Downs,
     Cornell '69: Liberalism and the Crisis of the American University (Ithaca, NY:
     Cornell University Press, 1999); Glasker, *Black Students in the Ivory Tower*; Joy
     Ann Williamson, *Black Power on Campus: The University of Illinois, 1965–1975*
     (Champaign: University of Illinois Press, 2003); Carl Fields, *Black in Two Worlds*
     (Princeton: Red Hummingbird Press, 2006); Fabio Rojas, *From Black Power to
     Black Studies: How a Radical Social Movement Became an Academic Discipline*
     (Charlottesville: University of Virginia Press, 2007); Peter Wallenstein, ed., *Higher
     Education and the Civil Rights Movement: White Supremacy, Black Southerners,
     and College Campuses* (Gainesville: University Press of Florida, 2008); Joe Turner,
     Sitting In and Speaking Out: Student Movements in the American South, 1960–1970
     (Athens: University of Georgia Press, 2010); Stefan Bradley, *Harlem vs. Colum-
     bia University: Black Student Power in the Late 1960s* (Champaign: University of
     Illinois Press, 2009); Martha Biondi, *The Black Revolution on Campus* (Berkeley:
     University of California Press, 2012); Ibram Rogers, *The Black Campus Movement:
     Black Students and the Racial Reconstitution of Higher Education, 1965–1972* (New
     York: Palgrave Macmillan, 2012); Robert Cohen and David Snyder, eds., *Rebel-
     lion in Black and White: Southern Student Activism in the 1960s* (Baltimore: Johns
     Hopkins University Press, 2013).

26   Vincent Harding, *There Is a River: The Black Struggle for Freedom in America*
     (New York: Harcourt, 1981).

27   Frantz Fanon, *Wretched of the Earth* (New York: Grove Press, 1963); Malcolm X,
     with Alex Haley, *The Autobiography of Malcolm X* (New York: Grove Press, 1965);
     Stokely Carmichael and Charles Hamilton, *Black Power: The Politics of Libera-
     tion* (New York: Vintage Books, 1967); Harold Cruse: *Crisis of the Negro Intellectual*
     (New York: Morrow Press, 1967); Nathan Wright, *Black Power and Urban Unrest*
     (New York: Hawthorn Press, 1968); Floyd Barbour, *The Black Power Revolt: A Col-
     lection of Essays* (New York: Collier Books, 1968).

28   Alford Dempsey, after starting his college career at Columbia, left in fall 1968 for
     Morehouse College, where he graduated in 1972. He received a Juris Doctorate
     from Harvard Law School in 1976.

29   For context on the Haverford Group, see Michael Lackey, ed., *The Haverford
     Discussions: A Black Integrationist Manifesto for Racial Justice* (Charlottesville:
     University of Virginia Press, 2013).

30 Author Allan Bloom referred to Keyes's incident in Allan Bloom, *The Closing of the American Mind* (New York: Simon & Schuster, 1987), 316; Downs, *Cornell '69*, 60–61.

31 Thomas Sowell, "The Day Cornell Died," *Weekly Standard*, May 3, 1999, 31.

32 Vera Marcus, interview by Brenda Tindal, tape recording, April 11, 2012, Seeley G. Mudd Manuscript Library, Princeton University. Hereafter, Vera Marcus interview II.

33 Synnott, *Half-Opened Door*, 201.

34 William Borders, "Ivy's Admissions Irk Prep Schools," *New York Times*, April 18, 1967, 64; Synnott, *Half-Opened Door*, 5.

35 Gene Hawes, "The Colleges of America's Upper Class," *Saturday Review Magazine*, November 16, 1963, 68–70; Synnott, *Half-Opened Door*, 201.

36 "Admissions Office Report, 1968," Minority Admissions folder, box 15, Carl A. Fields Papers, Seeley G. Mudd Manuscript Library, Princeton University.

37 FHM, "Students Give the Orders," *New York Times*, December 15, 1968, E9.

38 See V. P. Franklin and Bettye Collier-Thomas, *Sisters in Struggle: African American Women in the Civil Rights Struggle* (New York: New York University Press, 2001); Bettye Collier-Thomas, *Jesus, Jobs, and Justice: African American Women and Religion* (New York: Knopf, 2010); Paula Giddings, *When and Where I Enter: The Impact of Black Women on Race and Sex in America* (New York: William Morrow, 1984); Sherie M. Randolph, *Florynce "Flo" Kennedy, The Life of a Black Feminist Radical* (Chapel Hill: University of North Carolina Press, 2015); Dayo F. Gore, Jeanne Theoharis, and Komozi Woodard, eds., *Want to Start a Revolution?: Radical Women in the Black Freedom Struggle* (New York: New York University Press, 2009); Jeanne Theoharis, *The Rebellious Life of Mrs. Rosa Parks* (New York: Random House, 2013); Barbara Ransby, *Ella Baker and the Black Freedom Movement: A Radical Democratic Vision* (Chapel Hill: University of North Carolina Press, 2004); Vicky L. Crawford et al., eds., *Women in the Civil Rights Movement: Trailblazers and Torchbearers, 1941–1965* (Bloomington: University of Indiana Press, 1993); Kimberly Springer, ed., *Still Lifting and Still Climbing: African American Women's Contemporary Activism* (New York: New York University Press, 1999), and *Living for the Revolution: Black Feminist Organizations, 1968–1980* (Durham, NC: Duke University Press, 2005); Faith S. Holsaert et al., eds., *Hands on the Freedom Plow: Personal Accounts by Women in SNCC* (Champaign: University of Illinois Press, 2010); Stephanie Y. Evans, *Black Women in the Ivory Tower, 1850–1954: An Intellectual History* (Gainesville: University Press of Florida, 2008); Robyn C. Spencer, *The Revolution Has Come: Black Power, Gender, and the Black Panther Party in Oakland* (Durham, NC: Duke University Press, 2016); Anne Moody, *Coming of Age in Mississippi* (New York: Delta Trade Publishers, 1968); Ashley Farmer, *Remaking Black Power: How Black Women Transformed an Era* (Chapel Hill: University of North Carolina, 2017).

39 Robert Reinhold, "University Heads Weigh Disorders," *New York Times*, March 9, 1969, 73.

40 Ibid.
41 Ula Taylor, "Introduction: The Shaping of an Activist and Scholar," *Journal of African American History* 96, no. 2 (2011): 209.
42 Milton Mankoff and Richard Flacks, "The Changing Base of the American Student Movement," *Annals of the American Academy of Political and Social Science* 395 (May 1971): 57.
43 "Weary University Chief," *New York Times*, May 10, 1969, 14.

CHAPTER 1. SURVIVING SOLITUDE

1 Henry Arthur Callis, "Twenty-Five Years Hence," *Sphinx* (December 1931): 22.
2 Kevin Gaines, *Uplifting the Race: Black Leadership, Politics, and Culture in the Twentieth Century* (Chapel Hill: University of North Carolina Press, 1996), 2.
3 David Levering Lewis, *W.E.B. Du Bois: Biography of a Race* (New York: Henry Holt, 1993), 79–99.
4 W.E.B. Du Bois, *The Autobiography of W.E.B. Du Bois: A Soliloquy on Viewing My Life from the Last Decade of Its First Century* (New York: International Publishers, 1968), 135.
5 See Stephen Birmingham, *Certain People: America's Black Elite* (Boston: Little Brown, 1977); William Gatewood Jr., *Aristocrats of Color: The Black Elite, 1880–1920* (Fayetteville: University of Arkansas Press, 2000); Jacqueline Moore, *Leading the Race: The Transformation of the Black Elite in the Nation's Capital, 1880–1920* (Charlottesville: University of Virginia Press, 1999).
6 Robert L. Harris Jr., "Foreword," in *Part and Apart: The Black Experience at Cornell, 1865–1945*, by Carol Kammen (unpublished manuscript, 2009), x.
7 Ibid., xi.
8 Regarding the M Street (Dunbar High) School, see Mary Church Terrell, "History of the High School for Negroes in Washington," *Journal of Negro History* 2, no. 3 (1917): 252–266; Henry Robinson, "The M Street School, 1891–1916," *Records of the Columbia Historical Society* 51 (1984): 119–143.
9 Harris, in *Part and Apart*, xii.
10 Kammen, *Part and Apart*, 37.
11 Nathaniel Allison Murray, "Bro. N. A. Murray Recalls Experiences of the Jewels in Founders' Address," *Sphinx* (October 1936): 6.
12 Gaines, *Uplifting the Race*, 1.
13 George Biddle Kelley, "Reminisces of a Founder," in John H. Johnson, III, ed., *Centennial Book of Essays and Letters: Excerpts from the Brotherhood of Alpha Phi Alpha Fraternity, Inc.* (Baltimore: Foundation Publishers, 2006), 20. Originally published in *Sphinx* (November/December 1939).
14 "Negro Graduate Protests," *New York Times*, January 13, 1923, 5.
15 Kelley, "Reminisces of a Founder," 20.
16 See Elizabeth McHenry, *Forgotten Readers: Recovering the Lost History of African American Literary Societies* (Durham, NC: Duke University Press, 2002); Dorothy

Porter, "The Organized Educational Activities of Negro Literary Societies, 1828–1846," *Journal of Negro Education* 5, no. 4 (1936): 555–576.

17 Charles H. Wesley, *Henry Arthur Callis: Life and Legacy* (Baltimore: Foundation Publishers, 1977), 26.

18 N. A. Murray, "The Early History and Ideals of the Founders," *Sphinx* 60 (May–June 1974): 13; "Minutes of the Alpha Phi Alpha Society," December 4, 1906, in Wesley, *The History of Alpha Phi Alpha: A Development in College Life* (Baltimore: Foundation Publishers, 1996), 508.

19 See Charles H. Wesley, *History of Sigma Pi Phi: First of the Negro-American Greek-Letter Fraternities* (Washington, DC: Association for the Study of Negro Life and History, 1954); www.sigmapiphi.org, accessed November 14, 2016.

20 Stefan Bradley, "The First and the Finest: The Founders of Alpha Phi Alpha," in *Black Greek-Letter Organizations in the 21st Century: Our Fight Has Just Begun*, ed. Gregory S. Parks (Lexington: University Press of Kentucky, 2008), 25.

21 Stefan Bradley, "Progenitors of Progress: A Brief History of the Jewels of Alpha Phi Alpha," in *Alpha Phi Alpha: A Legacy of Greatness, The Demands of Transcendence*, eds. Gregory S. Parks and Stefan M. Bradley (Lexington: University Press of Kentucky, 2012), 69–72.

22 Wesley, *History of Alpha Phi Alpha*, 40–41.

23 George Biddle Kelley, "Jewel Kelley's Testimonial on Vertner W. Tandy," *Sphinx* 36, no. 1 (1950): 2.

24 Wesley, *Henry Arthur Callis*, 115.

25 Ibid., 44–45; *Who's Who in Colored America*, 1927 ed., s.v. "Myrna Colson Callis." *Negro Yearbook*, 1937–1938 ed., s.v. "Lorenzo J. Greene and Myrna Colson Callis."

26 Henry Arthur Callis, "Memorial Address for Brother Charles H. Chapman," *Sphinx* (February 1936): 14.

27 "Kinckle Jones Reports," *New York Times*, April 27, 1932, 16; "Roper Appoints E. K. Jones," *New York Times*, October 19, 1933, 20; "Urban League Cites Retired Executive," *New York Times*, May 22, 1951, 28.

28 "Death Claims the Body of Brother Jewel George Biddle Kelley . . . But His Spirit Marches On," *Sphinx* (October 1962): 2.

29 Henry "Skip" Mason, *The Talented Tenth: The Founders and Presidents of Alpha* (Winter Park, FL: Four G Publishers, 1999), 103.

30 Emory Smith, "Alpha Phi Alpha His First Love," *Sphinx* 23 (February 1937): 3.

31 Carson A. Anderson, *African American Architects: A Biographical Dictionary, 1865–1945*, 2006 ed., s.v. "Vertner Woodson Tandy"; Vertner Woodson Tandy, *Report of the National Negro Business League*, August 22, 1918, 313; Richard Peck, "Harlem: Valley of Myths," *New York Times*, April 11, 1976, 233; Christopher Gray, "After the Wooden Ceiling Came Tumbling Down," *New York Times*, January 21, 1996, RNJ7; Christopher Gray, "The Grand Mansion of an Early Black Entrepreneur," *New York Times*, April 24, 1994, 352; Milena Jovanovitch, "Committee Seeks to Turn Irvington Villa," *New York Times*, January 11, 1987, 24.

32 Kammen, *Part and Apart*, 55.

33 Carolyn Wedin Sylvander, *Jessie Redmon Fauset, Black American Writer* (Albany, NY: Whitson, 1981), 30–31.
34 Synnott, *Half-Opened Door*, 82.
35 Ibid.
36 Kammen, *Part and Apart*, 60–67.
37 "Color Lines Not Easy to Obliterate," *New York Times*, April 12, 1911, 12.
38 Kammen, *Part and Apart*, 57–70.
39 Ibid., 75–76.
40 Genna Rae McNeil, *Groundwork: Charles Hamilton Houston and the Struggle for Civil Rights* (Philadelphia: University of Pennsylvania Press, 1984), 51.
41 Ibid., 51–52; for more information on Pace, see David A. Canton, *Raymond Alexander Pace: A New Negro Lawyer Fights for Civil Rights in Philadelphia* (Oxford: University Press of Mississippi, 2010).
42 McNeil, *Groundwork*, 51–52.
43 Ibid., 52.
44 "Ralph Bunche-Biographical," The Nobel Peace Prize 1950, www.nobelprize.org, accessed August 20, 2017.
45 Kammen, *Part and Apart*, 102–103.
46 J. Saunders Redding, *No Day of Triumph* (New York: Harper & Brothers, 1942), 35.
47 Ibid., 35–36.
48 Ibid., 39.
49 William A. Smith, Walter Allen, and Lynette Danley, "Assume the Position . . . You Fit the Description: Psychosocial Experiences and Racial Battle Fatigue Among African American Male College Students," *American Behavior Scientist* 51, no. 4 (2007): 551–578.
50 Redding, *No Day of Triumph*, 37–39.
51 William H. Hastie, interview by Jerry N. Hess, January 5, 1972, transcript, Philadelphia, Pennsylvania.
52 John Hope Franklin, *Mirror to America* (New York: Farrar, Strauss, and Giroux, 2005), 62.
53 Ibid.
54 Ibid., 66.
55 Art Evans, "Joe Louis as a Key Functionary: White Reactions toward a Black Champion," *Journal of Black Studies* 16, no. 1 (1985): 95–111.
56 Charles Martin, *Benching Jim Crow: The Rise and Fall of the Color Line in Southern College Sports*, 1890–1980 (Champaign: University of Illinois Press, 2010), 3 and 19.
57 Ibid., 11. Paul Robeson experienced similar animosity on the field while playing for Rutgers and as a semiprofessional player. Racism in athletics leagues was endemic.
58 See Stefan M. Bradley, "The Southern-Most Ivy: Princeton University from Jim Crow Admissions to Anti-Apartheid Protests, 1794–1969," *American Studies* 51, no. 3/4 (2010): 109–130.

59 Dwayne Wiggins, ed., *Out of the Shadows: A Biographical History of African American Athletes* (Little Rock: University of Arkansas Press, 2006), 39–57.

60 John Carroll, *Fritz Pollard: Pioneer in Racial Advancement* (Champaign: University of Illinois Press, 1992), 100.

61 Joan Cook, "Jerome Holland, Former U.S. Envoy," *New York Times*, January 14, 1985, www.nytimes.com, accessed November 18, 2016; "Jerome H (Brud) Holland," Cornell Hall of Fame, cornellbigred.com, accessed November 18, 2016.

62 "Obituaries, George Gregory Jr., 88," *Columbia University Record* 19 (June 10, 1994); www.columbia.edu, accessed November 18, 2016.

63 "'No Racial Discrimination' at Harvard, Orders Corporation," *The Harvard Crimson*, April 21, 1941, www.thecrimson.com, accessed November 18, 2016.

64 Martin, *Benching Jim Crow*, 60.

65 James Axtell, *The Making of Princeton University: From Woodrow Wilson to the Present* (Princeton: Princeton University Press, 2006), 144.

66 Synnott, *Half-Opened Door*, 210.

67 C. Gerald Fraser, "J. Saunders Redding, 81, Is Dead; Pioneer Black Ivy Teacher," *New York Times*, March 5, 1988, 33.

CHAPTER 2. UPENDING OL' NASSAU

1 Paul Robeson, *Here I Stand* (Boston: Beacon Press, 1988), 11; Paul Robeson Jr., *The Undiscovered Paul Robeson: An Artist's Journey, 1898–1939* (New York: Wiley, 2001), 5–6. For more insight into black life in Princeton, see Eslanda Goode Robeson, *Paul Robeson: Negro* (London: Harper and Brothers, 1930); Lloyd Brown, *The Young Paul Robeson: On My Journey Now* (New York: Basic Books, 1998).

2 John Schwartz, "An Ivy-Covered Path to the Supreme Court," *New York Times*, June 8, 2009, nytimes.com, accessed November 13, 2010.

3 "In the nation's service and in the service of all nations" is a line from an 1896 Woodrow Wilson speech while he was a faculty member at Princeton. Since then, Princetonians have used the phrase as an unofficial motto.

4 For instance, shortly after Ivy League universities began looking to standardized tests to prevent class and social biases, other universities followed suit. See Nicholas Lehmann, *The Big Test: The Secret History of the American Meritocracy* (New York: Farrar, Straus, and Giroux, 1999). Similarly, several of the Ivy League universities maintained ties to the Department of Defense before many of the flagship universities of the states established relationships. See Jane Wilson, "Universities Act on the Institute for Defense Analysis," *Bulletin of Atomic Scientists* (May 1968): 40.

5 Donald Downs, *Cornell '69: Liberalism and the Crisis of the American University* (Ithaca, NY: Cornell University Press, 1999); Wayne Glasker, *Black Students in the Ivory Tower: African American Student Activism at the University of Pennsylvania, 1967–1990* (Amherst: University of Massachusetts Press, 2002); Stefan Bradley, *Harlem vs. Columbia University: Black Student Power in the Late 1960s* (Champaign: University of Illinois Press, 2009); Joy Ann Williamson, *Black Power on Campus:*

The University of Illinois, 1965–1975 (Champaign: University of Illinois Press, 2003); Fabio Rojas, *From Black Power to Black Studies: How a Radical Social Movement Became an Academic Discipline* (Charlottesville: University of Virginia Press, 2007); Peter Wallenstein, ed., *Higher Education and the Civil Rights Movement: White Supremacy, Black Southerners, and College Campuses* (Gainesville: University Press of Florida, 2008); Ibram Rogers, "The Marginalization of the Black Campus Movement," *Journal of Social History* 42, no. 1 (2008): 175–182; Carl Fields, *Black in Two Worlds* (Princeton: Red Hummingbird Press, 2006); Jerome Karabel, *The Chosen: The Hidden History of Admission and Exclusion at Yale, Harvard, and Princeton* (Boston: Houghton Mifflin, 2005).

6 See the outstanding documentary work of Marylou Tibaldo-Bongiorno, "Revolution '67," Borgiorno Productions, 2007. Also, there are several wonderful works discussing the northern civil rights and Black Power Movement. See Peniel Joseph, *Waiting 'Til the Midnight Hour: A Narrative History of Black Power* (New York: Henry Holt, 2006); Thomas Sugrue, *Sweet Land of Liberty: The Forgotten Struggle of Civil Rights in the North* (New York: Random House, 2008); Leonard Moore, *Carl B. Stokes and the Rise of Black Political Power* (Champaign: University of Illinois Press, 2003); Yohuru Williams, *Black Politics/White Power: Civil Rights, Black Power, and Black Panthers* (Maplecrest, NY: Brandywine Press, 2000); Matthew Countryman, *The Up South: Civil Rights and Black Power in Philadelphia* (Philadelphia: University of Pennsylvania Press, 2005); Jeanne Theoharis and Komozi Woodard, *Groundworks: Local Black Freedom Movements in America* (New York: New York University Press, 2005); Brian Purnell, "'Taxation without Sanitation Is Tyranny': Brooklyn CORE Dumps Racial Discrimination on the Steps of Borough Hall," in *Afro-Americans in New York Life and History* 31 (July 2007): 61–88.

7 Richard McCormick, *The Black Student Protest Movement at Rutgers* (New Brunswick, NJ: Rutgers University Press, 1990).

8 "Slavery at Princeton," princeton.edu, accessed November 6, 2009.

9 See William Selden, *Chapels of Princeton University: Their Historical and Religious Significance* (Princeton: Princeton University Office of Communications, 2005).

10 "A Negro at Princeton?" *Princeton Alumni Weekly*, March 29, 1935.

11 "Minutes of the Board of Trustees," September 25, 1792, Ethnic Diversity—African Americans (1791–1991) file, box 1, Minorities at Princeton Series, Historic Subject Collection, Seeley G. Mudd Manuscript Library, Princeton University.

12 Timothy Tyson, *Blood Done Sign My Name: A True Story* (New York: Crown Press, 2004), 131–135.

13 Melvin McCray, *Looking Forward: Reflections of Black Princeton Alumni*, documentary video, 2006, alumni.princeton.edu, accessed November 10, 2009.

14 Matthew Anderson, *Presbyterianism: Its Relation to the Negro* (Philadelphia: J. M. White, 1897), 168–169.

15 Arthur V. Bryan, *The Mirror: A History of the Class of 1878, of Princeton College* (Princeton: printed by Charles S. Robinson, 1878), 80–81; "A Race Trouble at Princeton College," *Nashville American*, September 27, 1876, page unknown.

16 Anderson, *Presbyterianism*, 175–176.

17 John M. Mulder, *Woodrow Wilson: The Years of Preparation* (Princeton: Princeton University Press, 1978), 137.

18 Woodrow Wilson to John Rodger Williams, September 2, 1904, Arthur Link et al., eds., *The Papers of Woodrow Wilson, Volume 15, 1903–1905* (Princeton: Princeton University, 1973), 463.

19 G. McArthur Sullivan to Woodrow Wilson, November 20, 1909, Ethnic Diversity—African Americans (1791–1991) file, box 1, Minorities at Princeton Series, Historic Subject Collection, Seeley G. Mudd Manuscript Library, Princeton University.

20 Secretary of Woodrow Wilson to G. McArthur Sullivan, December 6, 1909, Ethnic Diversity—African Americans (1791–1991) file, box 1, Minorities at Princeton Series, Historic Subject Collection, Seeley G. Mudd Manuscript Library, Princeton University.

21 William White (class of 1923), *Princeton Alumni Weekly*, May 14, 1948, Ethnic Diversity—African Americans (1791–1991) file, box 1, Minorities at Princeton Series, Historic Subject Collection, Seeley G. Mudd Manuscript Library, Princeton University.

22 Mark Bernstein, "A Princeton Pioneer: When Joseph Moss '51 Broke through the Color Line," *Princeton Alumni Weekly*, date unknown, Ethnic Diversity—African Americans (1791–1991) file, box 1, Minorities at Princeton Series, Historic Subject Collection, Seeley G. Mudd Manuscript Library, Princeton University.

23 Ibid.

24 Bruce M. Wright in Melvin McCray, *Looking Back: Reflections of Black Alumni at Princeton*, 1997, youtube.com, accessed November 6, 2016.

25 Radcliffe Heermance to Bruce M. Wright, regarding Princeton and Race, June 13, 1939, folder 6C, box 73, Historical Subject Collection, Department of Rare Books and Special Collections, Princeton University Archives.

26 McCray, *Looking Back*; Robert Schneller Jr., *Breaking the Color Barrier: The US Naval Academy's First Black Midshipmen and the Struggle for Racial Equality* (New York: New York University Press, 2005), 156.

27 For information on the "Double V" campaign, see Paul Burstein, *Discrimination, Jobs, and Politics: The Struggle for Equal Employment Opportunity in the United States since the New Deal* (Chicago: University of Chicago Press, 1998); Richard Dalfiume, *Desegregation of the U.S. Armed Forces: Fighting on Two Fronts, 1939-1953* (Columbia: University of Missouri Press, 1969); Lou Potter, *Liberators: Fighting on Two Fronts in World War II* (New York: Harcourt, 1992); Neil McMillen, ed., *Remaking Dixie: The Impact of World War II on the American South* (Jackson: University Press of Mississippi, 1997; Andrew Kersten, *Race and War: The FEPC in the Midwest, 1941-1946* (Champaign: University of Illinois Press, 2000); Paula Pfeffer, *A. Philip Randolph, Pioneer of the Civil Rights Movement* (Baton Rouge: Louisiana State University Press, 1990); John D'Emilio, *Lost Prophet: The Life and Times of Bayard Rustin* (Chicago: University of Chicago Press, 2004); John Hope

Franklin, "Their War and Mine," *Journal of American History* 77, no. 2 (1990): 576–579.

28 "Negroes," *Princeton Alumni Weekly*, March 29, 1940.

29 Ibid.

30 Alexander Leitsch, "Norman Thomas," *A Princeton Companion* (Princeton, 1978), etcweb.princeton.edu, accessed January 12, 2011.

31 "Negroes," *Princeton Alumni Weekly*, April 12, 1940.

32 "Ralph John Reiman '35," paw.princeton.edu, accessed January 27, 2011.

33 "Democracy Begins at Home," *Daily Princetonian*, July 31, 1942.

34 "White Supremacy at Princeton," *Daily Princetonian*, September 30, 1942.

35 For comprehensive discussions of Jackie Robinson's experiences, see Arnold Rampersad, *Jackie Robinson: A Biography* (New York: Ballantine, 1998), and Jules Tygiel, *Baseball's Great Experiment: Jackie Robinson and His Legacy*, expanded edition (New York: Oxford University Press, 2008); for discussion regarding the desegregation of the armed forces see Dalfiume, *Desegregation of the U.S. Armed Forces*; Potter, *Liberators*; for summaries of Morgan v. Commonwealth and Shelley v. Kraemer see Joseph Menez and John R. Vile, *Summaries of the Leading Cases on the Constitution* (New York: Rowman and Littlefield, 2004), and Joseph Tussman, ed., *The Supreme Court on Racial Discrimination* (New York: Oxford University Press, 1963).

36 In 1895, the Reverend Irwin William Langston Roundtree became the first to receive a graduate degree (M.A.). It took another half century for a black student to achieve such success at the undergraduate level. Bernstein, "A Princeton Pioneer," in *African Americans and Princeton University: A Brief History*, princeton.edu, accessed November 14, 2010.

37 "Looking Back: Reflections of Black Princeton Alumni," *Princeton Today*, Summer 1997.

38 Robert J. Rivers, "Sankofa: Looking Back as We Move Forward," *Princeton Alumni Weekly*, 16 July 2008, princeton.edu, accessed January 27, 2011.

39 Ibid.

40 "Looking Back: Reflections of Black Princeton Alumni," *Princeton Today*, Summer 1997.

41 Bernstein, "A Princeton Pioneer"; njleg.state.nj.us, accessed March 7, 2009.

42 "Growing up in a Neighborhood Where History Matters," in *Blacks at Princeton: The Black Experience at Princeton from 1746 to the Present*, blacksatprinceton.com, accessed November 6, 2016.

43 Maggie Shi, "First Black Students Face Isolation, Racism," *Daily Princetonian*, March 7, 1995, 1–2.

44 "Dr. Charles T. Davis Shatters Precedent," *Newark Herald*, July 3, 1955, 1.

45 Douglas Martin, "Robert Goheen, Innovative Princeton President, Is Dead at 88," *New York Times*, April 1, 2008, nytimes.com, accessed November 6, 2016.

46 "Ivy Colleges Encourage Negro Applicants," *Daily Princetonian*, November 14, 1963.

47 For a discussion of the history of African Americans in Trenton see John Cumbler, *A Social History of Economic Decline: Business, Politics and Work in Trenton* (New Brunswick, NJ: Rutgers University Press, 1989), 149–150.

48 Jonathon Livingston, "Negro Admissions Stay Static," *Daily Princetonian*, April 16, 1963, 1.

49 "Survey of Black Princeton Alumni" folder, box 16, Carl A. Fields Papers, Princeton University Archives.

50 Ibid.

51 Maggie Shi, "Black Alumni Recall 1960s," *Daily Princetonian*, March 9, 1995, 1.

52 Mel Masuda, "Ivy Colleges Encourage Negro Applicants," *Daily Princetonian*, November 14, 1963.

53 John Armstrong, "Group Promotes Segregation," *Daily Princetonian*, March 13, 1964.

54 Department of Public Information, Princeton University, August 16, 1966, Ethnic Diversity—African Americans (1791–1991) file, box 1, Minorities at Princeton Series, Historic Subject Collection, Seeley G. Mudd Manuscript Library, Princeton University.

55 Komozi Woodard, interview by author, tape recording, June 26, 2015. Hereafter, referred to as Woodard interview.

56 Dan Carlinsky, Director, News Office, June 26, 1966, folder 23, box 1, Double Discovery Center Records, Rare Book and Manuscript Library, Columbia University.

57 Woodard interview.

58 Michael R. Halleran, "Message on the Passage of Robert F. Engs," January 17, 2013, www.wm.edu, accessed November 6, 2016.

59 McCray, *Looking Forward*.

60 Bob Durkee, "New Era for the Negro at Princeton," *Daily Princetonian*, October 17, 1967.

61 Kushanava Choudhury, "University Administrators Remember First Black Dean," *Daily Princetonian*, October 26, 1998, 1.

62 Shi, "Black Alumni Recall 1960s," 1; Brent Henry, interviewed by Brendan Holt, tape recording, March 16, 2015, Seeley G. Mudd Manuscript Library, Princeton University. Hereafter, Henry interview.

63 Maggie Shi, "University Focuses on Integration," *Daily Princetonian*, March 8, 1995, 1 and 8.

64 "Survey of Black Alumni," box 16, Carl A. Fields Papers, Princeton University.

65 "Drewry Gets Guidance Job at Princeton," *Evening Times* (Trenton), March 20, 1968, 1; "Nassau Post to Drewry," *Trentonian*, March 20, 1968, 1; "Princeton Placement Post Filled," *Newark Herald*, March 20, 1968, 1.

66 "Negro Pair Join Faculty," *Philadelphia Inquirer*, October 3, 1968; "Princeton Gets Negroes to Teach Black Culture," *The Evening Bulletin* (Philadelphia), October 3, 1968; "Princeton Adopts 2 Negro Courses," *Evening Bulletin* (Philadelphia), September 30, 1968; "Black Couple to Teach Black Courses at Princeton," *Jet*, October 17, 1968.

67 Brent Henry interview.
68 "Both Sides Censured in Princeton Race Incident," *New York Times*, November 2, 1968.
69 Gerald Horne, interview by author, email, January 23, 2010. Hereafter, Horne interview.
70 "Black Collegians," *Princeton Alumni Weekly*, May 2, 1967.
71 "Department of Public Information," Ethnic Diversity—African American, Association of Black Collegians file, box 2, Minorities at Princeton Series, Historic Subject Collection, Seeley G. Mudd Manuscript Library, Princeton University.
72 Bob Schnell, "Second Negro Joins Student Aid Staff; ABC Sponsors Enrichment Program," *Daily Princetonian*, 1–2.
73 Stephen Dreyfuss, "Osander Discloses Tripled Black Admission," *Daily Princeton*, April 11, 1968, 1; "Department of Public Information," Ethnic Diversity—African American, Association of Black Collegians file, box 2, Minorities at Princeton Series, Historic Subject Collection, Seeley G. Mudd Manuscript Library, Princeton University.
74 Jerome Karabel, *The Chosen: The Hidden History of Admission and Exclusion at Harvard, Yale, and Princeton* (Boston: Houghton Mifflin, 2005), 9.
75 "Association of Black Collegians Conference, 1967," Ethnic Diversity—African American, Association of Black Collegians file, box 2, Minorities at Princeton Series, Historic Subject Collection, Seeley G. Mudd Manuscript Library, Princeton University.
76 "ABC to Boycott Tuesday," *Daily Princetonian*, April 8, 1968, 2.
77 Ibid.
78 Ibid., 1.
79 Francis Nesbitt, *Race for Sanctions: African Americans against Apartheid, 1946–1994* (Bloomington: Indiana University Press, 2004), 60–68. See also, Clayborne Carson, In Struggle: SNCC and the Black Awakening of the 1960s (Cambridge, MA: Harvard University Press, 1995).
80 Press release of American Negro Leadership Conference on Africa, September 5, 1962, Peter Weiss Collection, African Activist Archives, africanactivist.msu.edu, accessed February 10, 2009; "Recommendations for Action against Apartheid," ibid.
81 Donald Culverson, "The Politics of the Anti-Apartheid Movement in the United States, 1969–1986," *Political Science Quarterly* 111, no. 1 (1996): 134.
82 F.W. Lancaster and Lorraine Haricombe, "The Academic Boycott of South Africa: Symbolic Gesture or Effective Agent of Change?," *Perspectives on the Professions* 15, no. 1 (1995), www.ethics.iit.edu, accessed February 6, 2010.
83 Harry Edwards, *Revolt of the Black Athlete* (New York: Free Press, 1970), 55–56; 92–97. See also Amy Bass, *Not the Triumph but the Struggle: The 1968 Olympics and the Making of the Black Athlete* (Minneapolis: University of Minnesota Press, 2004).
84 Students at Cornell University also protested their school's ties to companies that operated in apartheid South Africa. Downs, *Cornell '69*, 131–134.

85 Department of Public Information, Princeton University, January 6, 1969.

86 Henry interview.

87 Department of Public Information, Princeton University, January 6, 1969.

88 Ibid.

89 "Malkiel Report," Department of Public Information, Princeton University, January 6, 1969.

90 "Goheen Investment Statement," Department of Public Information, Princeton University, March 4, 1969, 2 P.M.

91 Ibid.

92 "Princeton to End Credit in R.O.T.C.," *New York Times*, March 4, 1969, 29.

93 "South African Trade Views Outlined by Princeton," *Chicago Tribune*, March 5, 1969, 7.

94 For a recounting of events, see Philip Seib, "University Response to a Crisis Situation . . ." (senior thesis, Princeton University, 1970), 7–11.

95 Henry interview.

96 "Black Students End Princeton Takeover," Trentonian, March 12, 1969, 1–2.

97 *Princeton Alumni Weekly*, Demonstrations file, box 38, Photo Collection, Seeley G. Mudd Library, Princeton University.

98 Rose DeWolf, *Evening Bulletin* (Philadelphia), March 11, 1969, 1.

99 Ibid.

100 DeWolf, *Evening Bulletin*, March 13, 1969, 1.

101 Ula Y. Taylor, "Introduction: The Shaping of an Activist and Scholar," *Journal of African American History* 96, no. 2 (2011): 204–214.

102 Ibid., 204.

103 "Black Students End Princeton Takeover," *Trentonian*, March 12, 1969, 1.

104 "Princeton Sit-In Abandoned by Negro Students," *Philadelphia Inquirer*, 1.

105 "Students Occupy Princeton Hall," *New York Times*, March 12, 1969, 30.

106 "Negro Students Abandon Sit-In at Princeton Campus," *Evening Bulletin*, March 12, 1969, 1.

107 "Students Occupy Princeton Hall," 30.

108 "Long Winter for Nassau," *Trentonian*, March 13, 1969, 48.

109 "Negro Students Abandon Sit-In at Princeton Campus," 1.

110 Henry interview.

111 Quoted in Seib, "University Responses to a Crisis Situation," 33.

112 "On the Campus," *Princeton Alumni Weekly*, April 22, 1969, 18.

113 At Columbia, the trustees and administration were extremely rigid and left students with little to no voice in decision-making matters. Other universities were able to learn from the result of shutting students (and sometimes faculty) out of university governance. Bradley, *Harlem vs. Columbia University*, 133–154.

114 Horne interview.

115 Henry interview.

116 Ibid.

117 Ibid.

118 Brent Davis, *Princeton Alumni Weekly*, October 21, 1969.
119 "The President's Report of 1968–1969," Robert Goheen folder, box 16, Carl A. Fields Papers, Princeton University Archives.
120 Charles Hey, "Where Are the Alumni Now?," *Daily Princetonian*, January 17, 1977, 2.
121 Ralph Austin, interviewed by Brandon Holt, tape recording, February 19, 2015, Seeley G. Mudd Manuscript Library, Princeton University.
122 Ibid.
123 E.S. Hubbell, "Letter to the Editor," *Princeton Alumni Weekly*, April 22, 1969, 5.
124 Action, "Letter to the Editor," *Princeton Alumni Weekly*, April 22, 1969, 5.
125 Vera Marcus, interviewed by Brenda Tindal, tape recording, March 2012, Seeley G. Mudd Manuscript Library, Princeton University. Hereafter, Marcus interview II.
126 Ibid.
127 Jim Dorsey, "Black Panel Raps with Alumni," *Daily Princetonian*, March 2, 1970, 1.
128 Marcus interview II.
129 Ibid.
130 "Survey of Black Princeton Alumni" folder, box 16, Carl A. Fields Papers, Princeton University.
131 Marcus interview II.

CHAPTER 3. BOURGEOIS BLACK ACTIVISM

1 "Two and a Half Centuries of Learning," Brown University website, www.brown.edu, accessed October 3, 2015.
2 "Slavery, the Brown Family of Providence, and Brown University," Brown University News Service, www.archive.org, accessed October 3, 2015.
3 "Third World History at Brown," Brown Center for Students of Color, www.brown.edu, accessed October 3, 2015.
4 "Brown's Early African-American Alumni," Center for Digital Scholarship, www.lib.brown.edu, accessed October 3, 2015.
5 "Ethel Robinson," Third World History at Brown, www.brown.edu, accessed October 3, 2015.
6 "About Fritz Pollard," Brown's Early African-American Alumni, www.dl.lib.brown.edu, accessed October 3, 2015; Jay Barry, "A Rose Bowl Star 56 Years Ago," *Ebony*, January 1972, 100–101.
7 R.A.R., "The Painful Birth of Black Studies," Materials on Afro-American Studies file, Charles H. Nichols box, Brown University Archives.
8 Barry Beckham, "Listen to the Black Graduate, You Might Learn Something," *Esquire*, September 1969, 196–197.
9 Ibid., 98.
10 Ibid., 196.
11 Terry H. Schwadron, "Blacks at Brown: A Cross-Section," *Brown Daily Herald*, September 19, 1969, 1–2.
12 Ibid., 197.

13 Jonathon Livingston, "Negro Admissions Stay Static," *Daily Princetonian*, April 16, 1963, 1.
14 Terry Ferrer, "Negroe's Role in Ivy Colleges," *New York Herald Tribune*, April 16, 1965, page unknown.
15 Ibid.
16 Carnegie Commission on Higher Education, *Quality and Equality: New Levels of Federal Responsibility for Higher Education (A Special Report and Recommendations by the Commission)* (New York: McGraw-Hill, 1968).
17 Spencer Crew, interview by author, tape recording, April 25, 2014.
18 Gregory Parks and Stefan Bradley, eds., *Alpha Phi Alpha: A Legacy of Greatness, The Demands of Transcendence* (Lexington: University Press of Kentucky, 2012), 72–74.
19 Beckham, "Listen to the Black Graduate," 196.
20 Ibid., 198.
21 Robert Reinhold, "Negroes at Brown U. Begin Boycott of Classes," *New York Times*, December 6, 1968, 38.
22 Rogers, *Black Campus Movement*, 4–5.
23 Fred Hechinger, "More Negroes Accepted by Ivy League Colleges," *New York Times*, April 18, 1968, page unknown.
24 Ibid.
25 Leonard Moore, *Carl B. Stokes and the Rise of Black Political Power* (Champaign: University of Illinois Press, 2003); Rhonda Williams, *Concrete Demands: The Search for Black Power in the 20th Century* (New York: Routledge Press, 2015).
26 Quoted in Peniel Joseph, *Stokely: A Life* (New York: Basic Civitas, 2014), 184; for more information on Carmichael, see Kwame Ture, John Edgar Wideman, and Ekwueme Michael Thelwell. Ready for Revolution: The Life and Struggles of Stokely Carmichael (New York: Scribner, 2003).
27 Kwame Ture and Charles Hamilton, *Black Power: The Politics of Liberation* (New York: Vintage Books, 1992), 184.
28 Fred Hechinger, "Ivy League Colleges Short of Goal in Enrolling More Negroes," *New York Times*, May 13, 1968, 49; Fred Hechinger, "More Negroes Accepted by Ivy League Colleges," page unknown.
29 Ibid.
30 Spencer Crew interview.
31 Hechinger, "Ivy League Colleges Short of Goal in Enrolling More Negroes," 49.
32 Stefan Bradley, *Harlem vs. Columbia University: Black Student Power in the Late 1960s* (Champaign: University of Illinois Press, 2009), 114; Thulani Davis, interview by author, digital recording November 6, 2016; Robert Reinhold, "Negroes Stage Sit-In at Radcliffe; College Acts on Their Demands," *New York Times*, December 11, 1968, 32.
33 The Black Women in Pembroke College to Dean Alberta Brown, November 18, 1968, Brown University Archives.
34 Reinhold, "Negroes at Brown U. Begin Boycott of Classes," 38.

35 Ibid.

36 Geoffrey Kabaservice, *The Guardians: Kingman Brewster, His Circle, and the Rise of the Liberal Establishment*, 224-35; Karabel, *The Chosen*, 381-403; Rogers, *The Black Campus Movement*, 72.

37 Reinhold, "Negro Students at Brown U. Begin Boycott of Classes, 38.

38 Spencer Crew interview.

39 Reinhold, "Negro Students at Brown U. Begin Boycott of Classes, 38.

40 "Come to the Speak-Out: 12:00 Noon on the Green (Sayles Hall if Rain)," circa December 6, 1968, Black Students folder, Brown University Archives.

41 Marc Sacardy, "To White Brothers and Sisters," no date, Black Students, Newspaper Clippings folder, Brown University Archives.

42 Paul Rosenburg, "We White Students of Brown," no date, Black Students, Newspaper Clippings folder, Brown University Archives.

43 Ronald P. Malaya et al., "As White Students," no date, Black Students, Newspaper Clippings folder, Brown University Archives.

44 "News Conference with the Black Students of the College," Brown University, December 9, 1968," Black Students, Newspaper Clippings folder, Brown University Archives.

45 "Brown Corp. Backs Policy for Negroes," *Providence Journal*, December 11, 1968, 26.

46 "News Conference with the Black Students of the College, Brown University, December 9, 1968."

47 "H. Rap Brown-The Politics of Education," www.youtube.com, accessed June 15, 2016.

48 Afro-American Society to Ray L. Heffner, May 1968, date unknown, Black Students, Brown University Archives.

49 Ibid.

50 Reinhold, "Negro Students at Brown U. Begin Boycott of Classes, 38.

51 Bradley, *Harlem vs. Columbia University*, 145–148; Bradley, "The Southern-Most Ivy: Princeton University from Jim Crow Admissions to Anti-Apartheid Protests, 1794–1969, *American Studies* 51, nos. 3/4 (2010): 120; Ibram Rogers, *The Black Campus Movement: Black Students and the Racial Reconstitution of Higher Education, 1965–1972* (New York: Palgrave Macmillan, 2012), 120–22.

52 Philip Lord, interview by author, tape recording, June 17, 2013.

53 Ibid.

54 Peniel Joseph, *Waiting 'Til the Midnight Hour: A Narrative History of Black Power* (New York: Henry Holt, 2006), 174–176, 183–191.

55 Phil Lord interview.

56 "Brown U. Moves to Add More Negroes," *New York Times*, 31.

57 "News Conference with the Black Students of the College," December 9, 1968.

58 "7 of 8 Negro Demands Accepted at Radcliffe," *Providence Evening Bulletin*, page unknown.

59 "Brown U. Moves to Add More Negroes," *New York Times*, 31.

60 "Boycott at Brown U. Ends as Negroes Win Demands," *New York Times*, December 9, 1968, 42; "Negroes' Boycott at Brown U. Ends," *New York Times*, December 10, 1968, 43.

61 "Negroes and Brown Reach Agreement," *Providence Journal*, December 7, 1968, 13.

62 "Negroes' Boycott at Brown U. Ends," 43; For a discussion regarding the negotiation tactics of black workers, see James A. Geschwender, *Class, Race, and Worker Insurgency: The League of Revolutionary Black Workers* (New York: Cambridge University Press, 1977); Dan Georgakas and Marvin Surkas, *Detroit: I Do Mind Dying* (Boston: South End Press, 1998), 43–68; Sidney Fine, *Violence in the Model City: The Cavanaugh Administration, Race Relations, and the Detroit Riot of 1967* (Lansing: Michigan State University Press, 2007).

63 "Brown Corp. Backs Policy for Negroes," 26.

64 Ibid.

65 Title unknown, *Providence Sunday Journal*, December 15, 1968, T1.

66 Carol J. Young, "More Black Students for Brown," *Providence Sunday Journal*, December 15, 1968, T1.

67 Ibid.

68 "Concessions Accepted: Negroes Score Brown," *Evening Bulletin*, December 9, 1968, 1.

69 "Dean Eckelmann Refutes Charges of UH Response to Black," *Pembroke Record*, December 17, 1968, 1.

70 Young, "More Black Students for Brown," T1.

71 "Brown's Commitment on Black Students," *Providence Sunday Journal*, December 15, 1968, T3.

72 Reinhold, "Negroes at Brown U. Begin Boycott of Classes," 38.

73 John Kiffney, "Future 'Uncle Toms' Are Seen," *Providence Sunday Journal*, March 16, 1969, N20.

74 John Wideman, *Brothers and Keepers* (New York: Holt, Rinehart, and Winston, 1984), 33.

75 "Black Impressions," 1971, Black Students file, Brown University Archives.

76 Spencer Crew, interview by author, tape recording, April 25, 2014.

77 "Black Students at Brown: Amplifications and Recommendations," 1969, Blacks in Providence file, C. H. Nichols box, Brown University Archives.

78 Kiffney, "Future 'Uncle Toms' Are Seen," N20.

79 "Response to Student Demands," December 8, 1968, Black Students file, Brown University Archives.

80 "Black Impressions," 1971, Black Students file, Brown University Archives.

81 Ibid.

82 "Brown's Commitment on Black Students," T3.

83 Regarding intelligence tests, black psychologist Robert Williams discounted the efficacy of traditional tests and presented what he called the black intelligence test of cultural homogeneity. See Robert L. Williams, "The BITCH-100: A Culture-Specific Test, American Psychological Association Annual Convention, Honolulu,

Hawaii (September 1972); J. D. Matarazzo and A.N. Wiens, "Black Intelligence Test of Cultural Homogeneity and Wechsler Adult Intelligence Scale Scores of Black and White Police Applicants," *Journal of Applied Psychology* 62 (1977): 57–63.

84 Reinhold, "Negroes at Brown U. Begin Boycott of Classes," 38.

85 Hechinger, "More Negroes Accepted by Ivy League Colleges," 1.

86 Spencer Crew interview.

87 Jacqueline Fleming, *Enhancing Minority Student Retention and Academic Performance: What We Can Learn from Program Evaluations* (New York: Wiley Press, 2012), 43–49; George D. Kuh, "The Other Curriculum: Out-of-Class Experiences Associated with Student Learning and Personal Development," *Journal of Higher Education* 66, no. 2 (1995): 123–127.

88 Fred Hechinger, "Ivy League and Big 7 Take a Record Total of Nonwhites," *New York Times*, April 20, 1969, 67.

89 RAN to Mr. (James) Rogers, October 20, 1972, Brown University Archives.

90 Lloyd W. Cornell Jr. to Jacqueline A. Mattfield, November 7, 1972, Brown University Archives.

91 Terry H. Schwadron, "Blacks at Brown: A Cross-Section," *Brown Daily Herald*, September 19, 1969, 1.

92 Schwadron, "Blacks at Brown," 2.

93 Ibid.

94 Ibid.

95 Ibid.

96 Barry Beckham, "Listen to the Black Graduate, You Might Learn Something," *Esquire*, September 1969, 196.

97 Ibid., 197.

98 Office of Public Information, "For Immediate Release," December 6, 1968, Black Students file, Brown University Archives.

99 "Response to Student Demands," December 8, 1968.

100 "Black Students Position Paper," date unknown, Black Students file, Brown University Archives.

101 "Response to Student Demands," December 8, 1968.

102 Ibid.

103 Office of Public Information, "For Immediate Release," December 6, 1968, Black Students file, Brown University Archives.

104 Schwadron, "Blacks at Brown," 1.

105 Rich Geer, "Donations Up Despite Unrest," *Brown Daily Herald*, September 19, 1969, 1.

106 Janet Phillips, *Brown University: A Short History* (Providence, RI: Brown University, 2000), 81–87.

107 Jay Barry, *Gentlemen Under the Elms* (Providence: Brown Alumni Monthly, 1982).

108 "Black Impressions," 1971, Black Students file, Brown University Archives.

109 Spencer Crew, interview by author, tape recording, April 25, 2014.

110 "Black Studies: An Educational Imperative," November 11, 1971, 1, Brown University Archives.

111 "Courses in Negro History, Assertion—A New Afro-American Studies Major?," *Pembroke Record*, December 17, 1968, 1 and 4.

112 See John Thomas, *The Liberator William Lloyd Garrison* (Boston: Little, Brown, 1963).

113 Derrick White, *The Challenge of Blackness: The Institute of the Black World and Political Activism in the 1970s* (Gainesville: University Press of Florida, 2013), 19–33, 45–50.

114 F. Donald Eckelmann to Raymond Heffner, March 3, 1969, Brown University Archives.

115 "Black Students at Brown: Amplifications and Recommendations," 1969, Blacks in Providence file, C. H. Nichols box, Brown University Archives.

116 Martha Biondi, *The Black Revolution on Campus* (Berkeley: University of California Press, 2012), 46–51; Rojas, *From Black Power to Black Studies*, 45–92.

117 "Black Students at Brown," FPG Subcommittee Report, Black Students file, Brown University Archives.

118 Ture and Hamilton, *Black Power*, 37.

119 Merton Stoltz to Charles Nichols, March 24, 1969, Black Studies Committee, C. H. Nichols box, Brown University Archives.

120 Fabio Rojas, *From Black Power to Black Studies: How a Radical Social Movement Became an Academic Discipline* (Charlottesville: University of Virginia Press, 2007), 95–112.

121 "Tentative Statement for Meeting of Committee on Afro-American Studies," October 1, 1969, C. H. Nichols box, Brown University Archives.

122 council.nyc.gov; Janet I. Tu, "Episcopal Priest Ann Holmes Redding Has Been Defrocked," *Seattle Times*, April 1, 2009, seattletimes.com, accessed August 2, 2017; researchgate.net; nysba.org; law.utexas.edu.

123 Ambrose Dudley, "Beneficial Effects Found in Black Studies," *Westerly Sun*, November 2, 1969, 1.

124 Dudley, "Beneficial Effects Found in Black Studies," 1.

125 "Brown Appoints Afro-American Studies Head," *Providence Journal*, April 25, 1969, 1.

126 Richard Landau to Charles Nichols, February 20, 1970, Afro-American Studies Courses and Materials, 1970–71, C. H. Nichols box, Brown University Archives; "Budget Summary: Afro-American Research Center," Afro-American Courses and Materials, 1970–1971, C. H. Nichols box, Brown University Archives; John J. Scanlon to Merton Stoltz, January 22, 1970, Afro-American Studies Courses and Materials, 1970–71, C. H. Nichols box, Brown University Archives.

127 "Black Studies: An Educational Imperative," November 11, 1971, 1, Brown University Archives.

128 Document Untitled, February 22, 1971, BUA; Office of Communications, "Richard A. Lester Dies at 89; Influential Economist and Dean of the Faculty at Princeton

University," Princeton University, December 31, 1997, www.princeton.edu, accessed July 2, 2016.

129 Donald F. Hornig to Wendell A. Jeanpierre and Rhett S. Jones, March 22, 1971.

130 Lynora Williams, "Blacks Win Two Caucus Seats," *Uwezo*, November 10, 1972, 1.

131 Martha Allen, "Afro-American Studies," *Encyclopedia Brunonia*, www.brown.edu, accessed October 19, 2015; Charles H. Nichols to Merton P. Stoltz, "Blacks in the Community" folder, Afro-American Studies 1969–1970 file, C. H. Nichols box, Brown University Archives.

132 Open letter to Umoja (the Afro-American Society of Brown University), October 5, 1971, Brown University Archives; "Afro Rejects House," *Brown Daily Herald*, October 5, 1971, 1; Duane Robinson, James Hogan Jr., and Jesse McDade to Whom It May Concern, November 5, 1971, Brown University Archives; Peter Bernstein, "Afro Center Stalled, Hornig OK Awaited," *Brown Daily Herald*, November 11, 1971, 1; Jesse McDade to Dean Thomas Banchoff, November 11, 1971, Brown University Archives; "Afro Marches on UH over House Choice," *Brown Daily Herald*, November 12, 1971, 1.

133 Jesse McDade to Mr. (Milton) Noble, June 22, 1972, Brown University Archives.

134 Ibid.

135 Jesse McDade to Acting President Dean Jacquelyn Mattfeld, June 22, 1972, Brown University Archives.

136 Dean Rollins and Kenard McDuffie to Donald Hornig, May 13, 1971, Brown University Archives.

137 Ibid.

138 Queira Lige, Bridgette J. Peteet, and Carrie M. Brown, "Racial Identity, Self-Esteem, and the Impostor Phenomenon among African American College Students," *Journal of Black Psychology* 43, no. 4 (2017): 1–13; Bridgette Peteet et al., "Imposterism is Associated with Greater Psychological Distress and Lower Self-Esteem for African American Students," *Current Psychology* 34 (2015): 154–163; C. C. Austin et al., "Imposterism as a Mediator between Survivor Guilt and Depression in a Sample of African American College Students," *College Student Journal* 43 (2009): 1094–1109; Kimberly Ewing et al., "The Relationship between Racial Identity Attitudes, Worldview, and African American Graduate Students' Experience of the Imposter Phenomenon," *Journal of Black Psychology* 22 (1996): 53–66.

139 Richard Nurse to Donald Hornig, date unknown, Admissions file, 1970–1971, Brown University Archives.

140 "Statistical Report on the Distribution of Financial Aid for the Class of 1976 as of September 20, 1972," Brown University Archives.

141 William Brown, Anderson Kurtz, and Nanette Reynolds to All Deans, December 18, 1972, Brown University Archives.

142 "Recommendations for the Reaffirmation of Brown University's Commitment to Its Black Community Based upon the December 1968 Agreements with Its Black Students (Confidential)," March 28, 1973, Appendices-Reaffirmation of Univ. Commitment to Black Community, Brown University Archives.

143 Ibid.
144 Ibid.
145 Emma Harris and Joseph Zappa, "Differences in Faculty, Student Backgrounds Can Affect Advising and Classroom Dynamics," *Brown Daily Herald*, December 4, 2014, 2.
146 Ibid.
147 Phil Lord interview.
148 Spencer Crew interview.
149 "More Black Students for Brown," *Providence Sunday Journal*, December 15, 1968, T1.

CHAPTER 4. BLACK POWER AND THE BIG GREEN

1 Ibram Rogers, *The Black Campus Movement: Black Students and the Racial Reconstitution of Higher Education, 1965–1972* (New York: Palgrave Macmillan, 2012), 1–29; www.scholar.google.com, accessed July 8, 2013; Nick Disatnick, "Affirmative Action Promotes Inequality," *Dartmouth Review*, January 28, 2012, www.dartreview.com, accessed July 8, 2013; Kevin Francfort, "Francfort: Rethinking Diversity," *The Dartmouth*, February 22, 2012, www.thedartmouth.com, accessed July 8, 2013; Jamal Abdul-Alim, "Affirmative Action Argument by University of Texas Draws Praise, Invites Criticism," *Diverse Issues*, August 8, 2012; Adam Clark Estes, "Dartmouth Students Jump to Racist Conclusion about New President," *Ivy Gate*, March 4, 2009, www.ivygateblog.com, accessed July 8, 2013; Geoffrey Kabaservice, *The Guardians: Kingman Brewster, His Circle, and the Liberal Establishment* (New York: Henry Holt, 2004), 49, 66; Nicholas Lehmann, *The Big Test: The Secret History of the American Meritocracy* (New York: Farrar, Straus and Giroux, 1999); Jerome Karabel, *The Chosen: The Hidden History of Admission and Exclusion at Yale, Harvard, and Princeton* (Boston: Houghton Mifflin, 2005).
2 Groups of mostly white student activists at Dartmouth, on the other hand, seized campus buildings in protest of the Vietnam War and the presence of the Reserve Officers Training Corps (ROTC) at the college.
3 Quoted in Donald Downs, *Cornell '69: Liberalism and the Crisis of the American University* (Ithaca, NY: Cornell University Press, 1999), 8.
4 Jerry Avorn, ed., *Up Against the Ivy Wall: A History of the Columbia University* (New York: Atheneum Press, 1969); Lawrence Eichel et al., *The Harvard Strike* (Boston: Houghton, 1970); "The Fist and Its Clencher," *Harvard Magazine*, July 1998, www.harvardmagazine.com, accessed November 6, 2016.
5 Bobby Wright, "'For the Children of Infidels': American Indian Education in the Colonial Colleges," *American Indian Culture and Research Journal* 12, no. 3 (1998): 9–12.
6 "JBHE Chronology of Major Landmarks in the Progress of African Americans in Higher Education," *Journal of Blacks in Higher Education* 53 (Autumn 2006): 77.
7 "Black Alumni through 1920" and "Black Alumni," Blacks folder, Rauner Special Collections Library, Dartmouth College.

8   See the Papers of the Presidential Committee on Civil Rights 1946–47, Rauner Special Collections Library, Dartmouth College.

9   "The Wheelock Succession of Presidents," www.dartmouth.edu, accessed June 21, 2011; Charles Widmayer, *John Sloan Dickey: A Chronicle of His Presidency of Dartmouth College* (Hanover, NH: Dartmouth College, 1991), 275.

10 Widmayer, *John Sloan Dickey*, 15–19.

11 Information regarding Grayson Kirk comes from www.columbia.edu, accessed March 19, 2012.

12 It should be noted that while seven of the eight Ivy League schools had been admitting black students for decades, Princeton University, in Robinson's home state, had only just begun to admit black undergraduates during World War II. See Stefan Bradley, "The Southern-Most Ivy: Princeton University from Jim Crow Admissions to the Anti-Apartheid Movement, 1794–1969," *American Studies* 51, no. 3/4 (2010): 113–115.

13 C. K. Wolfson, "Brief Encounters: Julian K. Robinson-Picture Perfect," *The Martha's Vineyard Times*, February 7, 2008, www.mvtimes.com, accessed February 5, 2010; Peter Maas, "Here's to You, Mr. Robinson," *New York Magazine*, March 3, 1969, 8–9.

14 Bernard W. Harleston, "Higher Education for the Negro," *Atlantic Monthly* 216, no. 5 (1965): 139–143; Linda M. Perkins, "The First Black Talent Identification Program: The National Scholarship Service and Fund for Negro Students," *Perspectives on the History of Higher Education* 29 (December 2012): 173–186.

15 R. Harcourt Dodds, interview by Chris Burns, May 19–20, 2001, Oral History Collection, Rauner Special Collections Library, Dartmouth College.

16 Kabaservice, *Guardians*, 49 and 66.

17 Widmayer, *John Sloan Dickey*, 15–16.

18 Ibid, 60.

19 Ibid; "Paid Notices: Deaths, DODDS, R.," *New York Times*, July 19, 2009, www .query.nytimes.com, accessed June 20, 2011.

20 Charles B. Strauss Jr. and Mark E. Nackman, "Tabard Admits Rejecting Rushee for Racial Reasons on First Night," *The Dartmouth*, October 4, 1963, 1.

21 "UGC Discrimination Committee Plans Study of '54 Referendum," *The Dartmouth*, October 9, 1963, 1.

22 "Tabard Admits Rejecting Rushee," *The Dartmouth*, October 4, 1963, 2.

23 Terry Lee, to the editor, *The Dartmouth*, October 7, 1963, 2; David Johnston, *The Dartmouth*, October 7, 1963, 2.

24 Glenn Askew, *But for Birmingham: The Local and National Movements in the Civil Rights Struggle* (Chapel Hill: University of North Carolina Press, 1997); Horace Huntley and John W. McKerley, eds., *Footsoldiers for Democracy: The Men, Women, and Children of the Birmingham Movement* (Champaign: University of Illinois Press, 2009).

25 Christopher Langley, "Wallace Arrives Today for Speech; Harvard Visit Marred by Incident," *The Dartmouth*, November 5, 1963, 1.

26 Dan Dimancescu, to the editor, *The Dartmouth*, October 9, 1963, 2; Richard Joseph, *The Dartmouth*, October 9, 1963.

27 Langley, "Wallace Arrives Today for Speech," 1.

28 "Students . . . ," *The Dartmouth*, November 5, 1963, 2.

29 Widmayer, *John Sloan Dickey*, 216–217.

30 E. Michael Goodkind, "Faculty Plan Silent Protest for Wallace," *The Dartmouth*, October 25, 1963, 1. The Brotherhood of the Tabard has since become a coeducational fraternity that includes members of all races.

31 "More Cheer Than Jeer; Governor Speaks on States Rights," *The Dartmouth*, November 6, 1963, 1; Ruth Segal, to the editor, *The Dartmouth*, November 7, 1963, 2.

32 According to the U.S. Census, the total of number of black people inside and outside the central cities of New Hampshire was 312 in 1960 and 600 in 1970. The total population of New Hampshire in 1970 was 737,681, with "negro and other races" making up 4,575 of the total. Dartmouth's efforts to attract black students improved not just campus racial diversity but the state's and city's as well. *U.S. Census of Population and Housing, 1970: General Demographic Trends for Metropolitan Areas, 1960–1970: New Hampshire* (Washington, DC: Government Printing Office, 1971).

33 Stefan Bradley, *Harlem vs. Columbia University: Black Student Power in the Late 1960s* (Champaign: University of Illinois Press, 2009); Werner Sollors et al., *Blacks at Harvard: A Documentary History of African-American Experience at Harvard and Radcliffe* (New York: New York University Press, 1993); Eichel et al., *Strike*; Kabaservice, *Guardians*; Laura Kalman, *Yale Law School and the Sixties: Revolt and Reverberations* (Chapel Hill: University of North Carolina Press, 2005); Wayne Glasker, *Black Students in the Ivory Tower: African American Student Activism at the University of Pennsylvania, 1967–1990* (Amherst: University of Massachusetts Press, 2002).

34 Glasker, *Black Students in the Ivory Tower*, 23–29; similar activities took place on predominantly white public university campuses. See Joy Ann Williamson, *Black Power on Campus: The University of Illinois, 1965–1975* (Champaign: University of Illinois Press, 2003), 26–27; Richard McCormick, *The Black Student Protest Movement at Rutgers* (New Brunswick, NJ: Rutgers University Press, 1990), 35.

35 Karabel, *Chosen*, 9; McGeorge Bundy quoted in Kabaservice, *Guardians*, 265; Joseph A. Soares, *The Power of Privilege: Yale and America's Elite Colleges* (Redwood City, CA: Stanford University Press, 2007), 112–114; Morton Keller and Phyllis Keller, *Making Harvard Modern: The Rise of America's University* (New York: Oxford University Press, 2001), 284–289.

36 *Crisis at Columbia: Report of the Fact-Finding Commission Appointed to Investigate the Disturbances at Columbia University in April and May 1968* (New York: Vintage Books, 1968), 16.

37 James R. McLane Jr. et al., "Dartmouth College Report of the Trustees' Committee on Equal Opportunity, December 1968," folder 6-6, Errol G. Hill Papers, Rauner Special Collections Library, Dartmouth College, hereafter referred to as McLane Report.

38 Ibid.

39 Bradley, "Southern-Most Ivy," 117; Harleston, "Higher Education for the Negro," 141.

40 McLane Report; Marc Alden Branch, "A Firm Foundation," *Yale Alumni Magazine*, October 2002, *yalealumnimagazine.com*, accessed March 21, 2012; Harleston, "Higher Education for the Negro," 141.

41 McLane Report.

42 "He Thinks He's Ready for the Ivy League," Blacks folder, Rauner Special Collections Library, Dartmouth College.

43 John Adam Moreau, "1,000 Miles from Lawndale, The Good Life Beckons Eddie," *Chicago Sun Times*, September 19, 1969; for information about Dawley's experience with the Vice Lords, see David Dawley, *A Nation of Lords: The Autobiography of the Vice Lords* (Garden City: Waveland Production, 1973); E. J. Crawford, "Profiles from the Ivy League's Black History," ivy50.com, accessed June 21, 2011; "Conservative Vice Lords, Inc.," *Chicago Crime Scenes Project*, www.chicagocrimescenes.blogspot.com, accessed June 21, 2011.

44 Moreau, "1,000 Miles from Lawndale."

45 "Vice Lords Offer Scholarship Here," *Chicago Daily Defender*, September 23, 1968, 3; "Lawndale from White to Black," www.gangresearch.net, accessed June 21, 2011.

46 Moreau, "1,000 Miles from Lawndale."

47 John Thelin, *A History of American Higher Education* (Baltimore: Johns Hopkins University Press, 2004), 270–316.

48 Martin L. Kilson Jr., "Black Militancy on Campus: Negro Separatism and the Colleges," *Harvard Today*, Spring 1968, 30–33.

49 Lerone Bennett Jr., "Confrontation on the Campus," *Ebony*, May 1968, 28.

50 "The Constitution of the Afro-American Society Dartmouth College," folder 6-38, Errol G. Hill Papers, Rauner Special Collections Library, Dartmouth College.

51 "Negro Students Fighting Apathy," *New York Times*, December 20, 1964, 53; Bradley, *Harlem vs. Columbia University*, 11–12.

52 "Leaders Discuss Afro-American Society," *The Dartmouth*, April 25, 1966, 2.

53 Woody Lee, interview by author, February 7, 2013.

54 See *Organization of American Historians Magazine* 26 (January 2012).

55 Williamson, *Black Power on Campus*, 28; William Exum, *Paradoxes of Protest: Black Student Activism at a White University* (Philadelphia: Temple University Press, 1985), 42; Rogers, *Black Campus Movement*, 92–97.

56 See Tom Hayden, *The Port Huron Statement: The Vision Call of the 1960s Revolution* (New York: Public Affairs, 2005).

57 See the Port Huron Statement, www.coursesa.matrix.msu.edu, accessed July 30, 2009; also see Kirkpatrick Sales, *SDS: Students for a Democratic Society* (New York: Random House, 1974).

58 Phillip Rush, "Students Form Chapter of 'New Leftist' SDS," *The Dartmouth*, February 24, 1966, 1; An interview with Saul Alinsky regarding his role in the Eastman Kodak controversy can be found at www.progress.org, accessed July 31, 2009;

for additional context regarding the campaign against Kodak, see Laura Hill and Julia Rabig, eds., *The Business of Black Power: Community Development, Capitalism, and Corporate Responsibility in Postwar America* (Rochester, NY: University of Rochester Press, 2013), 57–60.

59 Carl Japiske, "Parkhurst Supports Kodak, Refuses to Withdraw Proxy," *The Dartmouth*, April 25, 1967, 1–2.

60 Widmayer, *John Sloan Dickey*, 221.

61 Ibid.

62 "Police Chief Terms Riot 'Worst Seen in 22 Years,'" *The Dartmouth*, May 4, 1967, 1; "Students, Faculty Condemn Rioting at Wallace Speech," *The Dartmouth*, May 5, 1967, 1; John H. Fenton, "Dartmouth Gives Wallace Apology," *New York Times*, May 5, 1967, 28.

63 "Committee Makes Decision to Suspend Demonstrators Who Participated 'Overtly,'" *The Dartmouth*, May 12, 1967, 1; "Students Facing Ouster," *New York Times*, May 12, 1967, 29.

64 "Blacks Quit in Furor," *Chicago Daily Defender*, December 11, 1969, 12; Widmayer, *John Sloan Dickey*, 278–279.

65 McLane Report.

66 National Advisory Commission on Civil Disorders, *Report of the National Advisory Commission on Civil Disorders* (New York: Bantam Books, 1968).

67 McLane Report.

68 Ibid.

69 Downs, *Cornell '69*, 46–47; Bradley, "Southern-Most Ivy," 116–17; Edward Rubenstein, "College Seeks Negro Applicants," *Columbia Daily Spectator*, October 15, 1963, 1; Edward Rubenstein, "CU Gets Few Negro Applications," *Columbia Daily Spectator*, October 17, 1963, 1.

70 McLane Report.

71 Dodds interviewed by Burns.

72 McLane Report.

73. "Dartmouth from the Black Perspective," folder 7–15, Errol G. Hill Papers, Rauner Special Collections Library, Dartmouth University; Glasker, *Black Students in the Ivory Tower*, 91; Bradley, *Harlem vs. Columbia University*, 123–129.

74 "Dartmouth," *Bay State Banner*, September 5, 1969, 11A.

75 Bradley, *Harlem vs. Columbia University*, 129; Glasker, *Black Students in the Ivory Tower*, 27; Kabaservice, *Guardians*, 330; Karabel, *Chosen*, 403, 636; Downs, *Cornell '69*, 4.

76 Quoted in "Dartmouth," *Bay State Banner*, September 5, 1969, 11A.

77 "Southside Dartmouth Graduate to London as a Rhodes Scholar, *Chicago Daily Defender*, September 30, 1969, 5.

78 Bennett, "Confrontation on the Campus," 34.

79 Widmayer, *John Sloan Dickey*, 224.

80 Ibid., 230.

81 Wallace Ford II, interview by author, May 9, 2012.

82 McLane Report.
83 Widmayer, *John Sloan Dickey*, 224–225.
84 Harding, "Educators' View," 144.
85 Quoted in "Mutual Sensitivity Wins the Day," *Dartmouth Alumni Magazine*, May 1969, 21.
86 "Academy Group Will Review Shockley Notion," *Scientific Research*, October 27, 1969, 11; Robert B. Graham, "Free Speech at Issue," *Dartmouth Alumni Magazine*, November 1969, 21; "Scientific Battle Rages over the Genetic Theories Put forward by Jansen and Shockley on Race Traits," *Valley News*, December 17, 1969, 12; "Students Heckle Shockley," *Chicago Daily Defender*, October 20, 1969, 5; "Blacks Quit in Furor," *Chicago Daily Defender*, December 11, 1969, 12.
87 Kristine Jiwoo Ahn, "Yale Criticized for Use of Dartmouth Indian Images," *The Dartmouth*, October 21, 2016, www.thedartmouth.com, accessed July 31, 2017; Chidi Anyadike, "40 Years of Native American Studies at Dartmouth," April 2, 2013, www.news.dartmouth.edu, accessed July 31, 2017.
88 "Report of the Trustees' Committee on Equal Opportunity—1975," folder 6-7, Errol G. Hill Papers, Rauner Special Collections Library, Dartmouth College, hereafter referred to as CEO Report, 1975.
89 Ibid.
90 Drew Newman, "Alpha Phi Alpha," *The Dartmouth*, April 27, 1973, 1; for information about the national fraternity, see Gregory S. Parks and Stefan Bradley, eds., *Alpha Phi Alpha: A Legacy of Greatness and the Demands of Transcendence* (Lexington: University Press of Kentucky, 2011); Stefan Bradley, "The First and the Finest: The Founders of Alpha Phi Alpha Fraternity, Inc.," in *Black Greek-Lettered Organizations in the 21st Century: Our Fight Has Just Begun*, ed. Gregory S. Parks (Lexington: University Press of Kentucky, 2008); Herman Mason, *The Talented Tenth: The Founders and Presidents of Alpha* (Winter Park: Four G Publishers, 1999); Charles H. Wesley, *Alpha Phi Alpha: A Development in College Life* (Washington, DC: Foundation Press, 1929).
91 McLane Report.
92 Richard Zuckerman, "Afro-Am Center Dedicated; Informal White Visits Barred," *The Dartmouth*, November 17, 1971, 1.
93 Malcolm X, interviewed by Ken Sharpe, WDCR Radio, Dartmouth College, Hanover, NH, January 26, 1965.
94 For comprehensive coverage of Malcolm X's post-*hajj* transformation, see William W. Sales, *From Civil Rights to Black Liberation: Malcolm X and the Organization of Afro-American Unity* (Cambridge, MA: South End Press, 1994); Marable, *Malcolm X: A Life of Reinvention* (New York: Penguin Books, 2011); Russell Rickford, *Betty Shabazz: Surviving Malcolm X: A Journey of Strength from Wife to Widow to Heroine* (Naperville: Sourcebooks, 2005).
95 CEO Report.
96 CEO Report; "Statement of Dartmouth College's Present Affirmative Action Hiring and Promotion Goals and a Ten-Year Review of Actual Hiring and

Promotion," folder 6-8, Errol G. Hill Papers, Rauner Special Collections Library, Dartmouth College.

97 "Violence on the Green," *Valley News*, April 24, 1969.

98 "Ford, Wallace L., II," Contemporary Black Biography, 2007, www.encyclopedia .com, accessed May 8, 2012.

99 "Mutual Sensitivity Wins the Day," 21.

CHAPTER 5. SPACE INVADERS

1 For a thorough analysis of battles over housing and space in West Philadelphia, see Matt Delmont, "Making Philadelphia Safe for 'WFIL-adelpi: Television, Housing, and Defensive Localism in Postwar Philadelphia," *Journal of Urban History* 38, no. 1 (2012): 89–113; Margaret Weir, "Urban Poverty and Defensive Localism," *Dissent* 41 (Summer 1994): 337–342.

2 Davarian Baldwin, "The '800-Pound Gargoyle': The Long History of Higher Education and Urban Development on Chicago's South Side," *American Quarterly* 67, no. 1 (2015): 82.

3 Ibid., 84.

4 Gary M. Stern, "The Colleges That Ate New York," January 21, 2015, www.commer cialobserver.com, accessed November 6, 2016.

5 John V. Conti, "Manhattanville Renewal Criticized," *Columbia Daily Spectator*, March 5, 1965, 1; Michael Garofalo, "Columbia Unfurls Manhattanville Campus," March 17, 2017, www.nypress.com, accessed June 12, 2017.

6 "Certificate of Incorporation of Morningside Heights, Inc.,"Morningside Heights Incorporated project files—M. H. Inc., Board of Directors and Committee Records, Certificate of Incorporation, 1947, folder 20, box 116, Columbia Rare Book and Manuscript Library.

7 "Copy of a Resolution Adopted by the Board of Directors of Morningside Heights, Inc.," Morningside Heights Incorporated project files—Resolutions, November 23, 1948, folder 34, box 116, Columbia University Rare Book and Manuscript Library.

8 David Rockefeller to Clarence Michalis, December 4, 1947, Morningside Heights Incorporated project files—Financial Participation 1947-1950, folder 47, box 97, Columbia University Rare Book and Manuscript Library.

9 "Morningside Heights, Inc.: Ratio of Underwriting Shares to Exempt Assessed Valuation Shares," Morningside Heights Incorporated project files—Financial Participation 1947–1950, folder 48, box 97, Columbia University Rare Book and Manuscript Library.

10 "Lawrence Orton, 89, New York City Planner," *New York Times*, September 13, 1988, www.nytimes.com.

11 "Cleveland E. Dodge, Businessman and Philanthropist, Is Dead at 94," *New York Times*, November 25, 1982, nytimes.com.

12 David Rockefeller to Father Thomas Brown, January 6, 1948, Morningside Heights Incorporated project files—Financial Participation 1947–1950, folder 47, box 97, Columbia University Rare Book and Manuscript Library.

13 "Report of the Executive Committee to the Board of Directors Re Continuing Program and Budget for Morningside Heights, Inc.," 1949, Morningside Heights Incorporated project files—Continuing Program and Budget, folder 22, box 116, Columbia University Rare Book and Manuscript Library.

14 Rockefeller to Father Thomas Brown, January 6, 1948.

15 Rockefeller to Michalis, December 4, 1947.

16 Ibid.

17 George B. Ford to Robert Moses, November 9, 1951, "Housing for Morningside," Morningside Heights Incorporated project files, folder 25, box 97, Columbia University Rare Book and Manuscript Library; New York Times, October 2, 1951, 26.

18 "Statement by the Morningside Committee on Cooperative Housing at a Conference Called by Borough President Wagner, City Hall," November 8, 1951, Morningside Heights Incorporated project files, folder 26, box 97, Columbia University Rare Book and Manuscript Library.

19 Ibid.

20 "An Inspiring Attack on Slums," New York Herald Tribune, October 2, 1951, page unknown.

21 "Morningside Street Patrol Posts," October 1, 1967, Morningside Heights Incorporated project files—Morningside: Street Patrol, Crime Statistics, Commendations, Mailings, 1967, 1969–1971, 1976–1979, 1982–1983, folder 6, box 11, Columbia University Rare Book and Manuscript Library.

22 Michael J. Fortner, Black Silent Majority: The Rockefeller Drug Laws and the Politics of Punishment (Cambridge, MA: Harvard University Press, 2015), 121–132.

23 Morningside Security Council, "Security," November 30, 1967, Morningside Heights Incorporated project files—GNRP, Public Safety, 1967–1988, folder 1—Security Notes and Bulletins, 1967–1973, box 11, Columbia University Rare Book and Manuscript Library,

24 "Morningside Street Patrol: Summary of Incidents by Post," Morningside Heights Incorporated project files—Morningside: Street Patrol, Crime Statistics, Commendations, Mailing, 1967, 1969–1971, 1976–1979, 1982–1983, folder 6, box 11, Columbia University Rare Book and Manuscript Library.

25 See Rashad Shabazz, Spatializing Blackness: Architectures of Confinement and Black Masculinity in Chicago (Champaign: University of Illinois Press, 2015).

26 "Celebrities Hail Morningside Heights Youth Center," April 22, 1966, Morningside Heights Incorporated project files—Community Services and Programs, 1966–1970, 1972, 1976, 1988, folder 11—Stone Gym, Community Playgrounds, and Neighborhood Youth Programs and Publications, box 11, Columbia University Rare Book and Manuscript Library.

27 Linda Perkins, "The First Black Talent Identification Program: The National Scholarship and Service Fund for Negro Students, 1947–1968, Perspectives on the History of Higher Education 29 (December 2012): 173–197.

28 Marcia Synnott, ed., The Half-Opened Door: Discrimination in Admissions at Harvard, Yale, and Princeton, 1900–1970 (Westport, CT: Greenwood Press, 1979), 208.

29 "Project Double Discovery Aids High School Students," *West Side News and Morningsider*, August 5, 1965, 1.

30 "Culturally Deprived Students Will be Aided at Columbia," *Bergen County Record*, June 21, 1965, 21; Office of Economic Opportunity, Memo to Educational Writers: Upward Bound Updated, July 28, 1965, folder 23, Series 1.2, Press Releases, 1965–1985, box 1, Double Discovery Center Records, Columbia University Rare Book and Manuscript Library.

31 "Project Double Discovery Aids High School Students," 1.

32 Ibid.

33 Gerald Fraser, "Kids Get Foothold on Life in Columbia Halls," *New York Daily News*, August 16, 1966, page unknown.

34 "Feeling Good: Project Double Discovery," *Columbia College Today*, September 1976, 28.

35 Mary Kelly, "Double Discovery Boosts High Schoolers," August 25, 1966, page unknown.

36 "Feeling Good," 27.

37 Office of College Relations, "PDD," Columbia University, 1968, folder 23, Press Releases, 1965–1985, Double Discovery Center Records, box 1, Columbia University Rare Book and Manuscript Library.

38 Robert L. Williams, "The BITCH-100: A Culturally Specific Test," paper presented at the American Psychological Association Annual Convention, Honolulu, Hawaii, September 1972.

39 "The Great Society's Legacy at Columbia," *Columbia College Today*, Fall 1987, 7.

40 "Kids Get Foothold on Life," page unknown; Mark Jaffee, "300 Scheduled to Arrive for Double Discovery," *Columbia Daily Spectator*, June 22, 1967, 1.

41 Samantha Carter, "Harlem," in *No Mask 1968* (Manhattan: Project Double Discovery, 1968), 35, Columbia University Rare Book and Manuscript Library, Double Discovery Center Records, box 16, folder 31, Student Publications—No Mask, 1968 Summer.

42 Frances Powell, "An Interview with Bill Sales," *Discoverer*, July 23, 1965, 2.

43 Dan Carlinsky, "The College's Unusual," *Columbia College Today*, Fall 1965, 58.

44 See Mark Naison, *White Boy: A Memoir* (Philadelphia: Temple University Press, 2002).

45 "Institutional Expansion Projects and Relocation in the Morningside Heights Core Area," January 24, 1967, Morningside Heights Incorporated project file—Buildings 1966–1968, Institution Expansion and Relocation, folder 20, box 11, Columbia University Rare Book and Manuscript Library.

46 Ibid.

47 Ibid.

48 Office of Public Information, April 17, 1969, Morningside Heights Incorporated project files—Public Relations Officers, Public Information, and Press Releases, 1968–1969, 1982, folder 10, box 11, Columbia University Rare Book and Manuscript Library.

49 "CORE Charges Bias at 440 Riverside," *Columbia Daily Spectator*, October 16, 1962, 4.

50 "CORE Holds Panel on Expansion," *Columbia Daily Spectator*, February 17, 1965, 3.

51 John Koutsos, "City Council Board Members Urge Reversal of Gym Policy," *Columbia Daily Spectator*, December 21, 1967, 2.

52 Davis interview.

53 Students' Afro-American Society, quoted in Joanne Grant, *Confrontation on Campus: The Columbia Pattern for the New Protest* (New York: Signet Books, 1969), 32.

54 Ibid.

55 Mark Rudd, *Underground: My Life with SDS and the Weathermen* (New York: William Morrow, 2009), 40–41; Alan Adelson, SDS: A Profile (New York: Scribner, 1972), 7; David, Gilbert, SDS/WUO, Students for a Democratic Society and the Weather Underground Organization (Oakland, CA: Abraham Guillen Press/ Arm the Spirit, 2002).

56 Bill Sales, quoted in Hilton Obenzinger, *Busy Dying* (Tucson, AZ: Chax Publishing, 2008).

57 William Sales, "Response to a Negro Negative," *Columbia Daily Spectator*, March 14, 1969, 5; David Barber, A Hard Rain Fell: SDS and Why It Failed, 43-44.

58 Grayson Kirk, "A Message to Alumni, Parents, and Other Friends of Columbia," June 1, 1968, Morningside Heights Incorporated project files—Public Relations Officers, Public Information, and Press Releases, 1968–1969, 1982, folder 10, box 11, Columbia University Rare Book and Manuscript Library.

59 Ibid.

60 Ibid.

61 "A Declaration of Confidence in Columbia's Future," May 16, 1968, Morningside Heights Incorporated project files—Education, Public Relations, Officers, Public Information, and Press Releases, folder 10, box 11, Columbia University Rare Book and Manuscript Library.

62 Office of Public Information, April 17, 1969, Morningside Heights Incorporated project files—Public Relations Officers, Public Information, and Press Releases, 1968–1969, 1982, folder 10, box 11, Columbia University Rare Book and Manuscript Library.

63 Ibid.

64 Office of Public Information, November 7, 1968, Morningside Heights Incorporated project files—Public Relations Officers, Public Information, and Press Releases, 1968–1969, 1982, folder 10, box 11, Columbia University Rare Book and Manuscript Library.

65 Office of Public Information, April 17, 1969, Morningside Heights Incorporated project files—Public Relations Officers, Public Information, and Press Releases, 1968–1969, 1982, folder 10, box 11, Columbia University Rare Book and Manuscript Library.

CHAPTER 6. THERE GOES THE NEIGHBORHOOD

1 Harvey Etienne, *Pushing Back the Gates: Neighborhood Perspectives on University-Driven Revitalization in West Philadelphia* (Philadelphia: Temple University Press, 2012), x.

2 Ibid., xiii.

3 Ibid., 11.

4 Judith Rodin, *The University and Urban Revival: Out of the Ivory Tower and into the Streets* (Philadelphia: University of Pennsylvania Press, 2007).

5 See also, George Nash, *The University and the City: Eight Cases of Involvement* (New York: McGraw-Hill Book Company, 1973).

6 Margaret O'Mara, "Building 'Brainsville': The University of Pennsylvania and Philadelphia," in *Cities of Knowledge: Cold War Science and the Search for the Next Silicon Valley* (Princeton: Princeton University Press, 2005).

7 Matthew Countryman, *Up South: Civil Rights and Black Power in Philadelphia* (Philadelphia: University of Pennsylvania Press, 2006), 164.

8 Jeanne Theoharis and Komozi Woodard, eds., *Freedom North: Black Freedom Struggles Outside the South, 1940–1980* (New York: Palgrave Macmillan, 2003); Martha Biondi, *To Stand and Fight: The Struggle for Civil Rights in Postwar New York City* (Cambridge, MA: Harvard University Press, 2003).

9 Rodin, *University and Urban Revival*, 29.

10 University of Pennsylvania Report of the Trustees Committee for the Physical Development of the University, October 25, 1948, UPA 1.51, UARC.

11 American Housing Act of 1949 (Title V of P.L. 81-171) Housing Act of 1949 S 1070—P.L. 171.

12 Scott Cohen, "Urban Renewal in West Philadelphia: An Examination of the University of Pennsylvania's Planning, Expansion, and Community Role from the Mid-1940s to the Mid-1970s" (senior thesis, University of Pennsylvania, 1998), 13.

13 John Mollenkopf, *The Contested City* (Princeton: Princeton University Press, 1983), 3–11.

14 Gaylord P. Harnwell, "Design for Excellence: University of Pennsylvania Report of the President, 1956," UPI 25.1, UARC, page 7.

15 "Biographical Note," Gaylord P. Harnwell Papers, 1889–1992, UPT 50 H289, UARC, University of Pennsylvania.

16 O'Mara, *Cities of Knowledge*, 78.

17 Carolyn Adams et al., eds., *Philadelphia: Neighborhoods, Division, and Conflict in a Post Industrial City* (Philadelphia: Temple University Press, 1991), 79.

18 "West Philadelphia Community History Center," www.archives.upenn.edu, accessed November 6, 2016. See also David Roediger, *The Wages of Whiteness: Race and the Making of the American Working Class* (New York: Verso Books, 1991), and *Working Toward Whiteness: How America's Immigrants Became White, The Strange Journey from Ellis Island to the Suburbs* (New York: Basic Books, 2005).

19 "Overview of Philadelphia's Post World War II Public Housing Projects and the Philadelphia Housing Authority," phmc.state.pa.us, accessed August 15, 2017.

20 Matt Delmont, "Making Philadelphia Safe for 'WFIL-adelphia': Television, Housing, and Defensive Localism in Postwar Philadelphia," *Journal of Urban History* 38, no. 1 (2012): 91.

21 Delmont, "Making Philadelphia Safe for 'WFIL-adelphia,'" 90.

22 "Down 'Da Bottom with Ardie Stuart Brown," www.funeralforahome.org, accessed November 6, 2016.

23 Bill Gaither, "Herman Wrice, 1939–2000, *Powelton Post*, poweltonvillage.org.

24 Ibid.

25 Belmont, "Making Philadelphia Safe for 'WFIL-adelphia,'" 92; Commission on Human Relations, "Philadelphia's Non-White Population 1960, Report No. 1, Demographic Data," folder 148.4, box A-621, Philadelphia City Archives.

26 Countryman, *Up South*, 65; Thomas Sugrue, "Affirmative Action from Below: Civil Rights, the Building Trades, and the Politics of Racial Equality in the Urban North, 1945–1969," *Journal of American History* 91 (June 2004): 152–54; Adams, *Philadelphia*, 81–87.

27 Rodin, *University and Urban Revival*, 30.

28 Trustees Minutes, April 12, 1957, vol. 26-355, UARC, University of Pennsylvania; Cohen, "Urban Renewal in West Philadelphia," 30.

29 Rodin, *University and Urban Revival*, 33.

30 Quoted in John Puckett and Mark Frazier, *Becoming Penn: The Pragmatic University, 1950–2000* (Philadelphia: University of Pennsylvania Press, 2015), 39; Harold Stassen, interview by Jeannette Nichols, 18 October 1971, UPP1, "Stassen" folder, box 3, UARC.

31 "A History of the University Science Center," UARC, www.archives.upenn.edu, accessed November 6, 2016.

32 Carolyn T. Adams, "Philadelphia Industrial Development Corporation," *Encyclopedia of Greater Philadelphia*, www.philadelphiaencyclopedia.org, accessed November 6, 2016.

33 Elijah Anderson, "The Iconic Ghetto," *Annals of the American Academy of Political and Social Science* 642 (November 2013): 8–24.

34 Etienne, *Pushing Back the Gates*, 23.

35 Puckett and Frazier, *Becoming Penn*, 61–63.

36 Len Lear, "Urban Renewal Means Negro Removal, Says Community Planning Official," *Philadelphia Tribune*, March 26, 1968, 4.

37 Countryman, *Up South*, 188.

38 Lear, "Urban Renewal Means Negro Removal," 4.

39 Len Lear, "Mantuans Will Soon Take Woes to 'Grief Centers,'" *Philadelphia Tribune*, February 15, 1969, 1.

40 Ibid.

41 Rodin, *University and Urban Revival*, 36.

42 See Sugrue, "Affirmative Action from Below," 145–173.

43 Countryman, *Up South*, 41.
44 Lisa Levenstein, *A Movement without Marches: African American Women and the Politics of Poverty in Postwar Philadelphia* (Chapel Hill: University of North Carolina Press, 2009), 121.
45 Ibid., 122.
46 Matthew Delmont, *Nicest Kids in Town: American Bandstand, Rock 'n' Roll, and the Struggle for Civil Rights in the 1950s* (Berkley: University of California Press, 2012), 68.
47 Countryman, *Up South*, 171.
48 Pamela Haynes, "Mother Escorts Boy to Girard for First Classes," *Philadelphia Tribune*, February 1, 1969, 3.
49 Gerald L. Early, interview by author, digital recording, July 10, 2015. Hereafter, Early interview
50 See National Advisory Commission on Civil Disorders, *Report of the National Advisory Commission on Civil Disorders* (New York: Bantam Books, 1968).
51 Countryman, *Up South*, 155–163.
52 Walter Palmer, interview by author, digital recording, July 16, 2015. Hereafter, Palmer interview.
53 Early interview.
54 Sheldon Hackney, "The University and Its Community: Past and Present," *Annals of the American Academy*, 488 (November 1986), 139; Wayne Glasker, *Black Students in the Ivory Tower: African American Student Activists at the University of Pennsylvania, 1967–1990* (Amherst: University of Massachusetts Press, 2002), 68.
55 John Wideman, *Brothers and Keepers* (New York: Holt, Rinehart, and Winston, 1984), 27–33.
56 Early interview.
57 Wideman, *Brothers and Keepers*, 31–32.
58 Ibid., 32.
59 Ibid.
60 Woody Lee, interview by author, digital recording, February 7, 2013. Hereafter, Lee interview.
61 "Negro College Grads More Intellectual than Whites," *Philadelphia Tribune*, January 30, 1968, 2.
62 Glasker, *Black Students in the Ivory Tower*, 25–27.
63 Ibid., 47.
64 Ibid., 46.
65 "Defiant Students," *Philadelphia Tribune*, March 26, 1968, 3; Lawrence Geller, "Mutinous Cheyney Students Demand Less Longfellow, More Malcolm X," *Philadelphia Tribune*, April 2, 1968, 1; John Wilder, "Temple Students Demand Apology for Blackface Minstrel Show," April 2, 1968, 1.
66 "Memorial Services Held Last Friday," *Philadelphia Tribune*, April 9, 1968, 1.
67 Glasker, *Black Students in the Ivory Tower*, 40.
68 Bayard Rustin, *Philadelphia Tribune*, April 9, 1968, 7.

69 Glasker, *Black Students in the Ivory Tower*, 29–32; Ibram Rogers, *The Black Campus Movement: Black Students and the Racial Reconstitution of Higher Education, 1965–1972* (New York: Palgrave Macmillan, 2012), 131.

70 *Black Power Conference Reports: Philadelphia, Aug. 30–Sept. 1, 1968; Bermuda, July 13, 1969* (New York: Afram Associates, 1970).

71 Armstead Robinson et al., *Black Studies in the University: A Symposium* (New Haven: Yale University Press, 1969), 38.

72 Ibid., 40.

73 Robinson, *Black Studies in the University*, 64.

74 Sue Chong, "University City Home Owners Fight Planners to Save Homes," *Daily Pennsylvanian*, December 6, 1966, 5.

75 Erasmus Kloman, "Citizen Participation in the Philadelphia Model Cities Program: Retrospect and Prospect," *Public Administration Review* 32 (September 1972): 402–408. Also, see Fred Powledge, *Model City* (New York: Simon and Schuster, 1970); Woodlawn Organization, *Woodlawn's Model Cities Plan: A Demonstration of Citizen Responsibility* (Northbrook, IL: Whitehall Company, 1970); Abigail, Perkiss, *Making Good Neighbors: Civil Rights, Liberalism, and Integration in Postwar Philadelphia* (Ithaca, NY: Cornell University Press, 2014).

76 Pennsylvania Higher Educational Facilities Authority Act 1967, the Act of Dec. 6, 1967, P.L. 678, no. 318 Cl. 64, www.legis.state.pa.us, accessed November 6, 2016.

77 Berl Schwartz, "Residents to Fight Center Demolition," January 27, 1969, 1.

78 Glasker, *Black Students in the Ivory Tower*, 53.

79 Lawrence Geller, "Trouble is Predicted Unless City Cracks Down Hard on Slumlords," *Philadelphia Tribune*, April 29, 1968, 5.

80 Puckett and Frazier, *Becoming Penn*, 84.

81 "In Mantua, Two People Are Battling 176,000 Rats—The Rats Are Winning," *Philadelphia Tribune*, March 4, 1969, 4.

82 Stuart Madden, "Relocation Plans are Rejected by Walnut Center," *Daily Pennsylvanian*, January 23, 1969, 1.

83 Stuart Madden, "GPH Meets to Tell Plans for Center," *Daily Pennsylvanian*, January 28, 1969, 1; Schwartz, "Residents to Fight Center Demolition," 1.

84 "Police to Tow Cars of Ticket Ignorers," *Daily Pennsylvanian*, January 23, 1969, 1.

85 David Cohen, conversation with author, handwritten notes, January 29, 2013.

86 "Student Nurse Attacked in Apartment Lobby," *Daily Pennsylvanian*, January 23, 1969, 1.

87 Len Lear, "Mantuan Will Soon Take Woes to 'Grief Center,'" *Philadelphia Tribune*, February 15, 1969, 4; Pamala Haynes, "Gang Murder Rate Zooms Up 600% over 1967," *Philadelphia Tribune*, February 15, 1969, 4.

88 "New Mantua Named for Late Stanley Workman," *Philadelphia Tribune*, January 21, 1969, 4.

89 Schwartz, "Residents to Fight Center Demolition," 5.

90 Puckett and Frazier, *Becoming Penn*, 83.

91 Richard A. Humphrey, "University of Pennsylvania 'Sit-In,' February 1969," *Report to the Special Committee on Campus Tensions, American Council on Education,* UPF 8.5, University News Bureau, Student Demonstrations—Sit-in at College Hall, American Council on Education Report to the Campus Tensions Committee, 1970, 4, UARC.

92 Schwartz, "Residents to Fight Center Demolition," 5.

93 "Cheyney State President Explained Why Students Were Expelled," *Philadelphia Tribune,* January 21, 1969, 3; Pamala Haynes, "Call Indictment of Cheyney Students 'A Railroad Job,'" *Philadelphia Tribune,* March 8, 1969, 1.

94 Susan Grober, "Liberation Week Starts on Saturday," *Daily Pennsylvanian,* January 26, 1969, 1.

95 "College Planning Afro-American Studies Major," *Daily Pennsylvanian,* January 22, 1969, 1.

96 "Educational Roundup," *Philadelphia Tribune,* February 4, 1969, 6.

97 J. L. Teller, "Poet Calls for Black Autonomy," *Daily Pennsylvanian,* February 18, 1969, 1.

98 "Disruption Marks Nation's Campuses," *Daily Pennsylvanian,* February 17, 1969, 1 and 5.

99 See Howard Zinn, *SNCC: The New Abolitionists* (Boston: Beacon Press, 1964).

100 "Review: The Battle of the Faculty," UPF 8.5 News Bureau, Student Demonstration—Sit-in at College Hall 1969 (II), UARC, University of Pennsylvania.

101 "Caution, Not Violence," *Daily Pennsylvanian,* February 18, 1969, 2.

102 Ibid.

103 Scot Brown, *Fighting for US: Maulana Karenga, the US Organization, and Black Cultural Nationalism* (New York: New York University Press, 2005), 96.

104 "Chronology of the Six-Day Sit-In," 1969, UPF 8.5 News Bureau, Student Demonstrations—Sit-In at College Hall, 1.

105 Puckett and Lloyd, *Becoming Penn,* 128.

106 Office of Vice Provost of Student Affairs, "On the Exercise of Free Speech and Lawful Assembly," November 1, 1967, UPF 8.5 University News Bureau, Student Demonstrations and Protests (subject), News Releases, etc., 1965–1971, UARC.

107 Clarence Greene, "Catto Tutorial Plan Aids Black Students," *Daily Pennsylvanian,* February 17, 1969, 5.

108 Ira Harkavy, interview by author, digital recording, July 24, 2015. Hereafter, Harkavy interview.

109 Grober, "Liberation Week Starts on Saturday, 1.

110 Harkavy interview.

111 "Chronology of the Six-Day Sit-In," 1969, 2.

112 Statement of Senate Advisory Committee of the University of Pennsylvania, 1969, Student Demonstrations—Sit-In at College Hall, UARC.

113 University of Pennsylvania News Release, February 29, 1969, News Bureau file—Student Demonstrations and Protests, 1965–1973, folder 7, box 2/5, Harnwell and Community Relations2, UARC.

114 Statement of the Board of Trustees, February 23, 1969, "The Day the Campus Demonstrations Ended," Harnwell and Community Relations5, UARC.
115 Ibid.
116 William L. Day to Gaylord Harnwell, February 24, 1969, Harnwell and Community Relations3, UARC.
117 University of Pennsylvania News Release, February 29, 1969.
118 Day to Harnwell, February 24, 1969.
119 "Chronology of the Six-Day Sit-In," 1969, page unknown.
120 Robert Rutman, "Letters to the Editor of the *Times*," *New York Times*, March 4, 1969, 42.
121 "A Reply to WCAU-TV Editorial," WCAU-TV, CBS TV10, Philadelphia, March 10, 1969, UPF 8.5 News Bureau, Student Demonstration—Sit-in at College Hall 1969 (II), UARC, University of Pennsylvania.
122 "Robert McClain, 91," Obituary, Charles F. Snyder Funeral Homes and Crematory, April 19, 2016, www.snyderfuneralhome.com, accessed November 6, 2016.
123 "Accord Reached at Pennsylvania," *New York Times*, February 24, 1969, 11.
124 "A Reply to WCAU-TV Editorial," March 10, 1969.
125 Paul Levy, "Mullen Warns Colleges to Control Disorders," *Evening Bulletin* (Philadelphia), February 20, 1969, 10.
126 Ibid.
127 "Residents of U. of P. Area Back Student Protest," *Philadelphia Tribune*, March 4, 1969, 2.
128 Ibid., 4.
129 Ibid.
130 Ibid.
131 Ibid.
132 Ibid.; Palmer interview; Harkavy interview.
133 Amiri Baraka, "Black People!," in *The LeRoi Jones/Amiri Baraka Reader*, eds. Amiri Baraka et al. (New York: Basic Books, 1991), 224.
134 "Residents of U. of P. Area Support Student Protest," 4.
135 Ibid.
136 "Accord Reached at Pennsylvania," *New York Times*, February 24, 1969, 11.
137 Rutman, "Letters to the Editor of *The Times*," 42.
138 "Accord Reached at Pennsylvania," 11.
139 Ibid.
140 David Holmstrom, "Six Tense Days at Penn," *Christian Science Monitor*, March 4, 1969, 4.
141 Harnwell to Our Alumni and Friends, February 29, 1969, Harnwell and Community Relations9, UARC.
142 Ibid.
143 Ibid.
144 Ibid.

145 Alistair Cooke, "Goodwill Guerillas in the City of Brotherly Love," *Guardian*, March 13, 1969, 13.

146 "Alumni Reaction to Campus Unrest," UPF 8.5 News Bureau, Student Demonstration—Sit-in at College Hall 1969 (II), UARC.

147 Humphrey, "University of Pennsylvania 'Sit-In,'" February 1969."

148 Richard A. Humphrey to Gaylord Harnwell, American Council on Education Report to the Campus Tensions Committee, March 12, 1970, Student Demonstrations—Sit-in at College Hall, UARC.

149 Bob Hoffman, "IAA to Run Student Power Conference Here," *Daily Pennsylvanian*, March 5, 1969, 1.

150 Glasker, *Black Students in the Ivy Tower*, 71–85.

151 Minutes of the Board of Trustees, December 19, 1969, UPA 1.1, UARC.

152 See Ira Harkavy and John Puckett, "Lessons from Hull House for the Contemporary Urban University," *Social Science Review* 68 (September 1994): 299–321.

153 Hackney, "The University and Its Community," 141. He boasted that the center employs 6,000 area locals and had become a "major business incubator." Further, the science center allowed "28 participating colleges, universities and academic health center in the Greater Philadelphia area."

154 Ibid., 142.

155 Elizabeth Strom, "The Political Strategies Behind University-Based Development," in David C. Penny and Wim Wiewel, eds., *The University as Urban Developer: Case Studies and Analysis* (New York: Routledge, 2005), 119.

CHAPTER 7. BLUE BULLDOGS AND BLACK PANTHERS

1 John Darnton, "8 Black Panthers Seized in Torture-Murder Case," *New York Times*, May 23, 1969, 24; Stuart Rosow, "Panthers to Rally on Jail Conditions," Yale Daily News, November 21, 1969, 1.

2 For a thorough history of the activities of the Black Panthers in New Haven, see Yohuru Williams, *Black Politics/White Power: Civil Rights, Black Power and the Black Panthers in New Haven* (New York: Brandywine Press, 2000).

3 "How Black Studies Happened," *Yale Alumni Magazine*, May 1969, 22.

4 Ibid.

5 Ibid, 23; James R. McLane Jr. et al., "Dartmouth College Report of the Trustees' Committee on Equal Opportunity, December 1968," folder 6-6, Errol G. Hill Papers, Rauner Special Collections Library, Dartmouth College, hereafter referred to as McLane Report.

6 John Darnton, "Yale Has Been Spared Campus Strife, But Some Administrators Are Nervous," *New York Times*, April 15, 1969, 71.

7 "How Black Studies Happened," 23.

8 Ernest Wilson, III, interview by author, digital recording, October 28, 2016. Hereafter, Wilson interview.

9 Ibid.

10 "On Being Black at Yale," *Yale Alumni News*, May 1969, 28.

11 Ibid.

12 Ibid.

13 John Darnton, "New Black Studies at Yale Go from Slavery to the Slums," *New York Times*, May 15, 1969, 49.

14 "On Being Black at Yale," 28–33.

15 Ibid., 28.

16 Ibid.

17 Ibid., 30.

18 Shaun Hauper, "Niggers No More: A Critical Race Counternarrative on Black Male Achievement at Predominantly White Colleges and Universities," *International Journal of Qualitative Studies in Education* 6 (Nov–Dec 2009): 697–712.

19 Sophie Yan and Grace Yoon, "Amidst Campus Dialogue, Students Confront Racial Perceptions," *Brown Daily Herald*, December 3, 2014.

20 "On Being Black at Yale," 29–30.

21 See Arnold Rampersad, *Jackie Robinson: A Biography* (New York: Ballantine Books, 1998), 219–220.

22 "On Being Black at Yale," 30.

23 Ibid., 31.

24 Ibid.

25 Martha Biondi, *The Black Revolution on Campus* (Berkeley: University of California Press, 2012).

26 Darnton, "New Black Studies at Yale," 49.

27 "On Being Black at Yale," 31.

28 "Ford, Wallace L., II," Contemporary Black Biography, 2007, *Encyclopedia.com*, accessed November 6, 2016.

29 "On Being Black at Yale," 32.

30 "How Black Studies Happened," *Yale Alumni Magazine*, May 1969, 22.

31 Kimberlé Crenshaw et al., eds., *Critical Race Theory: The Key Writings that Formed the Movement* (New York: The New Press, 1995), xi–xix, 5–28, and 302–314.

32 Ibid.

33 "How Black Studies Happened," 22–24.

34 "New Book: Symposium Published," *Yale Daily News*, November 19, 1969, 1.

35 Stefan Bradley, *Harlem vs. Columbia University: Black Student Power in the Late 1960s* (Champaign: University of Illinois Press, 2009), 55.

36 See Noliwe M. Rooks, *White Money, Black Power: The Surprising History of African American Studies and the Crisis of Race in Higher Education* (Boston: Beacon Books, 2006), 75–80, 93–122.

37 Gila Reinstein, "African-American Studies Revisits Origins, Imagines Future," *Yale Bulletin and Calendar* 30 (May 10, 2002), www.archives.news.yale.edu, accessed November 6, 2016.

38 "On Being Black at Yale," 29.

39 Reinstein, "African-American Studies."

40 Michael Thelwell, "Directions in Black Studies: A Political Perspective," *Massachusetts Review* 10, no. 4 (1969): 707.

41 Ibid., 708.

42 "Black Studies: An Educational Imperative," November 11, 1971, 1, Brown University Archives.

43 Darnton, "New Black Studies at Yale," 49.

44 Thelwell, "Directions in Black Studies," 711.

45 Vincent Harding, "New Creation or Familiar Death?: An Open Letter to Black Students in the North," *Negro Digest*, March 1969, 5–14.

46 Martin Kilson et al., *Black Studies: Myths and Realities* (New York: A. Philip Randolph Foundation, 1969), 26.

47 Kilson, *Black Studies*, 6.

48 Thelwell, "Directions in Black Studies," 709.

49 Ibid.

50 Quoted in *Black Studies USA*, directed by 'Niyi Coker (Birmingham, AL: Coker, 2005).

51 "On Being Black at Yale," 29.

52 Ibid.

53 Ibid.

54 Bradley, *Harlem vs. Columbia University*, 112.

55 "On Being Black at Yale," 29.

56 "On Being Black at Yale," 29–30.

57 Armstead Robinson et al., eds., *Black Studies in the University: A Symposium* (New Haven: Yale University Press, 1969), 5.

58 Ibid.

59 Gerald L. Early, interview by author, digital recording, June 30, 2015.

60 Reinstein, "African-American Studies."

61 "Yale University News Bureau," December 12, 1968, Misc. News Releases, Statements, Yale University Archives.

62 "How Black Studies Happened," 27.

63 "Afro Major, College Seminars to Go Before Faculty Today," *Yale Daily News*, December 12, 1968, 1.

64 "Yale University News Bureau," December 12, 1968, Misc., News Releases, Statements, Yale University Archives.

65 Max Gladstone, "First Black Profs Recall Challenges, Successes," *Yale Daily News*, February 15, 2005, www.yaledailynews.com, accessed November 6, 2016.

66 Robinson, *Black Studies in the University*, 6–11.

67 Darnton, "New Black Studies at Yale," 49.

68 Douglas Martin, "Roy S. Bryce-Laporte, Who Led Black Studies at Yale, Dies at 78, *New York Times*, August 9, 2012, B22.

69 Ibid.

70 "Afro-American Studies at Yale," in the Afro-American Studies: Courses and Materials, 1970–1971 file, Brown University Archives.

71 "How Black Studies Happened," 27.
72 Ibid.
73 Ibid.
74 Kilson, *Black Studies*, 33.
75 "On Being Black at Yale," 30.
76 Ibid., 33.
77 Ibid.
78 See Carol E. Anderson, "The Struggle for Human Rights: African Americans Petition the United Nations," in *Eyes Off the Prize: The United Nations and the African American Struggle for Human Rights, 1944–1955* , 58–112 (Cambridge: Cambridge University Press, 2003) 2; Andrew J. Young, "Whitney Young, "Working from the Middle," *Life*, March 26, 1971, 4; Robert E. Weems Jr., *Business in Black and White: American Presidents and Black Entrepreneurs in the Twentieth Century* (New York: New York University Press, 2009), 145–49; Jeffrey O. G. Ogbar, *Black Power: Radical Politics and African American Identity* (Baltimore: Johns Hopkins University Press, 2004), 150–152.
79 Reinstein, "African-American Studies."
80 *Marcus Garvey: Look for Me in the Whirlwind*, transcript, PBS American Experience, www.pbs.org, accessed November 6, 2016.
81 Reinstein, "African-American Studies."
82 Kilson, *Black Studies*, 35.
83 Ibid., 36.
84 Martin Kilson, "Anatomy of the Black Studies Movement," *Massachusetts Review* 10, no. 4 (1969): 720.
85 Kilson, *Black Studies*, 37.
86 Kilson, "Anatomy of the Black Studies Movement," 718–719.
87 Kilson, *Black Studies*, 9.
88 Kilson, "Anatomy of the Black Studies Movement," 723.
89 See Michael Lackey, ed., *The Haverford Discussions: A Black Integrationist Manifesto for Racial Justice* (Charlottesville: University of Virginia Press, 2013).
90 Cleveland Sellers, with Robert Terrell, *The River of No Return: The Autobiography of a Black Militant and the Life and Death of SNCC* (Jackson: University Press of Mississippi, 2003), 170–172; Peniel E. Joseph, *Stokely: A Life* (New York: Basic Civitas, 2014), 104–105, and 107–109.
91 See Richard Benson, II, *Fighting for Our Place in the Sun: Malcolm X and the Radicalization of the Student Movement, 1960–1973* (New York: Peter Lang, 2014).
92 Kilson, "Anatomy of the Black Studies Movement," 721.
93 Ibid., 722.
94 Ibid., 723.
95 Wesley C. Hogan, *Many Minds, One Heart: SNCC's Dream for a New America* (Chapel Hill: University of North Carolina Press, 2007), 240; Rhonda Y. Williams, *Concrete Demands: The Search for Black Power in the 20th Century* (New York: Routledge, 2015), 235.
96 Kilson, *Black Studies*, 38.

97 Ibid., 42.

98 Ibid., 43.

99 Ibid.

100 "Afro-Americans Must Blackwash Schools, Says Dr. Nathan Hare," *Philadelphia Tribune*, February 18, 1969, 8.

101 Kilson, "Anatomy of the Black Studies Movement," 723.

102 Thelwell, "Directions in Black Studies," 704–705.

103 Fern Marja Eckman, "Black Studies: A Report," *New York Post*, date unknown.

104 Ibid.

105 Ibid.

106 Ibid.

107 Ibid.

108 Ibid.

109 "On Being Black at Yale," 33.

110 Ibid.

111 "How Black Studies Happened," 27.

112 Ibid., 33.

113 "On Being Black at Yale," 33.

114 Williams, *Black Politics/White Power*, 92–93.

115 "Bomb Scare Stops Black Panther Chief," March 13, 1969, 1.

116 Williams, *Black Politics/White Power*, 8–9.

117 "Panther Aid Group Meets," *Yale Daily News*, November 3, 1969, 1; Rosow, "Panthers to Rally on Jail Conditions," 1; Thomas Kent, "Students Supporting Panthers Ask to Speak in Class; Disciplinary Action Considered," *Yale Daily News*, December 17, 1969, 1; Tom Latus, "Committee Suspends Five Students for Tuesday 'Panther' Disruptions," December 18, 1969, 1; Thomas Kent, "White Group Aids Panthers Here," *Yale Daily News*, April 6, 1970, 1.

118 Phillip M. Richards, "Black and Blue in New Haven: Memoirs of an African American at Yale in the late 1960s," *Journal of Blacks in Higher Education* 51 (Spring 2006): 67.

119 Tom Kuser and Ann Lopez, "May Day at Yale, 1970: Recollections," WSHU Public Radio, April 22, 2015, www.wshu.org, accessed April 29, 2017.

120 Ibid.

121 Joseph B. Treaster, "Brewster Doubts Black Fair Trials," *New York Times*, April 24, 1970, 1.

122 Reinstein, "African-American Studies."

CHAPTER 8. BLACK STUDIES THE HARD WAY

1 Henry Rosovsky, "A Happy Beginning," in *Department of Afro-American Studies, Harvard University: Thirtieth Anniversary Celebration* (Cambridge, MA: Harvard University Press, 2000), 31.

2 R. L. Worsnop, "Black, Blue, Crimson," no date, Blacks folder, Rauner Special Collections Library, Dartmouth College.

3 Ernest Wilson, III, "Afro-American Studies: Thirty Years Back, Thirty Years Forward," in *Department of Afro-American Studies, Harvard University*, 45.

4 Ernest Wilson, III, interview by author, digital recording, October 28, 2016. Hereafter, Wilson interview.

5 Robert L. Hall, interview by author, email, October 20, 2016. Hereafter, Hall interview.

6 Synnott, *The Half-Opened Door: Discrimination in Admissions at Harvard, Yale, and Princeton, 1900–1970* (Westport, CT: Greenwood Press, 1979), 208.

7 Hall interview; Wilson interview.

8 Wilson, "Afro-American Studies," 43.

9 Wilson interview.

10 William Cross Jr., "The Negro-To-Black Conversion Experience," *Black World* 20, no. 9 (1971): 13–27.

11 That phrase came from the contents and information page of *Liberator* IV (1964).

12 Hall interview.

13 Robert L. Hall, "SNCC's Call to Northern Black Students," *Harvard Journal of Negro Affairs* 2 (November 1968): 36.

14 Thulani Davis, interview by author, notes, November 6, 2016. Hereafter, Davis interview.

15 Hall, "SNCC's Call to Northern Black Students," 38; Charles J. Hamilton Jr., "SNCC: Brass Tacks," *Harvard Crimson*, May 4, 1968, www.thecrimson.com, accessed November 6, 2016.

16 Davis interview.

17 Griffin v. County School Board of Prince Edward County (1964), 377 U.S. 218.

18 Hamilton, "SNCC."

19 Hall interview; Seth Lipsky, "The Harvard Journal of Negro Affairs," *Harvard Crimson*, May 29, 1968, www.thecrimson.com, accessed November 6, 2016.

20 Hall interview.

21 Robert L. Hall, interview by author, email, March 26, 2017. Hereafter, Hall interview II.

22 Lawrence E. Eichel et al., *The Harvard Strike* (Boston: Houghton, 1970), 35–45.

23 Ibid.

24 "A Justified Demonstration," *Harvard Crimson*, October 26, 1967, www.thecrimson.com, accessed November 6, 2016.

25 Ibid.

26 Quoted in Eichel, *Harvard Strike*, 43–44.

27 Nathan M. Pusey, "Statement of President Nathan M. Pusey, News Office, Harvard University, April 11, 1969, Harvard University Archives.

28 "A Reply to Pusey," Harvard University Archives.

29 Eichel, *Harvard Strike*, 23.

30 For more information about the controversies regarding Harvard and housing in Cambridge, see Richard Sobel, *The Politics of Joint University and Community*

Housing Development: Cambridge, Boston, and Beyond (New York: Lexington Books, 2014), 57–68.

31 "A Reply to Pusey," Harvard University Archives.

32 Eichel, *Harvard Strike*, 66.

33 "Wilson's Report Harvard Can't Ignore the City," *Harvard Crimson*, June 12, 1969, www.thecrimson.com, accessed November 6, 2016.

34 Hall interview II.

35 Wilson, "Afro-American Studies," in *Department of Afro-American Studies, Harvard University*, 46.

36 Ibid., 41.

37 "Kilson Says Black Power Meaningless," *Harvard Crimson*, November 2, 1967, 1.

38 Wilson interview.

39 Wilson interview; Hall interview.

40 Wilson interview.

41 "Report of the Faculty Committee on African and Afro-American Studies," January 20, 1969, HUF 124.569.

42 "Report of the Faculty Committee on African and Afro-American Studies," January 20, 1969, HUF 124.569; "Afro-American Studies," Press Release, January 22, 1969, HUF 124.2, Harvard University Archives; "CEP Accepts Black Studies Degree; Virtually All Student Demands Met," *Harvard Crimson*, January 16, 1969, www.thecrimson.com, accessed November 6, 2016.

43 Wilson, "Afro-American Studies," 46.

44 "Report of the Faculty Committee on African and Afro-American Studies," January 20, 1969, HUF 124.569, Harvard University Archives.

45 Wilson, "Afro-American Studies," 42.

46 "Report of the Faculty Committee on African and Afro-American Studies," January 20, 1969, HUF 124.569; "Afro-American Studies," Press Release, January 22, 1969, HUF 124.2, Harvard University Archives.

47 "Report of the Faculty Committee on African and Afro-American Studies," January 20, 1969, HUF 124.569, Harvard University Archives.

48 "Tentative Proposal for Concentration in Afro-American Studies," April 14, 1969, HUF 124.2, Harvard University Archives.

49 Letter to the Faculty of Arts and Sciences from Association of African and Afro-American Students, April 21, 1969, HUF 124.2, Harvard University Archives.

50 "Tentative Proposal for Concentration in Afro-American Studies," April 14, 1969, HUF 124.2, Harvard University Archives; Letter to the Faculty of Arts and Sciences from Association of African and Afro-American Students, April 21, 1969, HUF 124.2, Harvard University Archives.

51 Letter to the Faculty of Arts and Sciences from Association of African and Afro-American Students, April 21, 1969, HUF 124.2, Harvard University Archives.

52 Henry Rosovsky, "Black Studies at Harvard: Personal Reflections Concerning Recent Events" *American Scholar* 38, no. 4 (1969): 569.

53 Jon Wiener, "Harvard Strike 40th Anniversary," *The Nation*, May 18, 2009, www.thenation.com, accessed November 6, 2016.

54 Jean Engelmayer and Melissa Weissberg, "Reflecting on the 1969 Student Strike," *Harvard Crimson*, April 9, 1984, www.thecrimson.com, accessed November 6, 2016.

55 Pusey, "Statement of Nathan M. Pusey," April 11, 1969.

56 Engelmayer and Weissberg, "Reflecting on the 1969 Student Strike," April 9, 1984.

57 Eichel, *Harvard Strike*, 175.

58 Ibid., 139.

59 "The Fist and Its Clencher," *Harvard Magazine*, July 1998, www.harvardmagazine.com, accessed November 6, 2016.

60 "AAAAS Position Paper," Harvard University Archives.

61 Ibid.

62 Ibid.

63 Rosovsky, "Black Studies at Harvard," 571.

64 Ibram Rogers, *The Black Campus Movement: Black Students and the Racial Reconstitution of Higher Education, 1965–1972* (New York: Palgrave Macmillan, 2012), 2.

65 Rosovsky, "Black Studies at Harvard," 571.

66 Ibid.

67 Stanley Hoffman et al., "Dear Sirs," Harvard University Archives.

68 Rosovsky, "Black Studies at Harvard," 562.

69 Ibid., 563.

70 Ibid., 568.

71 Israel Shenker, "Harvard Faculty Members Divided on Student Protests and Their Meaning," *New York Times*, April 25, 1969, 28.

72 Ibid.

73 "A Progress Report of the Standing Committee to Develop the Afro-American Studies Department," September 22, 1969, HUF 124.569.2, Harvard University Archives.

74 Ibid.

75 Norman Scott, "A Progress Report on Black Studies," *Boston Globe*, September 1, 1972, 18.

76 Harvard-Radcliffe AAAAS, "Whereas the Administration of Harvard University," November 18, 1969, Harvard University Archives.

77 "Checking Out the Blatantly Racist Employment Practices of Harvard University," Harvard University Archives.

78 L. Gard Wiggins to L. F. Griffin, November 19, 1969, Harvard University Archives.

79 Archibald Cox to Philip Lee, November 30, 1969, Harvard University Archives.

80 "Statement by Harvard University Regarding Discussions with the Organization of Black Unity," December 2, 1969, Harvard University Archives.

81 "Factual Report to the Harvard Community," December 15, 1969, Harvard University Archives.

82 Organization of Black Unity, "Press Release," December 11, 1969, Harvard University Archives.
83 "Factual Report to the Harvard Community," December 15, 1969, Harvard University Archives; "Excerpt from Temporary Restraining Order Issued by the Superior Court for the County of Middlesex," Harvard University Archives.
84 Association of Black Faculty Members, Fellows, and Administrators, circa December 15, 1969, Harvard University Archives.

CHAPTER 9. AFRICANA AMBITIONS

1 Thomas W. Jones, "Reflections on the Sixties and Nineties," speech delivered at Cornell University, April 19, 1994, Cornell University Archives.
2 "College and School Notes," *The Crisis*, March 1966, 179; George Lowery, "A Campus Takeover That Symbolized an Era of Change," *Cornell Chronicle*, April 16, 2009, www.news.cornell.edu, accessed November 6, 2016.
3 Robert L. Hall, personal memoirs, unpublished.
4 James A. Perkins, "A Paper Presented to the Tower Club of Cornell University," May 14, 1969, Cornell '69 file, 14/17/1821, folder 3, box 1, Rare and Manuscript Collection, Carl A. Kroch Library, Cornell University.
5 See Laura W. Hill and Julia Rabig, eds., *The Business of Black Power: Community Development, Capitalism, and Corporate Responsibility in Postwar America* (Rochester, NY: University of Rochester Press, 2012), 45–54.
6 Stefan Bradley, *Harlem vs. Columbia University: Black Student Power in the Late 1960s* (Champaign: University of Illinois Press, 2009), 145–146; Donald Downs, *Cornell '69: Liberalism and the Crisis of the American University* (Ithaca, NY: Cornell University Press, 1999), 3–4; John Leo, "Cornell is Seeking Nation's Best Negro Scholars," *New York Times*, October 29, 1968, 44.
7 Downs, *Cornell '69*, 54.
8 Gloria Joseph, "Dr. Gloria Joseph, PhD '67: COSEP Anniversary," November 13, 2014, youtube.com, accessed November 6, 2016.
9 Cleveland Donald, "Cornell: Confrontation in Black and White," in *Divided We Stand: Reflections on the Crisis at Cornell*, eds. Cushing Strout and David I. Grossvogel (New York: Doubleday, 1970), 165–166; Williamson, *Black Power on Campus: The University of Illinois, 1965–1975* (Champaign: University of Illinois Press, 2003), 30; Downs, *Cornell '69*, 57.
10 Donald, "Cornell: Confrontation in Black and White," 167–168.
11 Wilson interview; Donald, "Cornell: Confrontation in Black and White," 156–157.
12 Donald, "Cornell: Confrontation in Black and White," 157.
13 "Chronology: Spring 1968," Cornell '69 file, 14/17/1821, folder 5, box 1, Division of Rare and Manuscript Collection, Carl A. Kroch Library, Cornell University.
14 Cushing Strout and David I. Grossvogel, eds., *Divided We Stand: Reflections on the Crisis at Cornell* (New York: Doubleday, 1971), 7–9.
15 Ibid.

16 Daniel P. Moynihan, *The Negro Family: A Case for National Action* (Washington, DC: Office of Policy Planning and Research, U.S. Department of Labor, 1965).

17 Strout and Grossvogel, *Divided We Stand*, 7–9.

18 Downs, *Cornell '69*, 78–79.

19 "Chronology: Spring 1968," Cornell '69 file, 14/17/1821, folder 5, box 1, Division of Rare and Manuscript Collection, Carl A. Kroch Library, Cornell University.

20 Ibid.

21 Ibid.

22 Press Release, October 11, 1968, Cornell '69 file, 53/21/2745, folder AASP Miscellaneous, box 1, Division of Rare and Manuscript Collection, Carl A. Kroch Library, Cornell University.

23 "Chronology: Spring 1968," Cornell '69 file, 14/17/1821, folder 5, box 1, Division of Rare and Manuscript Collection, Carl A. Kroch Library, Cornell University; Downs, *Cornell '69*, 106–107.

24 For more information on Turner's activism as a student and scholar, see Jonathan Fenderson, "'Committed to Institution Building': James Turner and the History of Africana Studies at Cornell University, an Interview," *Journal of African American Studies* 16, no. 1 (2012): 121–167.

25 Strout and Grossvogel, *Divided We Stand*, 2.

26 Tom Jones, "Willard Straight Hall Speech," June 29, 1969, Division and Rare Manuscript Collection, Carl A. Kroch Library, Cornell University; Chronology: Spring 1968," Cornell '69 file, 14/17/1821, folder 5, box 1, Division of Rare and Manuscript Collection, Carl A. Kroch Library, Cornell University.

27 Afro-American Society to James A. Perkins, December 12, 1968, Cornell '69 file, 53/21/2745, box 1, Division of Rare and Manuscript Collection, Carl A. Kroch Library, Cornell University.

28 Ibid.

29 "Afro-American Studies at a White University—The AASP at Cornell," AASP folder, 53/21/2745, box 1, Rare and Manuscript Collection, Carl A. Kroch Library, Cornell University.

30 James A. Perkins, "An Agreement with Respect to the Future of the Afro-American Studies Program," December 11, 1968, Cornell '69 file, 53/21/2745, box 1, Division of Rare and Manuscript Collection, Carl A. Kroch Library, Cornell University.

31 "Chronology: Spring 1968," Cornell '69 file, 14/17/1821, folder 5, box 1, Division of Rare and Manuscript Collection, Carl A. Kroch Library, Cornell University.

32 "Afro-American Studies at Cornell: Information on Potential Teachers and Courses as of 12/16/68," Cornell '69 file, 53/21/2745, box 1.

33 Quoted in Downs, *Cornell '69*, 166.

34 Downs, *Cornell '69*, 161–162.

35 Ibid., 172–173.

36 Donald, "Cornell: Confrontation in Black and White," 182.

37 Quoted in Downs, *Cornell '69*, 174.

38   In an address to the alumni after the takeover, Vice President for Public Affairs
     Steven Muller explained that even university officials had heard the rumors about
     potential white armed invaders coming to campus. "Statement to the Alumni,"
     Cornell Alumni News, June 1969, 35.
39   Stephanie Dunn, *"Baad Bitches" and Sassy Supermamas: Black Power Action Films*
     (Champaign: University of Illinois Press, 2008), 39.
40   Donald, "Cornell: Confrontation in Black and White," 139–142, 149, and
     160–161.
41   For an insightful discussion regarding black self-defense, see Akinyele O. Umoja,
     We Will Shoot Back: Armed Resistance in the Mississippi Freedom Movement (New
     York: New York University Press, 2013); Charles E. Cobb Jr., *This Nonviolent
     Stuff'll Get You Killed: How Guns Made the Civil Rights Movement Possible* (New
     York: Basic Books, 2014); Robert F. Williams, *Negroes with Guns* (Detroit: Wayne
     State University Press, 1962); Timothy B. Tyson, *Radio free Dixie: Robert F. Wil-
     liams and the Roots of Black Power* (Durham, NC: Duke University Press, 1994);
     Donna Murch, *Living for the City: Migration, Education, and the Rise of the Black
     Panther Party in Oakland, California* (Chapel Hill: University of North Carolina
     Press, 2010).
42   Martin Kilson, "Black Power: Anatomy of a Paradox," in *Harvard Journal of Negro
     Affairs* 2 (November 1968): 32.
43   Donald, "Cornell: Confrontation in Black and White," 182.
44   Charles Frankel, *Education and the Barricades* (New York: W. W. Norton, 1970),
     18–19.
45   "A Statement by James A. Perkins, President of Cornell University," April 28, 1969,
     Cornell '69 file, 37/5/3049 K-115-I-2-C, box 1, Rare and Manuscript Collection,
     Carl A. Kroch Library, Cornell University.
46   Ibid.
47   Ibid.
48   Office of President, "Collection of Firearms," April 25, 1969, Cornell '69 file,
     37/5/3029 K-115-I-2-C, box 1, Rare and Manuscript Collection, Carl A. Kroch
     Library, Cornell University.
49   "Statement of the Cornell Community of Anthropologists," April 26, 1969, Cor-
     nell '69 file, 37/5/3049 K-115-I-2-C, box 1, Rare and Manuscript Collection, Carl A.
     Kroch Library, Cornell University .
50   "Some Professors Fight Back," *Cornell Alumni News*, June 1969, 26.
51   Ibid., 27.
52   "Pressure and Vote," *Cornell Alumni News*, June 1969, 21.
53   "Some Professors Fight Back," 28.
54   "Pressure and Vote," 22.
55   Original emphasis. "An Effort to Settle," *Cornell Alumni News*, June 1969, 19.
56   "Some Professors Fight Back," 27.
57   P.M.G, "Perkins Must Go," Cornell '69 file, 37/5/3049 K-115-I-2-C.
58   "Blood Free Campus," *Cornell Alumni News*, June 1969, 30.

59 James Turner, "An Approach to Black Studies: Concept and Plan of the Africana Studies and Research Center at Cornell University," 14/17/1821, folder 4, box 1, Rare and Manuscript Collection, Carl A. Kroch Library, Cornell University.

60 James Turner, *The Next Decade* (Ithaca, NY: Africana Studies and Research Center, 1984), 31.

61 For a thorough treatment of the Institute for the Black World, see Derrick A. White, *The Challenge of Blackness: Institute of the Black World* (Gainesville: University Press of Florida, 2011); Peniel E. Joseph, "Dashikis and Democracy: Black Studies, Student Activism, and the Black Power Movement," *Journal of African American History* 88, no. 2 (2003): 193–194.

62 Vincent Harding, "Vocation of the Black Scholar and the Struggles of the Black Community," in *Education and Black Struggle: Notes from the Colonized World*, ed. Institute of the Black World (Cambridge, MA: Harvard Educational Review, 1974), 16.

63 James Turner, "An Approach to Black Studies: Concept and Plan of the Africana Studies and Research Center at Cornell University," 14/17/1821, folder 4, box 1, Rare and Manuscript Collection, Carl A. Kroch Library, Cornell University.

64 See "Yale's Black Studies Said to Founder," *New York Times*, December 11, 1989, B3.

65 Robert L. Harris Jr., "In Memoriam: Dr. John Henrik Clarke," *Journal of Negro History* 83 (Autumn, 1998): 311.

66 Downs, *Cornell '69*, 65.

67 James Turner, "Student Perspective: Black Students and Their Changing Perspective," *Ebony*, August 1969, 137.

68 Alex Poinsett, "The Plight of Black Studies," *Ebony*, December 1973, 128–129.

CONCLUSION

1 Charles Frankel, *Education and the Barricades* (New York: W. W. Norton, 1970), 12.

2 James A. Perkins, "A Paper Presented to the Tower Club of Cornell University," Cornell '69 file, 14/17/1821, folder 3, box 1, Rare and Manuscript Collection, Carl A. Kroch Library, Cornell University.

3 "Manual for Student Strikes," Harvard University Student Strike, 1969, General File 969.100, Harvard University Archives.

4 Alex Poinsett, "The Plight of Black Studies," *Ebony*, December 1973, 130.

5 Peniel E. Joseph, "Dashikis and Democracy: Black Studies, Student Activism, and the Black Power Movement," *Journal of African American History* 88, no. 2 (Spring 2003): 182.

6 Mark Christian, "Black Studies in the 21st Century: Longevity Has Its Place," *Journal of Black Studies* 36, no. 5 (2006): 698–719.

7 Will Oremus, "Did Obama Hug a Radical: What's 'Critical Race Theory,' And How Crazy Is It?," *Slate*, March 9, 2012, www.slate.com, accessed November 6, 2016; Dorian L. McCoy and Dirk J. Rodricks, "Critical Race Theory in Higher Education: 20 Years of Theoretical and Research Innovations," *ASHE Higher Education Report* 41, no. 3 (2015): 5–10 and 18–31.

8 Carl A. Fields to Mr. Lawrence T. Ellis, Sr., September 15, 1983, box 16, "Correspondence," Carl A. Fields Papers, Seely Mudd Library, Princeton University.

9 Randall M. Jelks, Facebook post, January 4, 2017.

10 "Black First-Year Students at Nation's Leading Research Universities," JBHE Annual Survey 2014, *Journal of Blacks in Higher Education* (December 31, 2014), jbhe .com.

BIBLIOGRAPHY

ARCHIVES AND MANUSCRIPTS
Brown University Archives, John Hay Library
 Afro-American Studies: Courses and Material, 1970–1971
 Afro-American Studies: Rites and Reason Records, 1970–2006
 Papers of Charles H. Nichols, 1953–1990
 Papers of Ray Lorenzo Heffner, 1966–1969
Columbia University Archives, Rare Book and Manuscript Library
 Buildings and Grounds Collection
 Double Discovery Center Records
 Morningside Heights Incorporated Project Files
 Protests and Activism Collection
Cornell University Archives, Division of Rare and Manuscript Collections, Carl A.
 Kroch Library
 Alpha Phi Alpha Exhibition
 Cornell '69 File
 Papers of James A. Perkins, 1963–1969
Dartmouth College Archives, Rauner Special Collections Library
 Oral History Collection
 Papers of Errol G. Hill
 Papers of the Presidential Committee on Civil Rights 1946–1947
Harvard University Archives
 Nathan Marsh Pusey Library
 Abbott Lawrence Lowell Papers
 Widener Library
 Harvard University Strike Posters Collection, 1969
 Material on the 1969 Student Strike, 1969
 Papers of Abbott Lawrence Lowell
 Student Strike, 1969
Princeton University Archives
 Minorities at Princeton Series
 Papers of Carl A. Fields
 Robert Goheen Papers
University Archives and Records Center, University of Pennsylvania
 Papers of Gaylord P. Harnwell
 Papers of Robert F. Engs

Student Demonstrations—Sit-in at College Hall 1969 (II)
Trustees Minutes, 1957
University News Bureau, Student Demonstration—Sit-in at College Hall
Yale University Archives
Papers of Charles T. Davis
Records of Kingman Brewster, 1941–1983
Records of the Office of the President Concerning the May Day Rally

INTERVIEWS

Austin, Ralph. Interview by Brandon Holt. February 19, 2015. Tape recording, Seeley G. Mudd Manuscript Library, Princeton University.

Crew, Spencer. Interview by author. April 25, 2014. Tape recording.

Davis, Thulani. Interview by author. November 6, 2016.

Dodds, R. Harcourt. Interview by Chris Burns. May 19–20, 2001. Oral History Collection, Rauner Special Collections, Dartmouth College, Hanover, NH.

Early, Gerald L. Interview by author. June 30, 2015. Digital recording.

Ford Wallace, II. Interview by author. May 9, 2012.

Hall, Robert, Jr. Interview by author. October 20, 2016. Email.

Hastie, William H. Interview by Jerry N. Hess. January 5, 1972. Transcript. Philadelphia, Pennsylvania.

Henry, Brent. Interview by Brendan Holt. March 16, 2015. Tape recording. Seeley G. Mudd Manuscript Library, Princeton University.

Horne, Gerald. Interview by author. January 23, 2010. Email.

Lee, Woody. Interview by author. February 7, 2013.

Lord, Philip. Interview by author. June 17, 2013. Tape recording.

Marcus, Vera, Interview by Brenda Tindal, March 2012, Tape recording, Seeley G. Mudd Manuscript Library, Princeton University.

Perkins, James A. Interview by Keith R. Johnson. 1994. Archive 47-8-2795, Kroch Library Rare Books and Manuscripts, Cornell University Archives, Ithaca, NY.

Wilson Ernest, III. Interview by author. October 28, 2016.,

X, Malcolm. Interview by Ken Sharpe. January 26, 1965. WDCR Radio, Dartmouth College, Hanover, NH.

GOVERNMENT DOCUMENTS

Griffin v. County School Board of Prince Edward County (1964), 377 U.S. 218.

Morgan v. Commonwealth and *Shelley v. Kraemer*.

New Jersey State Constitution. www.njleg.state.nj.us, accessed November 6, 2016.

U.S. Census of Population and Housing, 1970: General Demographic Trends for Metropolitan Areas, 1960–1970: New Hampshire. Washington, DC: Government Printing Office, 1971.

NEWSPAPERS

Bergen County Record, 1965
Boston Globe, 1969

Brown Daily Herald, 1965–1971
Chicago Daily Defender, 1967–1969
Chicago Sun Times, 1969
Columbia Daily Spectator, 1954–1974
Cornell Chronicle, 2009
Daily Princetonian, 1941–1977
The Dartmouth, 1945–1975
Evening Bulletin (Philadelphia), 1968
Evening Times (Trenton), 1968
The Harvard Crimson, 1963–1970
The Martha's Vineyard Times, 2008
Nashville American, 1876
New York Daily News, 1966–1969
New York Post, 1968
New York Times, 1954–2017
Newark Herald, 1955
Philadelphia Inquirer, 1968–1971
Philadelphia Tribune, 1968–1971
Providence Journal, 1968–1969
Providence Sunday Journal, 1968
Trentonian, 1969
The Valley News (New Hampshire), 1969
West Side News and Morningsider, 1965
The Westerly Sun (Rhode Island), 1969
Yale Daily News, 1963–1971

MAGAZINES
Atlantic Monthly
Columbia College Today
Dartmouth Alumni Magazine
Ebony
Harvard Magazine
Jet
Life
The Nation
Negro Digest
Princeton Alumni Weekly
Organization of American Historians Magazine
Scientific Research
The Sphinx
Uwezo
Yale Alumni Magazine

FILMS / DOCUMENTARIES

Coker, 'Niyi, dir. *Black Studies USA*. Birmingham, AL: Coker, 2005.

Joseph, Gloria. *Dr. Gloria Joseph, PhD '67: COSEP Anniversary*. youtube.com. November 13, 2014.

McCray, Melvin. *Looking Back: Reflections of Black Princeton Alumni*. 1997. YouTube video. youtube.com, accessed November 6, 2016.

———. *Looking Forward: Reflections of Black Princeton Alumni*. Documentary video. 2006. http://alumni.princeton.edu.

Tibaldo-Bongiorno, Marylou. *Revolution '67*. Bongiorno Productions, 2007.

WEBSITES AND WEB PAGES

"About Fritz Pollard." Brown's Early African-American Alumni. http://dl.lib.brown.edu (accessed October 3, 2015).

"African Americans and Princeton University: A Brief History." http://www.princeton .edu (accessed November 6, 2016).

"Brown's Early African-American Alumni." Center for Digital Scholarship. http://dl.lib .brown.edu (accessed October 3, 2015).

"Conservative Vice Lords, Inc." Chicago Crime Scenes Project. http://chicagocrimes-cenes.blogspot.com (accessed June 21, 2011).

Crawford, E. J. "Profiles from the Ivy League's Black History." www.ivy50.com (accessed June 21, 2011).

"Ethel Robinson." Third World History at Brown." www.brown.edu (accessed October 3, 2015).

"Ford, Wallace L., II. "Contemporary Black Biography, 2007." www.encyclopedia.com (accessed May 8, 2012).

"Jerome H. (Brud) Holland." Cornell Hall of Fame. www.cornellbigred.com (accessed November 18, 2016).

Leitsch, Alexander. "Norman Thomas." *A Princeton Companion* (Princeton, 1978). http://etcweb.princeton.edu (accessed January 12, 2011).

Marcus Garvey: Look for Me in the Whirlwind. PBS American Experience, transcript. www.pbs.org (accessed November 6, 2016).

Mitchell, Martha. "Afro-American Studies," *Encyclopedia Brunonia*, www.brown.edu (accessed October 19, 2015).

Port Huron Statement. http://www.sds-1960s.org/PortHuronStatement-draft.htm (accessed March 17, 2018)."Ralph John Reiman '35." http://paw.princeton.edu (accessed January 27, 2011).

Reinstein, Gila. "African-American Studies Revisits Origins, Imagines Future." *Yale Bulletin and Calendar* 30, no. 29 (May 10, 2002). http://archives.news.yale.edu.

"Richard A. Lester Dies at 89; Influential Economist and Dean of the Faculty at Princeton University." December 31, 1997. Princeton University Office of Communications, www.princeton.edu (accessed July 2, 2016).

"Slavery at Princeton." www.princeton.edu (accessed November 6, 2009).

"Slavery, the Brown Family of Providence, and Brown University," Brown University News Service. http://web.archive.org (accessed October 3, 2015).

Stern, Gary M. "The Colleges That Ate New York." https://commercialobserver.com, January 21, 2015.

"Third World History at Brown." Brown Center for Students of Color. www.brown.edu (accessed October 3, 2015).

"Two and a Half Centuries of Learning." Brown University. www.brown.edu (accessed October 3, 2015).

Wesley, Charles H. "History of Sigma Pi Phi: First of the Negro-American Greek-Letter Fraternities." Washington, D.C.: Association for the Study of Negro Life and History, 1954. www.sigmapiphi.org.

"The Wheelock Succession of Presidents." www.dartmouth.edu (accessed June 21, 2011).

UNPUBLISHED MANUSCRIPTS

Carter, Samantha. "Harlem." In No Mask 1968, XX–XX. New York: Project Double Discovery, 1968, Columbia University Rare Book and Manuscripts, Columbia University.

Cohen, Scott. "Urban Renewal in West Philadelphia: An Examination of the University of Pennsylvania's Planning, Expansion, and Community Role from the Mid-1940s to the Mid-1970s." Senior thesis, University of Pennsylvania, 1998.

Robinson, Michelle L. "Princeton-Educated Blacks and the Black Community." Undergraduate thesis, Princeton University, 1985. www.politico.com.

JOURNAL ARTICLES

Abdul-Alim, Jamal. "Affirmative Action Argument by University of Texas Draws Praise, Invites Criticism." Diverse Issues (August 8, 2012).

Anderson, Elijah. "The Iconic Ghetto." Annals of the American Academy of Political and Social Science 642 (November 2013): 8–24.

Austin, C. C., E. M. Clark, M. J. Ross, and M. J. Taylor. "Impostorism as a Mediator between Survivor Guilt and Depression in a Sample of African American College Students." College Student Journal 43 (2009): 1094–1109.

Baldwin, Davarian. "The '800-Pound Gargoyle': The Long History of Higher Education and Urban Development on Chicago's South Side." American Quarterly 67, no. 1 (2015): 81–103.

Bradley, Stefan. "The Southern-Most Ivy: Princeton University from Jim Crow Admissions to Anti-Apartheid Protests, 1794–1969." American Studies 51, no. 3/4 (2010): 109–130.

Christian, Mark. "Black Studies in the 21st Century: Longevity Has Its Place." Journal of Black Studies 36, no. 5 (2006): 698–719.

Cross, William, Jr. "The Negro-To-Black Conversion Experience." Black World 20, no. 9 (1971): 13–27.

Culverson, Donald. "The Politics of the Anti-Apartheid Movement in the United
States, 1969-1986." *Political Science Quarterly* 111, no. 1 (1996): 127–149.

Delmont, Matt. "Making Philadelphia Safe for 'WFIL-adelpia': Television, Housing,
and Defensive Localism in Postwar Philadelphia." *Journal of Urban History* 38, no. 1
(2012): 89–113.

Evans, Art. "Joe Louis as a Key Functionary: White Reactions toward a Black Champion." *Journal of Black Studies* 16, no. 1 (1985): 95–111.

Ewing, Kimberly, Tina Q. Richardson, Linda James-Myers, and Richard K. Russell.
"The Relationship between Racial Identity Attitudes, Worldview, and African
American Graduate Students' Experience of the Imposter Phenomenon." *Journal of
Black Psychology* 22, no. 1 (1996): 53–66.

Fenderson, Jonathan. "'Committed to Institution Building': James Turner and the
History of Africana Studies at Cornell University, an Interview." *Journal of African
American Studies* 16, no. 1 (2012): 121–167.

Fields, Carl. "One University's Response to Today's Negro Student." *University: A
Princeton Quarterly* no. 36 (Spring 1968): 14.

Franklin, John Hope. "Their War and Mine." *Journal of American History* 77, no. 2
(1990): 576–579.

Hackney, Sheldon. "The University and Its Community: Past and Present." *Annals of
the American Academy*, 488 (November 1986): 137–145.

Hall, Robert L. "SNCC's Call to Northern Black Students." *Harvard Journal of Negro
Affairs* 2 (November 1968): 36–38.

Harkavy, Ira, and John Puckett. "Lessons from Hull House for the Contemporary
Urban University." *Social Science Review* 68 (Sept. 1994): 299–321.

Harleston, Bernard W. "Higher Education for the Negro." *Atlantic Monthly* 216, no. 5
(1965): 139–143.

Harris, Robert L., Jr. "In Memoriam: Dr. John Henrik Clarke." *Journal of Negro History*
83 (Autumn 1998): 311.

Hauper, Shaun. "Niggers No More: A Critical Race Counternarrative on Black Male
Achievement at Predominantly White Colleges and Universities." *International
Journal of Qualitative Studies in Education* 6 (Nov–Dec 2009): 697–712.

"JBHE Chronology of Major Landmarks in the Progress of African Americans in
Higher Education." *Journal of Blacks in Higher Education* 53 (Autumn 2006): 77.

Joseph, Peniel E. "Dashikis and Democracy: Black Studies, Student Activism, and the
Black Power Movement." *Journal of African American History* 88, no. 2 (Spring
2003): 182–203.

Kilson, Martin. "Anatomy of the Black Studies Movement." *Massachusetts Review* 10,
no. 4 (1969): 718–725.

———. "Black Militancy on Campus: Negro Separatism and the Colleges." *Harvard
Today* (Spring 1968): 30–33.

Kuh, George D. "The Other Curriculum: Out-of-Class Experiences Associated with
Student Learning and Personal Development." *Journal of Higher Education* 66, no. 2
(1995) 123–127.

Lancaster, F. W., and Lorraine Haricombe. "The Academic Boycott of South Africa: Symbolic Gesture or Effective Agent of Change?" *Perspectives on the Professions* 15, no. 1 (1995).

Lige, Queira M., Bridgette J. Peteet, and Carrie M. Brown. "Racial Identity, Self-Esteem, and the Impostor Phenomenon among African American College Students." *Journal of Black Psychology* 43, no. 4 (2017): 1–13.

Mankoff, Milton, and Richard Flacks. "The Changing Base of the American Student Movement." *Annals of the American Academy of Political and Social Science* 395 (May 1971): 54–67.

McCoy, Dorian L., and Dirk J. Rodricks. "Critical Race Theory in Higher Education: 20 Years of Theoretical and Research Innovations." *ASHE Higher Education Report* 41, no. 3 (2015): 1–117.

Perkins, Linda. "The First Black Talent Identification Program: The National Scholarship and Service Fund for Negro Students, 1947–1968." *Perspectives on the History of Higher Education* 29 (December 2012): 173–197.

Peteet, B., Brown, C., Lige, Q., and Lannaway, D. "Imposterism is Associated with Greater Psychological Distress and Lower Self-Esteem for African American Students." *Current Psychology* 34 (2015): 154–163.

Porter, Dorothy. "The Organized Educational Activities of Negro Literary Societies, 1828–1846." *Journal of Negro Education* 5, no. 4 (1936): 555–576.

Purnell, Brian. "'Taxation without Sanitation Is Tyranny': Brooklyn CORE Dumps Racial Discrimination on the Steps of Borough Hall." *Afro-Americans in New York Life and History* 31 (July 2007): 61–88. http://www.nyc.gov/html/cchr/justice/down loads/pdf/taxation_without_sanitation_is_tyranny.pdf.

Richards, Phillip M. "Black and Blue in New Haven: Memoirs of an African American at Yale in the late 1960s." *Journal of Blacks in Higher Education* 51 (Spring 2006): 67.

Robinson, Henry. "The M Street School, 1891–1916." *Records of the Columbia Historical Society* 51 (1984): 119–143.

Rogers, Ibram. "The Marginalization of the Black Campus Movement." *Journal of Social History* 42, no. 1 (2008): 175–182.

Rosovsky, Henry. "Black Studies at Harvard: Personal Reflections Concerning Recent Events." *American Scholar* 38, no. 4 (1969): 562–572.

Sugrue, Thomas. "Affirmative Action from Below: Civil Rights, the Building Trades, and the Politics of Racial Equality in the Urban North, 1945–1969." *Journal of American History* 91 (June 2004): 145–173.

Taylor, Ula Y. "Introduction: The Shaping of an Activist and Scholar." *Journal of African American History* 96, no. 2 (2011): 204–214.

Terrell, Mary Church. "History of the High School for Negroes in Washington." *Journal of Negro History* 2, no. 3 (1917): 252–266.

Thelwell, Michael. "Directions in Black Studies: A Political Perspective." *Massachusetts Review* 10, no. 4 (1969): 701–712.

Weir, Margaret. "Urban Poverty and Defensive Localism." *Dissent* 41 (Summer 1994): 337–342.

Smith, William A., Walter Allen, and Lynette Danley. "Assume the Position . . . You Fit the Description: Psychosocial Experiences and Racial Battle Fatigue among African American Male College Students." *American Behavior Scientist* 51, no. 4 (2007): 551–578.

Wilson, Jane. "Universities Act on the Institute for Defense Analysis." *Bulletin of Atomic Scientists* (May 1968): 40.

Wright, Bobby. "For the Children of Infidels": American Indian Education in the Colonial Colleges." *American Indian Culture and Research Journal* 12, no. 3 (1998): 1–14.

BOOKS

Adams, Carolyn, David Bartelt, David Elesh, Ira Goldstein, Nancy Kleniewski, and William Yancey, eds. *Philadelphia: Neighborhoods, Division, and Conflict in a Post Industrial City.* Philadelphia: Temple University Press, 1991.

Adelson, Alan. *SDS: A Profile.* New York: Scribner, 1972.

Anderson, Carol E. *Eyes Off the Prize: The United Nations and the African American Struggle for Human Rights, 1944–1955.* Cambridge: Cambridge University Press, 2003.

Anderson, Matthew. *Presbyterianism: Its Relation to the Negro.* Philadelphia: J. M. White, 1897.

Askew, Glenn. *But for Birmingham: The Local and National Movements in the Civil Rights Struggle.* Chapel Hill: University of North Carolina Press, 1997.

Avorn, Jerry, ed. *Up Against the Ivy Wall: A History of the Columbia Crisis.* New York: Atheneum Press, 1968.

Axtell, James. *The Making of Princeton University: From Woodrow Wilson to the Present.* Princeton: Princeton University Press, 2006.

Baraka, Amiri. "Black People!" In *The LeRoi Jones/Amiri Baraka Reader*, edited by Amiri Baraka et al. New York: Basic Books, 1991.

Barber, David. *A Hard Rain Fell: SDS and Why It Failed.* Oxford: University Press of Mississippi, 2010.

Barbour, Floyd. *The Black Power Revolt: A Collection of Essays.* New York: Collier Books, 1968.

Barry, Jay. *Gentlemen Under the Elms.* Providence, RI: Brown Alumni Monthly, 1982.

Bass, Amy. *Not the Triumph but the Struggle: The 1968 Olympics and the Making of the Black Athlete.* Minneapolis: University of Minnesota Press, 2004.

Benson, Richard, II. *Fighting for Our Place in the Sun: Malcolm X and the Radicalization of the Student Movement, 1960–1973.* New York: Peter Lang, 2014.

Biondi, Martha. *The Black Revolution on Campus.* Berkeley: University of California Press, 2012.

———. *To Stand and Fight: The Struggle for Civil Rights in Postwar New York City.* Cambridge, MA: Harvard University Press, 2003.

Birmingham, Stephen. *Certain People: America's Black Elite.* Boston: Little Brown, 1977.

Bloom, Allan. *The Closing of the American Mind.* New York: Simon & Schuster, 1987.

Bradley, Stefan. "The First and the Finest: The Founders of Alpha Phi Alpha." In *Black Greek-Letter Organizations in the 21st Century: Our Fight Has Just Begun*, edited by Gregory S. Parks, 19–40. Lexington: University Press of Kentucky, 2008.

———. *Harlem vs. Columbia University: Black Student Power in the Late 1960s*. Champaign: University of Illinois Press, 2009.

———. "Progenitors of Progress: A Brief History of the Jewels of Alpha Phi Alpha." In *Alpha Phi Alpha: A Legacy of Greatness, The Demands of Transcendence*, edited by Gregory S. Parks, 67–92. Lexington: University Press of Kentucky, 2012.

Brown, Lloyd. *The Young Paul Robeson: On My Journey Now*. New York: Basic Books, 1998.

Brown, Scot. *Fighting for US: Maulana Karenga, the US Organization, and Black Cultural Nationalism*. New York: New York University Press, 2005.

Bryan, Arthur V. *The Mirror: A History of the Class of 1878, of Princeton College* (Princeton: printed by Charles S. Robinson, 1878).

Burstein, Paul. *Discrimination, Jobs, and Politics: The Struggle for Equal Employment Opportunity in the United States since the New Deal*. Chicago: University of Chicago Press, 1998.

Canton, David A. *Raymond Alexander Pace: A New Negro Lawyer Fights for Civil Rights in Philadelphia*. Oxford: University Press of Mississippi, 2010.

Carmichael, Stokely, and Charles Hamilton. *Black Power: The Politics of Liberation*. New York: Vintage Books, 1967.

Carnegie Commission on Higher Education. *Quality and Equality: New Levels of Federal Responsibility for Higher Education (A Special Report and Recommendations by the Commission)*. New York: McGraw-Hill, 1968.

Carroll, John. *Fritz Pollard: Pioneer in Racial Advancement*. Champaign: University of Illinois Press, 1992.

Carson, Clayborne. *In Struggle: SNCC and the Black Awakening of the 1960s*. Cambridge, MA: Harvard University Press, 1995.

Cobb, Charles E., Jr. *This Nonviolent Stuff'll Get You Killed: How Guns Made the Civil Rights Movement Possible*. New York: Basic Books, 2014.

Cohen, Robert. *Freedom's Orator: Mario Savio and the Radical Legacy of the 1960s*. New York: Oxford University Press, 2009.

Cohen, Robert, and David Snyder, eds. *Rebellion in Black and White: Southern Student Activism in the 1960s*. Baltimore: Johns Hopkins University Press, 2013.

Collier-Thomas, Bettye. *Jesus, Jobs, and Justice: African American Women and Religion*. New York: Alfred A. Knopf, 2010.

Countryman, Matthew. *Up South: Civil Rights and Black Power in Philadelphia*. Philadelphia: University of Pennsylvania Press, 2006.

Crawford, Vicky L., et al., eds. *Women in the Civil Rights Movement: Trailblazers and Torchbearers, 1941–1965*. Bloomington: University of Indiana Press, 1993.

Crenshaw, Kimberlé, Neil T. Gotanda, Gary Peller, and Kendall Thomas, eds. *Critical Race Theory: The Key Writings that Formed the Movement*. New York: New Press, 1995.

Crisis at Columbia: Report of the Fact-Finding Commission Appointed to Investigate the Disturbances at Columbia University in April and May 1968. New York: Vintage Books, 1968.

Cruse, Harold. *Crisis of the Negro Intellectual*. New York: Morrow Press, 1967.

Cumbler, John. *A Social History of Economic Decline: Business, Politics and Work in Trenton*. New Brunswick, NJ: Rutgers University Press, 1989.

Dalfiume, Richard. *Desegregation of the U.S. Armed Forces: Fighting on Two Fronts, 1939–1953*. Columbia: University of Missouri Press, 1969.

Dawley, David. *A Nation of Lords: The Autobiography of the Vice Lords*. Garden City: Waveland, 1973.

D'Emilio, John. *Lost Prophet: The Life and Times of Bayard Rustin*. Chicago: University of Chicago Press, 2004.

Delmont, Matthew. Nicest Kids in Town: American Bandstand, Rock 'n' Roll, and the Struggle for Civil Rights in the 1950s. Berkley: University of California Press, 2012.

Department of Afro-American Studies, Harvard University. *Department of Afro-American Studies, Harvard University: Thirtieth Anniversary Celebration*. North Andover, MA: Free Press, 2003.

Donald, Cleveland. "Cornell: Confrontation in Black and White." In *Divided We Stand: Reflections on the Crisis at Cornell*, edited by Cushing Strout and David I. Grossvogel, 139–182 New York: Doubleday, 1970.

Downs, Donald. *Cornell '69: Liberalism and the Crisis of the American University*. Ithaca, NY: Cornell University Press, 1999.

Du Bois, W.E.B. *The Autobiography of W.E.B. Du Bois: A Soliloquy on Viewing My Life from the Last Decade of Its First Century*. New York: International Publishers, 1968.

Edwards, Harry. *Revolt of the Black Athlete*. New York: Free Press, 1970.

Eichel, Lawrence, Kenneth Jost, Robert D. Luskin, and Richard M. Neustadt. *The Harvard Strike*. Boston: Houghton, 1970.

Etienne, Harvey. *Pushing Back the Gates: Neighborhood Perspectives on University-Driven Revitalization in West Philadelphia*. Philadelphia: Temple University Press, 2012.

Evans, Stephanie Y. *Black Women in the Ivory Tower, 1850–1954: An Intellectual History*. Gainesville: University Press of Florida, 2008.

Exum, William. *Paradoxes of Protest: Black Student Activism at a White University*. Philadelphia: Temple University Press, 1985.

Fanon, Frantz. *Wretched of the Earth*. New York: Grove Press, 1963.

Farmer, Ashley. Remaking Black Power: How Black Power Transformed an Era. Chapel Hills: University of North Carolina, 2017.

Fields, Carl. *Black in Two Worlds*. Princeton: Red Hummingbird Press, 2006.

Fine, Sidney. *Violence in the Model City: The Cavanaugh Administration, Race Relations, and the Detroit Riot of 1967*. Lansing: Michigan State University Press, 2007.

Fleming, Jacqueline. *Enhancing Minority Student Retention and Academic Performance: What We Can Learn from Program Evaluations*. New York: Wiley Press, 2012.

Fortner, Michael J. *Black Silent Majority: The Rockefeller Drug Laws and the Politics of Punishment.* Cambridge, MA: Harvard University Press, 2015.

Frankel, Charles. *Education and the Barricades.* New York: W. W. Norton, 1970.

Franklin, John Hope. *Mirror to America.* New York: Farrar, Straus, and Giroux, 2005.

Franklin, V. P., and Bettye Collier-Thomas. *Sisters in Struggle: African American Women in the Civil Rights Struggle.* New York: New York University Press, 2001.

Gaines, Kevin. *Uplifting the Race: Black Leadership, Politics, and Culture in the Twentieth Century.* Chapel Hill: University of North Carolina Press, 1996.

Gatewood, William, Jr. *Aristocrats of Color: The Black Elite, 1880–1920.* Fayetteville: University of Arkansas Press, 2000.

Georgakas, Dan, and Marvin Surkas. *Detroit: I Do Mind Dying.* Boston: South End Press, 1998.

Geschwender, James A. *Class, Race, and Worker Insurgency: The League of Revolutionary Black Workers.* New York: Cambridge University Press, 1977.

Giddings, Paula. *When and Where I Enter: The Impact of Black Women on Race and Sex in America.* New York: William Morrow, 1984.

Gilbert, David. *SDS/WUO, Students for a Democratic Society and the Weather Underground Organization.* Oakland, CA: Abraham Guillen Press/Arm the Spirit, 2002.

Glasker, Wayne. *Black Students in the Ivory Tower: African American Student Activism at the University of Pennsylvania, 1967–1990.* Amherst: University of Massachusetts Press, 2002.

Gore, Dayo F., Jeanne Theoharis, and Komozi Woodard, eds. *Want to Start a Revolution?: Radical Women in the Black Freedom Struggle.* New York: New York University Press, 2009.

Grant, Joanne. *Confrontation on Campus: The Columbia Pattern for the New Protest.* New York: Signet Books, 1969.

Harding, Vincent. *There Is a River: The Black Struggle for Freedom in America.* New York: Harcourt, 1981.

Hayden, Tom. *The Port Huron Statement: The Vision Call of the 1960s Revolution.* New York: Public Affairs, 2005.

———. *Rebel: A Personal History of the 1960s.* Pasadena, CA: ReadHowYouWant, 2003.

Hill, Laura W., and Julia Rabig, eds. *The Business of Black Power: Community Development, Capitalism, and Corporate Responsibility in Postwar America.* Rochester, NY: University of Rochester Press, 2012.

Hogan, Wesley C. *Many Minds, One Heart: SNCC's Dream for a New America.* Chapel Hill: University of North Carolina Press, 2007.

Holsaert, Faith, Martha Prescod Norman Noonan, Judy Richardson, Betty Garman Robinson, Jean Smith Young, and Dorothy M. Zellner, eds. *Hands on the Freedom Plow: Personal Accounts by Women in SNCC.* Champaign: University of Illinois Press, 2010.

Huntley, Horace, and John W. McKerley, eds. *Footsoldiers for Democracy: The Men, Women, and Children of the Birmingham Movement.* Champaign: University of Illinois Press, 2009.

Jeffries, Hassan. *Bloody Lowndes: Civil Rights and Black Power in Alabama's Black Belt*. New York: New York University Press, 2009.

Johnson, John H., III, ed. *Centennial Book of Essays and Letters: Excerpts from the Brotherhood of Alpha Phi Alpha Fraternity, Inc*. Baltimore: Foundation Publishers, 2006.

Joseph, Peniel. *Stokely: A Life*. New York: Basic Civitas, 2014.

———. *Waiting 'Til the Midnight Hour: A Narrative History of Black Power*. New York: Henry Holt, 2006.

Kabaservice, Geoffrey. *The Guardians: Kingman Brewster, His Circle, and the Liberal Establishment*. New York: Henry Holt, 2004.

Kahn, Roger. *The Battle for Morningside Heights: Why Students Rebel*. New York: William Morrow and Company, 1970.

Kalman, Laura. *Yale Law School and the Sixties: Revolt and Reverberations*. Chapel Hill: University of North Carolina Press, 2005.

Kammen, Carol. *Part and Apart: The Black Experience at Cornell, 1865–1945*. Ithaca: Cornell University Library, 2009.

Karabel, Jerome. *The Chosen: The Hidden History of Admission and Exclusion at Harvard, Yale, and Princeton*. Boston: Houghton Mifflin, 2005.

Keller, Morton, and Phyllis Keller. *Making Harvard Modern: The Rise of America's University*. New York: Oxford University Press, 2001.

Kersten, Andrew. *Race and War: The FEPC in the Midwest, 1941–1946*. Champaign: University of Illinois Press, 2000.

Kilson, Martin, C. Vann Woodward, Kenneth Clark, Thomas Sowell, Roy Wilkins, Andrew Brimmer, and Norman Hill. *Black Studies: Myths and Realities*. New York: A. Philip Randolph Foundation, 1969.

Lackey, Michael, ed. *The Haverford Discussions: A Black Integrationist Manifesto for Racial Justice*. Charlottesville: University of Virginia Press, 2013.

Lehmann, Nicholas. *The Big Test: The Secret History of the American Meritocracy*. New York: Farrar, Straus, and Giroux, 1999.

———. *Promised Land: The Great Migration and How It Changed America*. New York: Vintage, 1992.

Levenstein, Lisa. *A Movement without Marches: African American Women and the Politics of Poverty in Postwar Philadelphia*. Chapel Hill: University of North Carolina Press, 2009.

Lewis, David Levering. *W.E.B. Du Bois: Biography of a Race*. New York: Henry Holt, 1993.

Link, Arthur S., et al., eds. *The Papers of Woodrow Wilson*. 67 vols. Princeton: Princeton University, 1973.

Marable, Manning. *Malcolm X: A Life of Reinvention*. New York: Penguin Books, 2011.

Martin, Charles. *Benching Jim Crow: The Rise and Fall of the Color Line in Southern College Sports, 1890–1980*. Champaign: University of Illinois Press, 2010.

Mason, Henry "Skip." *The Talented Tenth: The Founders and Presidents of Alpha*. Winter Park, FL: Four G Publishers, 1999.

McCormick, Richard. *The Black Student Protest Movement at Rutgers*. New Brunswick, NJ: Rutgers University Press, 1990.

McHenry, Elizabeth. *Forgotten Readers: Recovering the Lost History of African American Literary Societies*. Durham, NC: Duke University Press, 2002.

McMillen, Neil, ed. *Remaking Dixie: The Impact of World War II on the American South*. Jackson: University Press of Mississippi, 1997.

McNeil, Genna Rae. *Groundwork: Charles Hamilton Houston and the Struggle for Civil Rights*. Philadelphia: University of Pennsylvania Press, 1984.

Menez, Joseph, and John R. Vile. *Summaries of the Leading Cases on the Constitution*. New York: Rowman and Littlefield, 2004.

Mollenkopf, John. *The Contested City*. Princeton: Princeton University Press, 1983.

Moody, Anne. *Coming of Age in Mississippi*. New York: Delta Trade Publishers, 1968.

Moore, Jacqueline. *Leading the Race: The Transformation of the Black Elite in the Nation's Capital, 1880–1920*. Charlottesville: University of Virginia Press, 1999.

Moore, Leonard. *Carl B. Stokes and the Rise of Black Political Power*. Champaign: University of Illinois Press, 2003.

Moynihan, Daniel P. *The Negro Family: A Case for National Action*. Washington, DC: Office of Policy Planning and Research, U.S. Department of Labor, 1965.

Mulder, John M. *Woodrow Wilson: The Years of Preparation*. Princeton: Princeton University Press, 1978.

Mumford, Kevin. *Newark: A History of Race, Rights, and Riots in America*. New York: New York University Press, 2008.

Murch, Donna. *Living for the City: Migration, Education, and the Rise of the Black Panther Party in Oakland, California*. Chapel Hill: University of North Carolina Press, 2010.

Naison, Mark. *White Boy: A Memoir*. Philadelphia: Temple University Press, 2002.

Nash, George. *The University and the City: Eight Cases of Involvement*. New York: McGraw-Hill, 1973.

National Advisory Commission on Civil Disorders. *Report of the National Advisory Commission on Civil Disorders*. New York: Bantam Books, 1968.

Nesbitt, Francis. *Race for Sanctions: African Americans against Apartheid, 1946–1994*. Bloomington: Indiana University Press, 2004.

Obenzinger, Hilton. *Busy Dying*. Tucson, AZ: Chax Publishing, 2008.

Ogbar, Jeffrey O. G. *Black Power: Radical Politics and African American Identity*. Baltimore: Johns Hopkins University Press, 2004.

O'Mara, Margaret. *Cities of Knowledge: Cold War Science and the Search for the Next Silicon Valley*. Princeton: Princeton University Press, 2005.

Parks, Gregory, and Stefan Bradley, eds. *Alpha Phi Alpha: A Legacy of Greatness, The Demands of Transcendence*. Lexington: University Press of Kentucky, 2012.

Perkiss, Abigail. *Making Good Neighbors: Civil Rights, Liberalism, and Integration in Postwar Philadelphia*. Ithaca, NY: Cornell University Press, 2014.

Pfeffer, Paula. *A. Philip Randolph, Pioneer of the Civil Rights Movement*. Baton Rouge: Louisiana State University Press, 1990.

Phillips, Janet. *Brown University: A Short History*. Providence, RI: Brown University, 2000.

Potter, Lou. *Liberators: Fighting on Two Fronts in World War II*. New York: Harcourt, 1992.

Powledge, Fred. *Model City*. New York: Simon and Schuster, 1970.

Puckett, John, and Mark Frazier. *Becoming Penn: The Pragmatic University, 1950–2000*. Philadelphia: University of Pennsylvania Press, 2015.

Rampersad, Arnold. *Jackie Robinson: A Biography*. New York: Ballantine Books, 1998.

Randolph, Sherie M. *Florynce "Flo" Kennedy: The Life of a Black Feminist Radical*. Chapel Hill: University of North Carolina Press, 2015.

Ransby, Barbara. *Ella Baker and the Black Freedom Movement: A Radical Democratic Vision*. Chapel Hill: University of North Carolina Press, 2004.

Redding, J. Saunders. *No Day of Triumph*. New York: Harpers & Brothers, 1942.

Rickford, Russell. *Betty Shabazz, Surviving Malcolm X: A Journey of Strength from Wife to Widow to Heroine*. Naperville, IL: Sourcebooks, 2005.

Robeson, Eslanda Goode. *Paul Robeson, Negro*. London: Harper & Brothers, 1930.

Robeson, Paul, Jr. *Here I Stand*. Boston: Beacon Press, 1998.

———. *The Undiscovered Paul Robeson: An Artist's Journey, 1898–1939*. New York: Wiley, 2001.

Robinson, Armstead L., Craig C. Foster, and Donald H. Ogilvie, eds. *Black Studies in the University: A Symposium*. New Haven: Yale University Press, 1969.

Rodin, Judith. *The University and Urban Revival: Out of the Ivory Tower and into the Streets*. Philadelphia: University of Pennsylvania Press, 2007.

Roediger, David. *The Wages of Whiteness: Race and the Making of the American Working Class*. New York: Verso Books, 1991.

———. *Working Toward Whiteness: How America's Immigrants Became White, the Strange Journey from Ellis Island to the Suburbs*. New York: Basic Books, 2005.

Rogers, Ibram. *The Black Campus Movement: Black Students and the Racial Reconstitution of Higher Education, 1965–1972*. New York: Palgrave Macmillan, 2012.

Rojas, Fabio. *From Black Power to Black Studies: How a Radical Social Movement Became an Academic Discipline*. Charlottesville: University of Virginia Press, 2007.

Rooks, Noliwe M. *White Money, Black Power: The Surprising History of African American Studies and the Crisis of Race in Higher Education*. Boston: Beacon Books, 2006.

Rosovsky, Henry. "A Happy Beginning." *Department of Afro-American Studies, Harvard University: Thirtieth Anniversary Celebration*. Cambridge, MA: Harvard University Press, 2000.

Rudd, Mark. *Underground: My Life with SDS and the Weathermen*. New York: William Morrow, 2009.

Sales, Kirkpatrick. *SDS: Students for a Democratic Society*. New York: Random House, 1974.

Sales, William W. *From Civil Rights to Black Liberation: Malcolm X and the Organization of Afro-American Unity*. Cambridge, MA: South End Press, 1994.

Schneller, Robert, Jr. *Breaking the Color Barrier: The US Naval Academy's First Black Midshipmen and the Struggle for Racial Equality.* New York: New York University Press, 2005.

Selden, William. *Chapels of Princeton University: Their Historical and Religious Significance.* Princeton: Princeton University Office of Communications, 2005.

Sellers, Cleveland, with Robert Terrell. *The River of No Return: The Autobiography of a Black Militant and the Life and Death of SNCC.* Jackson: University Press of Mississippi, 2003.

Shabazz, Rashad. *Spatializing Blackness: Architectures of Confinement and Black Masculinity in Chicago.* Champaign: University of Illinois Press, 2015.

Soares, Joseph A. *The Power of Privilege: Yale and America's Elite Colleges.* Redwood City, CA: Stanford University Press, 2007.

Sobel, Richard. *The Politics of Joint University and Community Housing Development: Cambridge, Boston, and Beyond.* New York: Lexington Books, 2014.

Sollors, Werner, Caldwell Titcomb, Thomas A. Underwood, and Randall Kennedy, eds. *Black at Harvard: A Documentary History of African-American Experience at Harvard and Radcliffe.* New York: New York University Press, 1993.

Spencer, Robyn C. *The Revolution Has Come: Black Power, Gender, and the Black Panther Party in Oakland.* Durham, NC: Duke University Press, 2016.

Springer, Kimberly, ed. *Living for the Revolution: Black Feminist Organizations, 1968–1980.* Durham. NC: Duke University Press, 2005.

———. *Still Lifting and Still Climbing: African American Women's Contemporary Activism.* New York: New York University Press, 1999.

Strom, Elizabeth. "The Political Strategies Behind University-Based Development." In *The University as Urban Developer: Case Studies and Analysis,* edited by David. C. Perry and Wim Wiewel. New York: Routledge, 2005.

Strout, Cushing, and David I. Grossvogel, eds. *Divided We Stand: Reflections on the Crisis at Cornell.* New York: Doubleday, 1971.

Sugrue, Thomas. *The Origins of Urban Crisis: Race and Inequality in Postwar Detroit.* Princeton: Princeton University Press, 1996.

———. *Sweet Land of Liberty: The Forgotten Struggle of Civil Rights in the North.* New York: Random House, 2008.

Sylvander, Carolyn Wedin. *Jessie Redmon Fauset, Black American Writer.* Albany, NY: Whitson, 1981.

Synnott, Marcia, ed. *The Half-Opened Door: Discrimination in Admissions at Harvard, Yale, and Princeton, 1900–1970.* Westport, CT: Greenwood Press, 1979.

Tandy, Vertner Woodson. *Report of the National Negro Business League.* Bethesda, MD: University Publications of America, 1918.

Thelin, John. *A History of American Higher Education.* Baltimore: Johns Hopkins University Press, 2004.

Theoharis, Jeanne, and Komozi Woodard, eds. *Freedom North: Black Freedom Struggles Outside the South.* New York: Palgrave Macmillan, 2003.

———. *Groundworks: Local Black Freedom Movements in America*. New York: New York University Press, 2005.

———. *The Rebellious Life of Mrs. Rosa Parks*. New York: Random House, 2013.

Thomas, John. *The Liberator William Lloyd Garrison*. Boston: Little, Brown, 1963.

Trow, Martin, ed. *Twentieth-Century Higher Education: Elite to Mass to Universal*. Baltimore: Johns Hopkins University Press, 2010.

Ture, Kwame, and Charles Hamilton. *Black Power: The Politics of Liberation*. New York: Vintage Books, 1992.

Ture, Kwame, John Edgar Wideman, and Ekwueme Michael Thelwell. *Ready for Revolution: The Life and Struggles of Stokely Carmichael*. New York: Scribner, 2003.

Turner, James. *The Next Decade*. Ithaca, NY: Africana Studies and Research Center, 1984.

Turner, Joe. *Sitting In and Speaking Out: Student Movements in the American South, 1960–1970*. Athens: University of Georgia Press, 2010.

Tussman, Joseph, ed. *The Supreme Court on Racial Discrimination*. New York: Oxford University Press, 1963.

Tygiel, Jules. *Baseball's Great Experiment: Jackie Robinson and His Legacy*. 25th Anniversary Edition. New York: Oxford University Press, 2008.

Tyson, Timothy. *Blood Done Sign My Name: A True Story*. New York: Crown Press, 2004.

Tyson, Timothy B. *Radio Free Dixie: Robert F. Williams and the Roots of Black Power*. Durham, NC: Duke University Press, 1994.

Umoja, Akinyele O. *We Will Shoot Back: Armed Resistance in the Mississippi Freedom Movement*. New York: New York University Press, 2013.

Wallenstein, Peter, ed. *Higher Education and the Civil Rights Movement: White Supremacy, Black Southerners, and College Campuses*. Gainesville: University Press of Florida, 2008.

Weems, Robert E., Jr. *Business in Black and White: American Presidents and Black Entrepreneurs in the Twentieth Century*. New York: New York University Press, 2009.

Wesley, Charles H. *Henry Arthur Callis: Life and Legacy*. Baltimore: Foundation Publishers, 1977.

———. *The History of Alpha Phi Alpha: A Development in College Life*. Baltimore: Foundation Publishers, 1996.

———. *History of Sigma Pi Phi: First of the Negro-American Greek-Letter Fraternities*. Washington, DC: Association for the Study of Negro Life and History, 1954.

White, Derrick. *The Challenge of Blackness: The Institute of the Black World and Political Activism in the 1970s*. Gainesville: University Press of Florida, 2013.

Wideman, John. *Brothers and Keepers*. New York: Holt, Rinehart, and Winston, 1984.

Widmayer, Charles. *John Sloan Dickey: A Chronicle of His Presidency of Dartmouth College*. Hanover, NH: Dartmouth College, 1991.

Wiggins, Dwayne, ed. *Out of the Shadows: A Biographical History of African American Athletes*. Little Rock: University of Arkansas Press, 2006.

Wilder, Craig. *Ebony and Ivy: Race, Slavery, and the Troubled History of America's Universities*. New York: Bloomsbury Press, 2013.

Williams, Rhonda Y. *Concrete Demands: The Search for Black Power in the 20th Century.* New York: Routledge, 2015.

Williams, Robert F. *Negroes with Guns.* Detroit: Wayne State University Press, 1962.

Williams, Yohuru. *Black Politics/White Power: Civil Rights, Black Power, and Black Panthers.* Maplecrest, NY: Brandywine Press, 2000.

Williamson, Joy Ann. *Black Power on Campus: The University of Illinois, 1965–1975.* Champaign: University of Illinois Press, 2003.

Wright, Nathan. *Black Power and Urban Unrest.* New York: Hawthorn Press, 1968.

X, Malcolm, and Alex Haley. *The Autobiography of Malcolm X.* New York: Grove Press, 1965.

Zinn, Howard. *SNCC: The New Abolitionists.* Boston: Beacon Press, 1964.

INDEX

Adger, William, 24
affirmative action, 102, 121, 138–139, 165, 270, 326, 344
African American Studies, 9, 14, 17, 19–21; at Brown, 92, 124–138, 141; at Columbia, 185, 188, 272, 285–289; at Cornell, 12, 331–332, 337, 341–342, 344, 357–359; at Dartmouth, 142, 164–165; at Harvard, 11, 296, 301, 304–305, 310–317, 320–326, 330; at Penn, 212, 228–229, 234, 246; at Princeton, 47, 73, 83; at Yale, 20, 249–252, 259–290, 295; at San Francisco State, 5, 126, 164, 229, 261, 269, 284, 296; legacies of, 136, 162, 364, 369–374. *See also* Afro-American Studies; Africana Studies; and Black Studies
Africana Studies, 9, 14, 17, 19–21; at Brown, 92, 124–138, 141; at Columbia, 185, 188, 272, 285–289; at Cornell, 12, 331–332, 337, 341–342, 344, 357–359; at Dartmouth, 142, 164–165; at Harvard, 11, 296, 301, 304–305, 310–317, 320–326, 330; at Penn, 212, 228–229, 234, 246; at Princeton, 47, 73, 83; at Yale, 20, 249–252, 259–290, 295; at San Francisco State, 5, 126, 164, 229, 261, 269, 284, 296; legacies of, 136, 162, 364, 369–374. *See also* African American Studies, Afro-American Studies; and Black Studies
Afro: and Afro-American Studies, 304, 310, 316–317, 319–322; coalition with SDS, 319–321; and committees, 301, 314; protest for black employment at Harvard, 329–330; position paper,

319–320. *See also* Association of African and Afro-American Students (AAAAS)
Afro-America, 252
Afro-American Society at Brown (AAS), 97–99, 101, 132; and admissions, 121, 123, 125, 134–137; and Black Studies (Afro-American Studies), 126, 129, 131; and Churchill House (affinity space), 131–133; and walkout, 103–111
Afro-American Society at Cornell: and Africana Studies Research Center (ASRC), 344; and Black Studies (Africana Studies), 337, 341–342, 344–345; founding of, 336; and leadership, 331, 337–338, 342; and McPhelin incident, 337–339; and meeting with SNCC, 336–337; and Willard Straight Hall takeover, 346–355
Afro-American Society at Dartmouth: and admissions, 157–159, 161; founding of, 152–153; and Eastman Kodak demonstration, 153; and George Wallace protest, 154–155; and Trustees' Committee on Equal Opportunity, 155–156
Afro-American Studies, 9, 14, 17, 19–21; at Brown, 92, 124–138, 141; at Columbia, 185, 188, 272, 285–289; at Cornell, 12, 331–332, 337, 341–342, 344, 357–359; at Dartmouth, 142, 164–165; at Harvard, 11, 296, 301, 304–305, 310–317, 320–326, 330; at Penn, 212, 228–229, 234, 246; at Princeton, 47, 73, 83; at Yale, 20, 249–252, 259–290, 295; at San

Afro-American Studies (*cont.*)
Francisco State, 5, 126, 164, 229, 261,
269, 284, 296; legacies of, 136, 162, 364,
369–374. *See also* African American
Studies, Africana Studies; and Black
Studies
Alabama State Normal School, 94
Alexander, Raymond Pace, 36, 37, 367
Alexander, Sadie Turner, 212, 367
Alexin, Lucien, 42
Ali, Muhammad, 219
Alpha Kappa Alpha, 37, 94
Alpha Phi Alpha, 29–31, 35, 41, 44, 97, 163,
255, 335, 336
Alsion, Marvin, 197, 241
American Council of Education, 227, 237
American Housing Act of 1949, 173, 200,
210, 248
Amherst College, 35, 38, 140
Amsterdam, Gustave, 208
Ancient Eight, 1, 11, 15–16, 23, 40, 362–363,
365–366, 380n1
Anderson, Elijah, 209
Anderson, Sam, 190
Angola, 187
Antioch College, 274
apartheid, ix, 69–70, 89, 91; and protest
against Princeton investment, xi, 20,
47, 70–84
Aptheker, Herbert, 325
Area-Wide Council (AWC), 222
Arkansas Agricultural and Mechanical
Institute, 94
Armstrong, Samuel Chapman, 116
Association of African and Afro-
American Students (AAAAS): and
Afro-American Studies, 304, 310,
316–317, 319–322; coalition with
SDS, 319–321; and committees, 301,
314; protest for black employment,
329–330; position paper, 319–320
Association of Black Collegians (ABC):
and admissions, 67–68; founding of,

66–67; leadership of, 73, 76, 83–84;
and protests against apartheid, 69–83
Association of Black Princeton Alumni
(ABPA), survey, 58–59, 64, 90
Austin, Ralph, 86, 368
Axtell, James, 5, 47

Baker, Houston A., 246, 269
Baker, Jessie, 239
Baldwin, Davarian, 168
Baraka, Amiri, 158, 229, 241, 345
Barnard College, Barnard Organization
of Soul Sisters (BOSS), 100
Barry, Jay, 124
Beaubien, Michael C., 127
Beckham, Barry, 94–97, 106, 121, 137,
255–256, 368
Bell, Derrick, 2, 259, 329, 365
Beverly, John William, 94
bickering process, 56
Big Bill Boonzy, 215
Big Three, 15
Biondi, Martha, 5
Black Arts Movement, 132, 158, 245
Black Bottom, 198, 202, 204–205, 208,
214–215
black bourgeoisie, 7, 11, 24, 113–115, 152, 271
black campus movement, 5, 14, 104, 139,
275, 277
Black Coalition, 273, 291–292
black freedom movement, 5–6, 10, 16,
19, 21, 366; and Princeton, 48, 69; and
Brown, 92–93, 98, 100, 106, 121, 124;
and Dartmouth, 140, 151–152, 165; and
Columbia, 187; and Penn, 216, 224;
and Yale, 253, 275–276, 278, 289
Black Greek-Letter Organization
(BGLO), 31, 42, 180, 185; and Black
Greek-letter fraternity, 163
Black Intelligence Test of Cultural
Homegeneity-100 (BITCH-100), 179
black intelligentsia, xvi, 101, 112, 220,
304, 338

Cooke, Alistair, 24
Cooke, Michael, 270
Cooper, Anna Julia, 26
Cooper, Betran, 341
Cordier, Andrew W., 194–195
Cornell, Ezra, 332
Cornell University: Africana Studies and
  Research Center (ASRC), 358–359;
  and Alpha Phi Alpha, 29–31; black
  admissions, 26, 332, 339; and James
  Perkins, 4, 18–19, 141, 332, 333, 343,
  349, 352–357, 361; and Straight Hall
  takeover, 349, 352, 353–357, 361; and
  McPhelin incident, 337–339; and
  Sage College, 32, 34, 341; and Wari
  Cooperative House, 335–336, 345–346,
  350; and Willard Straight Hall
  takeover, 331, 333, 346–355
Corpus Christi Church, 170; and
  pastor, 173
Countryman, Joan, 210
Countryman, Matthew, 6, 199
Countryman, Peter, 303
Cox, Archibald, 294, 326–327
Cox, Mary, 184
Creed, Courtland Van Rensselaer, 24
Crenshaw, Kimberlé, 259
Crew, Spencer, 100, 107, 114, 117, 125, 138, 368
Critical Race Theory, 2, 259
Cross, William, 12, 300
Crozer Theological Seminary, 218
Cruse, Harold, 267–268, 270–271, 286
Culp, Daniel, 49
Cutter-Shabazz Center, 169

Dahl, Robert, 260, 269
Daily Pennsylvanian, 225, 230
Daily Princetonian, 57, 58
Daily Spectator, 185
Dartmouth College: A Better Chance
  program, 61, 149, 151, 162, 176, 333;
  "Big Green," 142, 162; Black Alumni,
  150, 162; Dartmouth Christian Union,
147, 153; "Dartmouth Indian," 161–162;
  El Hajj Malik El Shabazz Center,
  163; Foundation Years, 150–151, 176,
  333; Political Action Committee, 147;
  Judiciary Advisory Committee for
  Black Students, 155
Datcher, Jane Eleanor, 25
Davis, Charles T., 57–58, 272
Davis, Jerome, 76
Davis, Thulani, 185, 301, 303, 369, 376
Dawley, David, 150
Day, William L., 236, 238, 241–242
Deacons for Self Defense, 351
deChabert, Glenn E., 253–255, 258, 266,
  276, 291, 371
Declaration of Independence, 3, 47
Deerfield Academy, 119
deindustrialization, 199, 209
Delaney, Martin, 24, 374
Delmont, Matthew, 6, 33, 204, 212
Delta Sigma Theta, 298
Delta Upsilon, 333, 349–350, 352
Democratic National Convention (1968),
  221, 307–308
Dempsey, Alford, 13
Dial Lodge, 64
Dickey, John Sloan, 20, 141–144; and
  AAS, 154, 158–161; and Committee
  on Civil Rights, 142, 165; and Ivy
  presidents, 37, 274, 333; and "To Secure
  These Rights," 171
Dickinson College, 62
Diggs, Charles, 69
Dinkins, David, 369
Dinkins, William, 94, 369
Dodds, R. Harcourt, 144, 150, 157, 165
Doebler, Charles, 97–98
Donald, Cleveland, 339, 348, 350–351
Donaldson, Ivanhoe, 325
Doob, Leonard W., 269
Double Discovery, 61, 176–181. See also
  Project Double Discovery
double marginalization, 11, 113–115

Stefan M. Bradley is Associate Professor and Chair in the Department of African American Studies at Loyola Marymount University in Los Angeles. He is author of *Harlem vs. Columbia University: Black Student Power in the Late 1960s* and co-editor of *Alpha Phi Alpha: A Legacy of Greatness, The Demands of Transcendence.*

Lightning Source UK Ltd.
Milton Keynes UK
UKHW011935081120
372905UK00013B/181